Frances Farmer

ALSO BY PETER SHELLEY

*Grande Dame Guignol Cinema:
A History of Hag Horror from* Baby Jane *to* Mother
(McFarland, 2009)

# Frances Farmer
*The Life and Films
of a Troubled Star*

PETER SHELLEY

McFarland & Company, Inc., Publishers
*Jefferson, North Carolina, and London*

LIBRARY OF CONGRESS CATALOGUING-IN-PUBLICATION DATA

Shelley, Peter, 1962–
Frances Farmer : the life and films of a troubled star / Peter Shelley.
p.   cm.
Includes bibliographical references and index.

ISBN 978-0-7864-4745-9
softcover : 50# alkaline paper ∞

1. Farmer, Frances, 1913–1970.  2. Motion picture
actors and actresses—United States—Biography.  I. Title.
PN2287.F34S54   2011    791.43'028'0924—dc22 [B]    2010042814

British Library cataloguing data are available

© 2011 Peter Shelley. All rights reserved

*No part of this book may be reproduced or transmitted in any form
or by any means, electronic or mechanical, including photocopying
or recording, or by any information storage and retrieval system,
without permission in writing from the publisher.*

On the cover: Frances Farmer in 1941
(Universal Pictures/Photofest)

Manufactured in the United States of America

*McFarland & Company, Inc., Publishers
Box 611, Jefferson, North Carolina 28640
www.mcfarlandpub.com*

# *Acknowledgments*

As with my last book, *Grande Dame Guignol Cinema*, I must once again thank fellow film writer Barry Lowe for his continued assistance and support in the making of this book. Additional thanks are offered to Alex Broun, Jeffrey Kauffman, Anne-Louise Luccarini, Hugh Monroe, Kath Perry, Anita Plateris, and Stewart South.

# Table of Contents

Acknowledgments  vii
Preface  1
Introduction and Biography  5

························ THE FILMS ························

| | |
|---|---:|
| *Too Many Parents* (1936) | 69 |
| *Border Flight* (1936) | 74 |
| *Rhythm on the Range* (1936) | 80 |
| *Come and Get It* (1936) | 88 |
| *Exclusive* (1937) | 99 |
| *The Toast of New York* (1937) | 106 |
| *Ebb Tide* (1937) | 113 |
| *Ride a Crooked Mile* (1938) | 121 |
| *South of Pago Pago* (1940) | 127 |
| *Flowing Gold* (1940) | 135 |
| *World Premiere* (1941) | 143 |
| *Badlands of Dakota* (1941) | 151 |
| *Among the Living* (1941) | 158 |
| *Son of Fury* (1942) | 165 |
| *No Escape* (1943) | 174 |
| *The Party Crashers* (1958) | 180 |

························ TELEVISION ························

| | |
|---|---:|
| *Toast of the Town/The Ed Sullivan Show* (June 1957) | 191 |
| *Toast of the Town/The Ed Sullivan Show* (October 1957) | 193 |
| *Playhouse 90*—"Reunion" (1958) | 194 |
| *Matinee Theatre*—"Something Stolen, Something Blue" (1958) | 194 |

| | |
|---|---:|
| *This Is Your Life* (1958) | 195 |
| *Studio One*—"Tongues of Angels" (1958) | 200 |
| *Frances Farmer Presents* (1958–1964, including Indianapolis special) | 201 |

## BIOPICS AND DOCUMENTARIES

| | |
|---|---:|
| *Frances* (1982) | 207 |
| *Will There Really Be a Morning?* (1983) | 220 |
| *Committed* (1984) | 227 |
| *Broadway's Dreamers: The Legacy of the Group Theatre* (1988) | 232 |
| *Hollywood Scandals and Tragedies* (1988) | 235 |
| *Hollywood Undressed* (1991) | 238 |
| *E! Mysteries and Scandals* (1998) | 240 |
| *A&E Biography*—"Paradise Lost" (2000) | 242 |

Bibliography 247

Index 251

# *Preface*

I first learned about Frances Farmer from Kenneth Anger's book *Hollywood Babylon*, in his chapter "Daughter of Fury: Frances, Saint." Before I had any awareness of her as an actress, here was Frances as a shamed celebrity, unprotected and humiliated. Those horribly unflattering press photographs were the very definition of tabloid exploitation at a time when most movie stars were protected by studio contracts and publicists. How could this have happened to her?

It is interesting to compare Frances' arrest with that of Errol Flynn the year before for statutory rape. Flynn wasn't photographed being arrested or handled by police the way she was. Even Flynn's trial became a joke because the idea that Flynn had to resort to rape seemed farcical. However, Frances was not so fortunate. She couldn't laugh off this trauma, and the defiant look on her face in the photographs told you that this was no laughing matter. Surely the pleasure to be had from seeing Frances like this, and those photographs were taken because it was assumed that they would give pleasure, came from the perversity of seeing a beautiful woman sabotaged.

The photographs also made me want to see her films. If she was star enough to warrant this kind of press attention when she got into trouble, then she must have had a grace period from which to fall. When I did see her films, it made me see how doubly tragic her fate was. For Frances was a good actress. She was more than just beautiful, although her beauty was extraordinary. Her fast speaking voice indicated an intelligence and nervous sensitivity, and if she had trouble expressing emotion with tears, she did have the lightness to play comedy, a much underrated quality. She could act, and even if the trajectory of her film career is like a primer for career mismanagement, the fact that her private life completely overwhelmed her professional life in the Hollywood zeitgeist seemed unfair.

David Shipman, in his chapter on Frances in *The Great Movie Stars*, writes:

> Beauty and the Beast: the Beauty was Frances, and the Beast was Alcohol. It was a short and not dazzling career, but it's a shame because she was talented, intelligent, and gorgeous to look upon. She made very few films, and most of them were rotten: but she is unforgettable in the good ones.

In an article in *Time* magazine, February 15, 1982, entitled "Morning Comes for Frances" to publicize the making of the feature *Frances*, Richard Corliss writes that

> her life was one roiling curse. She was part of a movie age that glorified the strong-willed woman and punished the actresses who incarnated them. Hepburn, Davis, De Havilland were all mistreated by moguls who wanted their stars to behave like little women. Farmer was as willful as any of them—and far more troubled. The pressure drove her from the screen. It may have driven her mad.

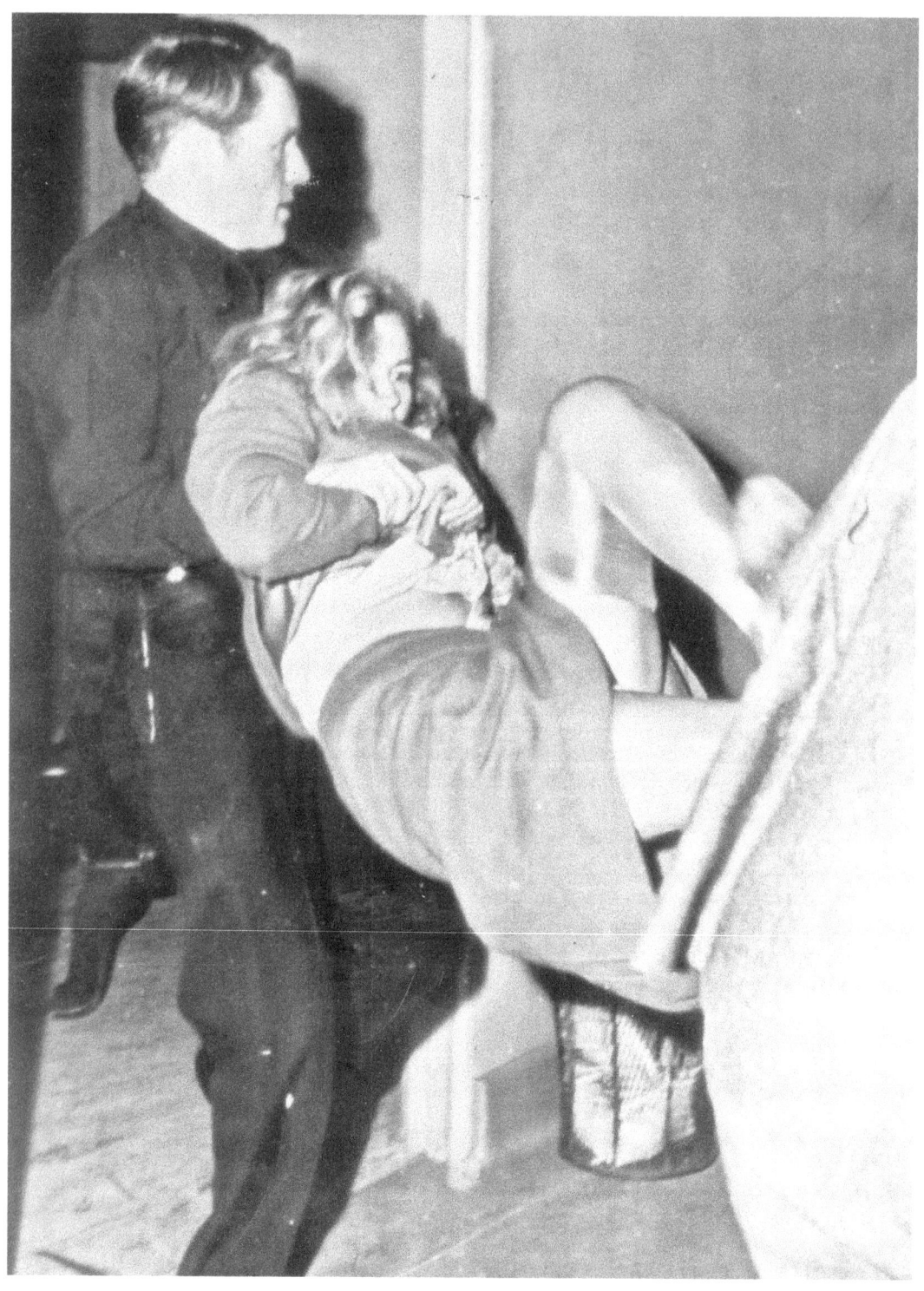

Frances brawling with police after her arrest on January 14, 1943, for assault and probation violation. This Wide World news photograph was reproduced in the alleged autobiography *Will There Really Be a Morning?*

# Preface

In the interview for Peter Bogdanovich's book *Who the Devil Made It*, Howard Hawks talked about Frances and what happened to her after the film they made together, *Come and Get It*:

> She began to get into real difficulties because the studio started dictating to her and throwing her into bad pictures. She'd fight and argue and make the directors hate her because they had to make the picture in so many days and they couldn't do it with a girl who'd argue about everything. She began to get herself into bad states and started drinking and became a complete drunk. A pitiful thing. She had an affair with Clifford Odets, which didn't help matters. When I knew her she never took a drink—never smoked a cigarette—was the cleanest physical thing you've ever seen.

Some film historians believe that Frances' movies are only interesting with hindsight—*because* of her private troubles—and that her reign as a leading lady in Hollywood was over before it really began. However, the culpability for the disappointment of her filmography can be shared equally between the actress and her studio. Paramount did not nurture Frances the way it did established stars like Carole Lombard, Claudette Colbert, Marlene Dietrich, or even Barbara Stanwyck and Jean Arthur on loan outs. And it quickly lost interest in her, preferring to promote newcomers like Paulette Goddard, Susan Hayward, and Veronica Lake. (The case for Frances to have been cast in the roles that Lake was is especially intriguing, given how Lake moved from working with Preston Sturges on the comedy *Sullivan's Travels* to her series of film noirs with Alan Ladd. However, as Lake's career would wind down at the end of the 1940s, so would have Frances', since it is most likely that Frances's liberal politics would have seen her branded a Communist and had her blacklisted.) While these ladies had their appeal, one could argue that Frances was equally talented, more beautiful and possessed greater range. But the extended career she might have had was not to be.

The existing biographical material on Frances mentions her films, but in a dismissive way, since that is not their focus. This book then is an attempt to provide an in-depth analysis of the films of Frances Farmer and to restore her place as a significant actress of the 1930s and '40s. If her career as a leading lady seems brief, her subsequent performances in supporting roles remain noteworthy. While the biographical chapter I have provided mentions the scandals of her personal life, this is mainly to give her professional life context. The biography also provides information about her work on stage, radio, and television. Any statement of fact is supported by common agreement in the accessed sources, with variations recorded according to the differing sources.

For each of her feature films, her work on television, and the biopics and documentaries on her or that mention her, I have created a chapter. I have viewed and listened to as much of her available work as possible to accurately describe the content and give my own opinions about her performances. The bulk of her films are not available commercially, and neither are her television dramas or "Frances Farmer Presents" (although I was able to see a special report entitled "Indiana Epilogue" which featured brief excerpts of Frances from her show). For what I have viewed, I make observations on how successful the films, television shows and documentaries are. I do not have the agenda of a biased fan, so I do not hesitate to point out elements that are disappointing or that I find downright bad, as well as praising things that I think good.

Each chapter has a cast and crew filmography taken from the actual film, television show or documentary, supplemented by the listings on the Internet Movie Database and Turner Classic Movies to include uncredited cast and crew members. For the titles not available commercially, I have accessed prints from auctions and collectors, and therefore have not judged the quality of photography in these sometimes less than ideal copies. The chapters also provide a plot synopsis and make mention of any songs, the filming dates of the production and location sites, the release or screening date and publicity taglines, and period and contemporary reviews. In my chapter notes I comment on Frances' performance in the film, give the history of the producers and director, highlight any noteworthy technique or plot narrative, and provide behind the scenes information. Additionally I have attempted to provide imagery to complement the chapters, with portraits of Frances and stills, lobby cards and posters for the films, television shows and documentaries when possible.

I hope I am successful in drawing attention to the work of Frances Farmer that has been critically neglected. While I have spent considerable time doing research to try to be as comprehensive as possible, ultimately my opinions and observations are subjective. I hope that what I have provided will encourage readers to seek out Frances' work and find all that I have found, and more.

# *Introduction and Biography*

Frances Farmer's story is clouded in myth and conjecture, scandal and gossip. Her life has been covered in an alleged autobiography, two biographies, a chapter in an anthology, and internet websites, but these versions sometimes offer conflicting views of the same incidents.

The supposed autobiography, *Will There Really Be a Morning?*, was published after her death, and although Frances was working on an autobiography in her last years, with writer Lois Kibbee, what was eventually released in 1972 is commonly thought to have been embroidered by Frances' companion, Jean Ratcliffe, and dramatized in order to make a movie sale. The William Arnold biography *Shadowland*, published in 1978, raised the idea that Farmer had been lobotomized at Steilacoom, the Washington state asylum where she had been committed and was held from 1945 to 1950. Arnold would later recant the lobotomy allegation in a court case, but the lobotomy rumor has stuck to Frances ever since, reinforced by it being presented in the biopic *Frances*. Arnold's court case arose from his suing the makers of *Frances*, Brooksfilms, because he felt the screenplay was based on his book, a case he lost since it was determined that his book was not entirely based on public record, which negated his claim to exclusive authorship rights. The biography of Frances' sister, Edith Farmer Elliot, entitled *Look Back in Love* and also published in 1978, is invalidated as hearsay by the fact of the author not being in the country when most of Frances' troubles with the law occurred. Jeffrey Kauffman has a website on Frances (www.jeffreykauffman.net), copyright dated 1999, which, after claiming to have researched her life for "decades," specifically debunks a lot of Arnold's claims. And Patrick Agan devotes a chapter to Frances in his book *The Decline and Fall of the Love Goddesses*, which was published in 1979. Agan claims to use quotations from the unpublished manuscript and correspondence between Lois Kibbee and Frances.

Therefore, what is true and what is fiction in relation to Frances' private life is anyone's guess, with the only person able to provide clarity having died in 1970. However, information related to her professional life is mostly consistent in all works, which can be referenced in this book, with its primary focus on Frances as actress. Her private life as a victim of Hollywood Babylon may have made Frances infamous, but fame as an actress came from her work in film more than on the stage, and this isn't what she set out to do.

## *Beginnings*

She was born Frances Elena Farmer in Seattle, Washington, on September 19, 1913. She was the youngest child of four, with sister Rita (a child of her mother's first marriage to William Mitchell), brother Wesley, and second sister Edith. Frances' parents were lawyer Ernest and Lillian Farmer, a boardinghouse operator, homemaker, dietician and sometime political activist. While they both possessed charm and intellectual curiosity, Ernest and Lillian also shared wills of iron, which would make them fight for the sake of the struggle. Frances would also inherit her mother's ambition and emotional volatility, which had resulted in Lillian herself nearly being institutionalized twice early in the marriage after the loss of a child, Little Zella, from pneumonia in between Wesley and Edith. While Lillian was the more outgoing of her parents, Frances possessed her father's interpersonal brusqueness, a quality that was often interpreted as stemming from arrogance. The marriage suffered when Lillian blamed the death of the child on Ernest, who had insisted that it be moved into a drafty room to accommodate his visiting mother.

When Frances was four her mother left Ernest in their home on 312 Harvard Avenue, North Seattle, and took her children to the home of her sister, Zella, in Los Angeles, Southern California. Lillian then moved the family to 853 Cole Avenue, Hollywood. The house near Hollywood and Vine was located directly opposite the original MGM studio, where the adult Frances would never get to act. Ernest supplied support payments, though they were often late. In 1925 Lillian moved her family to Chico Vecino, in the Sacramento Valley, where they could live rent-free since Lillian had inherited a house there from her late mother, Elizabeth Van Ornum. Edith says that Lillian sold the Chico "homestead" in order to buy a larger house outside the city limits on the Esplanade.

Then two years later the children were sent back to Seattle for an extended visit with their father, while Lillian worked on her nutritional research. Edith says the girls were initially placed in the home of one of Ernest's clients, on a Fauntleroy hillside, while Wesley stayed with their father in his downtown hotel room. They were then moved to an apartment in the Mage Apartments at the other end of West Seattle, where Frances started writing her own poetry.

After the Chico house burned down, destroying much of her material, Lillian, too, returned to Seattle, but only on the proviso that Ernest not live with them. They reached a compromise by buying a house to accommodate the family at 2636 Forty-Seventh Avenue S.W. (mid-block), and he becoming a weekend father. Having parents that shared a begrudging living arrangement and an unhappy marriage affected the sensitive Frances. She learned to become self-sufficient and an individual, mirroring Lillian's motto of "Decide for yourself." However, Lillian had another favorite saying: "Every living thing carries within itself the seeds of its own destruction."

Edith Farmer tells of Frances' stage debut when she was fifteen, in *The Pirate's Daughter*, a church fundraising operetta performed in May 1928. Interestingly, Frances played the male role of Hans, one of a pair of servants in love. As seen in a photo Edith included on her book's back cover, Frances is wearing a boyish bob that Edith says was then in vogue. Frances looks convincing as a boy, although Edith looks equally androgynous. Frances' femininity would be restored when she played the lead role of the Queen in *The Queen's Husband* in her senior high school class in 1931.

To counter Ernest's attempts to block Lillian's thirteen-and-a-half years efforts to divorce him, she moved out of the house in April 1929 and into a summer cottage in a village near Bremerton called Manette. It was now Lillian's turn to be a weekend mother. After six months the divorce was granted in October, and Lillian moved back with her children, with the divorce not seeming to create any improvement in the relationship between the two battling parents.

In childhood Frances demonstrated a talent for writing, something she inherited from her mother, who wrote letters to newspapers and printed pamphlets on the subject of dietetics. At the West Seattle High School, Frances worked on the student newspaper, though her participation in the debating team hinted at the dramatic performances to come. In April 1931 an essay she wrote for her creative writing class, entitled "God Dies," was chosen as the winner of a national high school essay contest. Edith claims that the teacher did not ask the permission of her students to enter the submissions, and reproduces the entire essay in her book. Sixteen-year-old Frances was awarded $100, and the essay was printed in the National Scholastic educational publication. The win headlined Seattle press—"Seattle Girl Denies God, Wins Prize"—and then the story was picked up by the national press. This became the first scandal of Frances' life, with her being denounced by a Baptist minister at a city-wide church meeting: "If the youth of Seattle are going to Hell, Frances Farmer is surely leading them there."

In 1932, at the age of eighteen, and continuing to write short stories and poetry, Frances entered the University of Washington in the School of Journalism and worked on the campus paper as a reporter. To support her studies she also worked as an usher at the downtown Paramount Theater, posed for art students, was a salesgirl at the Bon Marche Department store, a typist, and a singing waitress one summer at Mount Rainier National Park. Edith says that Frances also worked temporarily at the Golden Glint Shampoo Factory, though she proved allergic to the chemical hair dye that filled the air, which gave her nosebleeds so bad that she had to quit. Additionally, she was a dramatic counselor at the Camp Fire Girl's summer camp in July and August, putting the little girls through original skits and entertainments. This stage directing experience demonstrated her new interest in drama.

Frances supplied some of her own poetry when there was extra space to fill in the *University of Washington Daily*, but soon found journalism a chore. She befriended a fellow reporter who came from the university's Drama Department, and was introduced to the drama instructor, Sophie Weinstein (née Rosenstein). Edith says that Sophie would take her students to downtown speakeasies, and it was here that Frances' long-lasting taste for liquor began. Intrigued by Sophie and her classes, Frances transferred to the Drama Department. In May 1933 she was cast as the lead in *Uncle Vanya*, and Frances would also play Helen in their production of *Helen of Troy*. In the summer she was introduced to Mrs. Rivers by her uncle Frank and worked in a play at the Pasadena Playhouse with the Rivers theater group that had previously produced the avant-garde German lesbian play *Madechens in Uniform*.

During the Christmas vacation Edith and Frances moved out of their home and into a two-room penthouse apartment atop an older house in the residential section of the University District. In January 1934 Frances was cast in the Pirandello comedy *Right You Are—If You Think So*, which played at the Meany Hotel Hall, and she was singled out in the reviews. In February the Department's next production was *Everyman*, a modern adaptation of the medieval English morality play, with Frances' time divided between classes, rehearsals, her job at the Paramount Theater, and doing publicity for the Drama Department in Seattle newspapers and on radio. However, a smoldering cigarette she or one of her friends had left in a chair in the apartment resulted in a fire which forced the girls to move back home.

In the spring Frances won the lead in a student-written musical comedy farce, the annual Junior Girls' Vodvil production. In the summer she was a student summer assistant, and in the fall was cast in the Department's next play, Sidney Howard's *Alien Corn*. Frances played Elsa Brandt, a German musician stifled by a provisional environment, and her run was extended to an unprecedented college record of fifty nights (as confirmed by Glenn Hughes on the *This Is Your Life* show) over fourteen weekends in 1934, including a season off–Broadway. Frances was the star of the Drama Department, the one actor that Sophie thought had the best chance to succeed on Broadway.

## *From Seattle to Russia*

Sophie had contacts with the Group Theatre, the leading experimental theater in New York whose alumni included playwright Clifford Odets, directors Harold Clurman and Elia Kazan, and actors John Garfield, Lee J. Cobb, and Karl Malden. In order to finance the trip, Sophie had all her students buy subscriptions to the Communist newspaper *The Voice of Action*, which was running a competition in which the winner received an all-paid trip to Moscow via New York. It was announced on March 10, 1935, that Frances won. Edith says that Frances actually was runner-up, but that Sophie convinced *The Voice* to choose Frances as the younger and more attractive ambassador. The *Seattle Post-Intelligencer* had announced the news in an attempt to continue its policy of red-baiting, stating that the idea of an American coed being awarded a trip to Russia by a left-wing newspaper was pure propaganda.

Frances had been a supporter of demonstrations against the activities of The American Vigilantes of Washington who had raided bookstores, burned books, and perpetrated violence against anyone they saw as a Communist. She handed out leaflets, distributed petitions and attended meetings and pro–Communist rallies at the University commons. On news of Frances' win, fighting broke out between the vigilantes and *Voice of Action* people at the Seattle YMCA where she was scheduled to appear. To counter this hysteria, Frances wrote a statement for the *Seattle Times* under the heading "Why I Am Going to Russia," stating that her only interest in going to Russia was to see the Russian theater and that she was not a Communist.

What made this scandal worse for Frances was that, unlike with the "God Dies" incident, this time her mother opposed her. Lillian Farmer gave daily interviews to the newspaper declaring her daughter to be the dupe of Communists and announcing that she would attempt to legally restrain Frances from going; and if that didn't work, she would lay herself under the wheels of the bus. However, with Frances being twenty-one years old, Lillian had no such legal right; and on April 10, 1935, Frances drove out of Seattle, with Lillian nowhere near the bus' wheels.

Stopping at Spokane, Frances went to a luncheon at the Spokane Communist Party Headquarters and afterwards gave a press conference, again stating that she was not a Communist. She did the same in Chicago before arriving in New York five days later. Frances had three days before leaving for Russia. A representative of *The Voice of Action* informed her that part of the prize meant having to act as a contributing correspondent for the paper, ironically placing Frances back in the world of journalism. She also attended a party for the Group Theater, where she was briefly introduced to Clifford Odets. Edith claims that Frances was prepared to drop the trip to Russia part of the prize if the Group had asked her to stay in New York. But they were indifferent to her.

Frances sailed on April 10, having been accommodated in third-class steerage on the ship *Washington* (according to the autobiography, Patrick Agan, Edith, and Jeffrey Kauffman, although William Arnold claims the ship was called the *Manhattan*). It took her to Southampton, from which she boarded a Soviet ship to Bremerhaven and then a train to cross Eastern Europe, with brief stops in Berlin, Warsaw, and Leningrad. In Moscow Frances was taken by Party officials on a lengthy tour of showcase factories and collective farms. She watched the May Day parade, and attended a ballet and an army concert at the Bolshoi Theater.

Frances left Russia to go to Paris, then London. Edith quotes from a postcard Frances sent home from Berlin after she had left Moscow, citing her plan to go to Paris. Agan says she reunited with an Englishman, John McKenzie, who she had met on the ship. Edith says he was a lawyer and proposed marriage to Frances, though she declined. At the end of May she returned to New York aboard the ship *President Harding* (named as such by the autobiography, Edith, and Agan, although Arnold calls it the *Cleveland*). Frances held a press conference upon her arrival, telling what she saw in Russia, once again denying that she was a Communist, and declaring that her interest was in the theater and that she was an actress "or trying to be."

## New York

Frances cashed in her return bus ticket to Seattle and moved into the YWCA. After contacting her college classmate Jane Rose who was doing graduate work at Columbia University, she moved in with Jane to share a small Greenwich Village apartment on West Seventy-Fourth Street. Edith claims that Frances did not move into Jane's apartment until Frances was offered a seven-dollars-a-week sublet while Jane went on a European tour. Agan says that both of them earned some money modeling hats, but that times were tough. Frances tried the casting offices but was unsuccessful during Broadway's slow summer period, and not even the Group Theatre would see her.

She met Shepard Traube (Edith spells his name as Shephard), an agent who operated a small office on 42nd Street, who, according to the autobiography, signed her to a seven year personal contract on June 25, 1935. Edith quotes from a letter from Frances to the family dated June 15 which talks about Paramount offering Traube a contract. There are differing versions as to how she met Traube. One is that he was a friend of George Gladsman, a doctor Frances had met onboard the return ship and who had given her work reading manuscripts for him. This is the version Edith gives. Arnold claims that the more likely scenario is that Traube had seen her pictures in the *New York Times* and, being an ambitious man, had sought her out on her return to New York.

Agan describes Traube as a young Broadway producer who encouraged Frances to lose weight and dress better so that she could pursue a movie career. He rented her an expensive room at the Pierre Hotel for a press conference so that Frances could answer questions about her trip to Russia. Agan says Traube also had Frances speak on the differences between American and Soviet sports, something she claims she knew little about. Edith quotes from the *New York Post* and the *New York Herald Tribune*, which both state that Frances had attended a boxing match at Madison Square Garden. The *Tribune* says Frances had gone to contrast Soviet amateur athletics with American boxing. This illustrates the inaccuracy of the reports, since Edith says Frances had refused to attend the fight even though Traube had announced her going, since she was opposed to fighting in any form.

Traube got her an interview with Oscar Serlin, the New York talent chief for Paramount Pictures, who agreed to arrange a screen test for her. She was assigned to do scenes from *The Lake*, in the stage role originally created by Katharine Hepburn, and *The Second Man*. After weeks of rehearsal, in July she reported to Eddie Senz in the studio's make-up department on Long Island. Senz lightened her hair a shade blonder, cut it into a bob and gave her a permanent wave; he also shaved off her eyebrows and plastered a layer of pancake make-up on her face. Frances was recreated to resemble the top female stars in Paramount's stable—Carole Lombard, Claudette Colbert, and Marlene Dietrich.

Although this treatment angered her, since she did not recognize the person who looked back at her from the mirror, she still went through with the test. Frances' unprofessional behavior—her resistance and ingratitude for the opportunity made available to her—was a sign of things to come. She made the tests on August 9, 1935, with actor Allyn Joslin. The geocities internet website *The Misty One* reproduces a double-page article from a 1937 *Photoplay* magazine entitled "The Screen Test That Brought Fame to Frances Farmer," which includes screen captures and a 1937 publicity portrait. One close-up screen capture shows the gap in Frances' upper front teeth that she would later have capped to be an acceptable movie star. Although a slate identifies her as blonde, in spite of the lightening, Frances' hair color still reads as brunette, which will continue into her first films.

Waiting to hear back from Paramount, Frances took modeling work in New York, including a job for Chesterfield cigarettes. In September Traube advised that Paramount had offered her a seven-year contract, to start at one hundred dollars a week, with a six-month option. Frances accepted the offer, considering movies a stepping stone to working in the theater. She signed the contract on her twenty-second birthday in 1935 and boarded the train to Hollywood on September 29. Agan claims that Eddie Senz gave her an eight-week-old toy Boston Bulldog puppy as a parting gift, which Edith says was named Bozo but was a present from Traube.

Edith also claims that Frances went to Hollywood as one of seven "Wampus Babies," each groomed identically under the aegis of the now-defunct organization. The Western Association of Motion Picture Advertisers—WAMPAS—honored thirteen young women from 1922 to 1934 who it was believed had movie star potential. Some of the past Wampas Baby Stars were Clara Bow, Mary Astor, Joan Crawford, Dolores del Rio, Janet Gaynor, Fay Wray, Jean Arthur, Loretta Young, Joan Blondell, and Ginger Rogers.

## *Hollywood*

In *The Paramount Story*, John Douglas Eames writes that by 1935 the studio had emerged from the bankruptcy suffered as a result of the Wall Street crash and the Great Depression, and the mountain was beginning to rise again. Potential dark days had been leavened by the box office success of Bing Crosby musicals, Cecil B. DeMille spectacles and the sex comedies of Mae West. Although none of the studio's films were Academy Award winners, the patina of prestige was attained by the sophisticated styles of directors Josef von Sternberg, Ernst Lubitsch and Mitchell Leisen. A new female star had not been recruited since Sylvia Sidney and Tallulah Bankhead in 1931, and it seems the time was ripe for Frances to make her entrance as the next great white hope.

Arriving on October 5, she was photographed by the *Los Angeles Times*. Frances reported to the Talent Department on her arrival at Paramount Studios, where the norm

**This publicity portrait of Frances holding a perfume bottle, circa 1935, is one of her most repeated images.**

for the unknowns was a six-month contract. Frances took a modest Hollywood apartment and began the Paramount publicity regimen. She took classes in drama, ballet and voice, and disciplined herself in piano practice, voice drills, script memorizing, and exercise and diet to keep slim.

Edith says Frances put in long studio days that began at 5 A.M. and often ended at 10 P.M., and she endured long months of painful dentistry to cap her gap-spread front teeth. She wasted no time in social distractions but did befriend a handsome young man in the Paramount talent pool who had been seen as a vocalist with the Ted Fio Rito dance band in the shorts *The Sweetheart of Sigma Chi* (1933) and *Air Force* (1933). When he first came to Paramount, the blonde, six-foot-three Wycliffe Anderson changed his name to William Anderson, then Glenn Erikson and finally to Leif Erickson. (Frances, on the other hand, refused to change her name, even when the studio said it recalled the popular cook of the time, Fannie Farmer.) The potential stars were evaluated and photographed, and given instruction in how to walk, talk, sit, and lie down. Those deemed lacking were weeded out of the group, and the remainder educated in the techniques of making movies. A still exists of the line-up of seven actresses being built up by the studio as Paramount's Lucky 7, with Frances seen alongside Rosalind Keith, Betty Burgess, Marsha Hunt, Eleanore Whitney, Olympe Bradna, and Jane Rhodes.

Frances and Leif were given a scene to read together in drama class from Sidney Howard's *The Silver Cord*, and she liked working with him. After a month Frances was given her first film assignment, a Community Chest trailer. Her work impressed the front office who decided that she should be groomed as a starlet. While she hated the publicity dates set up for her in order to be seen in the right places, she agreed to go on them with Leif rather than the other leading men of the studio. Soon their names began to appear in the gossip columns as a couple, and they spent their time off together since he was her only friend. Featured articles also appeared about Frances in the fan magazines, but she was appalled by the fiction that was passed off as truth, and Edith claims Frances stormed the press office more than once to protest.

Arnold claims that Frances was about to leave and go back to Seattle when a director spotted her in a test and picked her for her first film. In November 1935 she was cast in

Frances with husband and fellow Paramount contract player Leif Erickson in a studio publicity portrait.

the B filler *Too Many Parents* (1936), starring Billy Lee and Carl "Alfalfa" Switzer, an account of the lives and heartaches of young boys in military school. The box office success of the film advanced Frances from being just a starlet to a *promising* starlet. Although she was miserable, Frances recognized that her relationship with Leif helped her cope with life in Hollywood, and while she was not in love with him, she agreed to marry him. Her reasoning must have included the acknowledgment that his career was not progressing as successfully as hers, so a marriage would benefit him.

They eloped on February 8, 1936, and married in Yuma, Arizona. She was twenty-two and he twenty-four. Edith claims that Frances told her she had slipped the wedding ring from her finger as they walked away from the Justice of the Peace and dropped it into a storm drain to demonstrate the nature of their relationship. They could be companions, friends, even lovers, but not marriage-bound captives. They moved into a small furnished bungalow in Laurel Canyon together, and their life continued in the same manner, though now Frances went into the desert on weekends with a sleeping bag to get away from work. Edith says Frances was also sending Lillian money every month to supplement the work Lillian did. During March and April Frances made her second film, *Border Flight* (1936), an action programmer of men at an air-patrol base, starring John Howard.

A week after the marriage the decision was made to give Frances a bigger part in a more important picture since Frances had come across so well in her first two efforts, receiving good notices despite the films' scathing reviews. She was cast in her first A film, *Rhythm on the Range* (1936), a light comedy about the cross-country trek of an heiress and a singing cowboy, opposite one of Paramount's main stars, Bing Crosby. Edith maintains that Crosby had asked for Frances to be cast, since he was always generous to newcomers at Paramount. Filming took place in May 1936, much of it on location on the edge of the Mojave Desert. Frances got along well with Crosby, perhaps because he came from Washington State. He reportedly gave her a diamond necklace which she cherished (Edith describes the gift as desert agate set in a gold friendship ring), and he saw how the nervousness and secrecy she demonstrated in preparation was due to her still mastering the technique of film acting, although the behavior was judged by others as arrogance.

Onscreen, Frances' patrician beauty and comic ability drew the attention away from veteran Crosby, with critics raving, "Frances Farmer is just a delight." The film was a huge hit, one of the industry's top twenty box-office successes of the year, and Frances rose from promising young starlet to rising young actress. She was working up to ten hours a day at the studio, filming and trying out for parts, studying, or exercising. Frances was considered for the part of Dian Turlon in 1936 during the early stages of planning *Spawn of the North* (1938), but the part would be taken by Louise Platt.

Called into the office of the studio's executive head, Adolph Zukor, Frances was scolded for her living habits and deportment. Zukor wanted her to present an image of glamour, but Frances resisted and remained antagonistic. In an age of sables and limousines, Frances wore ready-made slacks and drove a six-year-old jalopy. Considered by the studio as a valuable piece of property, the publicity department used Frances' attitude to peg her as "eccentric"—the star who would not go Hollywood. Things improved somewhat when a Los Angeles automobile agency agreed to give her a new Plymouth Dusenberg convertible in exchange for some publicity photographs. She accepted, and Zukor was pacified, since this car was the kind that he wanted her to drive.

Producer Sam Goldwyn asked that Frances be loaned out to appear in Edna Ferber's *Come and Get It* (1936), to be directed by Howard Hawks and co-star Joel McCrea, Edward Arnold and Walter Brennan (who would win the Best Supporting Actor Academy Award). Filming began in June, but Frances' good working relationship with Hawks ended when he left the film mid-production after a disagreement with Goldwyn over the picture's ending. William Wyler was brought in to finish the film, a man Frances did not get along with. She is quoted as saying, "Acting with Wyler is the nearest thing to slavery," while

**Frances as the Park Avenue heiress Doris Halloway in a publicity portrait for *Rhythm on the Range* (1936).**

he fired back with, "The nicest thing I can say about Frances Farmer is that she is unbearable."

The film was scheduled to premiere on November 6 at Seattle's Liberty Theater as a homage to Frances' advance as a star (Agan says the premiere was at the Paramount Theater); but she refused to go, as she claimed to be exhausted after making back-to-back films. She was also unhappy about the state of her marriage, which she recognized as a mistake. However, she did go to Seattle—after being pressured by the studio—and was reunited with her mother after having been away for fourteen months. Seattle's finest greeted Frances upon her return. Even the *Seattle Post-Intelligencer*, who had branded her a Communist for her trip to Moscow, now described her as the fair-haired daughter of the city. All was forgiven and forgotten. Frances was booked into a suite at the Olympia Hotel two days before the premiere, and publicity photographs were taken of Frances at her home with Lillian; at the university, where she spoke before an assembly and was guest of honor at a student production of *A Doll's House*; and at the Paramount Theater, where she used to usher.

Arnold says that Frances refused to autograph copies of *Come and Get It* at the Bon Marche, since she rightly claimed that she didn't write the book, although Kauffman claims that he possesses a copy of the book signed by her. Frances also tactlessly pointed out the hypocrisy of those who had previously railed against her but now praised her because she was a movie star. On the night of the premiere, Frances slipped out of the screening, changed out of the studio-furnished gown and into her own clothes, and ate a sandwich at the hotel's drugstore. Found by a woman from Paramount who had been sent to retrieve her, Frances agreed to go back to the theater for the reception, although she refused to change her clothes.

With the premiere a public relations disaster, Frances returned to Hollywood the next day. In spite of a magazine cover story describing her manners as "none too gracious," it was predicted that she would be "as great as, and perhaps greater than Garbo." *Come and Get It* was a smash hit, although Frances was not happy with her own performance. Interestingly, the title isn't even mentioned in the John Douglas Eames history of Paramount Studios, *The Paramount Story*. In his biography of Howard Hawks, *The Grey Fox of Hollywood*, Todd McCarthy says that it was suggested to Sam Goldwyn that he hire Frances for the title role in his production of *Stella Dallas* (1937), which apparently he was having trouble casting. McCarthy's timing may be off, however, since he calls it Goldwyn's next production—when the Turner Classic Movies notes indicate that filming had begun in April, around the same time as *Come and Get It*. This would have

**Publicity portrait of Frances as the hostess Lotta Morgan in a deleted scene from *Come and Get It* (1936).**

made Frances unavailable; but given the problems she would subsequently have with William Wyler when he joined that film production, Goldwyn was probably grateful he did not embrace this idea. Barbara Stanwyck would go on to play the role and be nominated for the Best Actress Academy Award for her performance.

Frances became very busy. She began production of *The Toast of New York* in December as a loan-out to RKO. The film was a big post–Civil War saga in which Frances starred opposite Edward Arnold and Cary Grant. During filming, *Colliers* magazine reporter Kyle Crichton interviewed Frances for an article titled "I Dress as I Like," which William Arnold calls her written declaration of war against the false image Hollywood was trying to impose on her. Arnold claims that the studio had previously deflected the controversy of her trip to Russia by referring to it in her official biography as "a prize she had won in a local popularity contest." Kauffman disputes this claim by citing fan magazine articles, Paramount's official biography of Frances, and the Screen Actors Guild biography. The trip to Russia aside, in the interview, Frances was candid. She also continued her interest in left wing political causes, doing volunteer work for various organizations which supported the Loyalists in the Spanish Civil War. Additionally, Frances organized rallies, made speeches, and asked for donations from other stars and producers to alleviate the plight of migrant farm workers in the San Joaquin Valley, who lived and worked in what she considered horrifying conditions.

Frances in a publicity portrait for *The Toast of New York* (1937). Her champagne toast is ironic given the box office bomb that the film turned out to be.

Before production of *The Toast of New York* was completed in April 1937, Frances began work on *Exclusive* (1937) in March, with Fred MacMurray in a drama of rival newspapers. Frances was a replacement for Carole Lombard. It appears that she worked double duty by signing to begin *Ebb Tide* (1937) in June, a sea yarn with Ray Milland (and the only film she made in Technicolor). Edith says that *The Toast of New York* was made at the same time as *Ebb Tide*, although her dates may be suspect. In June Frances also did two radio plays for *CBS Lux Radio Theatre*. On June 4 she co-starred with Spencer Tracy and Virginia Bruce in the thirty minute "Men in White," which was produced by Cecil B. DeMille; it was an adaptation of the MGM title released in 1934. In the film, Frances' Barbara Denham had been essayed by Elizabeth Allen, Bruce's Laura Hudson by Myrna

Loy, and Tracy's Dr. George Ferguson by Clark Gable. On June 7 Frances co-starred with Errol Flynn in the forty-five-minute "British Agent," directed by and produced by DeMille, and which was an adaptation of the First National–Warner Bros. picture from 1934. Playing Elena, the part that Kay Francis had essayed opposite Leslie Howard in the film, Frances' Russian accent prefigured the one she would use in *Ride a Crooked Mile*. During the broadcast, DeMille gave a potted biography of Frances; and when interviewed, she advised that she planned to go east to do summer stock after completing *Ebb Tide*. Frances also spoke of her pleasure in doing the radio play, which she equated with live theater, presumably because of the studio audience.

The autobiography says that Frances collapsed on the set during the filming of *Ebb Tide* because of the pressure of overwork, but it does not say that she was out for over a day for the hospital check-up. Agan claims that Frances was hospitalized twice, with Edith claiming that Frances' grueling schedule spared her the need to diet. At one hundred and ten pounds, Frances weighed the least she ever would, and at five-feet-six-inches tall she looked thin and wan. Edith also tells the story of how Frances was followed by a shark one day as she swam in the sea at the Catalina Island location, the experience putting her off swimming there again between shots.

Arnold says that the success of these last two Paramount films were evidence that the studio considered Frances to be good box office, and, as a result, the front office planned future co-starring projects for her with Gary Cooper, Ronald Coleman, and Clark Gable. Kauffman, on the other hand, claims that Frances' importance and her own haughtiness after the success of *Come and Get It* was out of proportion to the mixed reviews she received for *The Toast of New York* and *Ebb Tide*. Edith comments that jealous tension arose between Leif and Frances, since his career was not progressing as successfully as hers.

In August Frances opposed Paramount, who Agan says wanted her for *Beau Geste* (1939), presumably for the part of Isabel Rivers, which would be played by Susan Hayward. (This would not be the last time that Hayward would usurp Frances in a Paramount role.) Suspended without pay for her refusal, Frances went east to work in the summer stock theater. Frances starred in C. K. Munro's comedy *At Mrs. Beam's* at the Mount Kisco Playhouse in Westchester County, New York, and *The Petrified Forest* later in the month at Westport, Connecticut. Happy being in live theater again and away from the pressures of Hollywood, she regained her weight and peace of mind.

## Back to New York

Frances appeared in a picture spread in *Vogue*, which, according to Arnold, attracted the attention of Harold Clurman. Arnold claims, and Edith confirms it, that Clurman met her at a rally for the Spanish Civil War in Central Park. Arnold says Clurman had attended one of the stock performances, so his meeting with Frances was fortuitous, although Edith says Frances couldn't help but mention the Group Theater party where he had ignored her. Clurman telephoned her to invite her to his Manhattan apartment, where he asked her to join the Group Theater and offered her the female lead in Odets' play *Golden Boy*. Frances' autobiography claims that Odets himself had visited Frances at Westport and, having seen her performance there, offered her the part of Lorna Moon, the girl from the wrong side of the tracks. Edith notes that Frances' Hollywood success appealed to the struggling social revolutionary group, with Edith writing that Clurman "lured Frances into the fold and indicated that he might condescend to let her act with them."

*Golden Boy* was scheduled to have a production at the Belasco Theater on Broadway under the direction of Clurman. The cast included Luther Adler, Morris Carnovsky, Lee J. Cobb, Howard Da Silva, John Garfield (billed as Julius), Elia Kazan, and Martin Ritt. Publicity for Frances' performance appeared in the *Chicago Sun Times* in August, and she went into rehearsal in September, being paid a pittance for the privilege, according to Edith. Edith also says Leif flew to New York to join her in a Central Park West apartment, though the autobiography claims that the marriage had collapsed long before Frances left Hollywood and that the couple had announced a public separation. Agan claims that ten days before opening night, the budget of $19,000 had still not been raised. The play opened on November 4, and its successful run of 248 performances lasted until June 1938, landing Frances on the cover of *Life* magazine on January 17, 1938, in an article entitled "Frances Farmer: A Seattle Girl Reaches Broadway via Hollywood." She also became involved with Odets, who was married to actress Luise Rainer. Rainer was one of the backers of the production but left for Europe after the play opened, which gave Odets his chance to make advances toward Frances. Arnold calls the affair between Frances and Odets "one of the most curious romantic episodes in both their lives." He claims Odets was frightened of the depth of her feeling for him, and the relationship only highlighted his disdain for Hollywood actresses. Odets had ambivalent feelings about Hollywood, and no doubt being married to an actress who would walk away from a successful Hollywood career made him even more ambivalent. A misogynist, Odets was cruel to Frances, humiliating her in public and suggesting she should go back to Leif, whom she knew she didn't want to be with.

Edith describes Odets as "an unattractive man in looks, but his intense animal magnetism both attracted and repelled [Frances]." She continues, "His pretense of concern and sympathy found an easy target in her unhappiness.... For weeks he held her in the grips of emotional slavery." When Odets told her to go back to Leif, Edith reports that he said it would be the act of "a real woman, for her own good." In his autobiography, *A Life*, Elia Kazan would also comment on Odets' search for "a real woman"—being one who was "a peasant," self-effacing and servile—which neither Luise Rainer nor Frances was. Frances' autobiography states that Odets was

Portrait of playwright Clifford Odets, author of the play *Golden Boy*, with whom Frances had a turbulent affair.

a strange, almost ugly man, but he was everything I could ever imagine, at that time, admirable in a man. He was a fiery, fascinating intellect with strange sexual drives, and I reacted like a smitten schoolgirl.... Odets maneuvered me as he would a character in one of his plays. He toyed with my attitudes and reactions. He was a psychological button-pusher, able to crush me with a word or sweep me into ecstasy with a gesture.... I cannot say that I loved him; a more apt description would be a passionate hatred coupled with a physical fascination. Whatever it was, it did much to destroy me.

Kazan, who appeared in *Golden Boy*, wrote about Frances in *A Life*:

She had a special glow, a skin without flaw, lustrous eyes—a blonde you'd dream about. She also had a wry, and at times, rather disappointed manner, a twist of the mouth, which suited the part. She was a dramatic contrast to the dark up-from-under men she was playing with. As an actress, she was a beginner.

In *Selected Theatre Criticism Volume 3: 1931–1950*, Anthony Slide quoted a review written by Herbert Drake on November 13 for *Cue*, which says, "Frances Farmer turns in a simple and honest portrayal, completely in tune with the magnificent ensemble acting of the rest of the Group performance." Kauffman objects to Arnold's claim that Frances was singled out as the best thing in *Golden Boy*, as opposed to Odets' salty idiom of the street dialogue. He mentions reviews that considered her to be miscast as a tramp from Newark—*Time* magazine, for example, which noted "her fresh-faced prettiness belying every tough trait she tried to show." Brooks Atkinson in the *New York Times* (November 5, 1937) said, "Frances is sufficient to the part and excellent in the romantic scenes."

Kauffman also says that Frances' performance demonstrated her lack of stage experience. The latter point is questionable since Frances did have stage experience, and surely her performance was the responsibility of her director. Kauffman does acknowledge that the reviews for Frances in the national tour repeatedly mention her "intelligence and depth of characterization." Edith quotes from a *Los Angeles Herald Express* review that also questions her casting, since neither her look nor manner is that of a tramp. However, Edith is also quick to add that the Group treated Frances like one, and welcomed Leif to the fold. The autobiography claims that Leif followed Frances to New York because he was unable to find work in Hollywood. The truth is far more interesting. While he certainly didn't experience the meteoric rise that Frances had, Leif was appearing in films in supporting roles. He made a lot of Westerns with Buster Crabbe, but he was also featured in *Waiki Wedding* (1937), a musical comedy opposite Bing Crosby, Bob Burns and Martha Raye, an attempt by the studio to duplicate the success of *Rhythm on the Range*. He was even lent to MGM for their prestigious *Conquest* (1937), with Garbo and Charles Boyer. Leif wouldn't score a leading role at Paramount until *One Third of a Nation* (1939), but in the meantime was cast in several Broadway plays. Hardie Albright's *All the Living* ran from March 24 to May 1938 at the Fulton Theater under the direction of Lee Strasberg. Leif would also work for the Group Theater in Odets' *Rocket to the Moon* at the Belasco Theater under Harold Clurman's direction from November 24 to March 1939, and later do Irwin Shaw's *Retreat to Pleasure* in 1940/41.

Edith reports that Leif and Frances worked together doing improvisations in Stanislavsky technique, and they were used for publicity for the Group. They both contributed to the adoption of a ten-year-old orphan of the Spanish Revolution and made donations for his care. Perhaps to ward off suspicion by the House Un-American Activities Commission, who would be responsible for many Hollywood actors being blacklisted by the industry for being subversives, Leif would later speak out against the Group in an interview for American Mercury in 1955. He said that, in spite of the money he gave, and the use of his name, to causes like the Abraham Lincoln Brigade and a Rally for China, he never joined the Communist Party. In February 1938 Frances was in a full-page color photo spread in the *New York Sunday Mirror*, on the cover of *Ladies Home Journal*, and written about by columnists Walter Winchell and Danton Walker. Edith, however, notes that the reports erred in the color of Frances' eyes, which were grey-blue but invariably described as hazel. Edith also scoffs at the obvious pun used for Frances' many interviews as "The Farmer's Daughter." Edith also quotes a letter from Lillian to her that describes Frances at the Stork Club sitting with both Odets and Luise Rainer, which must have been odd if one is to believe that he and Frances were romantically involved. Perhaps this awkwardness was expressed in the copy of the play Frances sent Edith in March 1938, which was wrongly dated 1937.

Edith claims that the Group deliberately set out to halt any attempt at reconciliation between Leif and Frances, since they argued that her generosity and talents could be better used without a husband around. Nevertheless, the couple would subsequently make a film together called *Ride a Crooked Mile* (1938) about a Russian Cossack turned cattle rustler. Paramount was pleased to have Frances back, but Edith says Frances agreed to do the film only as a favor to Leif. Edith also reports that Frances discovered she was pregnant at this time, and with Leif showing more interest in his career than in being a father, she went to a back street Hollywood abortionist. This is something Edith claims Frances would regret the rest of her life, since the crude operation made her unable to become pregnant again, in spite of the autobiography's claim of another abortion. This claim of a botched abortion is repeated in the *A&E Biography* episode on Frances, "Paradise Lost." However, neither Edith nor the documentary questions the identity of the father—Leif Erickson or Clifford Odets?

During production on *Ride a Crooked Mile*, Edith, Lillian and Ernest visited Frances, and they posed for photographs. A photograph of Frances taken with her parents that Edith claims is often reproduced in newspaper and magazine articles about Frances appears in Edith's book. Edith claims that Frances kept a framed copy of the photograph as long as she lived, though presumably she was without it at Steilacoom. Frances returned to New York when the production wrapped and after she had attended a family reunion at the home of her sister, Rita, in Venice, California. Frances went on the road with *Golden Boy*, opening in Chicago in September and ending the run in Washington, D.C. in December. In Washington Frances met with Dr. Don Fernando de Los Rios, the Spanish ambassador to the United States, to publicize a national drive for food for the children of Spain.

Back in New York, Frances was struck three blows. Assuming that she would be going to London for the production of *Golden Boy*, she was devastated to learn that financial considerations had necessitated that another actress play Frances' part in London (since only she was able to provide the needed backing for the tour). The British published edition of the play lists American actress Lillian Emerson in the cast playing Lorna Moon when the production opened at the St. James Theatre in London on June 21, 1938. In his book *The Fervent Years: The Group Theatre & the '30s*, Harold Clurman claims that another factor that cemented the decision not to use Frances in London was her contractual obligation to Paramount to make another film. This film is presumably *Ride a Crooked Mile*, which went into production in July 1938, whereas the London production of *Golden Boy* occurred in June. The idea also puts a different spin on the Clurman character's attitude in the film *Frances*, in the scene where he tells her that she is not going to London. To

**Publicity portrait of Frances for** *Ride a Crooked Mile* **(1938). A close-up of Frances in this costume was used for the cover of William Arnold's biography** *Shadowland*.

Frances' question of "What am I going to do now?" he replies, "Hollywood wants you back," which doesn't seem as patronizing as it first appears.

The second blow came when Odets ended their affair in October and returned to his wife. This is described by Margaret Brennan-Gibson in her 1982 biography of Odets, who calls Frances "exquisitely beautiful, principled, and gifted," and describes her situation rather obtusely as "the tragic paradigm of a theatre artist in America." The biographer tells how Luise Rainer had been asked by reporters when she returned from Europe if she was aware of Odets' affair with Frances. Having filed for divorce from her husband, Rainer is quoted as responding, "I have been away a long time. A man has a right to do what he wants if a wife is gone so long." Odets' note to Frances—"The affair is now ended as my wife has returned from Europe"—would be quoted in the film *Frances*. However, in the *E! Mysteries and Scandals* television episode on Frances, *Frances* screenwriter Eric Bergren states that the telegram read, "My wife returns from Europe today. Best of luck." The *A&E Biography* episode on Frances, "Paradise Lost," claims the telegram said, "My wife returns from Europe today and I feel it is best for us never to see each other again." In his book *Clifford Odets and American Political Theater*, Christopher J. Herr advises that, in spite of the end of their affair, Odets remained fascinated by Frances, keeping a file on her and planning (but never succeeding) to write an "Actress" play loosely based on her story.

Then Shepard Traube sued Frances for seventy-five thousand dollars for breach of contract, maintaining that although he had helped her get the Paramount screen test, she had failed to pay him ten percent of her salary over the years of his representation. The case was decided in Frances' favor, since it was judged that Traube's representation was limited to that one contract, and her contract with Paramount invalidated his (Edith claims the court ruled Traube lacked an agent's license at the time he represented her). But the trauma of a court battle weighed on Frances, and she began drinking. In January 1939 she began rehearsals for *Quiet City*, an experimental piece by Irwin Shaw to be directed by Elia Kazan at the Belsco Theater. The production only ran for two performances, on the Sundays of April 16 and April 23, so naturally it was not considered a success. Kauffman says that the piece ran on the weekends, utilizing some of the Group's off-duty actors when another Shaw play was in season, and that it may have been extended if it was better received. In May Frances appeared on the radio on the *Kate Smith Dramatic Hour*, opposite Luther Adler in "Women in White." Edith claims Frances and Leif attempted reconciliation in July, which was not successful, although they continued to do workshops at the Group's Long Island abandoned school house.

Frances worked in summer stock until August. In September she began rehearsals for the Group's next play, Robert Ardrey's *Thunder Rock*, to be directed by Elia Kazan and co-starring Luther Adler and Lee J. Cobb. This fantasy set in a lighthouse in Michigan was about the spiritual renewal of a disillusioned writer, with Frances playing the supporting part of an immigrant maiden. It was known as *Tower of Light* up to the previews, and opened at the Mansfield Theater on November 14, 1939, running until December 2—a mere three weeks. In the *New York Times* on November 15, Brooks Atkinson wrote that Frances "is pleasant." The autobiography makes much of the antagonism that Franchot Tone expressed to Frances during the run, but Tone was not in the cast. In his book *A Method to Their Madness: The History of the Actors Studio*, Foster Hirsch says that around this time Frances began rehearsals for a Group production of Anton Chehkov's play *The Three Sisters*, adapted by Clifford Odets, with Frances cast as Olga. However, the production was soon abandoned because of a lack of funds to stage it. In his book *The Fervent Years*, Harold Clurman confirms that the Group did begin rehearsals in Long Island, but that the production felt apart because he, as the director, had lost faith in his ability, and also because of cast divisions that made working together impractical.

She accepted the role of Dorothy Bridges in the Theater Guild's production of Ernest Hemingway's play *The Fifth Column* about the Spanish Civil War, to be directed by Lee

Strasberg, but left while it was still in rehearsal, physically and emotionally exhausted. A brief affair with Harold Clurman didn't help. Arnold claims that it was the end of her affair with Odets that made Frances quit the play. She was fined fifteen hundred dollars for her walkout, and the play went ahead, with Catherine Locke cast in the part Frances would have played. The production ran at the Alvin Theater from March 6 to May 18; however, it was deemed a failure and signaled the end of the Group Theater company. Tone had been in this cast, so perhaps it was his antipathy towards Frances in rehearsal that contributed to her abandoning the production. Frances was now an outcast in the New York theater community, and it seemed Hollywood was her only alternative for paid work. The *A&E Biography* episode "Paradise Lost" sums up her situation with these two sentences: "She realized she would have to cave to conventionality if she wanted to survive. But for Frances Farmer, conformity was a four letter word."

Edith claims that Odets' rejection of Frances sent her to the F.B.I. to denounce the Group, who considered her an actress seeking publicity and did nothing. However, the Group saw her action as a betrayal and began a campaign of threats, innuendoes and terror tactics against her, which led to her leaving *The Fifth Column*. Edith says that footage of the slaughter and torture of prisoners of both the Russian Revolution and the Spanish Civil War were screened for her to illustrate the fate of anyone that wouldn't conform or dared to leave the Party. Supposedly this led to Frances locking herself in her hotel room and drinking away the Christmas week. Soon after that she fled home to Seattle. A letter from Ernest to Edith in January 1940 confirms Frances' presence. The letter also mentions that Frances had been asked to replace Marlene Dietrich in a Howard Hughes film, but that somehow the theater union Equity had stopped her from doing so. This claim is odd since the only film Hughes appeared to be planning at the time was *The Outlaw* (1943), which would not go into production until November 1940 and was distributed by RKO and not Paramount. It is conceivable that Hughes might have wanted Dietrich for the part of Rio McDonald, the sultry Mexican girl, after the success of Dietrich's saloon gal Frenchy in the western *Destry Rides Again* (1939). Though given that Dietrich was thirty-nine at the time, and Jane Russell (who would be cast as Rio) was only nineteen, the prospect of casting the twenty-seven-year-old Frances would seem more likely. The notes on the *Turner Classic Movie Database* tell how Howard Hawks was the original director chosen for *The Outlaw*, after he had directed Hughes' previous production, *Scarface* (1932). Since Hawks had directed Frances in *Come and Get It*, perhaps Ernest had meant to write about Howard Hawks rather than Hughes. However, what is most dubious about Ernest's tale is the idea that a theater union would have the power to stop a film producer hiring Frances for a film.

Another claim which may be equally misguided is made by Peter McNally in his book on Bette Davis, *The Performances That Made Her Great*. In it, McNally maintains that Frances was considered for the part Davis played in *The Letter* (1941). His claim is unsubstantiated, but what makes it ludicrous is the idea that director William Wyler would consider working with Frances again after their clash on *Come and Get It*.

## Back to Hollywood

Having been off-screen for two years, Frances returned to Paramount in 1940. In March she was on radio in a play called *Woman in the Wilderness*. Agan claims that by this time Paramount believed her potential as a star had crested, she had been forgotten in the constant rush of new talent that was drawn to Hollywood, and they no longer had an interest in giving her important roles. The studio could earn more for a loan-out fee, which explains why Frances was loaned to other studios for her next two films. At United Artists she made *South of Pago Pago* (1940), a South Seas drama about pearls in which she starred opposite Victor McLagen and Jon Hall. In their book *Hollywood Players: The Thirties*, James Robert Parish and William T. Leonard report that after making the film Frances did the radio play *Women in the Wilderness*, although this is not confirmed by other sources. In July at Warner Bros., Frances was cast in the oil picture *Flowing Gold* (1940) opposite former Group member John Garfield. Arnold says that it was Garfield who asked for Frances over the studio's objections.

Although the Group as a functioning theater company had disintegrated, members came to Frances for help in finding work in Hollywood. She remained generous, providing hand-outs and room and board when she could. Frances helped get Sophie Rosenstein a job as a drama coach at Warners, with Frances recognizing the hypocrisy of a woman who lectured against Hollywood at university accepting such a position. Frances also hired Sophie's husband, Arthur Weinstein, as her business manager, although his only previous business experience was as a hat salesman. Edith also claims that Frances paid for a cruise to Bermuda for one of the Group's women who was going through a divorce, and accompanied her on the trip.

Frances went back East to do summer stock—*Little Women* and *Our Betters* at the Cape Playhouse in Dennis, Massachusetts. She then went to New York in early 1941, driving alone for two months across the country and registering overnight under her married name, Mrs. William Anderson. The autobiography and Edith say that in April Frances returned to Hollywood and rented the former home of Dolores Del Rio in Santa Monica (Arnold says it was in Malibu). There she adopted the star lifestyle for the first time by employing a butler and a staff of servants. Kauffman maintains that contemporary news accounts state that the house Frances moved into was not Del Rio's but rather next door to it. The autobiography also states that Frances started writing an autobiographical novel entitled *God's Peculiar Care*. Sadly, the manuscript would be lost—Arnold says in a later fire.

She made her last two films for Paramount. *World Premiere* (1941) was a comedy about a Hollywood troupe junketing to Washington, D.C. for the premiere of a deluxe picture. Frances played opposite John Barrymore, and, as Kitty Carr, she abandoned her blondeness for a black Cleopatra wig. In May she played a supporting role in *Among the Living* (1941), with the starring femme part going to Susan Hayward. This B-movie drama about two murders in a small town had Frances as the wife of an accused maniac, played by Albert Dekker in a dual-role.

There is a rumor that director Preston Sturges wanted her for the part of the down-on-her-luck blonde actress "the Girl" in *Sullivan's Travels* (1942), which would be played by Veronica Lake, though this cannot be substantiated. In July Frances played Calamity Jane in a Universal Western about a Sioux uprising against new settlers, *Badlands of Dakota* (1941), opposite Broderick Crawford and Robert Stack. Agan says that Harold Clurman came to live with Frances during filming, as he was separated from his wife, Stella Adler, even though it appears that Clurman did not marry Adler until 1943.

*Opposite:* **Publicity portrait of Frances for** *South of Pago Pago* (1940).

After finishing the film, Frances went on a vacation to Mexico with Lillian, and then sent Lillian home to Seattle when Frances returned to Hollywood in August. In September Frances was hired by Twentieth Century–Fox to play Isabel Blake in the historical drama *Son of Fury* (1942), opposite Tyrone Power. In her autobiography, *Self-Portrait*, co-star Gene Tierney claims that it was on this film that Frances hit the studio hairdresser, though the event would actually occur nearly two years later. Agan says that Frances was cast in Mitchell Leisen's comedy *Take a Letter, Darling* (1942) in a supporting role, but was fired after failing to appear for makeup tests and costume fittings.

When the U.S. entered World War II after the attack on Pearl Harbor on December 7, 1941 (not witnessed by Edith, as Arnold claims), Frances worked to organize a group of movie actors to tour army bases and perform classic plays. She made an announcement to the press, but discovered that no studio was prepared to entrust their stars to someone with her bad reputation, so her plans came to nothing. Frances appeared in many magazine portraits, with the studio going overtime with publicity in spite of the quality of work it offered her. Subsequently she turned down proffered films in favor of seclusion in her home.

Frances spent the next six months mostly alone, unemployed and drinking. Edith says

**Sir Arthur Blake (George Sanders) in an almost romantic embrace with his daughter Isabel (Frances) at the masked ball in a still for a deleted scene from *Son of Fury* (1942). The masks represent the duplicity and perversity of both their characters.**

Frances occasionally visited her sister, Rita, and continued with her memoirs. Leif had arranged a divorce from her on June 12 so that he could marry actress Margaret Hayes the same day, although by this time Frances and Leif were long estranged.

Margaret Hayes, who bore some facial resemblance to Frances, also had the same penchant for name-changing as Leif. Originally Dana Dale when she made her feature debut at Warner Bros. in *The Man Who Talked Too Much* (1940), she became Margaret Hayes with *In Old Colorado* (1941), but changed to Maggie Haynes and then Maggie Hayes in the 1950s. She stayed Maggie Hayes until her death in 1977. Three years younger than Frances, Margaret had moved from Warners to Paramount in the 1940s and was a Paramount contract player when she married Leif. Ironically, she had appeared in a minor role in *Take a Letter, Darling*.

Publicity portrait of Margaret "Maggie" Hayes, whom Leif Erickson divorced Frances to marry. Interestingly, Hayes bears some facial similarity to Frances.

## *Arrest*

Both the autobiography and Arnold claim that on the evening of October 19, 1942, Frances was driving to a party at the house of Deanna Durbin. Agan, Edith and Kauffman all label this as untrue. Agan says Frances was coming home from the studio, presumably Paramount, where one imagines she would have been trying to restore faith in her after her behavior on *Take a Letter, Darling*. Edith and Kauffman both state that Frances had visited her sister Rita and was driving home in her black Plymouth convertible when she was stopped by a motorcycle policeman on the Pacific Coast Highway for driving in a dim-out zone with her lights on high beam. Kauffman references Frances' own account in a 1958 article for *American Weekly*, and also says contemporary news articles confirm this.

The autobiography claims that Frances was parked on the side of the road, but with her lights still on, when the policeman approached. Although it claims she had met Deanna Durbin once before, apparently she had mixed feelings about socializing with anyone and sat in her car crying. Amusingly, the autobiography also says that the officer did not believe that she was Frances Farmer, and rather thought she was trying to make a fool of him since he did not recognize her. Learning that she did not have her license on her, the policeman called a squad car, which took Frances to the Santa Monica station where she was charged with driving without a license and failing to observe a dim-out zone. Agan says she was also charged with drunk driving, and although Frances would admit to having had a few drinks, she would deny being drunk.

Agan also claims that Frances drove away from the policeman when he initially approached her, with Frances telling him, "You bore me." A chase ensued. When he caught up with Frances, the police officer took her into custody. This latter scenario seems to have fueled the re-enactment in *Frances* in which she and the policeman are shown to have physically fought (although there is no car chase). Her license was suspended, her car was impounded, and she was given a sentence of one-hundred-and-eighty days in jail, but put on a two-year probation as a first-time offender. Edith claims Frances was also fined $250.

Agan says Frances was held in a cell for eight hours until her agent arrived to bail her out, when she was photographed by the press with uncombed hair and looking "disheveled." It appears that Agan confuses this arrest with the press photographs of her arrest in 1943, since the photograph in Arnold's book of Frances at the police station has her looking neat, with her hair in an upswept style that could not be described as uncombed. The photograph is a candid, since Frances is not looking at the camera as she reads a piece of paper. It gives the impression that she is unaware that she is being photographed, which is possible since a flashbulb may not have been needed if daylight had broken.

## *Goodbye Paramount*

The arrest caused a scandal and made Frances even more of a pariah in Hollywood. She refused to talk to the press or studio representatives about the incident, and Paramount cancelled her contract. Few actors were able to survive in Hollywood at this time as freelancers without a studio contract.

Cary Grant and Loretta Young were about the only exceptions, and they were much bigger stars than Frances because they didn't share her interest in working in the theater and her contempt for making movies. No studio would now give Frances the necessary insurance backing to cover her reliable appearance in a film, and her agent advised her to leave town until things blew over. A producer had previously offered her the lead in an independent low-budget production to be shot in Mexico called *Five Were Chosen* (Arnold calls it *Hostages*, which is the working title on the Internet Movie Database). She now accepted the part.

**An uncharacteristically drag-glam portrait of Frances, circa 1943.**

Agan says the property was an adaptation of John Steinbeck's novel *Murder at Ludice*, whereas the listing on IMDB claims the screenplay and story about Yugoslav villagers fighting to free Nazi hostages was by Budd Schulberg, a member of the Group Theater. Edith says that their father Ernest came to see Frances when he received news of her arrest, and talked to her judge. She claims it was Ernest who talked Frances into doing the Mexican film after meeting the film's producer, and Ernest who persuaded the judge to put her on probation rather than impose a jail sentence.

When Frances arrived in Mexico City she changed her mind about doing the film. The autobiography says that Frances walked out after waiting for two weeks for a script re-rewrite that never came. Edith claims there was no script because the filmmakers had planned to improvise as they went. Kauffman claims that Frances may have done some master shots for the film. *Five Were Chosen* was directed by Herbert Kline, and the Spanish language version of the film, titled *Cinco fueron escogidos*, was helmed by Agustin P. Delgado. The Mexican actor Ricardo Montalban appeared in both versions, and Kauffman quotes from an interview with the actor archived by the Academy of Television Arts & Sciences. Montalban claims that a few days before filming began, Frances' mental problems caused her to roam the halls of the hotel naked and spray people with a seltzer bottle, although he doesn't specifically claim she was drunk.

Edith says that Frances had been unable to sleep in Mexico, and with her nightmares she was "an emotional bomb with a short fuse to go off at any spark." The spark was a quarrel with the director, and her being slapped by one of the male cast when Frances became sarcastic. She fought back, and a brawl ensued, with the police arriving. Frances went to bed and was ordered to leave the country the next morning. Protesting that she had not been paid, a government limousine and two policemen drove her to the border town of Laredo, Texas, where she wired her brother Wesley for travel fare. His wife Ruth flew down and accompanied Frances back to Hollywood.

Arnold, but not the autobiography, says that Frances became ill with dysentery. The American Embassy, rather than send her to a hospital, drove her to Laredo to recover in a hotel. Louella Parsons reported that Frances had had a nervous breakdown and was forced by the Embassy into a sanitarium. Agan claims that Frances had been deported after an all-night "rumpus" at the hotel where she was staying, something which Kauffman says Agan got from a Walter Winchell column. Agan claims that broken furniture and Frances throwing punches resulted in her being escorted by Mexican police to El Paso, Texas, and charged with being drunk and disorderly and disturbing the peace. Although he doesn't say what the consequences of these charges were, Agan does say that Frances caught a train back to California after being wired the fare by Wesley.

When she returned to Hollywood in November, Frances discovered that Arthur Weinstein had sublet her Santa Monica house to earn money while she was away (now "inhabited by a strange family," writes Agan), and had moved her possessions into a room at the Knickerbocker Hotel. The autobiography claims that the only possessions that she found in her room were her clothes, and that this is when the manuscript disappeared, though it's hard to know who else would want it, in spite of the "danger" she claims was in it. The autobiography also claims, as proof that she was purposely robbed, that an item was anonymously returned to her in the post three decades later, presumably something she had possessed in the Santa Monica house before leaving for Mexico.

Agan says that her things were taken by her mother and sister-in-law to store, although one wonders why they didn't place them in the hotel. He also says the item that was returned to her years later was a cut-glass decanter. Agan quotes from Kibbee that Frances didn't care about the loss of her possessions. Rather, the film *Frances* presents her as being devastated, especially by the missing manuscript, which Agan says Frances was using "as a means of therapy to solve the increasing puzzle her life was becoming." Kauffman claims that it was Wesley's wife Ruth who moved Frances' possessions, mainly because her financial situation would not allow her to stay in the house, since her not working had used up her savings. Edith says it was Ruth and Wesley (and possibly Weinstein) who moved her things, and that it was Wesley who burned the manuscript to keep it from "falling into the wrong hands." Edith also implies that Frances was aware or learned of the actions of her family, and that it sparked a distrust of the people who were supposedly concerned about her behavior.

Arnold claims that soon after moving into the Knickerbocker, Frances, in an effort to salvage her career, called Louella Parsons to try to correct the misinformation that had been published. She continued to use the amphetamine Benzedrine as an appetite suppressant and to bolster her energy, although its side effects included paranoia and erratic behavior. (Benzedrine was also the chosen drug of Judy Garland, though it had not had the detrimental result on her life as yet.) The effects of the drug on director Joseph L. Mankiewicz is noted in Kenneth L. Geist's biography *Pictures Will Talk* as "curbing the appetite, making him very talkative, kept him awake, [and] left a peculiar taste and dryness in the mouth." But Mankiewicz wasn't combining it with alcohol, a known depressant, as Frances was, which formulated a dangerous cocktail. In January she accepted a movie role in another low-budget effort, a Monogram melodrama produced by the King Brothers entitled *No Escape* (the autobiography calls it *There Is No Escape*), to be directed by Harold Young.

## *No Escape*

Edith oddly states that Frances had been "given a command to appear in the film," although she was in no condition to work. Agan says Frances' behavior on the set was erratic from the beginning, "alternating between fits of laugher and ear-shattering tantrums."

She demanded a total script re-write and flew into a rage when she was asked to do a scene that required she be bound and gagged. Kauffman says that in spite of this behavior she did manage to complete one day of filming, and she can be seen in the released feature in a one-second shot used during a montage sequence. The only existing publicity still that Frances did for the film shows her in another scene, with Dean Jagger, standing behind Jagger who sits in a chair.

On January 13, 1943, Frances got into an argument with the hairdresser, Edna Burge. Edna claimed that Frances slapped her, knocked her down, and dislocated her jaw. Agan also says Frances ripped off Edna's wig to add humiliation to her assault. Edith says that Frances grabbed the hairbrush from Burge, hurled it, and that it hit Burge. The autobiography doesn't mention the attack but does say that Frances was suffering head pains, and that it hurt to have her hair combed. The film *Frances* shows the actress storming off the set, and the next day Frances was replaced in the role of Helen, the amusement park employee, by Mary Brian. Brian was nicknamed "the Sweetest Girl in Pictures," which must have been a nice change for the film's producers in light of Frances' hostility.

The only still taken of Frances for *No Escape* (aka *I Escaped from the Gestapo*, 1943). Frances (left), with Dean Jagger and hatted Arthur Gardner (standing) and Norman Willis (seated). The scene was not recreated after Frances had been replaced in the film by Mary Brian.

Frances went back to the Knickerbocker and had drinks with friends at the hotel bar. Agan says she became drunk, slid out of her sweater, and threw a glass at a mirror behind the bar, smashing it. Burge, meanwhile, went to the police and filed an assault charge. As Frances had not paid the entire arrest fine, a warrant had already been issued for her arrest. Three police officers—one female—came to her room at the hotel at 3 A.M. Agan says Frances had taken a sleeping pill and gone to bed when she was awakened several hours later by pounding at her door. When Frances did not answer the door, they opened it with a passkey (Agan says the door was broken through). The police found her naked and hiding in the bathroom, and, after forcing her to dress, took her to the Santa Monica police station. Agan and Edith claim Frances was kicking and screaming as she left the hotel lobby, although the only press photograph of Frances acting this way was taken at the police station. Edith also says Frances was handcuffed. The autobiography defends Frances' resistance by claiming that the police did not tell her why she was being arrested, something she would only learn in court the next day. It also claims that it was the police who told the press of Frances' arrest, and that is how the photographers knew to be at the hotel and the station.

Held overnight in jail and denied counsel, according to Edith, Frances appeared in court the next morning. Agan says when Judge Marshall Hickson asked her about the hotel bar brawl she denied knowledge of it and taking part in it. It was when he asked about her drinking that Frances uttered the much quoted statement: "I put liquor in my milk. I put liquor in my coffee and in my orange juice. What do you want me to do, starve to death?" She also was heard to say, "Have you ever had a broken heart?" which Agan claims is a reference both to Leif and Clifford Odets. Edith claims the official opinion handed down by the court-appointed psychiatrist was that Frances' breakdown was due to the break-up of her marriage. Edith reports that Leif had heard about Frances' trouble and gone to Wesley to ask if he could help, but was told to stay away, as it was thought that he would upset her since he had remarried.

Frances was sentenced to one-hundred-and-eighty days in jail for violating probation. Without any legal counsel, Frances asked to use the telephone. When she was refused, she threw an inkwell at the judge and was restrained by officers and carried out of the courtroom. Agan says that during the struggle Frances hit a policeman and a matron. Frances was taken to the Los Angeles county jail where she was booked. Agan, Arnold and the autobiography all claim that Frances had been placed in a strait-jacket, but the press photographs do not bear this out. Agan's book includes a photograph of Frances on the telephone, in opposition to the idea that she was not allowed access. The look on her face shows surprise and disapproval at being photographed, with the angle not as unflattering as the other press photographs.

The photographs are fascinating for many reasons, although it is unclear where and when some of them were taken, apart from the ones obviously showing Frances in a cell. One is lurid in the image of Frances brawling with police, her flesh exposed as she is carried out. The most famous is a deliberately unflattering shot of her sitting in a chair, smoking, and with an apparent double-chin. That she was seemingly allowed to apply lipstick as she dressed but was not allowed to comb her hair seems rather perverse on the part of the officers who arrested her. Another photograph exists which shows Frances in close-up, glaring at the camera but looking beautiful, despite her disheveled hair. The autobiography uses the device of Frances looking at her mother's scrapbook to remember her past, with Frances becoming contemptuous of Lillian for keeping the "shocking" and "horrible" pictures carefully trimmed and pasted for posterity. The loss of memory is rationalized by blackouts, which is a convenient excuse for a ghost-writer.

Frances was transferred to the psychiatric ward of the Los Angeles General Hospital on January 20. A court order declared Frances mentally incompetent. Kauffman says news reports state that Ruth (not Lillian, as Arnold claims) was present at the hearing and agreed that psychiatric treatment would be preferable to jail. Kauffman also states that Wesley signed a commitment order for Frances. Edith claims that both Ernest and Lillian arrived to be with Frances, with Ernest working with her attorney to get the jail sentence changed to a sanity hearing. It was Weinstein's testimony on Frances' poverty that enabled her admission to a sanitarium. Edith says that Ernest went after Harold Clurman for repayment of six thousand dollars, which Clurman would state he considered donations and not loans, though Clurman would pay back five hundred dollars before fleeing California.

Frances was sent to the La Crescenta private sanitarium (Agan says it was called the Kimbel sanitarium—as does the *A&E Biography* episode on Frances, "Paradise Lost"— and located in the San Fernando Valley), paid for by the Screen Actors Guild. An article by John Rosenfield in the *Los Angeles Times* pointed out that Frances being left without legal counsel was unprecedented, although she was not under contract to a studio at the time. In opposition to Arnold's claim that news accounts of her arrest and commitment were unsympathetic, Kauffman notes that coverage in *Time* magazine, *Newsweek*, and *Variety* were uniformly sympathetic.

Agan says that Frances was left alone at first to rest. However, after several weeks, her doctors prescribed insulin shots for depression for ninety days, with permission granted by Lillian. Edith, however, says that Lillian knew nothing of the treatment and would not have approved it. Kauffman quotes a news report dated April 1943 which stated that Frances was to be released, and concludes that a relapse derailed said release. In the fall of 1943, Frances ran away because she was so alarmed by the effects the insulin had on her, making her more docile but wiping her memory. She hitchhiked her way to Venice and Rita's house, and contacted her mother. This led to Frances being released into Lillian's care in September.

## Back to Seattle

Frances stayed with Lillian in Seattle over the winter of 1943–44. Publicity over her troubles was limited to a column that Louella Parsons wrote which was capped by the pronouncement that the "Hollywood Cinderella Girl has gone back to the ashes on a liquor-soaked highway." Although her agent had advised Frances of a new film offer, it was at this time that Frances decided to give up her movie career. Lillian then filed a complaint at the Superior Court stating that her daughter was insane for rejecting her profession and livelihood. Kauffman claims that the idea of Lillian insisting that Frances resume her film career is untrue and quotes from an interview Lillian gave to the Seattle press: "[Frances] is going to rest before she goes back to work." This quote, of course, can be interpreted differently.

Edith claims that Frances' behavior at home became increasingly disturbing. She would go for long walks, then rush back home, paranoid and certain that someone was following her. Frances would pound on the piano and sing at the top of her voice, or play the radio loudly "to drown out the voices of fear." She was vulgar and abusive, pulling out a handful of hair from Lillian's head in a burst of temper. After flinging Lillian into a chair during an argument, Lillian and Ernest agreed to commit their daughter to an asylum, since they had no money to pay for a private sanitarium. Edith says Frances' use of vulgarity was a deliberate attempt to provoke her mother, whom Frances knew abhorred such language. This provocation recalls Frances' similar use of the word "cocksucker" when asked her occupation when arrested, as told by Arnold and recreated in the film *Frances*.

On March 21, 1944, attendants came to the house and took Frances to the psychiatric ward of Harborview Hospital. On March 23, after her guardian ad litem Charles Stone signed away her right to a jury trial, she was interviewed by psychiatrists Donald A. Nicholson and George Price, who determined that she was suffering from schizophrenia and was insane. On March 24 a commitment proceeding took place under the aegis of the Honorable Judge John A. Frater, a member of the American Vigilantes of Washington. While Arnold contends that it was Frater's membership in the right-wing militia that prompted his alleged sinister agenda, Kauffman denies the claim that the group orchestrated Frances' commitment. Frater ordered her to the Western Washington State Hospital for the Insane at Steilacoom.

## *Steilacoom*

At Steilacoom's receiving area Frances was stripped, numbered and fingerprinted. Interestingly, Arnold says that she had in her possession, apart from clothes, a radio and fifty books on various subjects. She spent the night in an auditorium that housed twenty-five other women. The next morning Frances received electric shock treatment, which was standard treatment for schizophrenics. Kauffman, however, denies that Frances received electroshock at this time, based on the Steilacoom records. During this confinement, Frances was also given hydrotherapy, which had her placed in a bathtub of icy water, naked, for up to eight hours at a time. Again Kauffman disputes this, stating that the hospital records show no time in which Frances underwent insulin or hydrotherapy treatments, although he admits that the records on patients who received hydrotherapy are incomplete. After months of treatment, her anger and resistance ceased, and her cooperation convinced her doctors that she had been cured.

Much is made in the autobiography about Frances' resolution to alter her attitude and behavior towards the doctors at Steilacoom in order to obtain her release. Since she would subsequently flee the day after she was released, this change in her outward behavior was considered to be Frances simply "acting" sane. One might think, however, that the doctors at Steilacoom could tell the difference; that they couldn't only added to their perceived humiliation. The film *Frances* presents the events that led to Frances' release in an interesting and apparently fictional way. She is visited by a sympathetic doctor the night before her hearing and shown to be incoherent, presumably as a result of her treatments. The doctor injects her with a drug which makes her lucid, so that she is able to impress the doctors at the hearing the next day as being sane and remorseful. Thus her "cure" is temporary; but the scenario demonstrates the counterproductive effects of the treatments, and the poor judgment and perhaps even perversity of her doctors, knowing how counterproductive such treatments are to her, by scheduling a hearing they know she cannot pass.

## *Parole*

Frances was paroled on July 2, 1944. Lillian had had herself appointed as Frances' legal guardian after Frances escape from the sanitarium in 1943, and the parole was granted on the condition that she was answerable to her mother. She needed to obtain Lillian's permission to leave the Seattle house, seek employment, or see anybody. At thirty years of age, Frances had no rights. Lillian called a press conference for Frances' return home, where photographs were taken. One shows Frances reading fan mail, and another reveals Frances and Lillian sitting together drinking tea. The smile on Frances' face in the latter photograph hides the hatred she must have felt for the woman who was responsible for her commitment, and Frances' intention to run away. (The re-enactment of the press interview that leads to the photograph being taken in the film *Frances* makes Frances' feelings much more transparent.)

Kauffman quotes from the press interview to further his argument that Lillian was not pressuring Frances to return to Hollywood. He claims that press accounts state that Lillian voiced the idea that her daughter had thought about pursuing a career as a nurse (which is almost farcical in light of her commitments), which Frances denied. That Frances never did show an interest in a nursing career is evidence, perhaps, that it was never her intention. In spite of telling the reporters and Lillian what they wanted to hear—that she would return to Hollywood to resume her career—Frances ran away the next day.

She was brought back by police, upon which her father took her to stay with her aunt, Lillian's sister and former practical nurse Edith Castaing, in Nevada Hot Springs. Frances' sister Edith says that Frances had hit Ernest during the trip, although he did not punish her for it. Frances ran away again and was returned. On July 15 she ran away a third time and was arrested in Antioch, California, and fined ten dollars for vagrancy. Reporters came to the police station, and Frances was photographed without make-up but tanned and wearing dungarees held up by a rope belt. The Associated Press reported that she had been seeking work in the fruit orchards when she was found, but also, ironically, that she had been offered the lead in a new film. Kauffman cites another ambiguous quote of the time by Lillian: "Frances will make her [comeback attempt] when she is ready."

In *The Enchanted Cottage* (1945) the character Frances might have played was that of Laura Pennington, a homely maid who is transformed into a beauty by the love of a disfigured veteran. Although she was in no fit state and had no desire to work in Hollywood again at this time, playing a role that didn't rely upon her physical beauty for at least part of the narrative might have provided the acting challenge that Frances had longed for. There is also a rumor that Frances was offered the part of the suffragette Victoria Woodhull in a Broadway production of the play *The Incredible Woodhull* at this time, although this appears dubious. The only play bearing that title appears to be the one written by Frederick Schlick, with a 1957 date attached, although no theater production information is known.

Edith Farmer claims that when Frances had worked harvesting garlic with migrants near Fresno, she had been beaten up by a co-worker whom she had slept with. When Frances fought back, the sheriff had been called, and this is how she had been found. Edith makes the outrageous claim that the migrant was somehow justified in beating Frances after she slept with him rather than rejecting him because of her "obvious superiority." Frances' submission to the man, Edith argues, was demeaning to them both.

Ernest Farmer came and took her back to her Aunt Edith's, where Frances remained for the next six months. The younger Edith tells a story of how Aunt Edith's puppy was bitten by a rattler when Frances took it for a walk in the desert. Frances brought the dead dog home, throwing it down with, "Here's your damn dog." Frances refused to answer questions about how the puppy had died, indignant at the suspicion that she could have killed it. Supposedly, Aunt Edith was also concerned with Frances being around her twelve-year-old asthmatic nephew, fearful that she would harm him in a violent rage.

Aunt Edith therefore told Lillian in December that Frances could no longer stay with her. Arnold maintains that during Frances' time with Aunt Edith she experienced the same kind of detention that occurred at home with Lillian, so that Frances rebelled and ran away on January 13, 1945. Arnold claims she was found, strangely enough, hiding in a movie theater, and was returned the same day, with Lillian bringing Frances back to Seattle in April. Edith Farmer says that Frances was back by December.

On April 27 Lillian told the press that her daughter was much improved and was soon headed back to Hollywood. Kauffman again quotes Lillian to present a different view: "Frances will make no attempt at a comeback" (although this statement could have been made after the subsequent events that led to Frances being recommitted). On May 5, Frances left the house to see a friend in Tacoma, without Lillian's permission. Upon her return she was met by Steilacoom attendants there to take her back to the asylum. The autobiography doesn't mention the Tacoma visit, but it does have Lillian announcing her intention—"I'm sending you back; and this time I'll see that you stay"—with Frances eschewing the opportunity to run away again before the men came for her the next day. It also gives the date she was recommitted as May 22, repeated by Agan, with Kauffman adding that the hearing to recommit Frances was held by Superior Court Judge Hugh C. Todd.

The autobiography adds more detail to the relationship between Frances and Lillian that led to Lillian having her daughter recommitted. It describes a world of hostility and violence, and of Frances physically attacking both her parents (the justification for Lillian's action). The book includes Frances' admission of her drinking, which released the rage inside her, and tells of Lillian's attempt to please her by asking the actress Zasu Pitts to visit, a woman neither of them knew but one Lillian admired. Regrettably, the book doesn't give Zasu's reaction to the spectacle she witnessed—of Frances' disinterest and Lillian's subsequent humiliation in having invited her to the house. Edith mentions Zasu Pitts by saying that the actress was in Seattle doing a play when Lillian asked her to visit Frances. Edith says Zasu waited an hour for Frances to appear, with Edith rationalizing Frances' refusal to see the actress as resentment towards Lillian's presumption. Edith says that she would talk to the actress years later about the incident, over which Zasu held no bad feelings toward Frances.

As opposed to the nurse's skill and sense of humor with which Aunt Edith initially managed Frances' tantrums and defiance (according to sister Edith), Ernest and Lillian could offer no such coping strategies. Edith thought Frances had a guilty conscience over her own perceived failure and the dashing of her parents' hopes for her. However, this did not make her behave any better towards them. They, in turn, were fearful of their daughter's restlessness and seclusion, and Edith claims this gave Frances an advantage. According to Edith, it was an incident in which Frances used money given her to buy groceries to go drinking at a beer parlor in Alki instead which led to an argument and the realization that Lillian could not handle her daughter, and finally to Lillian's decision to recommit. Edith claims that Lillian felt remorseful about recommitting Frances, and that both she and Ernest would visit her in the hospital weekly. Edith also quotes Bernice Frank, Lillian's hairdresser, as stating that Lillian brought Frances a basket of food every Sunday.

## *Back to Steilacoom*

With Frances considered incurable, no re-evaluation of her sanity took place at Steilacoom. Again Frances was stripped, her fingernails were cut, her hair was shaved, and she was placed in the violent ward—Ward T—which housed psychopathic criminals, senile old people, and the mentally retarded. In the autobiography, Frances refers to the ward as "the cage." Arnold leaves specific horror stories to the autobiography (and perhaps rightly so, no matter how embellished the tales may be), but claims that even the embellishments understated the inhumane conditions suffered by Frances and the other inmates. Arnold also provides some basic general information for context, which aids the reader's imagination. The wooden building was a hundred years old, with boarded up windows and cots spaced a foot apart (the autobiography says there were mattresses rather than cots). The autobiography describes the cage as eighteen feet wide and half a block long, surrounded by a steel fence. Arnold claims that the floors were dirt, something which Kauffman denies.

According to Arnold, the ward had secret rooms for killers who were chained by the ankles and wrists and deprived of light.

There was no discipline or order. Food was thrown at the patients, not served, and they vied with the rats and cockroaches for it. Every month they were washed down with a fire hose as a nominal attempt at sanitation (something else for which Kauffman can find no supporting hospital documentation). The autobiography confirms that "baths" were once a month (a budgetary restriction to conserve soap and water). Orderlies acted as pimps for soldiers at the nearby Fort Lewis camp. Kauffman disputes Arnold's claim about the (male) orderlies, however, stating that interviews with Steilacoom nurses confirm that the wards were gender separated, and that only female nurses and orderlies worked on female wards. The nurses also denied the accusation of pimping and that soldiers visited for illicit sex (something the film *Frances* presents). Kauffman further points out that it would have been logistically next to impossible for anyone to sneak onto the hospital grounds and into a locked and guarded ward. Of course, it's unsurprising that the nurses would deny such an accusation, considering the consequences of an admission. And access to the hospital and wards could certainly be granted by complicit insiders.

Some patients were given work detail, like cleaning up human waste and vomit that littered the floor after a feeding. Punishment for resistance was shock treatment, which Frances endured often, since she had the reputation of being steadfastly stubborn and uncooperative. Kauffman concedes that the hospital records show Frances receiving electroshock at this time for three months, shortly after her recommitment. This is in contrast to Arnold's claim of her routine and extensive treatment when she would refuse to work.

Arnold quotes from an article by Lucille Cohen in the *Seattle Post-Intelligencer*, dated February 8, 1949, which describes the overcrowding and understaffing at Steilacoom. While the article doesn't single out the violent ward, it would seem that this would be the one most prone to neglect. Cohen describes a canvas used as a roof to protect inmates from the rain. The autobiography says that vents in the roof provided air, but the roof did not protect from the rain or heat of the sun, or stop insects from swarming in summer. Arnold also tells of a student nurse who found Frances in the back wards and spoke to her on several occasions, but could do nothing to help her get out of her predicament.

The autobiography tells the tale of a cat who wandered into the cage and was torn apart and eaten. Frances was accused of the act because she was found with its bloody remains, although she claims to have tried to save it. The accusation was bolstered by the claim Lillian had made of how Frances had tortured their pet dog, which was evidence of her insanity and more justification for Lillian to have her daughter re-admitted (although the dog torturing may have simply been a retelling of the suspicions surrounding the death of Aunt Edith's puppy). Agan also tells this story and repeats the autobiography's contention that as punishment for the cat, Frances was put into one of the dark, "killer" rooms.

Kauffman quotes from an October 1945 news article which indicates that Frances was to be released, and that she had taken a job as a typist. This "imminent" release, Kauffman claims, occurred in 1946, when Frances was paroled from March 3 to April 30—in opposition to the claims made by Arnold, Agan and the autobiography of her five-year commitment. Kauffman says that the parole was approved by Lillian "to try to allow Frances to function outside of the hospital," and that Steilacoom and Lillian both kept the release quiet "so as not to add to Frances' pressures." However, Kauffman does not say what led to Frances being recommitted, since it is unlikely that she would have gone back to Steilacoom voluntarily.

Frances was notorious in the world of psychiatry as the most famous person to ever be committed to a public mental institution, and Arnold claims that doctors from around the world came to inspect her. Arnold says that in 1947 the hospital began testing experimental drugs on her, but it was found that they were only temporarily effective in altering her behavior. Kauffman states that hospital records show that the only experimental drugs Frances was given was a neurological agent designed as an anti-seizure medication. Kauffman refutes Arnold's claims that she was given anti-psychotic drugs, since Thorazine, the first anti-psychotic drug, was not introduced at Steilacoom, even in trials, until 1954—*after* Frances had been permanently released. Since Frances' spirit apparently could not be broken with conventional techniques, it was decided to take drastic measures.

## *Walter Freeman*

Arnold tells how a meeting he had with Frances' sister Edith in 1975 had given him additional information about Frances' treatment at Steilacoom. Edith said that their father had been told by a doctor at Steilacoom that because Frances was considered a hopeless case, it had been decided to give her a lobotomy in 1947. Edith said that the threat of legal action stopped this plan, since, legally, Frances' parents had to approve all treatments she received. However, Arnold contends that Frances was given a trans-orbital lobotomy without the permission of her family by Dr. Walter Freeman, who visited the hospital in 1948. (Interestingly, the autobiography makes no admission that Frances was lobotomized, although she does mention that other patients were. Given the extremity of the other treatments described, it would seem that a lobotomy would be prime material for more sensationalist claims.)

Perhaps some of the confusion surrounding the issue of the lobotomy comes from the kind of lobotomy that Frances was said to have received, since a trans-orbital lobotomy was different from a pre-frontal lobotomy. While the pre-frontal lobotomy was likely to leave the patient in a vegetable-like state, the trans-orbital was less likely to do so; therefore, its effects were less readily apparent. Freeman is said to have only slightly severed the nerves connecting the cortex to the thalamus, working directly on the part of the brain associated with violent and rebellious tendencies. The common term "ice-pick" lobotomy refers to the instrument used, inserted between the eye and eyeball and driven through the orbital plate to a depth of one-and-a-half inches.

Walter Freeman is said to have visited the hospital in late 1947, 1948 and 1949, and examined Frances three times. Arnold claims that when Freeman saw her in 1948 he had the nurses and orderlies leave the room after she had been administered electric shock, and then performed the procedure. This notion is refuted by the infamous photograph of Freeman allegedly giving Frances the lobotomy, since the woman in the photograph (whose face is obscured) is surrounded by people. The only evidence to support Freeman's and Arnold's claim is the argument that Frances' behavior altered after Freeman's visit with her.

Kauffman too rejects the notion of Frances being operated on privately, since archival records show that Freeman liked to operate with spectators and assistant doctors, as well as the press, in attendance. Kauffman says Freeman wanted publicity for his procedure to market it to hospitals nationwide—and what better "gimmick" could he have asked than Frances, a famous movie star, who he claimed he could cure. Regarding the photograph,

Kauffman says it was taken in 1949 and not 1948, as Arnold claims. He says a second shot of the patient, as she is being given electroshock before the procedure, accompanied an article in the *Seattle Post-Intelligencer* dated July 8, 1949. This second shot, and a close-up view of the woman provided by Kauffman, shows that she is not Frances. The article also provided a shot of the woman after the operation as further evidence.

Kauffman states that Steilacoom records prove who the patient was, but he declines to say in order to protect the woman's privacy. Additionally, Kauffman points out press coverage, and Freeman's own writing, that indicates Frances would make an unlikely candidate for the trans-orbital lobotomy. One of Freeman's criteria for operating on a patient was that the onset of mental illness had to be recent—i.e., less than six months. He claimed the procedure helped only the fixation aspect of the psychosis and not the psychosis itself. At Arnold's time of the alleged operation, Frances would have been manifesting psychosis for over four years; therefore, Freeman would have considered the procedure unhelpful to her and any effect it might have to be of a temporary nature. Kauffman, however, mentions that some long-term patients were given the trans-orbital procedure as a trial step towards a pre-frontal lobotomy.

Kauffman confirms that Freeman did visit Steilacoom and did perform trans-orbital lobotomies on August 19, 1947, October 15, 1948 and July 7, 1949, but denies Frances was one of his surgical subjects. Those that were operated on are named in archival data, and Frances' records state that she was not operated on by any doctor for any reason during her stay. Kauffman also quotes from Dr. Charles H. Jones, who was the psychiatric resident at Steilacoom and who assisted Freeman on some of the procedures. Jones confirms that Frances was not lobotomized (and insists that he had told Arnold that when contacted for research on *Shadowland*). Kauffman also quotes from Steilacoom surgery and lobotomy ward nurses in the *Seattle Post-Intelligencer* interviews that were published January 26, 1983, who also deny Frances' lobotomy.

Arnold claims that she was now meek and submissive, not even protesting when made to model hats at a fashion show given by one of the doctor's wives. Edith claims that when Ernest heard of this from Frances, he complained about his daughter's celebrity status being exploited, and this ultimately led to Ernest petitioning to have Frances released. The autobiography quotes from four hospital reports. On July 8, 1948, she is described as being mildly cooperative, though requiring restraint and confinement. On September 15, 1949, she is cooperative and has learned to answer pleasantly. On December 5, 1949, she is receiving routine treatment and restraint. And on March 22, 1950, Frances attended another hearing for parole. She was allowed to bathe and wash her hair, and given a clean dress to wear. (Agan says, however, that she was not allowed to shave the five-year growth under her arms and on her legs.) A nurse reports that she is helpful to other patients.

Agan claims that the hearing consisted of nothing more than Frances being asked about the weather and to count to fifty and back. The staff unanimously recommended that parole be granted. However, Frances' parole had come about primarily because her father had requested it, as she was needed at home to care for Lillian, who had suffered a stroke (Edith claims that Lillian experienced a stroke in 1947, and another in 1949). Arnold claims that the request came from Lillian, although the autobiography quotes the hospital's acknowledgment letter to Ernest. Edith says that Frances had triumphed over her struggles through a belief in God, and makes no mention of her parents requesting her release to help them in the home (though Edith claims Frances knew that they needed her).

## *Release*

Arnold gives the day of Frances' release as March 23, 1950, and says that she took a bus to Seattle alone. The autobiography states it was March 25 (as does Agan and Kauffman), and that Frances caught the bus back with her father. She was now thirty-six years old and had been in the Steilacoom violent ward for nearly five years. Lillian was now aged seventy-six, and Ernest seventy-nine. Frances served as a maid for her parents, and Arnold says she only left the house to go to church on Sundays. The autobiography paints a sad picture of Lillian's power over Frances and the constant threat of being sent back to Steilacoom. Edith paints a rosier picture of a period of peaceful happiness that they all enjoyed.

Arnold claims that in May 1953 Frances began to take walks in the neighborhood, and by June she was riding the bus downtown, making no mention of the psychological warfare that existed and which kept Frances frightened and isolated (since she believed she was still on parole). Arnold says that because of her perceived improvement the family decided that she was ready to get a job. Hollywood was not deemed an appropriate employer—or was it that there were no offers? Frances working was also seen as a way to add to the family coffers, since Ernest's poor health had stopped him from working. Edith says that Ernest was admitted to a nursing home in July 1951 to recover after abdominal surgery, although her timeline would suggest it was more likely 1953. Kauffman contends that it was Frances' idea that she work; while Edith claims that Frances wanted to work but was too timid to try, and that her parents didn't want her to.

The story of the voiding of Lillian's guardianship and the restoration of Frances' competency and civil rights differs between the autobiography and Arnold. Arnold claims that an attorney was hired to petition the Superior Court so that Frances could legally seek employment in Washington State. He says Frances was required to return to Steilacoom to have her parole ended and be fully discharged. After an examination in which she admitted to having overcome her problems and expressed her wish to work to support her parents, her competency and full civil rights were restored on July 27, 1953.

The autobiography claims that in 1953 Frances came across a letter from her father to the hospital advising of his intention to apply for a decree of competency. The hospital replied that no examination was required, and on March 25, 1951, the Superior Court had discharged Frances from the hospital, with her competency and civil rights restored. (Agan agrees with this version; while Edith denies the parents had any knowledge of same.) Frances wrote to Steilacoom in June and requested a hearing to end the guardianship. On July 1 she attended, accompanied by a testimonial from her brother concerning the care she had provided their parents and her ignorance of the end of her parole. On July 3, Frances and her attorney went before the Superior Court of Washington for "The Matter of the Insanity of Mrs. Frances Anderson," and her competency was restored by Judge Lloyd Sharett. On July 27 she secured an order that discharged Lillian as her guardian, a position her mother had held since October 1942 (i.e., for nearly eleven years).

With Frances living alone with Lillian (who the autobiography and Agan say remained hostile towards her), and Ernest no longer providing an income, the issue of Frances working rose again. Edith says Frances now suggested it. Using the name of Mrs. Bill Anderson supposedly helped Frances retain her anonymity, the loss of which was her greatest fear. She got a job as a valet girl doing laundry at the Olympic Hotel, where she had stayed for the premiere of *Come and Get It* sixteen years previously. Agan and the autobiography claim Frances earned seventy-five cents per hour for working ten hours a day, seven days a week. Edith quotes from a letter from Frances which says it was eight hours a day for five days a week, for which she earned forty dollars (as opposed to the fifty-two dollars of the other claim).

Edith reports that at this time Rita had tried to declare Lillian incompetent in order to sell the Seattle house. Lillian blocked this action legally because, according to Edith, Lillian wanted to retain the house to give Frances (and presumably herself) the security of property. Edith also claims that Lillian made her the executrix of Lillian's estate. In the Fall, Lillian and Frances visited the nursing home frequently, with Ernest's recovery enabling him to press that he be allowed to come home. A letter from Frances to Ernest dated November 23, 1953, has her telling him that she thinks he is better off in the home, saying, "This ain't a family life we've got, and I personally wouldn't like to see you being submitted again to that deadly grueling and dull routine out of a mistaken and useless sentimentality for what has never been." Edith had also commented to Frances that his living in the home where he had twenty-four-hour personal service was not a hardship, as he had lived in hotels most of his life.

Frances had begun dating. Arnold claims that Frances would frequent bars after work (which suggests her alcoholism had resurfaced) and was promiscuous (as she offered no resistance to admirers). The autobiography states that Frances was deliberately looking for a husband to liberate her from living with Lillian. She met a city engineer named Alfred Lobley (Agan calls him Alfred H. Lobley, Jr.) on a blind date set up by a co-worker. Edith describes him as husky, balding and personable, and aged forty-five to Frances' forty. Edith quotes Lobley as saying that he had met Frances when he saw her loaded down with groceries and offered to drive her home. He says after that he didn't see her for months, since she was going with another man (unnamed). But one night Lobley called her, and then they started going together.

Edith had moved back to the United States, to Springfield, Oregon, in March 1954. Frances and Lobley married on April 17, 1954, at the West Seattle Protestant church, with Edith having offered to take over arrangements for Frances, who was busy with work and family. Edith tells of how on the day the fruitcake wedding cake, which Edith had made and decorated herself, fell and squished against her shoes. She saw it as an omen of the marriage—along with Frances' choice of a black wedding dress. Ernest attended the ceremony as a respite from his nursing home residence. The couple honeymooned on Vashon Island.

The autobiography does not name Lobley as the man Frances married, and there is no photograph of him in the book (although there is none of Leif, either, or of any event post–1943). Kauffman's website features a 1954 wire service photograph of Frances with Lobley, which ran with a nationally published interview with both of them: "Former Film Actress to Marry." The interview describes Lobley as her fiancé, and the article includes the startling admission from Frances that she was not attracted to Lobley and had never loved him. Frances not being in love with Lobley is something confirmed by Edith.

Lobley moved into the Seattle house with Frances and her mother so that they could save for a home of their own. Frances quit her job, since Lillian could no longer be left alone (though Edith quotes Lillian as saying that Lobley had asked Frances to stop working because he wanted her home all the time). Lobley wanted Frances to buy a new home in the East Gate district across Lake Washington, and she imagined that Ernest should be liberated from the nursing home to live with them, while Lillian lived with Rita. Frances talked Rita into having Lillian visit her while the house went up for sale, though it appears Ernest was not liberated. Frances had Ernest accompany them to the airport to see Lillian off in July, and afterwards he returned to the nursing home. Although she did not know it at the time, this would be the last time she saw either of her parents alive.

When the house did not immediately sell, Frances offered the house to Edith, who declined to take it. Lillian suffered another stroke, so Rita decided she should stay with her. Edith claims that while emptying the house, Frances took Lillian's dog, Sheba, to the pound where it was destroyed. In a letter to Edith that winter, Frances claims to have learned of a report by Louella Parsons about Frances which was full of falsehoods. Louella had said that Frances had joined Alcoholics Anonymous and was living back in Santa Monica after having nursed a group of mental patients for the last eight years in Portland, Oregon. The latter claim is particularly transparent considering that Frances had only been out of Steilacoom for four years. Rita advised that Lillian had been beset by a new series of strokes and had become increasingly frail. Rita no longer wanted the responsibility of caring for her, and wanted Frances to assume control—just as Frances was planning to move into a new house in October. Edith claims Frances and Lobley argued over whether they should take Lillian in or have her institutionalized, with both Frances' and Lobley's drinking not helping.

Edith says that matters came to a head after a night out together when they had a tremendous quarrel that became physical. The autobiography claims that Lobley went into a drunken rage at Frances' indifferent attitude towards her parents, destroying the new furniture they had bought for the house. Agan claims this confrontation occurred the same day Lillian left. The comment that Frances was unimpressed with his violent outburst because she had lived years among violence in the asylum is insightful; and after he passed out, it is claimed that Frances took money from his wallet to finance her bus trip out of Seattle.

Agan says she took sixty dollars, Arnold says seventy-five, and Kauffman two-hundred-and-fifty (based on his being in possession of a loan document signed in Seattle in November). Arnold provides elaboration on Lobley's violent tendencies, claiming that he was physically abusive in reaction to her post-lobotomy state of haziness, and also that he threatened her with being recommitted. Arnold gives the month when Frances left as November. But Edith claims that she has a letter from Lobley which states that he hadn't seen Frances since late October, with Kauffman claiming she hid out in Seattle before obtaining the loan to leave. Edith says her letter from Lobley enclosed an undated one from Frances, saying goodbye, although Edith does not make it clear who Frances' note was intended for. Edith also does not mention, nor does Lobley, the notion of Frances taking money from his wallet. Rather, Edith says she scrounged all the money she could find around the house, adding it to the household expense money in her purse (with no mention of the loan Kauffman speaks of). With the cash she purchased a bus ticket. However, whether she took money from Lobley or not, and whether she left in October or November, the fact was that Frances had gone. And with Frances gone, Lillian would stay with Rita.

Edith defends Frances' leaving as a self-preservation mechanism, both in relation to her rejection of Lobley as an alcoholic and Frances' own recognition of an approaching nervous breakdown caused by her guilt feelings over her mother. Given Frances' history of running away, her doing so again did not surprise her sister, who assumed it would only be temporary while Frances thought things through. This notion seems to be in opposition to Edith's theory of Frances anticipating a nervous breakdown. Edith came to Seattle and found Lobley in an apartment, with the apparently un-destroyed new house furniture. It is not known what happened to the new house, but presumably the sale of the family home had not been finalized. Lobley supposedly ran personal advertisements and hired a private investigator to find Frances, but was unsuccessful. Edith also says that Lobley continued to visit Ernest and stay in touch with her.

## *Eureka*

Frances got off the bus at Eureka, a small town in California, because that was as far as her money could take her. Agan claims the trip would have cost her forty-two dollars. Frances got an inexpensive single room, without bath, in a typical small town hotel. Her funds only covered her for ten days at most, and she knew she needed a job. In a backstreet in the older part of town was a long established photographer and photography supply store, which had a help wanted sign in the window. Interviewed by the photographer, Oscar Swandlund, and his wife Arvilla, Frances was hired as a typist-clerk and office assistant, and required to organize graduation and wedding portraits. Perhaps no one could find her (Arnold claims that many looked) because she now went by the name Frances Anderson. The Swandlunds recommended an apartment she might rent in the nearby home of a friend, which was within walking distance of the shop, and she moved in.

Edith tells how in 1955 Swandlund became mayor of Eureka, which made him more reliant upon Frances as his personal secretary. The Swandlunds invited her to their home, and Frances became a member of their social family as much as their business one. Mrs. Swandlund is quoted as saying that there was never any problem with alcohol, although they were careful to respect Frances' privacy. Arnold claims that she attended church and was sociable with the townspeople, although she refused to speak of her past. The autobiography does not mention this social contact; rather, it concentrates on Frances' isolation and increased drinking. Agan also claims that she had no social life and adds the baroque idea that Frances took to locking her liquor in a suitcase chained to her bedstead.

Edith says Frances again wrote poetry, including a poetic quarter entitled "7," which would be published in a small poetry magazine in 1957 under the name Frances Farmer. Lillian died of a stroke on March 1, 1955, and was buried in Lake View Cemetery, sharing a plot with the infant daughter who had died prematurely. In April Edith moved to Portland to be nearer to Ernest, and in May Edith heard from Lobley for the last time. Ernest died July 15, 1956, of a stroke, and his ashes were placed beside Lillian's in the family plot. Edith makes the observation that her parents' parallel headstones brought them a unity that they never achieved in life. The autobiography, Agan, and Arnold all claim the Social Security office had tracked Frances to Eureka to tell her she was Lillian's sole heir and had inherited the Seattle house, though Edith claims it had already been sold. Edith says that she had contacted Social Security, guessing that Frances must be working, in order to get them to find her employment address. Edith subsequently wrote to Frances, and she replied.

Edith claims that a young advertising man from the local radio station came to the shop and recognized Frances but kept her secret. But perhaps it was no coincidence that the radio chain's advertising man from San Francisco also came to the shop in 1957, introduced himself to Frances, and invited her to dinner. His name was Lee Mikesell. The autobiography, Arnold, and Agan all say Frances met the entrepreneur Mikesell (though the autobiography leaves him nameless, á la Lobley) when he recognized her buying liquor one night. He encouraged her to make a show business comeback and offered to manage her. Edith says Frances initially declined Mikesell's offer, and he left town, urging her to contact him if she ever came to San Francisco. In April, Edith says, Frances left her job and took the bus to San Francisco. The autobiography, Arnold and Agan all say that Frances accepted Mikesell's offer, and they both caught a bus to San Francisco in May. Agan says Frances withdrew her savings of $400 before she left.

Arnold says Mikesell engaged an attorney in April to obtain a divorce for her from Lobley. The autobiography claims that it was Frances who instigated the divorce action, which was finally granted a year later, on March 7, 1958 (though Agan maintains she sued for divorce in July). The autobiography says they stayed in the house of his friends, who were all alcoholics. Frances moved out and alone to a small furnished apartment, and she looked for a job, securing one at the Park Sheraton Hotel as a reservation clerk earning seventy-five dollars a week. Notifying the couple whom she used to live with of her new address provided Mikesell with the chance to find her again. Edith quotes from an undated letter Frances wrote to Mrs. Swandlund that indicates Frances was working at the Sir Frances Drake Hotel as a clerk in the lobby shop before changing to the Park Sheraton Hotel. Arnold says it was Mikesell who got Frances the job—as a receptionist—at the Park Sheraton Hotel. Agan implies that the job (at the Park Sheraton) was part of Mikesell's "ground plan," so the inference is that he organized it.

## *Comeback*

Arnold and Edith claim that Mikesell began a press campaign to promote Frances' return to the industry ("Frances Farmer Found as Hotel Clerk"); whereas the autobiography claims it was the public relations director of the hotel who recognized Frances. Apparently he had her move into the hotel's best suite and planned a press conference. Returning to her apartment, Mikesell confronted her and drunkenly accused Frances of cutting him out of her new fame. She left him and moved into the hotel, although the autobiography stresses that Frances was hardly confident in her ability to succeed in a comeback. She also realized that any look back on her career was bound to include the ugly arrests and committals, the film images of the beautiful young woman tainted by the unflattering police photographs.

The press conference went well, and within days the hotel was flooded with letters and telegrams from people who remembered Frances. Edith says the publicity also brought legal pressure for financial settlements for various cases. They included a Seattle department store claiming assault damages on a hairdresser employed for the *Come and Get It* film premiere (an incident that is not mentioned in any other biography), and payment for the new furniture that Lobley had taken. Wesley, who was serving in South Korea, wrote to Edith suggesting that he become Frances' new manager to augment what he saw as her poor business judgment; however, Edith did not pass on the offer to Frances.

In May Frances received a letter from Michael Ellis, the director of the Bucks County Playhouse in New Hope, Pennsylvania. He was interested in her doing a summer run in the plays *The Chalk Garden*, *The Magic and the Loss*, and *The Jamison Affair*. She received a call from Ed Sullivan with an offer to appear on his television variety show in New York. The Sullivan show had been a Sunday night institution since its premiere on June 20,

1948, and would become the definitive and longest running live variety series in television history. Attempting to translate the principles of the vaudeville stage, the show's democratic mandate was to entertain all of the audience at least some of the time. To this end, it balanced legendary headliners with up-and-coming stars, and juxtaposed the highbrow with the lowbrow. Classical pianists and ballerinas would appear on the same episodes as novelty acts, and Sullivan would also capitalize on teenage interests and give opportunities to African American performers.

With Frances not able to afford the trip to New York, the hotel's manager offered Frances a loan, and she signed for two Sullivan shows, one in June and the other in October. Edith reported that the hotel offered to accommodate Frances in New York for a week, and a woman editor of the Christian Science Monitor also offered accommodation to discuss the possibility of doing a book on Frances. In a letter to Wesley, Edith made it known that *she* would rather be the one to do a biography on Frances, to control the content, since she considered the editor an outsider. Apparently Frances had already agreed to meet with the woman, so she felt she couldn't accept Edith's offer. This hesitancy on Frances' part regarding Edith writing her biography is interesting in lieu of Edith's subsequent book.

Edith says she supplied Frances with a written compilation of the highlights and significant aspects of their lives, and included a list of family pictures, school records, diaries and scrapbooks. That Edith also included a poem of her own indicates that she wanted the book by the Christian Science Monitor editor to be as much about Edith as it would be about Frances, something Edith ultimately achieved with *Look Back in Love*. However, the collaboration with the person Edith admitted was the better writer ended as soon it began. Frances did not volunteer what had happened. Unless this editor was Lois Kibbee, it is a coincidence that the book Kibbee and Frances would later attempt would also be abandoned.

Kauffman quotes from a June 1957 nationally syndicated article by Lloyd Shearer to argue that Lillian had *not* been hell-bent on having Frances resume her career at any cost, and that part of the stress of her breakdown had been due to her family's wishes that she quit show business, which she did not want to do. Considering the timing of the interview, it is more likely that Frances, via Mikesell, was putting a revisionist spin on her past in order to support their future ambitions. Two New York interviews labeled her an alcoholic, and the old photographs of Frances being hauled out of court by police were reprinted. However, the articles also said nice things, confirming that she had retained her beauty and quoting her intention to write her autobiography to correct the misconceptions about her. Whether these interviews took place before or after the proposed book project with the editor of the Christian Science Monitor was abandoned is unknown. If it was after, it demonstrates Frances' long held wish to write a memoir, with or without the assistance of a writer.

On August 12 Frances opened in Enid Bagnold's *The Chalk Garden*. Michael Ellis had to be aware of the cruel parallel between Frances' experience and the role he had asked her to play, Miss Madrigal. She is the strange and distant ex-prisoner who has been hired as the governess for Laurel, a sixteen-year-old child who may be mentally ill, though surely Frances could see herself as both Miss Madrigal and Laurel. During the run Frances visited Jane Rose in New York. Staying at the Alamac hotel, in September Frances was co-honoree at a banquet of the New York Gourmet Society, along with explorer, gourmet and author Hassoldt Davis, at Teddy's Restaurant. October marked Frances' second appearance on the Ed Sullivan show, and the reception she received was as successful as the first. She joined Mikesell in celebrating Thanksgiving with his family on their farm retreat near Indianapolis, Indiana. In December Frances was in a *Playhouse 90* television production called "*Reunion*," co-starring Charles Drake, Martha Hyer, Dane Clark, Jack Lord, and Hugh O'Brien, which would air on January 2, 1958. On January 27 she became one of the few celebrities to be warned in advance about an appearance on the television show *This Is Your Life*, which aired on January 29.

Edith reports that she and Rita had been asked to participate but that Wesley had declined out of public shyness. Edith was told by the program's producer, Janet Tighe, that the main goal of the show was to encourage others suffering from mental illness to renew their lives. Host Ralph Edwards had previously done shows spotlighting people with problems. On December 23, 1953, Eddie Cantor was featured, after recently having suffered a heart attack, with the tribute being pre-approved in case the shock might harm him further. In the same year Lillian Roth was welcomed back into the limelight after fifteen years, her personal life having been overshadowed by alcoholism, with the appearance perhaps inspiring her to write her autobiography, *I'll Cry Tomorrow*. An analysis of the show and Frances' appearance on it can be found in the television chapter.

Mikesell set up a series of interviews for her when no more film or stage offers were forthcoming. In February an article by Gerold Frank, entitled "The Return of the Actress," appeared in *Coronet* magazine. In April and May it was a three-part series by Edward Keyes entitled "I Climb Out of the Depths" in *American Weekly*. These articles told of her past in the asylum but also allowed Frances to express her faith in God and how it was He who had saved her from sin. Edith was pained and shocked at what she saw as the many lies in the copy, objecting to Lillian being made out as a villain and feeling Frances' faith had been given an "evangelical tent-show slant." She also thought Keyes had invented and embellished the hospital experiences for shocking effect. Edith expressed her dismay to Frances, who replied that she too was deeply upset but faced it with "defiant resignation, taking the blame herself." A quote from Frances was rather more ambivalent: "I'm sorry you didn't like the articles, but that was the story and now it is past. There is nothing as dead as yesterday's news."

Frances made another television anthology appearance, co-starring with Leon Ames, James MacArthur and Margaret O'Brien in *Tongues of Angels*, which aired on March 17. Arnold says Frances married Mikesell in Las Vegas during the filming of the show, although Edith cites the date as March 27 (the date also given in the book *Hollywood Players: The Thirties*, by James Robert Parish and William T. Leonard). Arnold also indicates that Frances made a guest appearance on the television crime drama series of former *Exclusive* and *South of Pago Pago* co-star Lloyd Nolan, *Special Agent 7*, though he and the autobiography call it *Treasury Agent*. On March 30, Frances starred as the murderous Lydia Haskell, opposite Cathy Lewis as Ellie, in the sixteen-minute CBS *Suspense* radio play entitled "The Sisters," written by George Wells, and produced and directed by William N. Robson. The play featured a memorably funny exchange. When told by a policeman that suicide was a crime, Frances' Lydia replied, "For which there is no punishment." This play had been performed on radio twice before, first on February 3, 1944, starring Ida Lupino and Agnes Moorehead, and next on December 9, 1948, starring Rosalind Russell and Lurene Tuttle.

Frances returned to films in a supporting role as Mrs. Bickford in a Paramount production, *The Party Crashers* (1958), which filmed from April 28 to mid–May. Agan makes much of the casting of Frances as the mother of Bobby Driscoll, the former child star who

Frances with Bobby Driscoll in her film comeback, *The Party Crashers* (1958).

would die ten years later of a drug overdose. After filming, Frances went east with Mikesell for their honeymoon, driving the Edsel around New Mexico and Oklahoma. She did summer stock, performing in *Yes My Darling Daughter* at the Ephrata Legion Star Playhouse, and *The Rainmaker* at the Cherry County Playhouse. Arnold says Frances repeated her role in *The Chalk Garden* at the Avondale Playhouse in Indianapolis, and the autobiography states she also played in Traverse City, Michigan.

Although the impending release of *The Party Crashers* in September did not secure Frances any more film offers, in Indianapolis she was offered work on television. Edith claims Mikesell arranged the deal, while Agan, Arnold and the autobiography all say the television station came to her, since by this time Frances' relationship with Mikesell had broken down. In the 1982 television special *Indiana Epilogue*, the station's general manager, Eldon Campbell, confirms that Frances had been approached by the station after their program director had seen her onstage in *The Chalk Garden* in August 1958. The autobiography claims that Frances moved from a hotel into the home of Jean's parents, Lunda and Lucy Ratcliffe. Lunda even paid Frances' outstanding hotel bill.

## *Indianapolis*

Though hosting an afternoon movie program from five to seven P.M. six days a week on a local NBC affiliate television station (WFBM-TV) may not have been Frances' ideal comeback vehicle, at least the show offered the cachet of being called *Frances Farmer Presents*. Edith claims Frances wrote her own introductions for the movie of the day after doing research on them, as well as chatting with visiting celebrities and politicians. She signed a contract on August 8 for thirteen weeks and renewal options, at a salary of two-hundred-and-twenty-five dollars a week. Edith says a hoped for job in radio management did not happen for Mikesell, and he was reduced to being an apartment husband to Frances, unemployed and living in the reflected glory of a famous wife. She was unable to pay for their mounting bills, added to by his cavalier spending.

It was at this time that, according to Edith, Frances met Jeanira "Jean" Victoria Ratcliffe, although Edith does not name her but rather refers to her as an "ingratiating, ambitious woman writer" and a "Plain-Jane plump loser with illusions of being a shrewd operator waiting for the right break." Edith claims that it was Jean's friendship that helped sow the seeds of Frances' divorce from Mikesell. The widowed interior decorator Jean was fifteen years Frances' junior. The autobiography says she and Frances had met at an after-show party that Frances had not wanted to attend. Arnold tells how Jean had discouraged Frances from working on her autobiography, which is ironic since it would be Jean that ended up authoring it. Edith claims that Jean's agenda was to ghost-write the autobiography; and although Mikesell did not like Jean, he agreed to let her start work on it with Frances in September because he saw the money-making potential.

Work began on the TV show on October 1. After Thanksgiving Frances and Mikesell traveled to New York to hobnob with the network bosses and for Frances to have more professional photos made. On her January 1959 television show with guest cowboy Curley Meyers, Frances sang three duets that earned the applause of stage hands and the camera crew. But while she was doing well professionally, Frances' private demons, says Edith, had been resurrected by the probing questions of Jean. The resurfacing memories prompted Frances to drink. Mikesell left her in February (Edith claimed that Jean had successfully separated them). His reason for leaving? He wanted Frances to see how she couldn't make it without him. After her husband left for the west coast without the Edsel, Frances mortgaged it for thirteen hundred and seventeen dollars and fifty-two cents to pay bills. Edith says that when Mikesell visited her, he labeled Jean a lesbian. Edith tells of how Frances had written about Jean moving in with her when Mikesell left, something which the autobiography denies. Edith later comments that Frances had moved into Jean's family home for two weeks but moved out again when she was besieged by Jean's friends and relatives who came to parties to meet the celebrity.

Edith says in May Mikesell filed a fifty thousand dollar breach of contract suit against Frances. Edith later quotes from an August letter from Frances in which Frances claims Mikesell had sued her for two hundred thousand dollars, and then one dated January 16, 1963, which states it was fifty thousand. Presumably this is the suit Arnold also speaks of, though Arnold claims it to be for one million dollars. Edith maintains that Mikesell's ten-year contract with Frances had required that she give him fifty percent of her earnings, and from her half she was required to cover accommodation, clothes, travel, and professional fees to the various unions. At this time Frances filed for legal separation, with the divorce granted in 1963. In May Frances' television duties included covering the Indianapolis 500 and all the celebrity interviews that accompanied the race.

By July Jean had finished the manuscript and showed it to Frances, who, Edith says, was appalled. Edith describes it as reading like a "true confessions shock-tripe story." Supposedly Frances demanded that it be rewritten, with Jean refusing because she insisted she knew what would sell. Frances refused to sign the release for publication. Edith claimed that Frances initially filed the manuscript away for a future revision, and then burned it before she died. Presumably Jean would use the tapes she had made of Frances to do her own posthumous rewrite, which became *Will There Really Be a Morning?* Edith says Jean found a new apartment, the upstairs of a house occupied by Ellen Glessing and her young Catholic family in N. College. This Catholic connection, Edith says, led to Frances regularly attending the St. Joan of Arch church.

In August Frances vacationed with Wesley and Ruth in Maine. The church instruction Frances took led her to being baptized on November 6, and she socialized in church. Frances joined the choir, went bowling with the parish women's league, and directed them in play productions. In March 1960 she sang in the Easter concert with the Indianapolis Symphony Orchestra, and Frances also MC'd fashion shows for Wasson's department store to promote her television program. Unless Edith's timeline is incorrect, Frances appeared to have covered the Indianapolis 500 again, since she includes a letter from Frances dated May 26, 1960, about the event on professional stationery with *Frances Farmer Presents* letterhead.

An undated letter from Frances to Edith indicate Frances signed to do the Noel Coward comedy *Present Laughter* in July as summer stock. A letter dated August 6 has Frances saying she planned to vacation in Michigan, and that she would file for divorce from Mikesell in the fall. In an October letter Frances reported that she spent the second half of her vacation back in Indianapolis working, doing another Wasson's fashion show and a station-sponsored antique car tour in September. Apparently she also lost her voice temporarily due to laryngitis, which threatened her ability to perform for the television show. This letter also states she decided to wait on the divorce proceedings, although she had heard that Mikesell was living in Oakland, California, and that he believed she was earning twenty thousand dollars annual income. Frances writes that this figure is incorrect, but Edith later states that it was accurate, with most of it coming from her show salary and the rest from investment bonds. Frances advises Edith that she has drawn up a will, and that Edith and Wesley are the heirs. She also writes that the television station is planning to create a monthly half-hour dramatic show for her to star in.

Edith does not quote from a letter from Frances again until May 1961, when Frances reported on having attended the Women in Television and Radio convention (location unknown). On July 17 Frances told of how Mikesell had come to Indianapolis to see her at the television station in May, although she managed to avoid him. Frances' letter speaks of her "new premises," which Edith says was a house on a half-acre lot at 5107 North Park Avenue. The purchase matches up with the autobiography's claim of her renewed television contract and prosperity, allowing Frances to buy a small house on the north side of the city only a block or two away from Jean's decorating studio. Edith does not mention the house's proximity to Jean; however, Edith does say that furnishings for the house were from a firm that "the writer" worked for. It is Edith's claim that the furnishings are what allowed Jean to reconnect with Frances, although the autobiography contends that there was never any disconnect (that would occur later).

Both Edith and the autobiography agree that Jean gave Frances a shepherd puppy she would call Sport as a housewarming gift, though only the autobiography claims Jean declined Frances' suggestion that they live together. Frances sent Edith a home movie of herself at the house, her first appearance on film since *The Party Crashers*. The autobiography claims Frances employed a housekeeper to come in once a week, and that her social life remained centered on Jean and the Ratcliffes, whose family home she visited in Virginia. Edith quotes a December letter from Frances that tells of driving to the country with an unnamed friend, but not the trip to Virginia. Edith's perception of Frances' Christmas in 1961 does not match that of the autobiography, perhaps because Frances did not tell her sister about it. While Edith states Frances had to work on Christmas Day, the autobiography claims that she was unable to appear because she had been on a drinking binge that had started in reaction to the receipt of poison pen letters.

The autobiography is the only source to mention the disturbing letters, which immediately makes the issue suspect; however, it does raise the rumor of lesbianism between Frances and Jean. The autobiography has Frances outraged by the accusation made in the letters, and claims that it led to Frances staying with Jean for ten days. When Frances supposedly told Jean of the accusation and the letters, the autobiography says that Jean was not alarmed by it (read into that what you may). However, since Frances *was* alarmed, she decided that the best thing to do was to distance herself from Jean, for Jean's own good. The autobiography says that Frances would not see Jean for two years, although presumably Frances would fill Jean in on what had occurred during that time at a later date.

In a letter to Edith dated April 14, 1962, Frances writes of giving up beer "and such" to lose weight, which either refutes the autobiography's claim that she was drinking or is perhaps ironic. Otherwise she spent her leisure hours building a rock garden in her backyard, with Edith commenting on Frances' perceived contentment living with Sport, Willie the cat, a garden and a job to support them all. Edith provides an extended transcript of the highlights of a radio interview Frances did with Dan Blocker on May 17. An August 31 letter has Frances speaking of how she did *Yes, My Darling Daughter* again, this time with the Madison County Dramatic Players in Anderson, Indiana, in the summer. The summer stock experience forced her to take two weeks off without pay. In August Frances broadcast a live show from the Indiana State Fairgrounds, which included a rodeo featuring Dan Blocker and the *Bonanza* boys.

In Frances' letter dated November 24 she writes how she plans to visit Edith in Portland around December 23 and to stay for a few days after Christmas. Apparently news of Frances' visit appeared in the December 5 *Indianapolis Times* society page, a clipping of which Frances sent Edith, although one wonders who planted the story. On Christmas Day Frances presented Edith with a jug of Brown County "Old Country Store" white lightnin' from Nashville, Indiana. Edith took her sister to see Portland's famous Sanctuary of Our Sorrowful Mother Grotto, which they had visited once before with their father. Edith also asked Frances about the woman writer and the abandoned autobiography, with Frances telling her that she might one day rewrite it herself. To that end Edith showed Frances her boxes of scrapbooks, photos and letters, and let Frances take what she wanted. Frances asked that Edith pack up and ship the rest to her. Interestingly, the photographs that Edith took of Frances and the family that Christmas were all lost by the mail-order photo developers Edith used. Frances sent Edith the ones Frances had taken, but naturally Frances was not in any of them.

In February 1963 Frances was rehearsing the part of Irina Trepleff in Anton Chehkov's play *The Sea Gull* at the Purdue University Loeb Playhouse; the play opened March 8. She commuted between Purdue and Indianapolis, and recorded her television show broadcasts at the playhouse during the seasonal run. WFBM had apparently posted a billboard in front of the theater which said "F.F. presents Festival of Premiers" to promote Frances' movie show. Her program's time was moved to an earlier slot in order to obtain better ratings in the war of the afternoon movie shows; it was advertised with a photograph of Frances on a couch being carried by her crew, with the headline "Frances Is Moving." Rival television station WISH-TV offered a petite blonde, styled glamorously in white fur, who had a pearly smile and a knack for saying the right thing at the right time. Both these blondes' appearances became as much about their wardrobes as their movies. A studio portrait was taken of Frances in which she looks slim and beautiful, like a woman not more than thirty-five (although she was forty-nine).

Edith reports that Frances was named Outstanding Business Woman of the Year by the Indianapolis Charter Chapter. Agan says that she was the 1964 Woman of the Year. Both the autobiography and Arnold mention the award, but neither gives the year. Frances received a certificate of recognition for outstanding service by the Department of Radio and Television at Indiana University, with the autobiography also claiming she was honorary chairwoman of the Red Cross drive. Arnold paints a more somber picture of Frances at this time. He calls her a minor celebrity who, apart from her television program, also hosted fashion shows, spoke at clubs and student assemblies, and opened supermarkets. Arnold says Frances spent her money on clothes and trips without a thought to savings, and hired a full-time maid and secretary. He also claims that she continued drinking—at night after her show, and alone.

WISH-TV's rival blonde was released from the station in May, the ratings loser. Frances interviewed Shelley Winters at a reception following the premiere performance of the play *The Days of Our Dancing*, in which Shelley appeared at the Avondale Tent Theater. Frances also interviewed Shelley's co-star, Robert Walker, Jr., the playwright Jim Bridges, and the producer-director Tim Everett.

Edith claims that Frances re-appraised the shelved autobiography manuscript after August with the intention of rewriting it, but she became insecure about her own ability as a writer. Edith says that Jean expressed interest in working again on the book, though Edith doesn't say whether Jean was successful in convincing Frances to let her do a rewrite (Frances remained mute on the subject in their correspondence for the rest of the year). In her letter dated January 6, 1964, Frances tells Edith how she is getting ready to do an original play for television, a two-character mother-daughter drama written by one of the television show's editors.

However, as the time came for the yearly renewal of Frances' contract, Edith notes that Frances became aware of a cooling condescension and subtle critical harassment of her. She was told by her manager of the town gossiping about Frances' relationship with Jean and her entourage. The poison pen letters now came to the station (the autobiography says they continued to come to Frances' home as well), with Frances believing Mikesell to be the culprit. Frances refused to distance herself from Jean (a suggestion made by a national network executive), and Frances feared that she would lose her job. According to Edith, rather than discharge her outright, the station used less obvious strategies in the hope that Frances would voluntarily resign. There were on-the-spot program changes, and evasion and avoidance tactics by the top brass when Frances asked to discuss her option renewal. Edith claims the stress made Frances start drinking again.

Edith reports that in March the station announced that Frances would make a guest appearance with Hugh Downs, hosting *The Today Show* in New York on April 22. Kauffman claims it was April 21, with Agan saying that Frances was unable to film on the day decided upon because she heard that Clifford Odets had died (although Odets' date of death is known to be August 18, 1963). The autobiography says the offer came from *The Today Show* itself and not via WFBM. She would be given an hour segment profile, with some filming done in Indianapolis, to be followed by a personal appearance on *The Today Show*. If the offer had come from the station, as Edith claims, Frances considered it as her triumph—as if she had won over the brass—and they might even promote her to a regular position in New York.

The autobiography says that in March Frances had been unable to do one show and had been temporarily replaced. Intoxication was suspected, although Frances claimed that was not true. Perhaps it was this kind of unreliable behavior that made the network wary about renewing her option, with *The Today Show* considered as a farewell gift. Frances returned to the show and continued to work competently until it was time to leave for New York. However, Frances was surprised that she was to be accompanied to New York by WFBM executives and PR men. When she arrived on the set, she was told the usual host had been called away suddenly, replaced by James Daly (Arnold says it was John Daly, the host of CBS' *What's My Line?*).

The show consisted of a flattering welcome, film of Frances in her garden with her pets, and footage from her program. Frances was not warned in advance that she would be asked about her arrests, mental breakdowns, drinking and reputation for temperament. Edith states that afterwards at her hotel Frances drowned her sorrows, declining the public appearances the PR men had arranged. She had seen out the humiliating interview to the end like the professional she was, but it had disturbed her. Again Edith claims Frances had been deliberately broadsided to get her to quit her job. The 1982 television special report on Frances, *Indiana Epilogue*, claims that her appearance on *The Today Show* was the beginning of the end for her television series, an appearance that the report says was "badly handled" and a "trigger to her deterioration." Former station manager Eldon Campbell says in the report that he blames himself for how Frances was treated and for her resultant "deterioration."

Frances stayed on in New York for a week to attend the World's Fair, and on leaving the Fair had been caught in a traffic jam. She mentioned it on one of her broadcasts, and that she understood that the jam was due to a demonstration led by the black Congress of Racial Equality (CORE) leader James L. Farmer, Jr. (no relation). The station said they received complaints about her comment, and she agreed to read a retraction statement. No new contract offer was made to Frances, and she was met with brush-offs, executive absences and avoidances. Edith says the stress kept Frances drinking. The autobiography claims Frances was suffering from dizzy spells in New York, and back in Indianapolis her doctor described her problem as low blood pressure, which Frances knew had been aggravated by her drinking.

News stories fed by the station's release stated that she had quit because of her embarrassment over the CORE faux pas. The *Indiana Epilogue* report claims that Frances failed to return to the station after New York, so they announced she had resigned. Days later she denied this and said she had been fired. Edith says that Frances was fired after she demanded a showdown with management, and quotes from Frances' comments to reporters that she had been fired for business and political reasons. Edith maintains that in retaliation, Frances threatened executives with violence. Since they had labeled her crazy on *The Today Show*, she would show them crazy—a line used in the film *Frances* (though not spoken by Frances). Edith claims that on April 30 a WFBM executive telephoned Edith and asked her to come to Indianapolis to help Frances. When Edith phoned Frances, she could tell she was drunk, so much so that Frances did not know who Edith was. Edith then had the executive wire her a ticket and flew into town in May.

Edith contacted her sister again, who this time recognized her, and they agreed that Edith would visit her the next day. Edith claims that she overheard men in the motel room next to hers celebrating "an axing," although Frances' name was not mentioned. The network executive told Edith that they had not renewed Frances' contract because of their concern over her, but implied that they might in the future "if she settles down." At her house, Frances held a glass of Scotch as she met Edith, "daring me to challenge her drinking at ten o'clock in the morning." Edith claims that Frances' defensiveness came after an explosive row that Frances had had with Jean over the manuscript, during which Jean had threatened to call Frances' family to have her recommitted. During Edith's visit, Frances carried on negotiations with a lawyer and Carl Baker, a station public relations man, but took a break to drive to Brown County where she hoped to buy some property. Frances had wanted to show Edith the property, but Edith would not drive with her sister when she was intoxicated.

Upon her return, claims Edith, Frances menacingly held a raised letter opener while asking what Edith had been doing, and lowered it only when Edith described the nondescript events of her day. Although her sister was near breaking point, Edith had no plan to recommit her but rather to be with her and help her if Frances would allow it. Frances told Edith that Jean had wrecked the upstairs bedroom because Frances wouldn't let her print the autobiography, although Edith did not look at the supposed wrecked room. Rather, Edith took a trip to see friends in Ohio; when she returned she found Wesley with Frances (Edith having invited him to come and assist in the station negotiations).

Edith had decided not to tell what had led to her visit, thinking Frances would be displeased to hear it had been instigated by the station. Edith went back home after eight days, leaving Wesley with Frances. Wesley would stay with her until May 17. A letter from Frances to Edith followed soon after in which she enclosed clippings from the *Indianapolis Times* about the "friendly reconciliation" negotiated by Baker and reporting that Frances would return to her show in June after a few weeks rest.

Frances had received an invitation to play Eliza Grant in a production of *Look Homeward, Angel* at Purdue in the summer, so her rehearsals would come before she could resume full-time work at WFBM. The play was directed by Dr. Joseph Stockdale, who also directed Frances in two other plays at Purdue—*The Sea Gull* and Friedrich Duerrenmatt's *The Visit*. The autobiography says that Frances was so happy to be back in the theater at this time that she stopped drinking during rehearsal and the run, and only resumed when she returned to her television program.

On July 26 Frances wrote that she would return to the station the next day. The autobiography calls the reports of Frances' firing a misunderstanding, since she returned to the program, and does not give details of the protracted negotiations Edith describes. However, with her return also came the dizzy spells, accompanied by an erratic heartbeat, momentary blackouts, and anxiety. Edith claims the station perceived her as being drunk on camera, so they bided their time, waiting for an excuse to dismiss her again. Edith says that the symptoms Frances displayed were due to hypoglycemia, for which she had never been tested. One morning while parking her car in the studio lot Frances overshot the space and hit a guard rail. Edith claims Frances had suffered an instant of confused dizziness, and that she was sober. Though the accident resulted in only slight damage, apparently Frances did not bother to challenge the accusation of intoxication and quit her job. The autobiography says that the end came after Frances was unable to appear on the program one day due to illness, and her director replaced her for the last time. The contract was ended—at Frances' request, according to the autobiography. Arnold claims she was fired, and Agan remains ambiguous. The *Indiana Epilogue* claims that it was Frances' frequent bouts with alcohol that ended her employment on the series, though it does not state whether she quit or was fired. Kauffman says a rival station hoped to hire Frances, but she did not follow up an initial telephone call. Former Channel 8 executive Dave Smith says in the *Indiana Epilogue* episode that Frances called him after leaving WFBM and wondered if she could work at his station. He told Frances he was interested, but as she wouldn't give him her telephone number he was reliant upon her to call him back, which she never did. Edith says Frances made applications to radio stations and the rival television station but was told there were no openings for her. Edith believes that the notion that Frances had been fired, coupled with the lesbian rumors, worked against her. It was at this low point, Edith claims, that Frances finally consented to let Jean rewrite the biographical manuscript.

The autobiography says that Frances' illness continued. She was told she had an ulcer and was going through menopause. Her state worsened when Alfred Lobley reappeared at her house late one night and admitted he wrote the poison-pen letters as a way to get even with her. After threatening that he would eventually kill her, Lobley left, and Frances went to Jean's studio the next day. After not speaking for two years, Frances asked for Jean's help. Jean moved into Frances' house, on Frances' request. As Frances was broke, Jean gave Frances access to her bank account, and Frances kept the house while Jean worked. Frances did not want to report Lobley to the police, since her fear of them was greater than her fear of him. One night Lobley reappeared, brandishing a butcher knife, and followed Frances when she fled in her car. Stopping at a gas station, Frances was protected by the attendant, Bob Jenkins, who doused Lobley in grease with his grease gun. Jenkins took down Lobley's license number. But when Frances still refused to involve the police, Lunda Ratcliffe said Jenkins tracked him down, and Frances never heard from Lobley again.

The autobiography says it was decided that Frances should join Jean's decorating business, although whose idea it was is not relayed. Edith reports that Frances, visiting in November 1965, had told her of the partnership, which involved Frances making a financial contribution and being used as a public relations front. Frances had sent Edith a photograph of herself in a white-vested black business suit, sitting on a baroque chair. Letters would be written in green ink on paper with the letterhead "FRANCES FARMER Presents GREENBRIER Gifts and Interiors." However, the shop and service was not a success, with the autobiography claiming that Frances meeting clients while drunk virtually ruined the business in three months. Jean and Frances had traveled to New Orleans on a buying trip, where they also visited Ruth. On December 7, Frances wrote to Ruth that she had lost her voice because of her illness, but that it had now come back. Although Frances would boast about how beautiful the shop looked for Christmas, Edith says that the business declared bankruptcy soon after.

Edith claims that Frances and Jean started a new business in the late spring of 1966, "Frances Farmer's Carriage Trade," leasing an antique and gift shop in downstate Brown County near Nashville, and adding some of the salvaged interior decorating stock. Edith says Frances mortgaged her house to meet the costs. The autobiography does not mention this new business but rather says that Jean agreed to live with Frances, and they rented a furnished cabin in the same area. It claims that Jean's small income from freelance work helped the couple survive. Edith tells the tale of Jean leaving the running of the gift shop to Frances. Edith claims Jean was preoccupied promoting an unnamed New York dancer-singer she had found, and cultivating the interest of wealthy women to bring city theater to Indianapolis, presumably vehicles for the singer-dancer. Although Edith does not state it overtly, there is the suggestion that Jean's interest in the singer-dancer was more than professional, since later Edith quotes from a letter from Ruth stating that "it was only a matter of time until Jean found another friend." The autobiographer spins the theater project as Jean taking a job working two to three days a week remodeling a theater in Indianapolis.

Frances' shop proved successful enough that she was able to hire a part-time assistant, although Edith says Frances was not psychologically suited to the work. In the summer she supposedly rebelled "violently and with force," and Jean counteracted this behavior by supplying Frances with liquor. At this time, Joe Stockdale asked Frances to play the eighty-year-old female lead, the richest woman in the world, in *The Visit* at Pardue for a two-week run. A reception at the university was given in Frances' honor, and she got through it without drinking. At a Sunday brunch during the first week's run, given by the Drama Department, Frances drank, and on the drive home she crashed her car. She was arrested because of her imperious attitude—the autobiography claims she was acting the role in the play—and booked for drunken driving, fingerprinted, and photographed. Jean was telephoned, and the Ratcliffes came. Frances would be fined seventy-five dollars and her license suspended for six months. Her behavior and the consequences mirror what had occurred more than twenty years previously.

The press got the story, and Pardue offered to cancel the second week of the play's run to spare Frances further embarrassment. Jean convinced Frances to go on, and the second week was a sellout, with the opening night audience giving Frances an ovation when she appeared onstage. After the season, Frances resumed her drinking. Lunda suggested sending her to a hospital, but Frances refused to go. Edith claims that Jean called Wesley to come, but since he was unavailable, he sent Ruth in his place. Jean agreed to close the shop and told Ruth that there was another television show prospect for Frances, though Ruth doubted it would happen given the past and Frances' seeming physical and emotional exhaustion. Ruth wrote to Edith of Jean complaining that Frances had not made a will (apparently, Frances had not told Jean that one existed and that Jean was not the major beneficiary).

## *Titicut Follies*

Although only receiving a limited theatrical release, Frederick Wiseman's documentary *Titicut Follies* (1967) evoked memories of Frances' commitment at Steilacoom. Vincent Canby, in his review of the film in the *New York Times* dated October 4, 1967, calls it "an extraordinarily candid picture of a modern Bedlam ... calm, cool and ultimately horrifying." Filmed in 1966 inside the Massachusetts Correctional Institution at Bridgewater, a prison hospital for the criminally insane, Wiseman's film would be banned from a wide release circulation by the Massachusetts Supreme Court who ruled that the film constituted an invasion of privacy. The documentary is now currently available for purchase on DVD from Zipporah Films on the internet (the website address is www.zipporah.com).

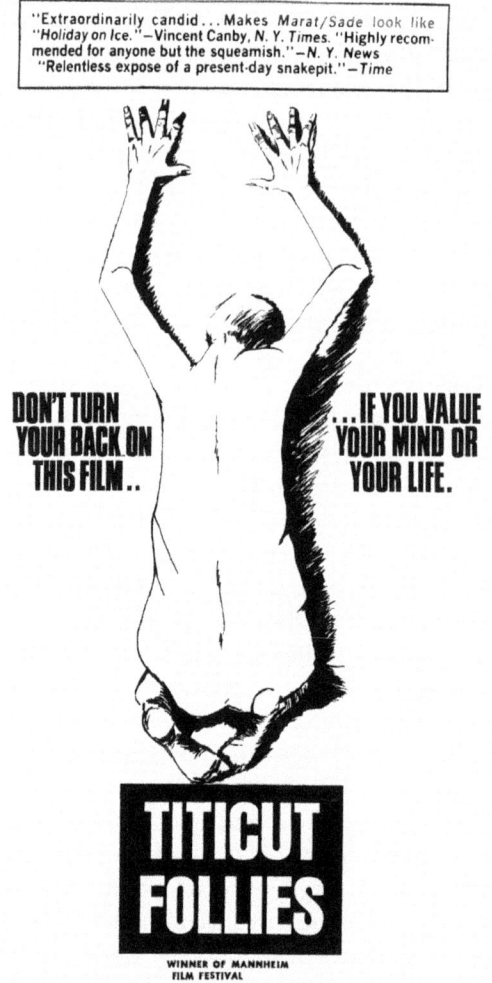

Poster for *Titicut Follies* (1967), a documentary about the Massachusetts prison hospital for the criminally insane which evoked memories of Frances' commitment at the Western Washington State Hospital from 1944 to 1950.

While the film makes no specific reference to Frances, a viewing of it raises several interesting points. The inmates presenting a follies performance highlights the disparity in people who have been judged unable to function in the normal world but who are still able to perform in a stage show, singing and dancing. It is not known how the follies came about, whether inmates were made to participate or whether it was voluntary; but the performances we see do not bear the mark of resistance. It's a shame Wiseman doesn't spotlight the behavior of any performers in their "natural" hospital environment, although we do see men singing and playing musical instruments, which we assume to be practice. The idea of singing the words of idealized songs and dancing as a preferred reality is in stark contrast to the humiliating reality of life for inmates, who are kept naked in their empty cells and treated without compassion by their guardians.

One inmate, Vladimir, voices his objection to being an inmate, claiming that the environment is doing more harm than good. He tells of the constant noise, with televisions blaring and other inmates babbling and screaming, which disturbs him, and challenges the logic of the diagnostic testing that has determined him to be a schizophrenic paranoid. We see him trying to reason with a panel of doctors, who only decide to increase his medication to alleviate what they see as paranoia. Vladimir echoes Frances in his misguided attempt to question those in control of his destiny. Clearly, they do not have the means for a natural improvement of his alleged condition. As Frances had deduced, it was better not to complain but rather accept the situation and fake improvement so that the doctors can believe their practices work, and that one can be cured to their approval and be released.

The film includes a postscript disclaimer indicating that, as per the Supreme Court, "changes and improvements" had taken place at Bridgewater since 1966. This prefigures a similar disclaimer that appears in *Frances*, which was required of director Graeme Clifford in exchange for being allowed to film on location at various hospitals. Although the controversy over *Titicut Follies* centered on the invasion of privacy issue, the idea that those compromised were only the patients may be short-sighted. While some patients look at the camera in resentment, the film's recording of the behavior of the doctors, nurses and guards is equally revealing. For those who are supposed to be the normal ones, their behavior seems as questionable as that of the patients. One example is the doctor who smokes as he force-feeds a patient, uncaring that the ash from his cigarette may drop into the food. Another involves the guards who bait a patient by repeating the same question over and over in a blatant attempt to defeat the patient's efforts to control his mounting anger.

## *Peace*

Edith reports that the shop was closed in November 1967, and Frances wrote that she was back in her Indianapolis house for Christmas, with exciting plans for the New Year. In January Frances wrote that those plans involved going into the cosmetics business, which the autobiography positions as occurring in the fall of 1968. Ruth advised Edith that the venture was named by Jean as Farmcliffe Enterprises, an amalgam of Farmer and Ratcliffe. *Will There Really Be a Morning?* would be published under the copyright of the same Farmcliffe Enterprises name. The autobiography says Frances and Jean worked with a laboratory for a year creating the products they wanted to market, with Edith stating that Frances again mortgaged her home to finance the new business. The autobiography also claims that additional funds were contributed by Lunda Ratcliffe. Arnold says that Frances used savings from her television show to finance the venture. Edith maintains that two years were spent struggling to make the venture a success, but that it failed. The autobiography, however, blames their company's accountant, who supposedly bungled the portfolio, and all funds were lost. Whatever the reason, the project was abandoned, and the autobiography indicates that Frances' house had to be sold.

The autobiography tells of another automobile incident. Lunda bought Frances a new car when her license was reinstated, but the death of Clifford Odets set Frances off on a drinking binge (again the time appears to be off in relation to the date of Odets' death). Jean could not console her, and Jean decided to leave Frances and stay in Indianapolis. Again Frances crashed her car, this time running, ironically, into the county jail and sheriff's office. Her license was revoked for a year and she was fined three hundred dollars. Frances moved back to Indianapolis, and Jean gave her kittens to Frances to care for, and also had her five nieces visit. This was Jean's strategy to get Frances to stop drinking—by giving of herself to others. In the spring they built a swimming pool in the backyard, which was used in the summer for get-togethers, and Frances worked in the garden.

In May 1968 Frances gave a series of poetry readings at the Indianapolis Art Museum, presenting Tennyson's "Enoch Arden" and her own favorite, Emily Dickinson's "Will There Really Be a Morning?" (the subsequent title of her alleged autobiography). She sought solace by attending the neighborhood church, Saint Joan of Arc, every Sunday. Frances eventually converted to Catholicism, and it was her faith in God that gave her the strength to stop drinking.

Edith had received fewer and fewer letters from Frances over the past two years. At first she reasoned that her sister had been busy with the cosmetics business, but in retrospect she came to suspect that her communications were being intercepted by Jean. An inquiry as to when Frances might visit went unanswered, and birthdays and holidays only brought brief greetings. When no letters came between January and June 1968, Edith became alarmed. Frances had once told her that she should contact her lawyer if anything happened, so Edith wrote to Frances advising that she would be writing to her lawyer as instructed. A jolting telegram was received on July 16. It was typed in capital letters, which was unusual for Frances, who usually wrote in small letters. It read: "Just because I don't write to you is no reason to suspect that I am not of sound mind and minding my own business. Hope you are the same." At the time, Edith was wounded by the sarcasm and waited for an apology or explanation that never came. It was only later that Edith came to suspect that the telegram was not written or sent by Frances.

In the Fall Edith sent a birthday letter to Frances and received only a Christmas card in reply, with no mention of the collapse of the cosmetics business. Frances' professional and financial crisis came at a time when Leif Erickson was enjoying his greatest success on television in the series *High Chaparral*. An Easter 1969 card arrived, with an image of the Tomb, which seemed to reflect death rather than the rebirth of the holiday. Edith was concerned when she learned that Frances' unlisted telephone number had been changed (Edith was unaware that Frances had left the Indianapolis house).

The autobiography reports that in November Frances and Jean leased a derelict farmhouse on a hill in the middle of a three-hundred-acre compound a few miles from town. (The 1982 *Indiana Epilogue* television special report says it was located at sixty-one-hundred Moller, in the new part of the city.) Destitute, they sought aid from Jean's family and comfort from their menagerie of animals. After Christmas, Frances decided to go back to working on the autobiography. The published autobiography says that Frances "drew heavily on Jean, and in mutual trust we began to formulate a book." Frances would write of her experience and Jean would edit. Arnold claims that Frances had met with Lois Kibbee, the biographer of Christine Jorgensen, earlier in the year, and they had taped some conversations. However, the Kibbee book was postponed when she was required to edit another book.

In January Edith had Wesley contact Jean's parents to obtain Frances' telephone number and new address. Frances told Edith that her Indianapolis house had been sold in December and described the farmhouse into which she and Jean had moved. Edith claims that she learned after Frances' death that the house had not been sold but actually deeded to friends of Jean for the sum of one dollar, subject to the unpaid balance of the original mortgage. Edith contends that Frances' decision to stop writing to her, and the move to the farmhouse, were indications of an awareness of her fatal illness. And, says Edith, Frances painted her oven black—a premonition, perhaps?

## *Death*

In March Edith says Frances consulted a doctor because of her weight loss and trouble swallowing. The autobiography indicates that Frances noticed a tightening in her throat in April, when she was also having headaches. It also says there was no money to pay for a doctor's consultation, and that their friend Ed Shaeffer, who was an orthopedic surgeon, arranged an appointment with a specialist. A week later Frances was in the Indianapolis Community Hospital having an esophageal biopsy. The results indicated an inoperable malignant tumor, and Frances had to be fed with a plastic tube sutured to her stomach. Edith did not receive any correspondence from Frances that revealed the illness, but she experienced a feeling of depression that overwhelmed her. Frances did not reply to the poems Edith posted to her, and Edith's own throat began to cause her irritation, as if she was suffering from a kind of empathetic pain for her sister.

After three weeks Frances was allowed to go home from the hospital. On June 30 Edith says she awoke to a feeling that whatever it was she had would be coming to an end soon. Thinking she was going to die, Edith wrote a farewell note "in case something happened." She also felt that Frances had written a similar note, since in July Frances was taken back to the hospital when blood came from her mouth. In an article written for *The Misty One* website in April 1999, Jennifer Steinberg would report that Jean had slept on the floor next to Frances for three months while Frances was ill, although other accounts suggest that Frances had not been in the hospital for three months nor could have afforded such an extended stay.

Edith says Wesley telephoned her on July 31 to tell her that Frances had died, although her date of death is given in the autobiography as August 1 at 3 P.M. Frances was fifty-six. Apparently Wesley had received a call from Frances' doctor, which led him to phone Jean at the funeral home. The autobiography gives the information about Frances' death as a coda, with nothing provided about her funeral. Edith insisted on going to Indianapolis for the funeral in spite of Wesley's opinion that Jean did not want any family there. Arnold doesn't give the date of the funeral but says it was held in a cemetery just outside Indianapolis, with six women as pallbearers. Edith reports that Frances had an open casket, which Edith says was Jean's idea as a publicity seeker. However, in spite of the perceived exploitative intent, Frances looked beautiful and serenely peaceful. Two songs were sung at the ceremony, "We Almost Made It, Didn't We?" and "Jean," with excerpts read from Chekhov plays by a Purdue drama friend.

Frances was buried in the Oak Lawn Memorial Gardens in Indianapolis in Hamilton County, Indiana. Seattle newspapers left her obituary in their back pages, and there was no national reportage. In the four-part article by Rita Rose that appeared in *The Indianapolis Star*, dated January 26, 1983 (reproduced on *The Misty One* website), Rose claims that Frances died nearly penniless, and that it was said she and Jean used to collect pop bottles along the road for money during Frances' final months. However, Rose also points out that the burial was far from that of a pauper. Edith says Frances' lawyer told her that Frances had never signed the will she had sent Edith a copy of, or that the copy she had signed was missing, although her estate only held clothes and her small library. Frances' jewelry, furs, piano and the house had all gone to pay debts. Jean had a signed will that left everything to her and made her executrix, which, Edith claims, was only important to Jean for one reason—to allow her the freedom to publish the contentious autobiography.

## Life After Death

According to Arnold, after Frances' death Kibbee withdrew from the autobiography project and Jean took over, even dedicating it to herself, although that may have been Frances' intention. Arnold claims that Jean also invented scenes and glorified her own character in the book, which was published in 1972 by Putnam. Rita Rose's article also has Jean answering the claim that she wrote the entire book by stating she wrote only the last chapter.

The cover of the Putnam first edition is a haunting, disturbing photograph of the older Frances in close-up. With darkness surrounding her face, her pale skin makes her countenance resemble a death mask. Her beauty ravished by her experiences, this Frances, unintentionally or not, brings a police mug shot to mind. The image being torn down the middle presumably represents her divided and broken psyche, and adds a science fiction creepiness which prefaces the horrors to be read inside. The lettering of the title also parallels Frances' trauma, with the color going from brown to orange to red. Later editions would change the cover image to those of the younger Frances, with the 1974 Fontana United Kingdom paperback sporting what appears to be a publicity shot taken around the time of *Son of Fury*. This picture makes Frances' face resemble a marble statue, her expression frozen and her countenance that of an unsmiling and unapproachable goddess.

The book only includes four photographs, with none of Frances and Jean together. Two of the photos are police shots of Frances being arrested in 1943, one being the infamous picture of Frances struggling, with her mid-riff and thigh exposed. Frances' shame and embarrassment over these photographs makes one think that she would not have wanted them to appear in her published autobiography. Edith describes *Will There Really Be a Morning?* (a title she never quotes) as Jean "cashing in on her exploitative friendship, an autobiography of Jean's own writing, full of salacious lies and libelous fiction." Edith's outrage and contempt for the published book is the reason she wrote her own—in order to "set the record straight"—which she states in her book's postscript, entitled "Of Truth and Freedom."

In the *A&E Biography* episode on Frances, "Paradise Lost," David Farmer says of the autobiography, "You can hear a couple of voices going in it. And some of the more sensationalized passages don't sound like Frances." In the same documentary, director Joe Stockdale comments, "I think that Jean embellished all the business about Steilacoom, the mad ward and the lesbian attack and all of those things. That was from her mind, and she thought it would enhance a possibility for a sale of a movie." The *New York Times* book review of August 20, 1972, misquotes the name of the book as *Will There Really Be a Tomorrow?*, and calls it "a Ghastly tale, not easy to forget." The first paperback edition published by Dell in July 1973 uses a quote from an unauthored review by the *Library Journal* as an inside cover blurb: "Her book is the most astonishing movie star autobiography I have ever read ... a hard bitter summing up of a terrible life ... its treatment of insanity and mental institutions resembles that of the best fictional treatment of the subject." The second Dell paperback edition, published in May 1979, uses four quotes, all undated, as inside cover blurbs:

> "A magnificent book, an autobiography of dashed hopes, unjust terrors, and finally, of solitary strength. Frances Farmer has left us a legacy of truth."—Author unnamed, *Woman's Wear Daily*
>
> "A shocker."—Author unnamed, *Publisher's Weekly*

"Begin anywhere and the reality of the human spirit's will to survive assaults you."—Author unnamed, *Newsday*

"Intriguing, candid and chilling."—Joyce Haber, author of *The Users* (publication unknown).

Joyce Haber was a gossip columnist for the *Los Angeles Times*, and her best-selling novel *The Users*, published by Delacorte in 1976, included passages on the exploits of seventy real and fictional Hollywood characters. In 1970 Haber had written about Jean Seberg (her identity given as "Miss A") having become pregnant by a prominent Black Panther, and the story was picked up by *Newsweek* three months later, naming Seberg. The story is said to have been part of the FBI's plot to discredit Ms. Seberg as a supporter of radicals, and is blamed for her continued attempts and final successful suicide on the anniversary of the death of the baby, who was born prematurely.

In 1973 Jean was also the ghostwriter of *The Kennedy Case, the Intimate Memoirs of the Head Nurse to Joseph P. Kennedy During the Last Eight Years of His Life*, by Rita Dallas, also published by Putnam. Registered nurse Josephine F. Goldsmith, in the letters section of *The American Journal of Nursing* of October 1973 (Volume 73, Issue 10, page 1699), defended the book against criticism that indicated Ms. Dallas violated the nursing code of ethics. Ms. Goldsmith contended that much of what Dallas wrote about had already appeared in the public domain as rumor, although Ms. Goldsmith did argue that the nurse "obviously did not assert her professional responsibilities to the patient."

In 1974 Rita Rose claims that Jean announced she was writing the screenplay for an all-woman production of *Will There Really Be a Morning?* to be filmed in Indianapolis and to star the British actress Glenda Jackson, with Ida Lupino directing. While Jackson is the same height as Frances, she would have been aged 38 at the time, but was considered good box office, having recently won the 1973 Best Actress Academy Award for *A Touch of Class* (1973). Kauffman says that actress-turned-director Ida Lupino, Frances' former friend, was close to optioning the book to direct the film, although Lupino had not helmed a feature since *The Trouble with Angels* (1966). In his biography of Lupino, William Donati comments that around 1972 she was enthusiastic about the project but never found the opportunity. The project was dropped when Jean couldn't obtain the necessary financial backing.

Kenneth Anger's tome *Hollywood Babylon* was published in the United States in 1975 and featured a chapter on Frances, which returned her plight to the American consciousness. J.J. Pauvert had originally published Anger's book in

This publicity portrait of Frances was used by Kenneth Anger in his chapter on her in *Hollywood Babylon*.

France in 1959 as *Hollywood Babylone*, giving it an underground cult status (enhanced by Anger's reputation as an underground avant-garde filmmaker). The first American edition published by Associated Professional Services in 1965 was subject to a series of copyright conflicts, which had been resolved for the 1975 second American edition published by Straight Arrow Books and distributed by Simon and Schuster.

Anger had continued the scandal-mongering that periodicals like *Confidential* had begun in the 1950s, and that *The National Enquirer* and internet blogger Perez Hilton continue with today; however, Anger's material went all the way back to the silent era. If the Hollywood studios publicity mills had worked to raise actors to the level of gods and goddesses—American royalty, if you will—Anger and his ilk wanted to prove that they were undeserving of such adoration. Exposing the underbelly of Hollywood success, the gossips reported on the stars that were caught by the media in compromising positions, after hours or unprotected by the studio spin doctors.

While Anger produced press and police photographs among the studio glamour shots for comparison, he also traded in rumor and conjecture. Naturally, this kind of coverage added a layer of resentment and envy to the idea of reportage, with the implication that the stars were just plain ordinary folk who happened to have found themselves in extraordinary circumstances. The sour grapes that the gossips overtly expressed was a way to bring the stars down to the level of the masses, but it also denied the extraordinary talent that is required to attain stardom in the first place or the magic that some possessed when captured on celluloid. After all, if anyone could do it, then everyone would be a Hollywood movie star and there would be no one left to do the gazing.

Anger's chapter lists some of the titles of Frances' films but in the incorrect order. He claims that Frances had streaked topless through traffic down Sunset Strip after the incident with the hairdresser, and that she spent ten years in the Snake Pit. Anger snidely comments that Lillian Farmer had never wanted a child, which none of the biographies confirm, as a way to enforce his presentation of Frances' mother as "her mortal enemy, her Nemesis," and someone "who seems to have crawled out of some very grim fairy tale." Finally, Anger nominates Frances as the patron saint for other troubled actresses, such as Clara Bow, Gail Russell and Gene Tierney. Clara Bow is mentioned in her own chapter in Anger's book, where he claims she suffered a series of nervous breakdowns and was institutionalized. However, neither Russell nor Tierney are mentioned elsewhere in the book.

Anger's chapter also offers four press photographs of Frances' 1943 arrest, including the infamous Wide World Photos shot of her grappling with an officer that appears in the autobiography and one in which Frances defiantly sneers for the photographer. Anger also includes a photo taken of Frances when she was arrested for vagrancy in Antioch in 1944, an image which also appeared in William Arnold's book. This last photo is interesting in the way Frances is barely recognizable, without the little makeup she used for the 1943 arrest, and sporting a bruise on her lower lip, presumably from the aforementioned scuffle she had had with the migrant worker. The rope she wears as a belt for her jeans and the serious look on her face completes the image of an actress who could not be less interested in Hollywood or looking like a star. Anger also reproduces publicity portraits of Frances from *Rhythm on the Range* and *Son of Fury*, although neither is identified as such, and an article on Frances' arrest from the *Philadelphia Record* dated January 14, presumably to give his claims added weight.

Arnold's *Shadowland*, published in 1978 by McGraw-Hill, uses a portrait of Frances from *Ride a Crooked Mile* for its cover, with lines drawn around and on her face and neck to suggest pencil-drawn shadows. This altered portrait is reproduced to introduce the collection of 37 photographs in the book's center, which also includes the original studio shot. Arnold's photographs of note from the "Author's collection" are a publicity picture for *Alien Corn*; Frances at 20 standing on the ship she would take to Russia; the 1938 family portrait of Ernest, Frances, and Lillian, which Arnold dates as 1936; Frances and Leif shortly before their separation; Frances at the police station in October 1942; Frances as a ward at Steilacoom in the 1940s; and shots of electroshock and Walter Freeman performing a lobotomy at Steilacoom.

Arnold reproduces the March 29, 1935, front page of the *Seattle Post-Intelligencer*, which features a photograph of Frances with the article headline "A Seattle Mother's Warning Against Red Teachers" and subtitled "Parent Unable to Halt Girl's Trip to Russia." What is interesting about the photo is that Frances' face is devoid of makeup, presumably to make her look younger, whereas the Author's collection shot of Frances as a freshman in 1931 shows her airbrushed and styled to look older and more glamorous. Other photographs in the collection are credited to the *Seattle Post-Intelligencer*, the *Los Angeles Times*, International News Service, and Wide World Photos. Of note among these are the mirrored image of Frances as an usherette at the Paramount Theater, the 1958 wedding of Frances and Mikesell, and shots of Frances and others looking at photographs. The first is Frances, Ernest and Lillian looking at a glamour studio portrait; the second shows Lillian gazing at a picture of Frances being arrested in Antioch. The second Antioch shot of Frances from Arnold's collection has Frances looking more attractive, sporting a tan that is not apparent in the first. Sitting with a police officer, she also expresses more of her contemptuous attitude than the relatively expressionless image of her in longer shot. In the *New York Times* book review on July 2, 1978, Caroline Seebohm wrote, "He [Arnold] tends at times to hype up an already painful story with journalistic techniques.... But his portrait is poignant in the extreme, and his messages at the end are chilling ones." As stated in the *A&E Biography* episode on Frances, "Paradise Lost," the book introduces the possibility of a lesbian relationship between Jean and Frances, and the lobotomy allegation.

Edith Farmer's *Look Back in Love* would appear to be self-published in 1978 by Gemaia Press. Rita Rose's article says that Edith paid $5,000 to have 1,500 copies of her book printed, and that she ended up giving away more than she sold. The uncredited cover photograph of Frances is a studio portrait, with her face half in shadow and her expression determined and unsmiling. As expected from a family member's biography, Edith supplies a plethora of family

**Edith Farmer Elliot used a variation of this publicity portrait of her sister Frances for Edith's book *Look Back in Love*.**

pictures, including one of her grandparents and plenty of Frances as a child. Edith also provides the 1938 shot of Ernest, Frances and Lillian, but from a different angle than the one in *Shadowland*. There is a signed program for the 1963 production of *The Seagull*; a collage of studio portraits (courtesy of T.J. Boris); a 1964 guide to Purdue Summer Theater productions, with Frances' bio; a 1964 photograph of Frances with Wesley; and publicity shots for *Frances Farmer Presents*. Patrick Agan's *The Decline and Fall of the Love Goddesses*, published in 1979 by Pinnacle Books, includes three photographs of Frances: a still for *Come and Get It*; a United Press International photo of Frances, said to be dated 1943, making a telephone call at the Los Angeles jail; and a Pictorial Parade shot of Frances supposedly playing a guitar and singing on *The Ed Sullivan Show* in 1957. The last photograph shows Frances' face and dark hair resembling the cover picture of the first edition of *Will There Really Be a Morning?* so one wonders whether that shot came from a photo session circa 1957.

The biopic *Frances*, starring Jessica Lange, was released on December 3, 1982; the made-for-TV movie *Will There Really Be a Morning?* was broadcast on February 22, 1983; and the independent drama *Committed*, starring co-director Sheila McLaughlin as Frances, was released in 1984. Parts of Frances' story also received coverage in the documentaries *Broadway Dreamers: The Legacy of the Group Theater* (1988), *Hollywood Scandals and Tragedies* (1988), *Hollywood Undressed* (1991), and the television series *E! Mysteries and Scandals* in 1998. Frances would receive her episode on *A&E Biography* when "Paradise Lost" was broadcast in 2000. She also inspired several literary works, was the subject of three produced plays (and two un-produced ones by the author of this book), and inspired several songs.

Yugoslavian poster for the biopic *Frances* (1982).

*The Canvas Prison*, by Gordon DeMarco, was published in 1982 by Germinal Press; it is a detective novel set around the time of the HUAC hearings, when Frances was in Steilacoom. *God's Peculiar Care*, the title of Frances' lost biographical novel, was published by Viking in 1991 as a novel by Patrick Roscoe about a group of social misfits obsessed with the spirit of Frances. *Las Fotografías de Frances Farmer*, by Peruvian author Ivan Thays, is a collection of nine short stories published in 1992 in Spanish. *The Frances Farmer Story*, by Sebastian Stuart, a play produced off–Broadway in New York in 1982, starred Elizabeth

Hess as Frances, and covers the years 1931 to 1964. *Golden Girl*, by Peter Occhiogrosso, is a character study of Frances' relationship with Clifford Odets; Frances was played by Maria Duvall. *Saint Frances of Hollywood*, by Sally Clarke, was produced in New York in 2005 and starred Sarah Ireland as Frances; Phoebe Hoban, in her *New York Times* review dated July 30, 2005, called this Frances "a crude caricature of a martyr to American values."

Perhaps the most widely recognized reference to Frances in popular culture is the song "Frances Farmer Will Have Her Revenge on Seattle" by the Seattle-based grunge band Nirvana, appearing on their 1993 album *In Utero*, although the song lyrics do not reference Frances specifically. It is believed that composer and vocalist Kurt Cobain is expressing his own difficulty with his record label rather than likening himself to Frances, although some of the song's lyrics can be applied to her if one is so inclined. A link between Cobain and Frances can also be made through his dislike of the media and his emotional problems, the latter leading to his suicide in 1994. Other musical artists who have written songs about Frances include The Men They Couldn't Handle, with the song "Lobotomy Gets 'Em Home"; Patterson Hood, with "Frances Farmer"; Culture Club, with "The Medal Song"; Everything but the Girl, with "Ugly Little Dreams"; and the French-Canadian singer Mylene Farmer, who chose her stage name in homage to Frances with "Maman a Tort" (My Mum Is Wrong).

Two references to Frances in popular culture have come in the animated television series *The Simpsons*. The biography of C. Montgomery Burns, first mentioned in the episode "Blood Feud" in Season 2 in 1991, is entitled "Will There Ever Be a Rainbow?" which seems to be a parody of "Will There Really Be a Morning?" In Season 5 in 1994, in the episode "Lady Bouvier's Lover," the following exchange occurs when Jackie Bouvier shows Abe Simpson an old photo of herself on a beach with her ankles indecently exposed:

> JACKIE: And here's a picture of me getting arrested for indecent exposure. It was the most embarrassing day of my life.
> ABE: [*Whistles*] Lift those gams. You were one nifty number!
> JACKIE: Boys all paid attention to me and it drove my friends crazy.
> ABE: Who were your friends?
> JACKIE: Oh, Zelda Fitzgerald, Frances Farmer, and little Sylvia Plath.

Jennifer Steinberg's article says that after Frances' death Jean lived in seclusion to avoid the "slanderous" and nasty things printed about her in the local paper. She refused to see the film *Frances*, although she was consulted about the made-for-TV movie. Another article on *The Misty One* website, dated April 1999, is written by Jack Randall Earles and entitled "The History of My Encounter with Jeanira Ratcliffe." In it he claims Jean told him that she had been working with Vivian Vance, who played sidekick Ethel Mertz on the *I Love Lucy* television sitcom, on an autobiography. The book was to be called *There Is a Mountain Beyond a Mountain Beyond a Mountain*, but supposedly Jean abandoned it because she thought Vivian would not be honest about certain parts of her life. Earles claims that this "ordeal" was mentioned in a biography of Vance, though Jean's name was recorded as "Radcliffe." The biography Earles references may be *Meet the Mertzes: The Life Stories of I Love Lucy's Other Couple*, by Rob Edelman and Audre Kupferberg, which was published by Renaissance Books in 1999. Earle reports that Vivian Vance's husband, John Dodds, had edited *Will There Really Be a Morning?*, and said Frances' name alone should appear as author to increase sales for critical attention. Earles also reports that Jean claimed that Edith left the funeral early and went back to the Indianapolis farmhouse to take things that Jean subsequently found missing. Apparently Edith was confronted at the hotel where she was staying, and later appeared at the house, throwing a suitcase of clothes at Jean that Jean did not recognize. For those who like parallels, Earle felt that Jean resembled a young Sophie Rosenstein. Earle says he was uncertain about Jean's sexual orientation, and advises that she died in 1987, although she was not buried in Oak Lawn with Frances.

The internet tribute website *The Misty One*, quoted earlier, was launched on April 9, 1988, as francesfarmer.com and copyrighted to David Kortegast. The contributors include David Farmer (Frances' nephew) and Jeffrey Kauffman, as well as Kristin Craig, Jack Randall Earles, Ulrich Fritzsche, Anthony Hale, Randi Massingill, Andrew McLaughlin, Dario Recla, Mike Ringenberger, George Snow, and Jennifer Steinberg. The site was a cornucopia of Frances material and an invaluable resource. It provided hyperlinks to a biography; transcribed articles from 1931 to 2001; offered a filmography with portraits, stills and lobby cards; and featured studio portraits and private collectors photos, theater memorabilia, post–Hollywood memorabilia, multimedia sound bites for radio, movies, television, and other audio, a resource guide to magazine publications, coverage of the books and movies on Frances, and examples of her own poetry and writing. I had intended to devote a chapter to an analysis of the site for this book until I learned that, regrettably, it was closed in October 2009 by geocities, who housed it. Being no longer available to access, as opposed to the other material I have sourced, I decided to only mention it here in the introduction.

In 2005, Jack El-Hai's book on Water Freeman, *The Lobotomist*, was published. Frances and the issue of whether she had been lobotomized is referenced in the book. Interviewed by psychosurgery historian David Shutts around the time of the release of the film *Frances* (1982), Freeman's son Franklin declared that the woman being lobotomized by Freeman in the photograph of William Arnold's book *Shadowland* was Frances, who was his father's patient. However, twenty years later, Franklin Freeman felt less certain and recalled for El-Hai that he had made the identification of Frances in the photograph secondhand. El-Hai claims that there is no mention in Walter Freeman's writings that he ever met Frances, or that she ever had a lobotomy. In the account of their lobotomy program published in *Northwest Medicine*, Western State physicians describe nearly fifty of their psychosurgery patients. El-Hai says that only one matched Frances' gender and age, and this patient was discharged at least two years before Frances' release. El-Hai also claims that, given Frances' accomplishments after her release—marriage, hosting her own television show, appearing on *This Is Your Life*—Freeman would probably have mentioned her with pride had she been his patient.

El-Hai concludes that because of Arnold's book and the film *Frances*, Frances Farmer had been turned into a symbol of the excesses of psychosurgery, a patient supposedly selected for her non-conformist political opinions who was operated on with the consent of a vindictive mother, and with her soul and spirit vanquished after surgery. That image, El-Hai says, was reinforced by the portrayal of lobotomy in Ken Kesey's book *One Flew over the Cuckoo's Nest* (which was also adapted into a widely seen film) and other literary works. El-Hai's book *The Lobotomist* would be the inspiration for the American Experience documentary of the same name by Barak Goodman and John Maggio on Walter Freeman, released in 2008 with the tagline "Sometimes medicine is a stab in the dark."

With a tone that suggests a study of a serial killer (it helps that Freeman has a Hitleresque moustache), this fascinating documentary provides grisly footage of insulin seizures, shock therapy and Freeman's trans-orbital lobotomy. The film also presents the dualities attached to him. Was he an angel of mercy or a medical monster? Was his procedure a medical breakthrough or a monstrous mistake? These dualities extend to the case studies which alternate between stories of success and failure. Freeman's most notorious failure is considered to be Rosemary Kennedy, the twenty-three-year-old daughter of the former United States ambassador to Britain, Joseph P. Kennedy, in 1941. She went from displaying symptoms of mental illness while being relatively independent before the treatment to being seriously disabled and requiring full-time care after it. Freeman's career only survived because of the context of history.

The end of the war saw traumatized veterans overwhelm the overcrowded state hospitals. A *Life* magazine article by Albert Q. Maisel entitled "Bedlam" included photographs of patients at the mental wards of two state hospitals that paralleled concentration camp footage. The author

**Publicity portrait of Frances for *Rhythm on the Range* (1936).**

of the obscure monograph that Freeman had appropriated for his work, Egaz Moniz, won the Nobel Prize. And by the end of the 1940s the lobotomy was being performed at elite medical institutions, with Freeman having won the acceptance of mainstream medicine. It is the 1950s that saw Freeman's rapid decline and dwindling opportunities, when long-term clinical studies in medical journals began to disavow his procedure as destroying the brain, and when, most significantly, Thorazine was marketed in 1954 as a "chemical lobotomy." Freeman would retire in 1967 when his last patient died of a brain hemorrhage, after having performed 2900 trans-orbital lobotomies during his career. Freeman ended his life a desperate man, criss-crossing America in search of former patients and seeking redemption for his good intentions.

The documentary's postscript states that Freeman died on May 31, 1972, and that the lobotomy, in modified form, is still performed in rare cases of obsessive compulsive disorder at hospitals around the world. Interestingly, the filmmakers show the image of Freeman's car driving into the horizon after this coda, as if he is still out there. While the film does not mention Frances or the Western State Hospital specifically, it does show the alleged photograph of her operation three times. The symptoms of mental illness described here as making a patient eligible for Freeman's lobotomy only partially match Frances' behavior, since she may have been anxious and depressed but not suicidal, and it is her alcoholism that would have made her appear hallucinatory. However, the known side effects of successful cases would seem to match Frances' demeanor after her release: unmotivated, uninhibited and childlike. The film displays before and after photographs of patients, where the unsmiling is replaced by the smiling, and one is tempted to compare Frances upon being arrested and Frances after her release from Steilacoom.

The issue of informed consent is raised. Although some case studies show how some families of patients agreed to Freeman's procedure being performed on their loved ones, others indicate that doctors in state hospitals did not always seek permission. Theoretically, this could have given Freeman the means and opportunity to have operated on Frances. The film repeatedly accuses him of being a man hungry for fame, one who courted the press for recognition of his work and bypassed the process of peer review. However, it also casts Freeman as an idealist, his motive being to reduce and remove the pain from which patients were suffering. If it was said that he shone a light into the snake pit, it can also be said that he tried to empty the snake pit and change the snakes into rabbits.

Kauffman reports on his website that Edith Farmer has died, though the year of her death is unknown. Rita Rose had commented that Edith was age seventy in 1983 when Rose had written her article. Both William Arnold and Patrick Agan appear to be still living.

## *Legacy*

In his review of the made-for-TV movie *Will There Really Be a Morning?* in the *New York Times*, John J. O'Connor states that Frances Farmer was never in the same league as Bette Davis, who can be considered a contemporary and who also had her share of troubles with the Hollywood studios. O'Connor calls Farmer a modestly talented performer who never made an important film, and that a nagging imbalance in the perception of her has developed. While this author agrees that Frances did not have the range of Davis, Frances Farmer was still an impressive performer given the material and a strong director, and her movies remain interesting because of her presence. It can often be said that she is the best thing about any film in which she appeared, which is an achievement unto itself and a value judgment that can also be applied to Davis, Crawford, Garbo, and Katharine Hepburn. Frances was an original, and like those other great movie stars, her face remains unforgettable.

# THE FILMS

## *Too Many Parents* (1936)

Paramount Pictures

**Credits:** Adolph Zukor Presents. Director: Robert F. McGowan; Associate Producer: Jack Cunningham; Screenplay: Virginia Van Upp, Doris Malloy, from stories by George Templeton and Jesse Lynch Williams; Photography: Karl Struss; Editor: Edward Dmytryk; Art Director: Hans Dreier, Robert O'Dell; Interior Decorations: A E. Freudeman; Sound: Earl Hayman, Walter Oberst; Choreography: Ethel Meglin. Black & White, 73 minutes.

**Cast:** Frances Farmer (Sally Colman); Porter Hall (Mr. Saunders); Lester Matthews (Mark Stewart); Henry Travers (Wilkins); George Ernest (Phillip Stewart); Douglas Scott (Morton Downing); Sherwood Bailey (Clarence Talbot, Jr.); Buster Phelps (Clinton Meadows); Callen Jader (Alfred); Carl "Alfalfa" Switzer (White Gardenia); Billy Lee (Billy Miller); Howard C. Hickman (Colonel Colman); Anne Grey (Miss Allison); Doris Lloyd (Mrs. Martha Downing). Uncredited: Colin Tapley (Miller); Jonathan Hale (Judge); Mabel Forrest (Clinton's Mother); Lillian West (Clinton's Stepmother); Frank Mayo (Clinton's Father); Bradley Metcalfe (Cadet Williams); Lois Kent (Morton's Sister); Russ Clark (Coach); Henry Roquemore (Belcher); Jack Norton (Drill); Sylvia Breamer (Malloy); Freeman Wood (Clinton's Stepfather); Al Burke (Motor Cop); Floyd Criswell (Motor Cop); George Magrill (Chauffeur); Rex Moore (A.D.T. Boy); Fred Anderson (Messenger); P.E. "Tiny" Newland (Fields); Harry Tenbrook (Guard); Norman Ainsley (Private tutor); John Nasboro (Doorman); Phillips Smalley (Second Man); Edward LeSaint (Trustee); William Norton Bailey (Trustee); Arnold Gray (Trustee); Fred Williams (Trustee); Clive Morgan (Trustee); Bruce Wyndham (Secretary); Don Roberts (Stage Manager); Howard Mitchell (Bailiff); Billy Butts (Cadet Adjutant); Lee Van Atta (Cadet); Gene Reynolds (Cadet); Hollis Jewell (Cadet); Terry Powers (Cadet Sergeant); Irene Bennett (Mabel); Ann Evers (Clara); Jerry Tucker (Mike the Bartender); Fred Winter (part unknown).

**Song:** "White Gardenia" (author/s unknown), sung by Carl "Alfalfa" Switzer.

**VHS/DVD:** Not available in either format.

## Synopsis

Obnoxious rich boy Clarence "Butch" Talbot Jr. accepts a bet to survive a week at the Colman Military Academy, and enrolls on the same day as Billy Miller, the son of actors, and Clinton Meadows, the child of divorced parents. At the Academy they meet eleven-year-old Lieutenant Philip Stewart, who is estranged from his neglectful engineer father, Mark. The boys befriend the school janitor, Mr. Wilkins, and are watched over by the receptionist, Sally, the commander's daughter. Clarence stays on after his week is up and gradually stops behaving badly. Philip's father sends a telegram to advise he is taking a week's leave from his travels to go to New York. Sally goes with Phillip to see Mark, but the visit is cut short when Mark is called back to Washington.

Phillip writes fake letters from his father to himself on the stationary Mark had given him. At Christmas, Clinton's mother, Mrs. Downing, takes in the abandoned Clarence, Billy, Philip, and Clinton, as well as Morton, to celebrate the holiday. Mr. Wilkins dresses as Santa and gives Philip a fishing rod, pretending that the gift has come from Mark, who has only sent his son a check. For the father-son dinner, Philip has written a play, but Mark telegrams that he cannot attend. All the boys act in the play, but Philip is heartbroken and is comforted by Sally. Mr. Wilkins discovers the boy's charade when he finds letter drafts in the trash, and reports him. In a ceremony before the other students, Philip is demoted for lying as conduct unbecoming an officer. Sally wires Mark, and he finally comes to the academy to witness Philip's humiliation. The boy runs away and hides in a canoe, which goes over a waterfall at the top of a dam. Mark jumps into the water and saves Philip, and then takes him and his friends on a camping trip. When we hear Philip address Sally as mother we realize she has married Mark.

A variation of this publicity portrait was used as a framed photograph of Frances as Sally Colman in *Too Many Parents* (1936).

## Notes

This B-movie programmer is Frances' film debut, in which she plays a supporting part (although top-billed). While she makes a strong impression, it is hardly a star-making role, since the boys of the academy are the focus of the narrative. Ironically, the film serves as a wonderful opportunity for eleven-year-old George Ernest as the protagonist, whose sensitive performance steals the show. One's enjoyment is reliant upon an appreciation of child stars, although director Robert F. McGowan supplies a pleasing, if melodramatic, action climax, and the camerawork has moments of note.

Early on, the film makes some attempts at humor. Director Robert McGowan cuts from a man saying of Clarence, "Just a poor little orphan, that's all in the world he's got," to a sign outside the Talbot Trust Company which reads "Capital $50,000,000, Resources

$250,000,000." An exchange between Mr. Saunders and an unnamed Trustee continues the thread:

> MR. SAUNDERS: Some sort of discipline is sadly needed.
> TRUSTEE: What that lad needs is a good old-fashioned spanking.
> MR. SAUNDERS: You can't spank ten million dollars.
> TRUSTEE: I'd like to try it.

McGowan employs a silent gag when Clarence jumps to sit on the window ledge of a high rise building and nearly falls back out the window. In response, the Trustees watching him all react in shocked concern. Billy's first scene with his parents (both actors) offers another mild laugh:

> MOTHER (TO FATHER): What did you cut in my laugh for? Every time I get a chance for a laugh you kill it.
> FATHER: Laugh? Huh, I saved you.
> MOTHER: From what?
> FATHER: From a laugh.

Publicity portrait of George Ernest, the juvenile lead in *Too Many Parents* (1936).

Clarence scores a laugh himself in the way he retreats at the sight of knives that Mr. Wilkins removes from a medical cabinet. Wilkins is described by Philip as the "judge of the rookie court" but never does anything in this capacity. Rather, his informing on Philip's fake letters would seem to be a personal betrayal. Wilkin's pratfalls over the coal left on the staircase and floor, and when, as Santa, he falls down Mrs. Downing's chimney, fail to amuse. However, the narrative effectively uses Billy for comic relief when he slips on the grass and drops a pail of water onto fellow cadets, and especially in his exasperation at the intellectual pronouncements and correcting of Morton. Billy Lee's affecting portrayal makes Billy so cute that he redeems these stale antics, and his dancing in the father-son dinner show is a highlight, since he is so accomplished. Said show, however, loses points for using a 1930s musical orchestration in the context of the western play, though that is not nearly as offensive as the sheer awfulness of Carl "Alfalfa" Switzer's singing of "White Gardenia."

The western play that Philip has written is a sign of his interest in creative writing, which dovetails nicely with his writing letters supposedly from his father. Clarence dressed in drag for the play is an interesting touch—rationalized by the academy being an all-boys school—in light of his preferred "butch" nickname and general testosterone-fuelled mischief. That he accepts the part without any apparent resistance is a sign of his maturing and new open-mindedness.

Mark's awkwardness with Philip is a problematic issue in the screenplay. Although Mark may see some self-justification in his behavior because the birth of his son resulted in the death of his wife, Mark should have resolved this by the time Philip has reached eleven. Sending your child to a military academy may have been an ordinary occurrence for the period, especially in light of Mark's determined pursuit of his career. However,

Publicity portrait of Lester Matthews and Frances for *Too Many Parents* (1936).

while his fear of his son when Philip visits is played for comedy, it actually reads as poor parental behavior and a lack of caring. Mark is presented as a weak and unlikable character, which makes the viewer's expected change of heart towards Mark after he rescues Philip from the waterfall an empty victory. One can interpret Mark's dive as accepting his parenthood, but we don't see him ask for his son's forgiveness, which he surely owed him. This papering over of an important character point is as arbitrary as Mark's romance with Sally.

Frances' first appearance has Clarence acknowledging her beauty. His "Hello Cookie" is answered with her "Hi ya, toots." That Sally only receives flattery from a child is an indication of her environment, and even her marriage to Mark in the last reel doesn't include any admission of Mark's feeling for or attraction to her.

McGowan makes sparing use of close-ups on Frances until the scene where Sally confronts Mark. Sally comforts Philip when Mark is a no-show at the dinner, more as a tomboy pal than an empathetic female, although she does give Philip a hug at the end. Frances is regrettably styled to resemble Carole Lombard in her big scene with Mark, though Farmer's snarl is a nice touch. She uses the raised eyebrow for the first time, a mannerism she will employ in later films, and the over-the-shoulder shot of Sally as she berates Mark displays the steely gaze of anger. Her line that they are taking away Philip's sword has an emasculating connotation, and McGowan noticeably uses the music score for the first time in the film to dramatize Philip's emotion.

The music tempo increases for the waterfall sequence, and we don't mind the melodrama since it's the only strong action sequence in the entire film. It's a pity that the narrative includes the cliché of the canoe stopping at the top of the dam, though the fall looks good, and it is not readily apparent whether Philip is in the canoe when it goes over. McGowan rewards Frances with perhaps her loveliest reactive close-up when she is listening to Philip and Mark reconcile, and it's a relief that Sally is included in the film's conclusion.

Director Robert F. McGowan utilizes various camera techniques to enhance the scenario. The vertical wipe transitions that McGowan repeatedly employs later culminates in a dividing split-screen shot at the father-son dinner, and he also uses a montage to indicate the passage of time after Christmas. The father-son dinner features a tracking shot past tables, though an earlier image of the four boys in shadowed profile as Taps plays for lights out is perhaps the film's most evocative shot.

McGowan had been directing comedy shorts since the silent era, achieving success for producer Hal Roach with the Our Gang comedy series, which utilized the talents of the Little Rascals, a cast of children who included *Too Many Parents* stars Billy Lee, Sherwood Bailey, and Carl "Alfalfa" Switzer. (Switzer's cameo appearance here was an attempt to present him in his first feature film.) However, after his last Our Gang title, *Divot Diggers* (1936), McGowan had moved on to make features. He would only direct one film for Paramount, and after three titles for Monogram Pictures, McGowan's career ended, with his final credit being one of the directors for the 1955 syndicated television series of *The Little Rascals*, which broadcast the shorts made between 1929 and 1938.

*Too Many Parents* was the first film for uncredited producer A.M. Botsford, who would also produce Frances' next picture, *Border Flight*. The TCM database lists Henry Herzbrun as the *Too Many Parents*' executive producer, although he also goes uncredited on the film print. Herzbrun was an executive producer for A and B titles at Paramount in 1935 and 1936. Credited associate producer Jack Cunningham was a screenwriter who had previously produced *The Iron Mask* (1929) for United Artists, and was the associate producer of *Woman Trap* (1936) for Paramount.

Editor Edward Dmytryk would graduate to directing Bs at Paramount, then move to direct A films at RKO Radio Pictures, like the film noir classics *Murder, My Sweet* (1944) and *Crossfire* (1947). His career was adversely affected when he was fired from RKO after being named by the House Committee on Un-American Activities (HUAC) and blacklisted as one of the infamous "Hollywood Ten." Co-screenwriter Virginia Van Upp would experience her greatest success when she became a producer at Columbia Pictures and made the Rita Hayworth classic *Gilda* (1946).

Choreographer Ethel Meglin had produced and directed *The Land of Oz*, a sequel to the 1932 *Wizard of Oz*, made for her Meglin Kiddies company. *Too Many Parents* was the only film on which she was credited as dance director. George Ernest had appeared as Roger Jones in 20th Century–Fox's comedy *Every Saturday Night* (1936) and would repeat the character in the Jones family movies until the last of the series, *On Their Own* (1940).

There is a scene in the *Will There Really Be a Morning?* made-for-TV movie which is supposed to be from the set of *Too Many Parents*, but the dialogue, characters, costumes and scene presented do not appear in the original film. Errors aside, the TV movie offers a point of interest by showing Frances to be unhappy with her performance, and her request for a retake being refused. The autobiography quotes Frances as stating that making the film was a "dull, professionally humiliating experience," although she doesn't say why.

## Release

March 20, 1936, with the tagline, "Children hungry for love ... caught in the mill of divorce!"

## Reviews

"Don't miss this excellent picture of juvenile life in a military academy full of entertainment and heart interest ... all of the cast is effective."—*Photoplay* magazine, author and date unknown

"Although her lines were almost embarrassingly inane, she [Frances] was utterly fascinating to watch. Audiences went away remembering that face and that voice and with the feeling they had seen someone very much on the way up."—William Arnold, *Shadowland*

"Well-intentioned."—Jay Robert Nash and Stanley Ralph Ross, *The Motion Picture Guide 1927–1983*

"Frances shines through beautifully.... You can see why she was considered star material. The talent was there."—Conrad Lane, *Indiana Epilogue*

# *Border Flight* (1936)

### Paramount Pictures

**Credits:** Adolph Zukor Presents. Director: Otho Lovering; Associate Producer: Dario Faralla; Screenplay: Stuart Anthony, Arthur J. Beckhard, based on a story by Ewing Scott; Photography: Harry Fischbeck; Editor: Chandler House; Art Direction: Hans Drier, Robert Odell; Interior Decorator: A. E. Freudeman; Sound: Jack Goodrich, Louis Mesenkop; Technical Adviser: Commander R. L. Jack; Technical Supervision: Lieutenant Stanley C. Linholm. Black & White, 68 minutes. Filming February–March 1936, some scenes filmed at the U.S. Coast Guard base in San Diego.

**Cast:** Frances Farmer (Anne Blane); John Howard (Lt. Dan Conlon); Roscoe Karns (Calico Smith); Robert Cummings (Lt. Bob Dixon); Grant Withers (Lt. Pat Tornell); Samuel S. Hinds (Commander Mosely); Donald Kirke (Heming); Matty Fain (Jerry); Frank Faylen (Jimmie); Ted Oliver (Turk); Paul Barrett (Radio Operator). Uncredited: Edgar Dearing (Smuggler's Pilot); Emily Fitzroy (Old Maid); Ralph Lewis (Boat Captain); Gertrude Simpson (Maid); Eddie Dunn, Jack Raymond (Mechanics).

**VHS/DVD:** Not available in either format.

## Synopsis

Lieutenant Pat Tornell and Lieutenant Bob Dixon are sworn into the United States Coast Guard Air Patrol, West Coast Division. Pat is a daredevil pilot and now joins his former rival from school, Lieutenant Dan Conlon, who is devoted to the service. Pat sees Dan's girlfriend, Anne Blaine, and pursues her romantically, much to the annoyance of Dan. When Commander Mosely is criticized for having allowed fur smugglers to elude the Coast Guard, he rallies his men to bring the smugglers in. During the attempt, Dixon is shot and goes down with his plane. This prompts the Guard to outfit planes with machine guns. During gunning practice, Pat makes daredevil maneuvers with his plane and is reprimanded by Mosely. Mosely warns Pat and Dan to end their rivalry, but Pat does not listen.

On patrol, Dan shoots down a smuggler's plane. As officer of the day, Pat tells Dan he can leave his post early so that Pat can skywrite a message to Anne over her returning ship, the *Seneca*. Pat's buzzing makes the captain complain to Mosely about him, and Mosely asks Pat to resign, which he does. Pat becomes the new pilot for the smugglers, although Anne believes he is actually working undercover, something which the smugglers also suspect. Following him on a date with Anne, the smugglers take the couple to their hideout, a shack on the beach twenty-five miles from the Coast Guard station. Outsmarting the kidnappers, Anne calls Dan on a short-wave radio and alerts him to their location. Dan flies out to meet them, and gunfire is exchanged between Dan, Pat and Anne, and the smugglers, who have retreated to their ship. Dan is wounded and his plane explodes, but the arrival of Calico Smith allows Pat to fly out and crash his plane into the smuggler's ship, killing the smugglers and himself.

## Notes

An aviation drama with a Boy's Own mentality, the B status of this title is betrayed by the fact that it lacks a single close-up. Director Otho Lovering seems more interested

**Publicity portrait of Grant Withers, Frances, and John Howard for *Border Flight* (1936).**

in presenting the aerial photography, resulting in the ground drama being pedestrian and dull. Matters aren't helped by the lack of charisma in the leading male actors. The *Hollywood Reporter* had announced that Cary Grant had been cast in the film, presumably in the role of Pat, which may have improved the dynamic. However, part of the problem is the screenplay's decision to make Pat the far more appealing male in the love triangle and to reduce his rival Dan to a cipher who only becomes interesting when he becomes the temporary protagonist at the film's climax. As the comedy relief, Roscoe Karns steals the picture.

Again looking brunette, as she had in *Too Many Parents*, Frances suffers from a lack of close-ups, and Lovering makes no attempt to highlight her beauty. However, Frances does manage to make Anne's banter with Pat work, and the climactic fight is directly instigated by her actions.

Farmer's character is modern and liberated in her reluctance to commit to Dan, and her willingness to consider the affections of another man. If Anne had rejected Pat's advances, her character would have been far less interesting. Even when Anne's dialogue is unremarkable, Farmer still creates the illusion that she is speaking spontaneously—the mark of a good actor. Lovering disappoints by offering our first sight of Anne in long shot, a decision that also undermines the plot point of this also being Pat's first glimpse of her. Granted, Anne is the only woman seen at the base, and only two other women appear in

Mechanic Calico Smith (Roscoe Karns) with Coast Guard pilot Lt. Dan Conlon (John Howard) in *Border Flight* (1936).

the screenplay, but it would have been preferable to have seen Anne from Pat's point of view. As it is, Pat is reduced to being a womanizer, with Anne simply a victim.

The screenplay makes much of Pat being a Taurus, and this allows Anne to insult him during their first exchange. After she initially rejects his offer of a date, the following exchange occurs:

> PAT: Mrs. Tornell's boy makes a specialty of laughing last.
> ANNE: Doesn't Taurus mean ... bull?!

Farmer's pause before the word bull makes the joke. That Anne should be kidnapped when she finally goes on a date with Pat is an indication of what a mistake it is, as much as Pat being a daredevil flyer and pursing a woman he knows is seeing a supposed friend of his prefigures Pat's doomed fate. Pat's opportunism is also commented on by Commander Mosely when Pat tells Mosely that he is a school friend of Dan's:

> MOSELY: You say you were friends?
> PAT: Yes sir.
> MOSELY: Well, I'd hate to have you as an enemy.

Of course, Pat's disregard of Dan's interest in Anne makes him practically an enemy to Dan. Pat's hostility also affects their work together when Pat flies too close to Dan in the air, which leads Pat to threaten, "The next time we fly together I'm going to come so close you'll land with your hair parted in the middle." This witticism is one of many in the screenplay which heightens the dialogue.

When Dan first lands on the base's runway with a damaged plane, the predicament is commented on by a mechanic and Calico. Part of the humor of Calico's disinterested replies as he works on another plane stems from the fact that Calico makes no eye contact with the mechanic and doesn't even look at the landing aircraft until after the exchange:

> MECHANIC: Calico, it's him. He's lost his wheels.
> CALICO: He hasn't lost his head.
> MECHANIC: He's going to try to land. He's almost sure to crack up.
> CALICO: I know it.
> MECHANIC: You're a funny guy, Calico.
> CALICO: I know it.

Calico's repeated use of "I know it" becomes a running gag in the treatment. Calico also introduces an element of homoeroticism into the scenario. Calico is the screenplay's most subversive character. Roscoe Karns' androgynous persona daringly combines the sissy, a man with no sexual appeal to women, with the passive-aggressive hostility of the retired and frustrated older man among the younger

Publicity portrait of Robert Cummings, who has a small role in *Border Flight* (1936).

pilots. When Dan calls Pat "an old sweetheart of mine" from school, Calico sings, "School days, school days," which is repeated after the flying-too-close confrontation. After Pat dresses in civilian clothes for his date with Anne, Calico straightens the hang of his suit and adjusts the handkerchief in Pat's jacket pocket. These actions play off the sexual innuendo begun when Pat claimed, "There's two things I can do. One of them's flying." When Calico joins the fight at the film's climax, his return to flying is the restoration of his self-esteem and masculinity, even though his actions allow for Pat's heroics and death.

When Mosely scolds Pat for his maneuver during gunning practice, the exchange is both funny and truthful:

> PAT: I know how to fly a plane.
> MOSELY: Well, you wouldn't be here if you didn't, so there's no need to prove it.

The conventions of radio broadcasting are parodied when the smugglers' pilot is ready to land with his booty, and the chief of operations is standing by the radio operator listening to the pilot's message:

> PILOT TO RADIO OPERATOR: Tell the chief everything's ready. We've got the stuff off the steamer and we're coming in.
> RADIO OPERATOR: He says—
> CHIEF SMUGGLER: Please! I hate repetition.

The climactic battle, while incorporating more aerial photography, also creates the film's best sequence in the gunfire exchange. Farmer's mussed hair, as Anne is bound, adds some realism and breaks the convention of the perfectly-coiffed-under-any-circumstances Hollywood actress. Her using a gun to hold off the smugglers when she radios for Dan, and her firing at the smugglers with Pat and Dan, makes Anne an equal-partner protagonist and adds dignity to what otherwise might have been just another Woman in Peril. The narrative seems to be indecisive about whether Pat or Dan will be the eventual hero, alternating opportunities for both. This mirrors Anne's switching allegiance, although her final choice of staying with the wounded Dan presents her as the empathetic nursing female rather than a suicidal, self-sacrificing heroine.

The notion that the smugglers have abandoned one of their group because he is unable to untie himself in time to escape indicates their heartlessness, even if their criminal activity had already pointed in that direction. The dropping of what looks like flour over the abandoned smuggler during the battle adds to his humiliation.

Pat's death gives the film a morally ambiguous ending. Although it is coated in supposed heroics in victory over the smugglers, this murder/suicide is celebrated by the surviving Dan, Anne and Calico, who display no remorse. The last line is Calico's: "I bet he got a kick out of doing that." There is an implied assumption that Pat is a fatalistic character, and his selfishness is redeemed by what is considered to be a noble act. It also removes the obstacle to the romance between Dan and Anne, and demonstrates that fighting was ultimately more important to Pat than his feelings for Anne.

There is a beautiful shot of Calico's plane landing on the beach, although the crash of Pat's plane into the ship, utilizing a zooming point-of-view camera, makes it obvious that models were used for the impact. Lovering's use of rear projection for medium shots of the pilots in their planes is standard Hollywood convention, but one angled screen wipe from a plane in the air to the craft landing on the runway offers some variety among the film's other vertical screen wipes. Publicity for the film claimed that Amelia Earheart's monoplane was rented to appear as the smuggler's plane.

Publicity portrait of Frances with John Howard for *Border Flight* (1936).

Otho Lovering was an editor who had only started directing in 1935. He debuted with the Western *Wanderer of the Wasteland* (1935), whose cast included Leif Erickson. 1936 saw the release of three of Lovering's films. Apart from *Border Flight*, he had made another Western, *Drift Fence* (1936), again featuring Erickson, and another aviation drama, *Sky Parade* (1936), which also starred Grant Withers. All the films he directed were made for Paramount, and *Border Flight* would be his last, after which he returned to being an editor. *Border Flight* was the first title that Dario Faralla associate produced. A.M. Botsford, who served as *Border Flight*'s uncredited producer, had produced Frances' prior (and first) film, *Too Many Parents*.

John Howard had previously played a pilot in Paramount's *Thirteen Hours by Air* (1936), and would go on to play Captain Hugh "Bulldog" Drummond in a series of Paramount titles. Although his character died in *Border Flight*, Robert Cummings, ironically, would serve as a flight instructor during World War II, and make a memorable appearance as a pilot in *The Twilight Zone* television episode "King Nine Will Not Return" (1960). Howard and Cummings had previously co-starred in Paramount's comedy *Millions in the Air* (1935).

## *Release*

May 29, 1936.

## Reviews

"Melodramatic trifle ... just another program picture."—Frank S. Nugent, *The New York Times*, June 22, 1936

"Good cast, good direction, and a fast-moving script.... The costume department didn't do any too well by Miss Farmer, a looker who could have carried a softer wardrobe."—*Variety*, June 24, 1936

"Interesting for old planes and Frances Farmer at her freshest."—Jay Robert Nash and Stanley Ralph Ross, *The Motion Picture Guide, 1927–1983*

"Full of fast and furious action, but poorly directed, this rates as an average programmer.... You'll enjoy the stunt-flying and the big climax, otherwise it's ordinary."—*Photoplay* magazine (author and date unknown)

## *Rhythm on the Range* (1936)

### Paramount

**Credits:** Adolph Zukor Presents. Director: Norman Taurog; Producer: Benjamin Glazer; Screenplay: John C. Moffitt, Sidney Salkow, Walter DeLeon, and Francis Martin, based on a story by Mervin J. Houser; Photography: Karl Struss; Art Direction: Hans Drier, Robert Usher; Editor: Ellsworth Hoagland; Music: John Leipold; Sound: Gene Merritt, Don Johnson; Costumes: Edith Head; Interior Decorations: A. E. Freudeman; Musical Direction: Boris Morros. Black & White, 87 minutes. Filmed in May 1936 on location at Alabama Hills, Lone Pine, California.

**Songs:** "Empty Saddles" (Billy Hill, J. Keirn Brennan), sung by Bing Crosby; "Roundup Lullaby" (Bager Clark, Gertrude Rose), sung by Bing Crosby; "I Can't Escape from You" (Leo Robin, Richard A. Whiting), sung by Bing Crosby; "Mr. Paganini" (Sam Coslow), sung by Martha Raye; "If You Can't Sing It (You'll Have to Swing It)" (Sam Coslow), sung by Martha Raye; "Drink It Down" (Ralph Rainger, Leo Robin), sung by Leonid Kinskey and Bing Crosby, accompanied by Bob Burns, Louis Prima and the Sons of the Pioneers; "I'm an Old Cowhand from the Rio Grande" (Johnny Mercer), sung by Bing Crosby, Leonid Kinskey, Martha Raye, Bob Burns, and Louis Prima, accompanied by the Sons of the Pioneers; "Love in Bloom" (Ralph Rainger, Leo Robin), sung by Martha Raye.

**Cast:** Bing Crosby (Jeff Larabee); Frances Farmer (Doris Halloway); Bob Burns (Buck); Martha Raye (Emma); Samuel S. Hinds (Robert Halloway); Warren Hymer (Big Brain); Lucille Webster Gleason (Penelope Ryland); George E. Stone (Shorty); James Burke (Wabash); Martha Sleeper (Connie Hyde); Clem Bevans (Gila Bend, Cowboy); Leonid Kinskey (Mischa); Charles Williams (Gopher); Beau Baldwin the 50th ("Cuddles" the Bull). Uncredited: Charles Amt (Driver); Herbert Ashley (Brakeman); Irving Bacon (Rodeo Announcer); Hank Bell (Rodeo Cowboy); James Blaine (Conductor); Harry C. Bradley (Minister); Jim Corey (Rodeo Cowboy); Frank Dawson (Butler); Ellen Drew (part unknown); Hugh Farr (Hugh, Sons of the Pioneers); Karl Farr (Karl, Sons of the Pioneers); Sam Garrett (Rider/Roper); Ben Hendricks, Jr. (Rodeo Trickster); Sam McDaniel (Porter); Robert McKenzie (Farmer); Bob Nolan (Bob, Sons of the Pioneers); Dennis O'Keefe (Heckler); Bessie Patterson (bit part); Sons of the Pioneers (Ranch Hands); Louis Prima (Trumpet Player); Jack Rice (Train Station Smoocher); Roy Rogers (Leonard, Sons of the Pioneers); Syd Saylor (Gus);

Oscar Smith (Waiter); Tim Spencer (Tim, Sons of the Pioneers); Frank Sully (Splashed Rodeo Cowboy); James Thompson (Porter); Otto Yamaoka (Houseboy).

**VHS/DVD:** DVD released May 6, 2003, by Universal Studios.

## Synopsis

Ranch owner Penelope Ryland comes to New York to visit her niece Doris Halloway, a Park Avenue heiress engaged to be married to a Wall Street vice president. Accompanying Penny to a rodeo contest at Madison Square Garden, Doris is touched by a speech Penny makes to the crowd about marrying the man you love, convincing Doris to abandon New York and her fiancé (whom we never meet), and go to Penny's ranch, the Frying Pan. At the rodeo, cowboy Jeff Larrabee wins the singing contest, enabling him to purchase Cuddles, a bull. Doris hides in the same boxcar that Jeff travels in, but they quarrel and Jeff only allows her to stay because of the rain. Attracted to Jeff, she lies to him about her identity, telling him she is a cook named Lois Hall. The next day Doris pays another boxcar passenger, Shorty, to send a telegram she has written to her father. However, Shorty and his two friends, Big Brain and Wabash, decide to cash in on Doris' notoriety and pursue her. Doris is chased off the train when Cuddles sees her red scarf, and Jeff rescues her. However, the train continues on without them. When Doris steals a car, she persuades Jeff to drive with her, and they rest in a barn that night.

The three men lock Jeff and Doris in the stable, but Jeff uses the scarf to entice Cuddles to break them out. They drive on to Jeff's house in Green Pastures, Arizona, which is close to Penny's ranch, where Jeff works. In the meantime, Jeff's partner Buck, who had missed the train that Jeff had caught, meets Macy's salesgirl Emma Mazda on another

Publicity portrait of Frances in a suit for *Rhythm on the Range* (1936).

train. Emma is also headed for Penny's ranch, where her brother Gopher works. Overwhelmed by Emma's attention, Buck proposes to her, and they announce their engagement at the Frying Pan. Jeff also proposes to Doris, who has delayed telling him who she really is. Penny and Doris' father interrupt the subsequent celebration, and Doris' real identity is revealed. Jeff leaves on his horse, offended that he is considered a fortune hunter, and Doris convinces the three men to pursue him. As Jeff packs, Doris appears in his house and they reconcile, with the help of Cuddles.

## *Notes*

This mix of musical, Western and romantic comedy features a screenplay with an abundance of slapstick and a performance by Martha Raye that steals the film from headliners Bing Crosby and Frances. Looking lovely in close-up and dressed attractively, Frances differentiates Doris' behavior in tune with the character's change. Acting understated and controlled at the beginning, Doris becomes more assertive and funny when she leaves her New York lifestyle, and Frances adds convincing moments of romantic longing and romantic disappointment. The standard convention of a battling romantic comedy—the joining of opposites—is met, with Frances' modern sophisticated woman positioned as secondary to the rather juvenile antics of cowboys and the women attracted to them. However, in spite of the lowbrow tediousness of most of the humor, an occasional genuine laugh emerges, and director Norman Taurog provides some interesting filmic touches.

The opening credits play over cartoon pencil sketches of a rodeo, and Penny Ryland is introduced in mannish attire, including jacket and tie (which is rationalized by her being a cowgirl and pioneer woman). The latter quality recalls Lillian Farmer, Frances' real-life mother, although Lillian would suffer through two failed marriages. Penny's love life is questionable; in spite of her promoting romantic and presumably heterosexual love, it is easy to read Penny as a lesbian. However, this reading is diluted somewhat by Penny being presented as a comic figure. The Charlie the "China boy" houseboy standing in as the groom stand-in at Doris' wedding rehearsal inspires a laugh primarily from Penny's shocked reaction, and Penny has funny exchanges with Doris' friend Connie.

When Connie laughs over the houseboy being the groom's stand-in, Penny disapproves:

> PENNY: Who are you?
> CONNIE: Well, if you're not too literal, I'm the matron of honor.

Connie's admission of a lack of morals leads her to make a cynical remark to Doris that Penny overhears. Connie reappears after Doris changes out of her satin wedding gown with it's lengthy train. Connie's "Doris darling, I'm off" receives a "Is there any doubt of it?" from Penny, and the following exchange reveals Connie's cynicism about marriage and men:

> CONNIE: For a wedding gift, I'll give you the name of a good detective agency.
> PENNY: What?!
> CONNIE: Oh. We're shocking your aunt. Life is like that, Miss Ryland, in the social jungle. The Flower Girl precedes the bride and the detective follows the groom.

The mirror reflection of Doris that Taurog focuses on when Penny leaves suggests both that Doris is not going to marry her fiancé and also the duplicitous nature of Doris, which will become evident when she later lies to Jeff about her name and occupation.

Further amusement arises early on when Buck tries to milk a resisting wild cow, and comments to Jeff, "Stop that rumba; keep it simple; we want milk not a milkshake." The comic payoff to the line is Jeff being squirted in the face with the cow's milk, which is an interesting treatment for Jeff since he is hardly the rodeo cowboy type.

While the film's runaway heiress plot may be derivative of *It Happened One Night* (1934), Bing Crosby's Jeff is not the protagonist that Clark Gable was. Although Crosby's later gruffness with Doris approximates masculine behavior, Jeff's shyness and sexual passivity challenges the notion of him as a standard Hollywood leading man of the period. Although the screenplay never suggests homoerotic feelings between Jeff and Buck, Jeff losing the rodeo ride but winning the singing contest can be interpreted as casting aspersions on Jeff's manhood. If anything, Jeff is more an asexual figure than a potential homosexual one, with even the film's closing embrace forced by Cuddles pushing him into Doris.

Taurog's having the horse Jeff is mounted on walking during the song "Empty Saddles" works both to enervate this dreary number and give Jeff a more controlling activity to counter-balance the admiring cutaways of cowboys and cowgirls reacting to Crosby's singing. We are not shown any other contender for the singing contest, which implies that there are none, and perhaps puts a different spin on those stunned audience cutaways. That winning the song contest does not win Jeff the prize money is more irony, since it is left to Buck to wrassle a steer so that Cuddles can be purchased by Jeff. Buck's ease in wrassling the steer in four seconds reaffirms Buck's masculinity, with Taurog inserting a close-up of the steer looking at Buck in fear.

Doris does not seem to be aware of Jeff (or Buck) at the rodeo, which works against the standard romantic expectation, although why Doris leaves is initially unclear. We have to wait until a good way into the narrative before she reveals that she is not in love with the man to which she is engaged; and although this presents her as morally ambiguous, our never having met the fiancé softens this judgment a little. The slapstick device of having the train lurch and people fall together is utilized in both the meetings of Doris and Jeff, and Buck and Emma. Doris' fall, in which she is knocked unconscious, is suggestive of Dorothy in *The Wizard of Oz* (1939), whose adventures in Oz are all a dream. However, the bull acting aggressively towards her adds a primal element to her pursuit, with the bull's heft contrasting with Jeff's lightweight demeanor.

Jeff poking her with a pitchfork when she is buried under toppled hay is a coded violation—but diluted, since it is unintentional, as he is unaware of her presence in the boxcar. Jeff's telling Doris to stick out her tongue after she has requested a cigarette when she sees him rolling one is more comic than sexual, though still a radical idea and perhaps indicative of Jeff's lack of sophistication. The cigarette gag receives a payoff when Doris loses it after another lurch and then throws water into Jeff's face by mistake, recalling the milk from the rodeo. Doris having to walk in the rain after she has left the boxcar is punishment for her invading Jeff's space and behaving haughtily towards him, as well as continuing the theme of characters getting wet. Rain will also factor into the narrative later.

Doris being sexually harassed by the three men in another boxcar is a more typical reaction to a beautiful woman, and their aggressiveness stands as counterpoint to Jeff's disinterest. Her seeking solace from Jeff continues to cast him in the role of a less-threatening male, while the introduction to the three men establishes their awareness of Doris' proximity (which later becomes important to the plot). The use of Doris' red scarf to excite the bull is repeated four times as a game of one-upmanship between Jeff and Doris, although the last time it helps them escape from the barn. Doris gets a laugh over the

Frances' New York heiress transformed by cowgirl drag in a publicity portrait for *Rhythm on the Range* (1936).

scarf after the bull chases her out of the boxcar the next day when she says, "I don't dress to please bulls."

Jeff singing a lullaby and stroking the bull, which is male, has a homoerotic undertone, and parallels Doris' frustrated expectation that Jeff will make a pass at her. It is interesting that Doris changes from her wet clothes into a rather severe negligee behind a haystack as Crosby sings, while Taurog (and the audience) never peeks at Farmer's body. Doris lying to Jeff about her name and occupation suggests some moral ambiguity, although being an heiress may make the lie more acceptable (to avoid the attentions of perceived fortune hunters). Since Jeff is unaware of the reward offered for Doris' return, this narrative point shifts to the three men.

The exploits of Jeff and Doris are played against a subplot involving Buck and Emma. Buck's oafishness gets a subtle laugh from a comment Emma makes. When he tells her how he doesn't want to ride a pulman to Green Pastures, he says, "I can get accommodated in a boxcar with a load of hogs." At this, Penny replies, "Well, of course, you wouldn't be so lonesome." Martha Raye's entrance as Emma establishes the broadness of her performance, where she pulls faces and invades other characters' personal space. Though plain awful in terms of realistic acting, Raye gets away with it because she is a comic force of nature. Emma's introduction as she disembarks from a taxi at the train station makes us like her instantly, even if her response indicates she is none too bright:

> PORTER: Want a red cap, lady?
> EMMA: What, with a brown jacket and checkered skirt? Are you kidding?!

Emma's pursuit of Buck is that of the conventionally unattractive woman who compensates with humor and sexual aggressiveness. Emma's lack of beauty in comparison to Doris is pointed out in a later scene when Emma rides in a car with Jeff and is spotted by the three men:

> BIG BRAIN: That's the cowboy we've been trailing. But he's switched girls on us.
> WABASH: He has, huh? Well, maybe you think you could get five grand on this one.
> BIG BRAIN: Did you see her?! Not in confederate money!

Emma and Buck's arrival at Green Pastures includes a funny exchange:

> EMMA: Taxi! Taxi!
> BUCK: The closest taxi stand is in Tucson. They can probably hear you alright, but it'd take 'em two days to get here.

Emma and Buck's meal on the train begins with him reading a newspaper sporting the headline "Knife Murderess Still at Large!" Then the train lurches, making Emma drive her knife through the paper. This inspired piece of slapstick is soon ruined by drawing it out past the breaking point, as subsequent lurches have Emma eating Buck's food and him taking her check. Emma may overwhelm Buck with her attention, but it never becomes mean-spirited because Buck is as unconventional as she is and therefore as deserving of her as she is of him. Buck's measured speech (which makes the street-corner routine nearly unwatchable) seems to match Crosby's languorous delivery of most of his songs, which must explain why Buck and Jeff are friends. Also, since Buck is basically a comic character, there exists no concern as to whether he feels any genuine affection for Emma.

Emma and Buck are not the only characters generating laughs. When a hitchhiking Doris tries to wave down a passing car, the occupants wave back at her as if she is only waving hello. After she steals a car, Doris' explanation to Jeff gives Frances a chance to be funny, with the humor arising as much from her delivery as the dialogue: "Funny thing, I didn't have any intention of getting a new car this year. But when I saw this I just couldn't resist it."

Taurog gets another laugh when the film cuts from Jeff's repeated "No," to him getting in the car with Doris, to Jeff then seen in the car next to her, sitting with his arms crossed. More slapstick ensues when Wabash hangs Shorty upside down so that he will hand over the money Doris has given him to send her telegram. Doris' admission to Jeff that she has never been in love comes after he sings the song "I Can't Escape From You." The song may be referencing Doris, but it does not operate as a romantic ballad—rather as a reminder of the burden she has become by accompanying him. Jeff here is more loner (or at least a loner with a pet bull) than romantic figure. This will be reinforced when he and Doris come to the barn and he fails to respond to her observation of the "perfect moon," which Taurog emphasizes via a close-up of Frances, whose expression changes from wistfulness to disappointment in the face of Jeff's greater interest in Cuddles.

The rain motif continues, turning comical when it begins to rain just after Buck's pronouncement, "I want to tell you honey, this is God's country—nuthin' but sunshine." The rain also causes Doris' car to get stuck in the mud; and Doris falling in the mud prefigures Frances doing the same in *Flowing Gold* (a scene repeated in *Frances*). This sequence provides Doris with a speech that might have engendered pathos if Taurog hadn't favored Crosby in over-the-shoulder close-ups. Despite this, Frances imbues the speech with emotion, even if only the back of her head can be seen:

> What are you yelling at me for? You're in your beloved West, aren't you? Well, why don't you lie down and wallow in it. Out where the gears shift a little harder, and the dust is a little thicker and the mud a whole lot deeper. Where a girl rates a little lower, and a bull rates a little higher. And the men are a whole lot awfuller. That's where the West begins.

When Doris and Jeff arrive at Green Pastures, we see Frances riding a horse for a scene in which Doris asks Buck about Jeff. Frances' apparent horsemanship may be due to

Pressbook advertising for *Rhythm on the Range*. Note the phallic bazooka blown by cowboy Bob Burns.

her habit of horse riding in her private life; and although she's wearing jeans, her glamour remains intact. Emma, on the other hand, suffers the indignity of falling into a well. The scenes at Green Pastures feature several vertical swipes as transitions, a technique not seen in the film otherwise. Additionally, the inclusion of four subsequent songs signals a shift in the film's tone.

These musical numbers seem to have been designed to showcase the talents of Martha Raye (though, oddly, up to now there had been no mention of Emma being a singer). In the book *The Slapstick Queens*, James Robert Parish and Michael R. Pitts report that Raye was cast in this, her film debut, after production had already begun, when Adolph Zukor and Taurog saw her performing at the Trocadero Club, which explains this late-hour shift in narrative focus.

While "Mr. Paganini" and "If You Can't Sing It (You'll Have to Swing It)" provide context for Raye's rambunctiousness, "Drink It Down" offers a running gag of "I can't take it" as her reaction to drinking moonshine. Buck also gets a laugh in his reaction to Emma's singing with, "I wonder what the coyotes are going to do on the night you're singing." Unlike with Jeff and Doris, this is the closest Buck and Emma get to sweet talk, and Emma is last seen drunk and singing "Love in Bloom" to Doris' father, Robert. Her drunkenness hopefully rationalizes this behavior, rather than presenting Emma as having dumped Buck.

The number "I'm an Old Cowhand from the Rio Grande," perhaps the film's best known song, is disappointing to Frances fans in the way Emma and Buck and Jeff all get a chance to sing a verse but Doris does not. Frances' next film, *Come and Get It*, will show that she has a serviceable voice, and she is only seen here singing with the chorus.

One wonders what the future has in store for Doris, presumably after she marries Jeff, given that she remains an heiress. A sequel never materialized, so we will never know. However, the film was loosely remade as *Pardners* (aka *When Men Are Men?*), with Taurog directing again, and starring Dean Martin in the Crosby role and Jerry Lewis in the sex-changed Frances role.

The *Hollywood Reporter* advised on October 4, 1935, that the rodeo sequences for *Rhythm on the Range* were shot at the real Madison Square Garden in New York, and, in a news item on January 30, 1936, that Paramount had wanted Merle Oberon to play Doris. Oberon was not cast because negotiations for a loan-out from Sam Goldwyn, to whom she was under contract, fell through. In his book *Bing Crosby: A Pocketful of Dreams*, Gary Giddins advises that Frances Langford and Jack Oakie were initially proposed to co-star with Crosby. Jean Arthur, Olivia de Havilland, and Marsha Hunt were also considered for the part of Doris. Additionally, Giddins claims that Frances' hair (and also Martha Raye's) was dyed red to accommodate the cinematography, and he says Frances' "glimmering frankness brought depth to a shallow role." Frances had recorded a duet with Bing Crosby, entitled "The House That Jack Built for Jill" (by Frederick Hollander and Leo Robin), that was cut from the released film. In the 1982 television special report on Frances entitled *Indiana Epilogue*, Conrad Lane quotes Frances as saying that *Rhythm on the Range* is the only film that she enjoyed making.

Norman Taurog had previously directed Crosby in *We're Not Dressing* (1934) and *The Big Broadcast of 1936* (1935), both of which had been produced by this film's producer, Benjamin Glazer. Glazer had also overseen *The Big Broadcast* (1932), which had made Crosby a star. Crosby would become the most popular film star of the 1940s and remained with Paramount for twenty-four years, with *Anything Goes* (1956) being his last title for the studio. In their entry for this film in *The Motion Picture Guide, 1927–1983*, Jay Robert Nash and Stanley Ralph Ross report that *Rhythm on the Range* proved to be one of Paramount's most profitable pictures of the year.

## Release

July 31, 1936, with the tagline, "A whirlwind round-up of romance, songs and gags, with Bing singin' and Bob Burns tootin' on the old Bazooka!"

## Reviews

"Our screen introduction to Martha Raye, a stridently funny comedienne who steals the picture from the laryngeal Mr. Crosby and the decorative Frances Farmer."—Frank S. Nugent, the *New York Times*, July 30, 1936

"Pleasant entertainment.... Miss Farmer is just the ingénue in this one, but a nice looking girl."—*Variety*, August 5, 1936

"Amiable.... Martha Raye is spectacular and steals every scene she is in."—Jay Robert Nash and Stanley Ralph Ross, *The Motion Picture Guide, 1927–1983*

"A good-humored, well-paced musicomedy in which Bing Crosby's nonchalant but thoroughly mellifluous baritone is pleasantly used to punctuate a mildly satiric investigation of the rodeo business.... Martha Raye's enthusiastic display of her most distressing facial characteristic will doubtless endear her to that large portion of the cinema public which finds physical abnormalities funny."—*Time* magazine, August 10, 1936

"Bing Crosby is almost completely overwhelmed by one of his co-stars. His easy-does-it crooning is simply no match for the side-splitting antics of the twenty-seven-year-old Martha Raye."—Robert Bookbinder, *The Films of Bing Crosby*

"An easygoing Western musical which rounded up a huge herd of profitable grossers ... but if it was Bing's singing that drew the crowds in, it was Martha Raye's clowning that gave them something to talk about."—John Douglas Eames, *The Paramount Story*

# *Come and Get It* (1936)

(aka *Roaring Timber*; aka *Roaring Timbers*)
Paramount

**Credits:** Howard Productions, Inc., presents. Directors: Howard Hawks, William Wyler; Producer: Samuel Goldwyn; Screenplay: Jane Murfin, Jules Furthman, based on the famous novel by Edna Ferber; Photography: Gregg Toland, Rudolph Mate; Art Direction: Richard Day; Music: Alfred Newman; Costumes: Omar Kiam; Editor: Edward Curtiss; Sound: Frank Maher; Special Effects: Ray Binger; Logging Sequences: Richard Rosson. Black & White, 99 minutes. Filming June 21 to September 1936. Portions shot on location in northern Idaho.

**Songs:** "Aura Lea" (George R. Poulton, W.W. Fosdick), sung by Frances Farmer, reprised by Edward Arnold and Walter Brennan; "The Bird on Nellie's Hat" (Alfred Solman,

Arthur J. Lamb), sung by Frances Farmer, Edward Arnold, Mady Christians, and Walter Brennan; "Jeanie with the Light Brown Hair" (Stephen Foster).

**Cast:** Edward Arnold (Barney Glasgow); Joel McCrea (Richard Glasgow); Frances Farmer (Lotta Morgan, Lotta Bostrom); Walter Brennan (Swan Bostrom); Mady Christians (Karie); Mary Nash (Emma Louise); Andrea Leeds (Evvie Glasgow); Frank Shields (Tony Schwerke); Edwin Maxwell (Sid LeMaire); Cecil Cunningham (Josie); Charles Halton (Mr. Jed Hewitt). Uncredited: Clem Bevans (Gunnar Gallagher); Stanley Blystone (Lumberjack); Harry C. Bradley (Thomas Gubbins); Ed Brady (Barfly); Egon Brecher (Mr. Schwerke); Don Brodie (Restaurant Customer); Heinie Conklin (Barfly); Phillip Cooper (Chore Boy); Gino Corrado (Waiter); Frances Dee (Restaurant Patron); Jesse Graves (Servant at Party); Kit Guard (Lumberjack in Saloon); Al K. Hall (Goodnow); Ben Hall (Barfly); Earle Hodgins (Shell Game Operator); Robert Homans (Cookie); George Humbert (George); Bud Jamison (Man in Saloon); Rollo Lloyd (Train Steward); Robert Lowery (Diner in Chicago Restaurant); Jack Pennick (Foreman); Constantine Romanoff (Rowdy); Lee Shumway (Diner); Harry Tenbrook (Lumberjack); Fred "Snowflake" Toones (Snowflake); Max Wagner (Lumberjack); William Wagner (Wine Steward); Fred Warren (Pianist); Harry Wilson (Barfly); Hank Worden (Lumberjack).

**VHS/DVD:** DVD released February 9, 1999, by HBO Home Video, and March 8, 2005, by MGM (video & DVD).

## Synopsis

In 1884 Wisconsin, Bernard "Barney" Glasgow is a lumberjack with corporate ambitions that involve marrying the boss' daughter, Emma Louise. He falls in love with Lotta, a saloon singer, but leaves her in favor of his marriage of convenience. Lotta marries Barney's best friend, the Swede Swan Bostrom. In 1907 we find the unhappily married Barney the rich owner of the Glasgow Mill and living in Bewdamore with Emma Louise and two adult children. Encouraged by his daughter Evvie to visit Swan after Barney receives a letter from him, Barney travels back to Iron Ridge. By this time Lotta has died, but not before bearing Swan a daughter, also named Lotta. When Barney meets Lotta, he sees that she is the spitting image of her mother and becomes infatuated with her. He takes the Bostrom family to Chicago and brings them back to Bewdamore. When gossip starts about Barney and Lotta, Barney's son Richard confronts her. However, Richard's antagonism soon turns to love. When Barney learns about Richard's interest in Lotta, he tries to have his son sent to the New York factory. The climax occurs at the company party, with the two men fighting until Lotta urges Richard to stop, as his father is an old man. Hurt and ashamed, Barney retreats as Richard takes Lotta away. Barney is comforted by Emma Louise, who confides that she was afraid that Barney was going to abandon her. Barney rings the dinner chime, calling out "Come and get it" with tears in his eyes.

## Notes

Frances' most prestigious film is famous among film historians as the picture co-directed by Howard Hawks and William Wyler. While which director helmed what scenes remains a point of contention, there is no doubt that the film gives Farmer the opportunity to make a memorable impression playing two parts. The narrative assumes the heights of Greek tragedy in its morality tale of choosing ambition over love, with the central character left disappointed in love twice. If the film's drama never quite matches the romance and beauty of the early logging sequences (with their odd, logic-defying action), at least Frances supplies the reason for a man to be his son's rival for her affections.

The opening scene of Barney chiming the dinner triangle is repeated for the film's end, providing a cyclical presentation of him trapped as a man of working class origins. Although Barney is presented as the reactor and not the instigator of the violence that erupts around him in two fights, Edward Arnold's blustering arrogance cannot engender audience sympathy, in spite of his jolly fat-man's laugh. Arnold, however, redeems himself in the quietness of his intimate scenes with Swan and Lotta, and with his tears at film's end. Walter Brennan is more successful at bringing Swan to life, despite the part being written as a cartoon with a Swedish accent, even if Swan's role becomes less important during the film's second half.

Frances' entrance as the first Lotta provides a revealing exchange with Barney. When he asks the gum-chewing harlot, "Are you going to bring me luck?" at the fixed shell game at the saloon, she replies, "If I do, it'll be the first time." Lotta agreeing to spike Barney's drink so she can retrieve the money he has won from her boss, Sid LeMaire, reveals her moral corruption, so that her singing the sentimental song "Aura Lea" creates irony. Lotta singing about the golden-haired Aura Lea is also ironic because Lotta Morgan is brunette, and the maid in the song abandoning one who loves her prefigures the actions of both Barney and Lotta Bostrom. In her book *Fast-Talking Dames*, Maria DiBattista quotes Hawks saying that Frances wore a wig to play Lotta Morgan, and that this informed the actress' interpretation of the character.

As she sings in her deep contralto voice, Farmer is photographed in close-up, with the shadow of the open parasol she holds darkening half her face, visually reinforcing the notion that Lotta is an immoral character. However, that fact that she is only half in shadow suggests the ambiguity that will surface when she deliberately knocks the spiked beer out of Barney's hand to stop him from drinking it. The beer splashes onto Swan, the man who will later marry her. The song is reprised after the crowd won't stop applauding her (although her voice is unremarkable), and the second rendition is shot from an unusually angle—looking up at Lotta as she leans over a balcony, with the four-man chorus at the bottom of the frame.

Why Barney thinks Lotta doesn't belong in the saloon is a mystery, although perhaps he imagines that there is more to her than the world-weariness she affects. Although he may say that he is helping her, he comes off as a man trying to impress a woman with his money, and her siding with him against her employer in the saloon brawl shows her as someone with poor judgment, since Barney will ultimately use and abandon her. His gift of a new dress, and his suggestion of changing her hairstyle, presents him as a Pygmalion character, as does her willingness to change for him.

Barney, unwilling to say goodbye to Lotta, further displays his moral cowardice (as does his using Lotta). Since he is prepared to sacrifice her (as the woman he claims to love) in favor of a loveless marriage to further his career ambitions, he will receive universal retribution in the form of a dashed second chance and the humiliation of being cuckolded by his own son. It is interesting that the dress that Barney buys for Lotta is a more conservative one than what he has seen her in, with a high-necked collar to cover her previously exposed bosom. The change in hairstyle he suggests also makes her less obviously someone

*Come and Get It* (1936) 91

French movie card for *Come and Get It* (1936).

with little money and poor taste. Ironically, Barney will provide the same service to Lotta's daughter.

Frances is touching in the scene in which she is to be married to Swan, far more so than in the previous scene when Swan tells her that Barney is not coming back. Hawks presumably directed these early sequences, and in the former he has Lotta express her anger by repeatedly attempting to strike the match for her cigarette on her bed railing, a device that is upstaging yet also perhaps true to a character who guards her emotions. However, in the next scene it is her stillness that is the key to Farmer's effectiveness. The camera begins with Lotta sitting on a bed, and when she stands she looks away from Swan and down at the floor in shame, aware that she is repeating Barney's act of marrying a person she does not love. This shame is also an awareness of the corner she has put herself in, after becoming reliant upon Barney.

Swan may love Lotta, although she has not given him any reason to, and her disappearance from the narrative after this sequence is like a moral banishment. We hear from Swan's letter that she has died before we even know about their daughter, and the memory of Lotta is invoked twice when her "Aura Lea" vocal is reprised for Barney's recall of her. Additionally, the sunniness of Frances playing Lotta's daughter reminds us of how briefly we saw Lotta happy. The original Lotta is a sad figure, the stereotypical bruised prostitute with a heart of gold who must suffer, and it is almost shocking to see Frances sink into the lower depths after the relative lightness of her troubles in *Rhythm on the Range*.

The second half of the narrative in placed twenty-three years later, in 1907, by which time Barney is aged fifty and Lotta Bostrom is presumably twenty-three, if not younger. Barney's relaxed relationship with Evvie prefigures the one he will want with Lotta Bostrom, with the point being made that Lotta is young enough to be his daughter. It is Evvie (and Richard) who are honest enough to challenge Barney about his relationship with Lotta, when Emma Louise cannot speak about it. Evvie's forthrightness is also made apparent by her addressing her father by his Christian name.

Additionally, it is Evvie's relationship with the mill worker Tony Schwerke that is paralleled with the one Barney had had with Lotta Morgan, with Evvie vowing not to make the same mistake that her father did in sacrificing love. Barney's efforts to talk to Tony, who is as obstinate as Barney, is evidence that Barney appreciates Evvie's point. A still exists showing a deleted scene of Evvie with her first fiancé, Orville Bremmer (Maynard Holmes), whom Richard describes as a "stuffed shirt" and who Barney calls a "fat can of lard." The latter insult is only funny because of Orville being a dead ringer for Barney. Orville's conventional unattractiveness is paralleled with that of Emma Louise, although we don't see Emma Louise in her younger days. She is unfavorably compared to Lotta Morgan, but her money makes her the wiser choice for marriage. Emma Louise's looks become the butt of a joke with a comment she makes, unaware of its intended sting (and the director has the tact not to provide a ham-handed reaction shot to it): "The Reverend Paley said to me only yesterday—he took one look at my face and he said, 'Mrs. Glasgow, if ever I saw a woman who is a martyr to her family, that woman is you.'"

Lotta's singing of "Aura Lea" on the soundtrack takes Barney back to Iron Ridge, and the information that Swan and Lotta have had a daughter. As the second Lotta, Frances is blonder than the brunette first, and she differentiates the characters in attitude and speech. Lotta's awareness of Barney's interest in her presents her as a more manipulative character than her mother was, but her youthful ambition makes it forgivable. Also, this

Lotta's ignorance of the history of her mother and Barney also establishes Lotta Bostrom as one who is being equally manipulated. Barney's agenda becomes apparent at the dinner he shares with the Bostroms, even if Karie is shocked at Lotta's idea to deliberately keep Barney waiting for her.

Barney gets angry when Lotta sings "Aura Lee" at the urging of Swan, which Frances performs this time as a soprano; but his anger gives way to passion when he kisses her. Lotta's retreat from the kiss tells us that she is out of her depth, and her discomfort is misread by the family to be virginal embarrassment rather than a rejection of Barney. Barney's re-costuming of Lotta in black fur as people at the Chicago restaurant turn to look at her pays off the earlier scene where she claims other people were looking at she and Karie when they wore gauche Iron Ridge dresses and hats. The difference between the two Lottas here is that Lotta Bostrom is more aware and more vocal in expressing when she is dressed inappropriately, but also more ambitious than her mother was.

Barney's happiness about bringing the Bostroms back with him to Bewdamore is noticed by his secretary, Josie. He tells her, "Fishing has made a new man of me," and she replies, "Fishing? You look as though you just shot a lion."

The scene where Richard goes to Lotta to warn her off seeing his father begins with mutual face slapping and Lotta's oddly respectful reaction when he yells at her. The pulling of taffy is a sexual metaphor for their romantic tug of war, with its melting when they are both too preoccupied with each other to pay attention to the candy. Lotta liking the candy is an example of her sweet childishness, and a warning that she must be handled carefully or is liable to become a mess. The taffy sequence also offers a nostalgic bit of Americana along with its slapstick (the latter matching the tone of the earlier fight scenes).

Lotta rejecting Barney's suggestion that she go to Chicago where he can visit her is more evidence of her lack of interest in him, with Frances' expression of fear matching Arnold's pathetic desperation. Although by this time Lotta has become interested in Richard, there is not the same opportunism attached to their relationship that she had initially fostered with Barney, in spite of Richard being Barney's heir. A confrontation between Richard and Barney features a deep-focus shot of Barney standing facing Richard, with Barney's hand in the bottom left of the frame revealing Barney's struggle to control his urge to strike his son. This urge will be given full reign at the film's climax.

Richard proposes to Lotta in an upstairs room before they are found by Barney, and in this scene Frances is photographed in close-up to look luminously beautiful standing at a window, with the shadow from her opaque black hat darkening her face. Before she can answer, Barney interrupts, and his entrance turns the scene to melodrama, which is not helped by Arnold's lack of subtlety in his playing. The slaps he gives Richard recall the slaps he administered in earlier fights and the slap Lotta had given him. However, the scene is saved by Richard's refusal to fight with his father, with Lotta coming between them and labeling Barney an old man. Barney's subsequent look at Lotta, to say "Get out of here," reveals his anger over his perceived humiliation. This drama is capped by two superb moments: Emma Louise's comforting Barney as an expression of her love for him, and Barney's final chiming of the dinner triangle. The last moment becomes one of tragic hysteria, with Barney's eyes full of tears as he sees Richard hurry Lotta away against the oncoming crowd that answers the call to eat.

Frances had been initially cast as Evvie, the role eventually played by Andrea Leeds. Leeds attracted her own publicity for the film as Hollywood's "kiss champion" after she reportedly spent more than nine hours kissing three young actors to test their ability to play the role of her fiancé. Ironically, in the film she is not seen to kiss Frank Shields' Tony—or anyone else, for that matter.

It was always envisaged that the same actress would play the double roles of Lotta, and Miriam Hopkins, who had just worked with producer Sam Goldwyn on *These Three* (1936), had been announced for them. Howard Hawks had directed Hopkins in Goldwyn's *Barbary Coast* (1935), but he vetoed Hopkins' casting in the new film, according to Jeffrey Kauffman, because he disliked her. Kauffman also says that Hawks had Leeds in mind for the role until he saw Frances. Leeds had been playing anonymous supporting roles under the name Antoinette Lees prior to this, with her last two titles being for Paramount.

William Arnold claims that Hawks saw Frances in rushes for *Rhythm on the Range* when looking to cast small parts, and was so impressed by her that she got the plum dual roles. The autobiography claims that Frances had asked to be considered for the starring roles, which had been pegged for Virginia Bruce. Bruce had been one of the original Goldwyn Girls (the most successful of which would be Lucille Ball), but was under contract to MGM, who it appears were unwilling to loan her out. In his book on Hawks, Scott Breivold reports that the unnamed actress Goldwyn had hired was paid off with $30,000, and Frances was hired as a loan-out from Paramount. Todd McCarthy, in his book on Hawks, *The Grey Fox of Hollywood*, writes that Frances was paid a salary of $75 a week (confirmed by Joseph McBride in *Hawks on Hawks*) and received a total of $562.50—in contrast to the salaries of Edward Arnold, who was paid $52,500, and Hawks, who received $73,150.

Hawks' casting of Farmer was an opportunity to discover an actress he considered essentially unknown and "put her definitively on the map." McCarthy writes about this, with Hawks allegedly having discovered Frances, or used her effectively for the first time on the screen, as he would later do with actresses like Carole Lombard, Rita Hayworth and Lauren Bacall, among others. McCarthy clams that Frances inspired Hawks in his most concentrated effort to create a feminine screen persona from scratch, for which he required not only sufficient artistic inspiration and erotic stimulation, but also total cooperation from her. Because of this, McCarthy would claim, *Come and Get It* "remains most compelling as the one film that reveals Farmer as an alluring personality and might-have-been great star. Despite her literally breathtaking beauty, she was bland, and blandly used, in every other film she made, but she came entrancing to life for Hawks."

To research the role of Lotta, Frances went to the red-light districts of Los Angeles to observe prostitutes, and Frances' relationship with Hawks extended to socializing with him after hours. McBride cites an anecdote about Frances going to see Hawks on his boat: "She had no phoniness about her at all. She came wearing her sweatshirt and her dungarees and carrying a toothbrush in her pocket." William Arnold quotes Hawks saying of Frances, "I think that she had more talent than anyone I ever worked with." Hawks reiterates this notion in Peter Bogdanovich's interview book *Conversations with ...* when the director says that Frances was "probably the best actress—outside of Lombard and Rosalind Russell—I've ever worked with. She had looks and ability—she could do anything—had a great personality." Hawks also tells Bogdanovich how Frances had come in to play Lotta Bostrom but was more interested in Lotta Morgan. Hawks did a screen test, but she was unhappy with it. McCarthy reports that after Frances and Hawks had worked intensively to prepare for the first test, she decided to wear heavy make-up to play the whore—against his advice. Hawks let her do what she wanted, as she "acted up a storm," and when he screened the result, Frances recognized how badly she had come across and from then on accepted his advice.

Hawks took her to cafés to find someone who acted the way he wanted the part played. Said Hawks:

> She found a waitress in a beer joint and I told her, "Now come in here every night for ten days. Get picked up. The worst that'll happen to you is that you'll get your legs felt up." [Frances] was a big husky girl who could take care of herself, you know. Then we made another test without makeup or anything, and she was marvelous.

*Will There Really Be a Morning?* says that Frances thought Hawks was "one of the finest and most sensitive directors in the business.... He gave every scene a minute examination, both psychological and visual, and under his direction I was secure and full of anticipation." After Hawks walked out and Wyler came in, Frances said, "I was basically satisfied with my interpretation of the trollop, but the daughter role of a gentle, innocent girl was in no way challenging. My only concern was to bring out the innocence, yet let a shade of the mother shine through, and it worked." McCarthy reports that Frances would clash with Wyler's directorial technique, which she saw as brusque, uncommunicative bullying and endlessly repeated takes—a far cry from Hawks' quiet, attentive support. McBride quotes Hawks on Frances' first day of shooting:

> I remember her working with Edward Arnold, who was a real trouper, and she said, "If you'd only speak that line a little quicker I could keep this thing going." And he looked at her, and he spoke it quicker, and the scene was better. [Arnold] said, "Hey, look, she's pretty good." I said, "She's so good that you'd better get right to work or she's going to take it and walk off with it."

Breivold cites a conversation between Hawks and Frances over a crying scene, which is interesting in light of Frances' difficulty in providing tears in all her films:

> HAWKS: Get the methol.
> FRANCES: What's that for?
> HAWKS: To make you cry.
> FRANCES: An actress does not need to use those things.
> HAWKS: Ok.

The scene was done her way. Hawks needed close-ups, medium shots, and another shot, and she had to cry all the way through. Hawks said, "Now Frances, we'll try it my way. I'll show you both, show you what happened." She saw it and said, "Kick me. You're right." The difference was that Hawks' method had her nose running, which is what happens when people cry.

The reason for Hawks' premature departure from the production differs depending on who is telling the story. Goldwyn apparently had switched

**Publicity portrait of Frances as ingénue Lotta Bostrom in *Come and Get It* (1936). Frances played dual roles in the film.**

Hawks and Wyler before, with Hawks brought to replace Wyler on *Barbary Coast*. William Arnold claims that Goldwyn fired Hawks from *Come and Get It*, and that Wyler did not even want the job. Goldwyn would say that he fired Hawks, whereas Hawks would say that he quit. Both Arthur Marx' book on Goldwyn and Axel Madsen's authorized biography of Wyler claim that Goldwyn asked Hawks to re-shoot the second half of the film, which Hawks had rewritten without Goldwyn's approval. In his book *Romantic Comedy in Hollywood, from Lubitsch to Sturges*, James Harvey says that Lotta Morgan in the Ferber book was a little lame girl who sang so badly that she was booed. Harvey says that Hawks changed her into a "good lusty girl" who sings better, if not well, and is cheered. Breivold writes about Hawks' rewrites:

> Goldwyn had told Hawks, "I want you to make this. Do anything you want to do." Hawks told Ferber, "This isn't such a good story that you wrote. You really ducked around all the issues.... You're writing about my grandfather and the people in his class—they were the lumber barons of the time." Goldwyn told Hawks that the new scenes were just what he wanted and he asked Hawks who wrote them. "I said I did," and he said, "Directors shouldn't write." And I said, "You stupid son-of-a-bitch. I don't want to work with you any longer." And Hawks quit. "He had everybody in town call me to come back. And I said I won't come back." Ironically, when Wyler came in, he used the scenes Hawks had written.

Hawks told Goldwyn that he couldn't re-shoot, as he was already committed to starting *Bringing Up Baby* (1938). The Turner Classic Movies database quotes *The Hollywood Reporter* saying that Hawks began preliminary tests and process photography on *Bringing Up Baby* in August 1937 and that Wyler didn't finish *Come and Get It* until September. Marx and Madsen state that, in light of Hawks' refusal, Goldwyn "fired" him and went to Wyler.

In his biography of Goldwyn, A. Scott Berg claims that the rift between Hawks and the producer began early. Goldwyn had hired Hawks because Edna Ferber had said that the character of Barney Glasgow was partly based on Hawks' own grandfather. However, Hawks soon began to disregard Goldwyn's instructions, including casting the bony Walter Brennan in the part that Ferber had described as "the strongest man in the North woods," and increasing the budget by $100,000 (the amount Goldwyn had paid for the rights to the book). According to McCarthy, Goldwyn had been absent from the set with pneumonia and was therefore unaware of the changes Hawks had made to the screenplay, including moving away from Ferber's environmental message about the damage the logger barons were doing to the forests. (This message still exists in the film, as voiced by Richard to Barney, but is dropped after Barney rejects the idea of replanting.) A. Scott Berg concurs that Wyler was reluctant to take over from Hawks, and that he only agreed when Goldwyn threatened to take him off *Dodsworth* (1936), which was in its final stages at the time. Hawks left on the forty-second day of production, on August 8, with only twelve days left in the shooting schedule. Wyler came onboard on August 19 after an eight day shutdown to shoot for twenty-eight days, finishing the film on September 19. Apparently Goldwyn had wanted to give Wyler full director credit, but the film ended up with the two filmmakers jointly credited. Interestingly, the film's trailer names no director.

It is believed that Wyler directed the picture's last thirty minutes, which includes the employee party scene, and that the reason for the climactic fight being so anti-climatic is Wyler's distaste for violent sequences. This seems likely when one compares the finale to the earlier fight scenes (presumably directed by Hawks), which revel in the machismo violence. Hawks' preferred milieu was one of competition and male companionship, which featured high-spirited banter that engendered male bonding. The relationship between Barney and Swan is indicative of this milieu. The taffy-pulling scene is also more Hawks than Wyler in light of Hawks' screwball comedy titles like *Twentieth Century* (1934) and *Bringing Up Baby*. Hawks told Scott Breivold that he would have changed the last scene of the film, believing that Barney should have been happy that Richard had taken Lotta away, which would have altered the permanent father-son separation in the completed film.

Lotta Morgan is viewed as the first prototype of the Hawksian woman, who would later be perfected by Lauren Bacall in *To Have and Have Not* (1944). This woman was honest and straightforward, game, smart, funny, and insolent. A masculine woman, she preferred the company of men to women, which made it easy for her to integrate into Hawks' world. However, Hawks would tell Bogdanovich that Marlene Dietrich had accused Hawks of appropriating her persona to create his Hawksian woman, an idea repeated in Clark Branson's book *Howard Hawks: A Jungian Study*: "Deep-voiced Lotta is rendered in a moderate pastiche of Dietrich imported from the genteel expressionism of [Von] Sternberg."

McBride quotes Hawks saying that he had wanted to remake *Come and Get It* as a Western in the 1970s, perhaps with Clint Eastwood in the Arnold role (since by now his favorite male actor, John Wayne, was too old to have played the younger Barney). However, McBride pointed out to Hawks that he had already remade the film as *Red River* (1947) — the story of an older and a younger man who battle over the love of the same woman, who is a surrogate for the woman the older man had previously left.

*Come and Get It* is not mentioned in the 1986 Aviva Slesin–directed documentary *Directed by William Wyler*, which was written by A. Scott Berg. Neither is it mentioned in writer/director Richard Schickel's Turner Classic Movies chapter on Hawks in Schickel's series *The Men Who Made the Movies*. The film *is* referenced by a camera pan over some books in the title sequence of the excellent 2001 documentary *Goldwyn: The Man and His Movies*, directed by Peter Jones and Mark Catalena, and co-produced and co-written by A. Scott. Berg. The documentary gives on-camera screen time to Berg, as well as Hawks and Wyler, although they do not talk specifically about *Come and Get It*. However, it does provide the history of how Goldwyn was forced out of Paramount Studios after he had been in partnership with the founder, Adolph Zukor, and also describes the themes that are repeated in many of Goldwyn's titles. These themes of the love of an (often blonde) unattainable woman, and the morally ambiguous mother, can be seen in *Come and Get It*. Goldwyn's distaste for seeing characters dead onscreen may be another reason why we are deprived of seeing Lotta Morgan's demise.

Richard Rosson, who is credited for directing the logging sequences, had been Hawks' co-director on *Scarface* (1932) and *Today We Live* (1933). In its review of the film, *Time* magazine reported that he was forced to recruit fake lumberjacks in Hollywood to photograph the sequence, since real lumberjacks of that time no longer rode falling trees or broke up log jams because it was considered "unsophisticated generosity" to their employers.

Spencer Tracy was courted for the part of Barney but turned it down. At this time, Tracy had just started a new contract with MGM, so was presumably reluctant to be loaned out. A. Scott Berg also suggests that Tracy's rejection was due to the fact that he wanted to change his image, and after having played a series of petty racketeers and ordinary guys, he was only interested in sympathetic and heroic roles.

After enacting an alcoholic millionaire in MGM's Joan Crawford melodrama *Sadie*

A still for another deleted scene from *Come and Get It* (1936), featuring Maynard Holmes (who is not in the existing film) and Andrea Leeds.

*McKee* (1934), Edward Arnold's persona as the florid, heavily-jowled financial tycoon was cemented when he played the title role in the biopic of gambler Diamond Jim Brady in Universal Pictures' *Diamond Jim* (1935). His role as Barney, and later Jim Fisk in *The Toast of New York*, are variations on the same character. Apart from the fact of Arnold being middle-aged and portly, his career as a leading man was also somewhat diminished when he was included in the infamous 1937 exhibitors list of "box office poison," alongside high profile names like Fred Astaire, Joan Crawford, Marlene Dietrich, and Katharine Hepburn. Arnold would go on to co-star with Frances in *The Toast of New York* (1937).

Under contract to Sam Goldwyn, and known as the preeminent character actor of his day, Walter Brennan is the only person to have ever won three Best Supporting Actor Academy Awards. His signature southern old-coot accent was the result of two factors — an accident in 1932 which cost him most of his teeth, and an exposure to gas during World War I which ruined his vocal chords and gave him a high-pitched voice. Although these would make him suitable to play eccentric rural parts and men older than himself, he also had the range to play sophisticated businessmen, con artists and military officers as easily as cowhands and yokels. Brennan had previously appeared in Paramount's romantic comedy *The Moon's Our Home* (1936); Wyler's *These Three*, (1936) with Joel McCrea; and Hawks' *Barbary Coast*, which also featured McCrea.

## Release

November 6, 1936.

## Reviews

"For the first half hour [the film] is a smashing, slam-bang entertainment. Then it fades.... Farmer is much more efficient in the less colorful daughter part. As the dance hall lady, she overdoes the hardboiled stuff to an extreme and tends to make it a burlesque rather than a sincere study."—*Variety*, November 18, 1936

"While not a thoroughly Ferber work, it is still genuinely satisfying and a vividly toned portrait of a man.... Frances Farmer is not merely a delight to the masculine eye, but an actress of more than usual merit."—Frank S. Nugent, the *New York Times*, November 12, 1936

"A simple disjointed story that doesn't stick together though the movie has many fine scenes...overlong and often bogs down in uncertain destination.... Arnold gives a powerhouse performance, doing a great job with an unwieldy role.... Farmer is fascinating to watch."—Jay Robert Nash and Stanley Ralph Ross, *The Motion Picture Guide, 1927–1983*

"An extraordinarily warm and lively picture of one of the few romantic aspects of the U. S. which the cinema has so far neglected."—*Time* magazine, November 16, 1936

"[T]echnically fine, beautifully directed, superbly synthesized.... Farmer is sensationally brilliant."—*Photoplay* magazine (author and date unknown)

## Awards

Walter Brennan—Best Supporting Actor Academy Award, 1937

•••••••••••••••••••••••••••••••••••••••••••••••••••••••••••

# *Exclusive* (1937)

(aka *Things Began to Happen*)
Paramount

**Credits:** Adolph Zukor Presents. Director: Alexander Hall; Producer: Benjamin Glazer; Screenplay: John C. Moffitt, Sidney Salkow, and Rian James, based on a play by John C. Moffitt; Photography: William C. Mellor; Music: Boris Morros; Art Direction: Hans Dreier, Ernst Fegte; Editor: Paul Weatherwax; Sound: Walter Oberst, Louis Mesenkop; Costumes: Edith Head; Interior Decorations: A. G. Freudeman; Black & White, 85 minutes.

**Cast:** Fred MacMurray (Ralph Houston); Frances Farmer (Vina Swain); Charlie Ruggles (Tod Swain); Lloyd Nolan (Charles Gillette); Fay Holden (Mrs. Swain); Ralph Morgan (Horace Mitchell); Edward H. Robine (Colonel Bogardus); Harlan Briggs (Springer); Willard Robertson (Mr. Franklin); Horace MacMahon (Beak); William Mansell (Formby); Gaylord Pendleton (Elliott); Chester Clute (Garner); Irving Bacon (Dr. Boomgarten); Frank Bruno (Lollipop); James Blakeley (Mr. Walton); Sam Hayes (Radio Announcer); Ann Marsters (Girl Reporter). Uncredited: Mariska Aldrich (Policewoman); Ricca Allen (bit part); Richard Allen (Policeman); William

Arnold (Reporter); Sam Ash (Elevator Starter); Benny Bartlett (Boy); Jack Chapin (Reed); Jack Cheartham (Rioter); Edward Churchill (Advertising Manager); Ethel Clayton (bit part); Joe Cunningham (Editor); Jack Daley (Policeman); Max Davidson (Tailor); Joe De Stefani (Foreman); James Dime (Rioter); Margaret Fealy (Rioter); Almeda Fowler (Mrs. Mitchell); Billy Franey (News Vendor); Mack Gray (Secretary); Frank Hammond (Switchman); Harry Hayden (City Editor); Edward Heam (Policeman); Oscar "Dutch" Hendrian (Janitor); Tex Higginson (Rioter); Carol Holloway (Rioter); Erskine Johnson (Reporter); John Kelly (Cab Driver); Billy Lee (Beaks' Child); Robert Milasch (Gangster); Frances Morros (Beak's Wife); Spec O'Donnell (Telephone Boy); Frank Puglia (Johnny); James Quinn (Rioter); Dick Rush (Policeman); Lou Salter (Rioter); Allan Sears (Rioter); Antrim Short (Messenger Boy); Gertrude Simpson (bit part); Libby Taylor (Maid); Ray Turner (Bellboy); Pat West (Santa Claus); Cornel Wilde (Reporter); Gloria Williams (bit part); Charlene Wyatt (Girl in Elevator).

VHS/DVD: Not available in either format.

## Synopsis

When Mountain City racketeer Charles Gillette is acquitted of criminal charges, he arrives at the *Mountain City World* newsroom, beats up reporter Tod Swain, and vows to take revenge on the men who had him arrested. Gillette buys a rival newspaper, the *Sentinel*, and offers a better paying job to *World* editor Ralph Houston, who turns Gillette down. A bill collector, Garner, comes to the Swain house, chasing a debt owed by Ralph for financing the college education of his fiancé, Vina, who is also Tod's daughter. Vina is furious that Ralph rejected Gillette's offer, and she telephones Gillette to warn him of a forthcoming police raid that Ralph and Tod have been tipped off about. Gillette offers her a job, which she accepts in order to pay Ralph back, but Ralph breaks up with her when she tells him about it. Gillette uses strong-arm tactics to secure advertising for his new paper, and assigns Vina to find evidence of scandal in the house of Horace Mitchell, who is running for mayor. Vina masquerades as a maid to obtain information about Mitchell being an ex-convict, and the *Sentinel* runs it.

Tod tells Vina that the *World* previously had refrained from printing the story because Mitchell's public service record has proven him to be a good man. Mitchell visits Vina and shoots himself in front of her, so Ralph encourages Tod to write a story that blames Vina for the death to teach her a lesson. Gillette changes Vina's next story about the elevators at the department store of Mr. Franklin to imply that they are unsafe. The *World* stages a public safety test of the elevators, which is initially a success. However, people are subsequently killed and Ralph is injured when one elevator falls six stories because of cables that have been sabotaged by Gillette's henchmen. Trying to hide his real agenda from Vina, Gillette has Vina rushed out of town with his top muscle, Beak, who is then told to kill her. Tod finds Beak and Vina, and tells Beak that he has found his ring at the scene of the accident. Tod gets Beak to sign a confession, then has him arrested. Gillette's men chase Tod and Vina, and Tod is wounded by gunfire. Tod writes the story, then dies.

The owner of the *World*, Colonel Bogardus, announces that he has sold the paper to Gillette, but when Ralph sees Tod's story he has the newsmen print the headline that Gillette is to blame for the elevator accident. When the paper is distributed around town, a mob storms the *Sentinel* headquarters and chases Gillette. The police save Gillette from

Publicity portrait of Charlie Ruggles, Frances, and Fred MacMurray for *Exclusive* (1937).

the mob and arrest him. Ralph is appointed the new head of the *World* and leaves the office, reunited with Vina, as the next day's edition is prepared.

## Notes

A newspaper drama appropriating the milieu of United Artists' hit comedy *The Front Page* (1931), this title begins promisingly, with fast-paced ensemble acting and witty dialogue. However, it soon deteriorates into tedious melodrama, which ultimately leads down the path to B-movie disappointment. Charlie Ruggles probably comes off best, since he gets an opportunity to show the versatility of his acting, ranging from comedy to pathos, but even he cannot save a scene in which he and Fred MacMurray alternately get inside a refrigerator to see if the light stays on when the door is closed. The film features two interesting montages—the harrowing elevator fall and an exciting penultimate scene of mob violence—but Frances' performance is as uneven as the narrative.

As with *The Front Page*, which was based on a play by Ben Hecht and Charles Macarthur, *Exclusive*'s script was also based on a play, which may explain some of the humor of the early dialogue. When Ralph sends Tod out to harangue Gillette, Ralph tells him to "pour it on," to which Tod replies, "Pour it on—but don't get wet yourself." Tod *does* get "wet," since he returns with a black eye. Ralph asks him who gave it to him, and Tod answers, "Nobody gave it to me, I had to fight for it." Gillette coming to the *World* news office protected by his muscle inspires Ralph to comment, "You know, if you had a flute you would look like the Pied Piper with those rats behind you." After Vina tells her mother that she has been fired from her modeling job, Mrs. Swain advises, "The finer jobs are hard to get," to which Vina replies, "That's what Spitzer said about blondes." There is also a funny if ironic exchange between Tod and the ambulance doctor, after he delivers Ralph to Tod's house:

> DOCTOR: That was a long fall.
> TOD: The fall was nothing. It was the sudden stop.

Director Alexander Hall inserts slapstick into the early half of the film to good effect. Tod amusingly employs a backwards mule kick to take out Beak, Gillette's muscleman (who had given him the black eye), causing Beak to fall, unseen, down a flight of stairs. Frances' first scene shows Vina tumbling to the floor of a taxi that stops suddenly in front of her house. Garner and Mrs. Swain assisting Vina with some dropped groceries gets a laugh when the house's front door handle comes off in Garner's hand. The arrival of Ralph and Tod in an ambulance turns amusing when they are dumped from a stretcher for being drunk.

Frances employs a repeated hand-through-her-hair gesture as a character mannerism in the film, and flashes her legs when checking her stockings for runs after the taxi fall. Her fast-talking wisecracks transition to a lovely close-up moment of reactive tenderness when Vina learns Ralph has paid for her to go to college, and she has a believable rapport with Ruggles as her father. Vina Swain is an interesting contrast to Frances' former role as Lotta Bostrom in *Come and Get It*, since Vina is more sophisticated and contemporary. It's a pity that Fred MacMurray doesn't have the romantic appeal to match her. Lloyd Nolan's suave Gillette is a better match, even though we know his character to be untrustworthy and ultimately lethal. MacMurray's Ralph is presumably an older man (particularly since he has financed Vina's college attendance), and the mismatch can be considered as a prefiguring of their split.

A supposedly romantic scene in a restaurant, with accompanying music, begins with director Alexander Hall photographing Vina and Ralph gazing at the stars, with their faces side by side, although she will turn to look at Ralph when he voices his objection to her working for Gillette. Ralph hits Vina's head with what are presumably chopsticks as a sign of affection, and although she is not hurt, the action stamps him as misguided and unsuitable for Vina. The narrative demands she relinquish her independence to him in order for him to accept her again. Although Vina's actions are not as hurtful as those of Ralph, who blames her for Horace Mitchell's suicide to "teach her a lesson," his criticism of her even in the restaurant scene reads as odd. He says she is "opinionated, disrespectful of her betters, and has a filthy temper," qualities deemed inappropriate for a woman—and traits some maintain the real Frances possessed in her private life.

Vina's alliance with Gillette has her pretend to be a maid for Mitchell and a nurse for the story she is pursuing when Gillette sends her away with Beak. While such duplicity is morally ambiguous, it seems to be nothing extraordinary for the staff of a "yellow" tabloid paper like the *Sentinel*. And such subterfuge highlights Vina's ingenuity.

Mitchell's suicide is imaginatively staged. Vina's white pants suit, with black ascot and diamond pin, presents her as a goddess, standing higher on the staircase when Mitchell enters the house. His death has him fall and lay at her feet, as if in worship. Her scream

Hoodlum Beak (Horace MacMahon) and racketeer Charles Gillette (Lloyd Nolan) pretend concern for Vina Swain (Frances) in *Exclusive* (1936).

in reaction to the gunfire is punctuated by Hall's quick cutting, which makes the shooting a sudden surprise (even if he stays too long on her stunned reaction afterwards).

At this stage of her acting career, Frances had trouble with tears and crying scenes. Witness the scene of her sobbing in *Come and Get It* (when Lotta Morgan is told Barney has left her), where her face is buried under Walter Brennan's arms. In *Exclusive*, Hall will twice have her turn from the camera to mask her inability to express real sorrow, although her scene with Gillette recalling Mitchell's shooting repeats the same stunned focus that marks her close-up at the end of the suicide scene. When Ralph rejects her for the second time, Hall again has Frances turn her back to the camera to sob (as a more effective device for the actress).

The afore-mentioned attempted comic scene with Ralph and Tod getting into a refrigerator indicates a change of tone in the narrative, moving from newspaper adventure to family saga, and the time devoted to the sequence only makes it read as treading water. The scene is also strange for its use of music which starts as comic and then mutates to melodrama. Ralph and Tod initially come to the house to face Vina, perhaps accepting that they have gone too far in blaming Vina for Mitchell's death. However, since Vina has left with Mrs. Swain and gone to a hotel, the scene becomes one of comedy when, they are inexplicably, presented as drunk. Although an earlier scene has established that Ralph and Tod are drinkers, them being drunk to appease Vina is not logical.

Vina Swain (Frances) shows her reluctant love interest, Ralph Houston (Fred MacMurray), the libel summons she has received in this still for *Exclusive* (1936).

Frances has another good moment in which she becomes frantic to open a door to get to the injured Ralph, and her crying turning to laughter in relief over the (false) news that Ralph has not been harmed works because her beginning laughter shows an awareness of how ridiculous her crying has seemed. The transition is aided by Lloyd Nolan's Gillette, who joins her in laughter.

The car chase scene employs an obviously still car in which Tod and Vina sit, but the stunt of a real car crashing through a barrier is impressive, even if it is stock footage. Tod asking Vina to turn off the car's front lights during the pursuit prefigures Frances' real-life dim-out zone arrest in 1942 (though for the opposite action). Tod's death scene is to be praised for the excess it avoids, with Ruggles only giving a few sputtered utterances before falling onto his used typewriter; and the montage of the *World* staff hurriedly preparing the next edition includes superimposed close-ups, including one of Vina as she finishes Tod's story. The subsequent montage of men distributing newspapers tops the film's first montage, which uses a subjective camera to show cars driving to various street sellers to coerce them to advertise in the *Sentinel*. This second montage uses vertical slide edits and creates a renewed energy in the film for the climactic mob scenes.

While Gillette climbing upwards when chased by the mob seems like a silly thriller convention, the expectation of him being killed when he falls onto the paper rollers remains refreshingly unfulfilled, with only his jacket being caught in the machinery. One feels empathy for the hunted Gillette and relief when the police prevent the mob from hurting him, although having Gillette try to bribe them is unnecessarily demeaning. Ralph and Vina walking out of the newsroom would seem to be an incongruous act, as one would think that this is the time when they would be most needed, although the music and their attitude suggest a noble triumph.

In *Fred MacMurray: A Biography*, Charles Tranberg claims that Jean Arthur was first announced for the role of Vina, but Columbia's chief, Harry Cohn, decided against the loan out. William Arnold says that Frances had been a last-minute replacement for Carole Lombard, who had dropped out of the film. Arnold claims that Frances had been around enough journalists to know how absurd the script was, but she accepted the role, nonetheless. Other members of the production team had experience in journalism and the newspaper business. Co-screenwriter John C. Moffitt worked for the *Kansas City Star*, co-screenwriter Rian James worked for the *Brooklyn Daily Eagle*, and producer Benjamin Glazer worked for the *Philadelphia Press*.

The Turner Classic Movie Database notes that the story was inspired by the real-life political scandal in Los Angeles at the time in which Mayor Frank Shaw was investigated by Clifford Clinton and his Citizens Independent Vice Investigating Committee. The scandal involved rival newspapers the *Los Angeles Times* and the *Citizen News*. Shaw would eventually be thrown out of office for corruption.

Alexander Hall was a contract director at Paramount who had begun helming features in 1932 after making four shorts in 1922 and working as an editor from 1926 to 1933. He specialized in light comedies and showcases for female stars like Alison Skipworth, Claudette Colbert, Shirley Temple, and Mae West. *Exclusive* was his last effort for Paramount, and he would enjoy his greatest success at Columbia Pictures with *Here Comes Mr. Jordan* (1941), for which he was nominated for the Best Director Academy Award. Producer Benjamin Glazer had previously produced *Rhythm on the Range*.

Both Lloyd Nolan and Fred MacMurray were under contract to Paramount, and Charlie Ruggles had been seen in Hall's previous film, *Yours for the Asking* (1936). Among the large uncredited supporting cast is Frances' *Too Many Parents* co-star Billy Lee, and Cornel Wilde in only his second film appearance in an anonymous part.

## Release

August 6, 1937.

## Reviews

"Hodgepodge of racketeering and newspaper yarn...a disappointment lacking in originality and without benefit of good workmanship in direction or writing.... Hall has directed without assurance and the film lacks conviction at any point."—*Variety*, July 20, 1937

"Gratifyingly authentic in journalistic detail, swift and engrossing in its essential story, and failing only when the boys let their imaginations ramble too far.... Miss Farmer is an apt and credible beginner."—*The New York Times*, July 22, 1937

"Decent newspaper yarn with a good cast."—Jay Robert Nash and Stanley Ralph Ross, *The Motion Picture Guide 1927–1983*

"A rather typical newspaper melodrama directed with a cynical flourish.... [Frances] turned in a light and likeable performance and made a particularly strong romantic team with MacMurray."—William Arnold, *Shadowland*

"Charles Ruggles had a rare chance to show what he could do with a dramatic part, and it was enough to lift Benjamin Glazer's production out of the routine B category.... Farmer also impressive.... Best sequence: the crash of a department store elevator."—John Douglas Eames, *The Paramount Story*

## *The Toast of New York* (1937)

(aka *The Robber Barons*)
RKO Radio Pictures

**Credits:** An Edward Small Production. Director: Rowland V. Lee; Screenplay: Dudley Nichols, John Twist, Joel Sayre, based on *Book of Daniel Drew* by Bouck White, and the story "Robber Barons" by Matthew Josephson; Music: Nathaniel Shilkret; Photography: Peverell Marley; Special Effects: Vernon L. Walker; Art Director: Van Nest Polglase; Costumes: Edward Stevens; Set Dressing: Darrell Silvera; Sound: John L. Cass; Montage: Douglas Travers; Editors: George Hively, Samuel Beetley. Black & White, 109 minutes. Filmed December 14, 1936–April 1937. Buget $1, 072,000.

**Songs:** "The First Time I Saw You" (Nathaniel Shilkret, Allie Wrubel), sung by Frances Farmer; "Ooh, La, La" ( Nathaniel Shilkret, Allie Wrubel), sung by Thelma Leeds; "Temptation Waltz" (Nathaniel Shilkret, L. Wolfe Gilbert).

**Cast:** Edward Arnold (Jim Fisk); Cary Grant (Nick Boyd); Frances Farmer (Josie Mansfield); Jack Oakie (Luke): Donald Meek (Daniel Drew); Thelma Leeds (Fleurique); Clarence Kolb (Vanderbilt); Billy Gilbert (Photographer); Stanley Fields (Top Sergeant); George Irving (Broker); Russell Hicks (Lawyer); Dudley Clements (Collins); Lionel Belmore (President of Board); Robert McClung (Bellhop); Robert Dudley (Janitor); Dewey Robinson (Beef Dooley). Uncredited: Oscar Apfel (Wallack); Joyce Compton (Mary Lou); Frank M. Thomas (Fisk's Lawyer); Richard Alexander (Stabbed Actor in Play); William Arnold (Broker); Reginald Barlow (Mr. Taylor); James Barnes (Broker); Clem Bevans (Hungry Panhandler); Stanley Blystone (Sheriff); Lynton Brent (Reporter); Tyone Brereton (Southern Cracker); Robert Brister (Broker); Tom Broweer (Taylor Hotel Waiter-Workman); Daisy Bufford (Heather); James Carlisle (Broker); Virginia Carroll (Virginia Lee); Allan Cavan (Stock Market Loser); Tom Chatterton (Fisk Broker); Harvey Clark (First Tailer); George Cleveland (Perkins); Tom Coleman (Sergeant); Ginger Connolly (Call Boy); Hal Craig (Broker); Frank Hall Crane (Second Tailer); Frank Darien (Member of the Board of Directors); Wally Dean (Man in New York); Joe De Stefani (Astor House Headwaiter); Homer Dickenson (Toastmaster); Charles Dorety (Reporter); Emile Durelle (Buyer); Earl Dwire (Member of the Board of Directors); Jay Eaton (Man in New York Restaurant); Jack Egan (Reporter).

**VHS/DVD:** DVD released.

## Synopsis

In 1861 Georgia, on the eve of the Civil War, Yankee peddlers Fisk & Boyd operate a scam selling soap with gold pieces out of a wagon. Fleeing from a hostile crowd, the trio of Jim Fisk, Nick Boyd and Luke are saved by crossing the Mason Dixie line into the North. When war breaks out, the trio think they have made two million dollars by smuggling Southern cotton but discover that the confederate bonds Luke has traded the greenbacks for are now worthless. Jim devises a scheme to use the bonds to finagle Daniel Drew into selling his shipping business. To celebrate their deal, Jim, Nick and Luke attend a musical revue, "Mlle. Pleurique and Her Dimpled Darlings in Playtime in Paris." Nick cheats at a coin toss game in order to get to Mlle. Pleurique before Jim, although she proves to be an uncontrollable flirt with other men. Jim takes her beautiful maid, Josie Mansfield, to dinner instead.

Jim decides to form a corporation to promote Josie as an actress, which annoys Nick (who also appreciates Josie's beauty). Daniel proposes a plan to Jim to prevent his longtime rival Cornelius Vanderbilt from buying his Erie railroad company, but Jim outmaneuvers both Vanderbilt and Daniel. In retaliation, Vanderbilt tries and fails to block the sale of Jim's stock. Investors resent Jim's increasing wealth, and a mob advances on his company. He and Daniel flee to the Taylor Hotel in New Jersey, along with the regiment he has purchased as a defense militia. At the opening of Josie's show, the New York audience turns on her because they have lost money to Fisk's schemes; and Josie accepts Jim's marriage proposal out of gratitude for furthering her career. Heartbroken and frightened of

Josie Mansfield (Frances) is first employed as a maid by entertainer Mlle. Pleurique (Thelma Leeds), seen here flirting with Nick Boyd (Cary Grant) in *The Toast of New York* (1937).

Jim's lust for power, Nick dissolves their partnership as Jim buys gold to corner the market. President Ulysses S. Grant releases the government's gold supply to the public market to save the economy, and Jim is ruined. He is shot by an angry riotous investor, and dies with Josie and Nick by his side.

## *Notes*

The large budget of this film is apparent in the use of countless extras for crowd scenes; however, its failing is a misguided screenplay that places more emphasis on the monetary machinations of its protagonists than their romantic triangle. Director Rowland V. Lee can't save the bulk of his scenario from becoming tiresome, although he supplies a couple of noteworthy montage sequences. In what is essentially a supporting part, Frances gives a quiet, honest performance, even when handicapped by playing a character that is almost mute. Her beauty is highlighted with a series of ravishing close-ups, and we get to hear her sing onscreen once again.

Under the opening credits, which glitter like the gold that is so important to the film's narrative, Lee features the imagery of raised champagne glasses and falling coins. He begins the montage of the four-and-a-half-year war with gunshots announcing each successive year and closes with "Peace," the lettering enlarged for emphasis.

Frances appears twenty-five minutes into the narrative, and she is first scene shielding herself from objects being thrown at her by Mlle. Pleurique. Josie is not seen by Nick when he comes for Mlle. because Josie stands behind the door she opens to let him in; and Jim actually benefits from being tricked by Nick cheating in the coin toss because Josie turns out to be more attractive and considerate than Mlle. Jim's idea for Josie to wear Mlle.'s dress, and his later refashioning of Josie, recalls the Pygmalion relationship Edward Arnold and Frances had in *Come and Get It*, and their second screen teaming shows the ease of their playing together.

Jim encourages Josie to wear Mlle's dress by advising, "When you're fighting for corn and another chicken comes along and shoves you out of the way, get right back into that circle and make the feathers fly." This analogy receives some amusing visual play via the feathered coat that Josie wears. Lee intercuts between Josie and Jim, with close-ups of Nick revealing *his* infatuation with Josie, although it will take him the

Publicity portrait of Frances for *The Toast of New York* (1937).

length of the narrative to admit these feelings. Lee's use of reactive close-ups is often jarring, however, since they break the natural flow of scenes in a film where he seems more comfortable with action sequences and long shots.

Although Josie is presented as a girl less blatantly ambitious than Lotta Bostrom was, Josie still declares her wish to be a "great actress." Josie's ambiguity about her relationship with Jim is expressed by how she initially declines the necklace he offers her, and then accepts it when he makes it part of their business arrangement. Jim's "investment" in Josie removes romance from their relationship, perhaps because he is aware of her lack of emotional feeling towards him. He acknowledges her assets as "looks, talent and ambition," and is more comfortable being a corporate admirer. Ironically, this scene allows Frances to give subtle line readings and reveal an untainted honesty when, in close-up, she says, "I've always been hungry for pretty things."

The screenplay takes a stab at humor with the series of inventors who visit Jim for backing. Such feeble amusement is matched by the broad mugging of Jack Oakie's performance as Luke, whose demeanor prefigures that of Lou Costello in the 1940s. Other failed attempts at levity include Jim and Daniel being tossed around the inside of a wagon, ending with Daniel sitting on Jim's lap; Luke barking ridiculous instructions to Jim's militia, who eventually advance on him in revolt; and Jim and his men hosing down infiltrators at the New Jersey Taylor Hotel headquarters.

Josie playing "The First Time I Saw You" on the piano (since we don't see Frances' hands, we assume someone else tickled the ivories) in the scene with Nick has him deliver the stereotypically expected line that "Women and business don't mix." While this attitude demonstrates his alliance with and protection of Jim, it is also his first in a series of denials of his feelings for her. Josie accepting Jim's investment in her soon becomes apparent in the two shimmery, bustled gowns she wears (the white one particularly unusual, since it also has a fur-trimmed collar). Nick positioned as Josie's bodyguard forces him to spend more time with her while Jim is out of town, with his ignorance of the technique of the photographer in her gallery session allowing for another broad and unfunny performance — that of Billy Gilbert as the photographer, who fusses in European exasperation like a stock sissy.

The scene of Josie playing "The First Time I Saw You" on the harp as she sings the song features close-ups of Frances singing after initial long shots to show the harp. Her contralto recalls her "Aura Lea" and elevates the film to a new emotional plane. That she is singing to herself is funny, since this number is not featured in Josie's "Twelve Temptations" show, and because she denies singing the song to Nick, who is with her.

Lee intercuts Frances' singing with reaction shots of Nick, so it is obvious he is affected by her display; and his second denial is followed by a third after the newspaper reporters come with the accusation against Josie. His initial response to them—"I've never known a finer woman"—is rationalized by his telling her he said it for Jim. Josie tells him that he's in love with her, and Frances has a look of provocation on her face in close-up, which causes Nick to kiss her.

Jim telling Nick that he intends to marry Josie comes with Jim's self-awareness: "Maybe she don't love me...yet she likes me." The scene is complemented by a painting of Josie in the background, looking the way she did when he first met her—though her wearing Mlle.'s feathered outfit is an indication that Josie is not being truthful. A confrontation between Josie and Nick follows, with Josie admitting that she doesn't love Jim, and Nick telling her that she has to marry Jim because of Jim's investment in her. Nick lies that he doesn't love her in order to push her towards marrying Jim, an act of self-sacrifice and further denial. In the scene, Josie's loveliness is heightened by wearing her long hair undone for the only time in the film, even though Frances obviously wears a wig. Her golden hair gives her a kind of angelic aura, and Frances inserts thoughtful pauses into what she is telling Nick, as opposed to the quick speech pattern she employed in her previous film roles. "Once I thought that a star on a dressing room door would be worth any sacrifice," she says. "But there's one sacrifice I never figured on. I'm going to make that, Nick." This is as close as Josie gets to revealing to Nick that she loves him, although the way she has been looking at him has informed us—and informed him too. Perhaps if Josie and Nick were more honest about their feelings it would spare Jim the heartache—and his death to come. While Josie is not the transparent whore that Frances wanted to play, Josie's stage show presenting her as the Twelve Temptations implies that she is deceitful and dangerous, a notion that is borne out at the Grand Opening when it is sabotaged by men claiming that Jim's focus on Josie has cost them their money.

For the supposed stage show, director Rowland V. Lee uses montage effects and the clever device of a program booklet's page turning for each temptation. We are only shown seven of the twelve temptations, with Lee including footage of crowds that could never

Luke (Jack Oakie) is seen in the background, as Jim Fisk (Edward Arnold) talks with his mistress, Josie Mansfield (Frances), in *The Toast of New York* (1937).

fit onto a stage. The idea that these performances are designed to showcase Josie as a great actress is naturally laughable, since they are all simply visual displays, with her supposed range only expressed in terms of hair and wardrobe.

In "Vanity: The Hall of Mirrors," she is Madame Pompadous, who screams at the sight of herself in multiple mirrors, with diamonds and the glass reflecting and glittering over the image. In "Flirtation: The Masked Ball," white dots of light are used. In "Desire: The Embreadaro of Barcelona," Josie has long black hair as Seniora Conchita, who kisses the man she dances with. In "Luxury: Egyptian Moonlight," she is a semi-naked Cleopatra with a headdress. A curtain falls for intermission. The audience applauds, and the break is presumably to change the setting for the epics to come. In "Revelry: Carnival in Venice," she is billed as Maria (but not seen in the crowd). In "Jealousy: The Cellar of Despair," she is dark-haired Kiki, who's being strangled by a man whom she stabs in the back (the way Grace Kelly will do in *Dial M for Murder*). In "Death: In Cathedral of Shadows," she is the Victim, singing as she stands by a lamp post on a bridge before jumping into the river. And in the "Finale: Pageant of Life," we are only shown the title card, perhaps to give Josie time to change into the white gown and large feathery hat that she wears when Jim brings her out onto the stage.

For Jim's gold-buying spree, Lee employs a montage of newspaper headlines and shots of the agitated stock exchange crowd. A subsequent montage uses further headlines and crowd shots, as well as close-ups of the smiling Jim, a rising tower of coins, expressionist angles of men falling into the camera, and men collapsing onto the stock exchange floor. Nick's opposition to Jim's greed is voiced as moral outrage, although his jealousy of Jim winning Josie must be a contributing emotional factor. A dialogue scene between Nick and Josie has Frances, in extreme close-up, raising her right eyebrow as she speaks, juxtaposed with an ordinary close-up of Cary Grant.

Josie's confrontation with Jim over his gold avarice finally gives Frances an opportunity to be assertive and play a forceful scene, and she implores with earnest honesty. Lee caps the scene with the shadow of a window frame falling across Jim's face when he realizes that he has lost Josie; and his facing down the crowd is an act of suicide that serves as punishment for his madness. Jim's fall down the staircase when he is shot is appropriately clumsy, and Arnold's playing of his death scene is pleasingly subtle and empathetic.

The film's original director, *Exclusive*'s Alexander Hall, was replaced in January 1937 after he fell ill. The *Hollywood Reporter* stated that two-thirds of the film had been shot before Hall left, but it is believed that Lee re-shot most of what Hall had done. It is unknown how much, if any, of Hall's original footage remains in the final film. This transition recalls the Howard Hawks/William Wyler situation during the making of *Come and Get It*, although the original director of that production left under better circumstances. Both Cary Grant and Frances were borrowed from Paramount for the film. In *Cary Grant: Haunted Idol*, Geffrey Wansell says that William Powell and Ginger Rogers were initially cast opposite Edward Arnold.

William Arnold claims that Frances held up production of the film as she argued over the interpretation of her character, though she finally acquiesced to the studio's milder take. Patrick Agan also says that Frances fought with the director. The autobiography has Frances complaining:

> Instead of a cheap vixen, they wanted an ingénue fresh from Sunnybrook. So I rebelled. I argued with the producer. I fought with the director, and got into verbal knockdown drag-out battles with the writers.... But they won, and I ended up beautifully costumed, and Josie Man-

sfield was safely tucked into a chastity belt.... The interesting acting challenge changed into a sugar-coated distortion.

Even Josie's involvement in the death of Jim Fisk was changed to make her a mere bystander rather than the center of the argument over which Fisk is shot. Frances' vision of Josie as a prostitute recalls her Lotta Morgan in *Come and Get It*, albeit a whore with a heart of gold—a type Frances will also play in *South of Pago Pago*. Additionally, the autobiography recounts Frances' disparaging impression of Cary Grant. "He was an aloof, remote person, intent on being Cary Grant playing Cary Grant playing Cary Grant.... I considered him a personality, not an actor.... Our love scenes had been mutually detached and void of any emotional kickbacks."

In his book *Cary Grant: The Light Touch*, Lionel Godfrey answers the comments supposedly made by Frances about Grant:

> Frances, almost throughout her life, was suspicious and resentful in her feelings towards others. Furthermore, it would have been characteristic of her to look to Grant, however inarticulately, for help that he could not have given even had he been aware of her mute appeal.... Her behavior on the set was punctuated by neurotic outbursts to which Grant, to his credit, reacted with stoical detachment. He weathered the storms with self-discipline and an appropriate distance. For, whether he was aware of the fact or not, neither he nor anyone else on the set could have helped poor Frances Farmer.

Patrick Agan maintains that the film was a success, as does Frances in the autobiography. These claims are in opposition to that given by Jay Robert Nash and Stanley Ralph Ross in *The Motion Picture Guide, 1927–1983*, and *The RKO Story*, by Richard B. Jewell and Vernon Harbin; both books label the film a flop. Jewell and Harbin call it "the year's biggest financial disaster," with its failure attributed to Arnold's insufficient box-office appeal. They say it lost $530,000 at the box office, on a budget of $1,072,000 (this last figure cited by Nash and Ross). Jeffrey Kauffman, too, insists that the film was a "notorious" flop. As the most expensive movie made in 1937 at RKO, its failure caused the studio major financial problems.

Rowland V. Lee had worked on Wall Street as a stockbroker before his theatrical career, which must have flavored the film's tale. He even directed a drama for Paramount entitled *The Wolf of Wall Street* (1929). Lee had been an actor, screenwriter and director in silent films, and his prior picture, *Love from a Stranger* (1937), had been made in England for Trafalgar Film Productions. Producer Edward Small had founded this company in 1929 (which was also known as Reliance Pictures). Among the British studio's notable titles are another Wall Street drama, *Clancy in Wall Street* (1930); and the Lee-directed *The Count of Monte Cristo* (1934). Small's prior production, *Super-Sleuth* (1937), featured Jack Oakie; and Small would go on to produce Frances' *South of Pago Pago*. *The Toast of New York*'s uncredited executive producer, Samuel J. Briskin, was second-in-command to Harry Cohn at Columbia Pictures, and had been the uncredited associate producer of *Super-Sleuth*.

After *Come and Get It* and before *The Toast of New York*, Edward Arnold had appeared in the drama *John Meade's Woman* (1937) for B. P. Schulberg Productions, and the romantic comedy *Easy Living* (1937) for Paramount. Jack Oakie had been under contract to Paramount from 1928 to 1932, and would continue to appear in the occasional Paramount title. He would go on to be nominated for the Best Supporting Actor Academy Award for *The Great Dictator* (1941).

Cary Grant had been under contract to Paramount for five years, from 1932 to 1937, and from then on he worked as a freelance actor for the rest of his career. It is said that he had arranged an agreement to work for Columbia Pictures and RKO Radio Pictures every eighteen months on a rotating schedule. *The Toast of New York* is situated during Grant's transition period of experimentation, when he evolved from a colorless, plump contract player to the streamlined, perfect foil for the hijinks of the wacky heroines of screwball comedies, with his star-making performance coming in the Columbia comedy *The Awful Truth* (1937). Richard Torregrossa, in his book *Cary Grant: A Celebration of Style*, calls *The Toast of New York* a "tuxedo romance in which Grant was more mannequin than movie star." In *Cary Grant: A Class Apart*, Graham McCann claims that Grant filmed *The Toast of New York* at night while he made the musical *When You're in Love* (1937) for Columbia during the day. This claim is only partially supported by the information on the Turner Classics Movies Database, which lists the production period for the latter film as October 5 to December 20, 1936, and *The Toast of New York* beginning December 14, 1936.

## Release

July 30, 1937.

## Reviews

"[A]bsurd biography but good entertainment despite its inanities, extravagances and exaggerations.... [D]irection is straightforward and well paced. Lee keeps reasonable check on the slapstick, which does not get too wild. Production has size, if not much class.... Farmer conveys innocence as the love interest, having very little to do."—*Variety*, author unknown, July 13, 1937

"[T]he picture is only moderately entertaining.... Miss Farmer comes as close to justifying a place in the picture as any one could [in this] familiar, formula Arnold show, with a vigorous period to lend it interest, a tendency toward opera bouffe to weaken it. Fair is still the word."—Frank S. Nugent, *The New York Times*, July 23, 1937

"Entertaining though thoroughly distorted biography gives Arnold a wonderful opportunity to display his solid acting ability...atmospheric direction."—Jay Robert Nash and Stanley Ralph Ross, *The Motion Picture Guide 1927–1983*

"Arnold brought a refreshing vigor to his role, Jack Oakie added humor, and Frances Farmer made a fitting object for Arnold's (and Grant's) affections. Only Grant came off poorly in a part that was not well-drawn."—Richard B. Jewell and Vernon Harbin, *The RKO Story*

"[M]arvelous entertainment, with Grant and Arnold almost perfect and stunning art direction.... Frances gave a tight and convincing performance."—William Arnold, *Shadowland*

# *Ebb Tide* (1937)

Paramount

**Credits:** Adolph Zukor Presents a Lucien Hubbard Production. Director: James Hogan; Screenplay: Bertram Millhauser, based on a story by Robert Lewis Stevenson and

Lloyd Osbourne; Photography: Ray Rennahan; Associate: Leo Tover; Color Art Direction: Natalie Kalmus; Associate: Morgan Padelford; Music: Victor Young; Musical Direction: Boris Morros; Art Direction: Hans Dreier, Earl Hedrick; Special Photographic Effects: Gordon Jennings; Editor: LeRoy Stone; Sound: Gene Merritt, Louis Mesenkop; Costumes: Edith Head; Interior Decorations: A. E. Freudeman; Technicolor, 94 minutes. Filmed in June 1937 on location at Santa Catalina Island and on the Paramount ranch in Malibu.

**Song:** "Ebb Tide" (Ralph Rainger, Leo Robin); "Rock of Ages" (the Rev. Augustus Montague Toplady), sung by Frances Farmer.

**Cast:** Oscar Homolka (Capt. Jakob Thorbecke); Frances Farmer (Faith Wishart); Ray Milland (Robert Herrick); Lloyd Nolan (Attwater); Barry Fitzgerald (Hulsh); Charles Judels (Port Doctor); Charles Stevens (Uncle Ned); David Torrence (Tapena Tom); Lina Basquett (Attwater's Servant); Harry Field (Taniera). Uncredited: Arthur B. Allen (Native Sailor); Eugene Beday (Port Officer); Nancy Chaplin (Woman); Sonny Chorre (Attwater's Guard); Jack Clark (Tourist); Stella Francis (Tourist); Jack George (Band Leader); Robert Haines (Man); Elizabeth Hartman (Tourist); David Hope (Sailor); Olaf Hytten (English Tourist); Manual Kalili (Fiji Islander); Al Kikume (Native Policeman); Joe Molina (Native Sailor); Inez Palange (Native Woman); George Piltz (Sally Day); Antrim Short (Man); Bernard Siegel (Waiter); James P. Spencer (Cook); Leonard Sues (Native Boy); Jacques Vanaire (Assistant Port Doctor); Don Wayson (Man); Gloria Williams (Woman).

**VHS/DVD:** Not available in either format.

## *Synopsis*

On the island of Tehua in the South Seas in 1890, three beachcombers are hired by the ruling French government to sail the *Golden State*, a schooner bound for Sydney, Australia, whose captain has died of smallpox. German Captain Jakob Thorbecke assumes command and appoints his British friends Robert Herrick and Hulsh to join him. Thorbecke decides to change the ship's course to Peru, where he can sell the cargo of champagne, but is opposed by Faith Wishart, the deceased captain's daughter, who holds a gun on the three. However, when Faith accidentally shoots Thorbecke, she is overpowered and the ship heads for Peru. Recovering from his flesh wound, Thorbecke soon joins Hulsh in a drinking spree. When a typhoon hits. Robert and Thorbecke save the ship, which is now off-course, and Thorbecke resolves to stay sober. Hulsh discovers that the rest of the cargo is actually water and not champagne, and the discovery of a jug of acid makes the men realize that Captain Wishart had planned to sabotage the ship for the insurance money.

The island of Kanaki appears on the horizon, and the men sail to it. An American named Attwater has taken charge of the few inhabitants and has mined pearls from the local waters. Thorbecke and Hulsh plan to rob Attwater, but Attwater outsmarts them at a dinner he gives for his visitors. Faith follows the men onto the island, where Robert confesses his love for her—despite her rejection of him during their previous days together when he refused to betray his two friends and return control of the ship to her. Hulsh suggests using the acid in a bottle of champagne to kill Attwater, and he and Thorbecke come back to the island while Attwater entertains Faith and Robert. The plan fails, and Attwater shoots both Hulsh and Thorbecke; however, his native bodyguards rebel against him after he trips and falls over the body of Hulsh—evidence to them that Attwater is not a god.

The natives join Faith and Robert back on the *Golden State*, which sails away, leaving Attwater alone on the island with his pearls.

## Notes

A vehicle for the dubious talents of Oscar Homolka, who had been borrowed from Gaumont British Pictures Corporation Limited to make his American film debut, this south sea island effort by director James Hogan is waterlogged by sluggish pacing and static scenes. On the plus side is the tinted technicolor, some interesting camerawork, and the enactment of a typhoon (the highlight of the film). Again, Frances appears in what is a supporting role, although Hogan gives her some good reaction shots, and she makes a dazzling appearance coming out of the sea wearing a sarong.

Ray Milland and Frances in a publicity portrait for *Ebb Tide* (1937).

Director Hogan and cinematographer Ray Rennahan offer the occasional inventive flourish. For instance, the dialogue for the first scene with Thorbecke, Robert and Hulsh is upstaged by the sight of falling white petals, but this doesn't matter because what is being said is unremarkable. When a storm hits, Hogan's camera follows the men entering a building, lifts above them, crosses the ceiling, and moves down to them again on the other side of the room.

Hulsh's habit of spitting will later come into play when it leads to the discovery of water being in the champagne bottles, but Barry Fitzgerald's often impenetrable accent overstates the eccentricity of his character. Additionally, the screenplay's attempts to spotlight Hulsh's drunkenness by having him repeatedly falling backwards fails to endear him to viewers.

Ray Milland and Homolka face the same problem. Although they are playing men of questionable moral character, which isn't necessarily a bad thing in acting terms, they both lack the charisma here to make the narrative interesting. Homolka's accent is not as

Barry Fitzgerald, director James Hogan, and Oscar Homolka on location for *Ebb Tide* (1937).

thick as Fitzgerald's, but it is still occasionally hard to understand. Additionally, he grimaces melodramatically, and his voice carries an unfortunate association with Bela Lugosi's Dracula (both Homolka and Lugosi were born in Austria-Hungary).

Milland's English accent is the most accessible of the three, but he is a wan presence in spite of his handsomeness. He comes off as weak in his refusal to defy Thorbeke and honor Faith's request. The scenes with the three men—and between Hulsh and Thorbecke in particular—remain dull (and not helped by the lack of underscoring).

The *Golden State*'s yellow pestilence flag is a premonition of danger, and foreshadows the fates of Thorbecke and Hulsh. Hulsh finding a woman's stocking on the ship prefigures the entrance of Faith, whom Hogan allows us to hear before he pans the camera over to reveal her presence. This confrontation provides one of the film's two successful attempts at humor.

> THORBECKE (to Faith): Do you intend to stand there and point that pistol at me till we berth in Sydney?
> HULSH: You'll have a stiff arm, miss, if you wait that long.

Hogan utilizes the location filming to provide scenic shots of the ship at dusk and dawn, although the picture's color scheme seems to include a yellow, and later red, tint. The music score includes a theme that recalls "The First Time I Saw You" from *The Toast of New York*, and Hogan stops the sentimental music suddenly when Thorbeke slams down the wooden-framed photograph of his former ship before Homolka states, "I was drunk in my berth when she struck."

When Thorbecke finds Hulsh drinking champagne from the cargo, Thorbecke has a strange reaction to the bubbling alcohol. Since we later learn that Captain Wishart had replaced the champagne with water, the slim chance of Hulsh finding one genuine bottle of champagne can be forgiven as narrative expediency. Hogan presents the champagne discharge as if it is Hulsh's erotic climax, an analogy that will be continued later when a bottle he has in his trouser pocket pops its cork while he is dancing. The homoerotic suggestion is underlined by the disgust of Thorbecke, who wipes the discharge from his hand. Ostensibly, this disgust is based on Thorbecke being an alcoholic, something which isn't necessarily known to Hulsh; it is Hulsh's release that makes Thorbecke drink again.

Frances wears a blue sheer wrap around her white dress that matches the color of the sea, although Hogan fails to provide a close-up so that we can also see her blue eyes. Faith (how's that for a symbolic name?) delivers a stinging rebuke to Robert after he speaks to her on deck: "Excuse me, I'll go in to the cabin; I think the air is better." Robert follows her and delivers one of his own: "You're a stuck-up little prude out of boarding school with no more judgment than a kitten." The kitten part is not only funny but apt, since she has shot Thorbecke by mishandling her gun. Unfortunately, Faith's English accent becomes more pronounced in response to Robert's.

Frances' yellow-blonde hair is highlighted by the photography's yellow tinting, and Logan has her rise into a close-up for a speech in which she chastises Milland. The camera begins and ends on Robert when Faith begins and ends her tirade, but it remains on her for the most part:

> You're proud of being decent in little things, aren't you? The fine English gentleman. Different from that horrible little Cockney or your drunken captain. Well, you're worse than both of them. They're scum. They never knew any better, but you—you've had something and you've gone against it. You're doomed and done for.

This speech does not motivate Robert to become a hero, although he does ward off Attwater at the film's climax and assumes the role of captain after the death of Thorbecke. Faith is wrong about Robert being doomed, since he survives the narrative and wins Faith, whose opinion of him improves.

The typhoon sequence begins with impressively violent clouds, which look to be animated, and the storm's assault is portrayed by crashing waves and the billowing sails of the ship. On the distaff side, Hogan uses laughable speeded-up movement for the actors scrambling to save the ship from sinking, with Faith shown being hit with water as she climbs some stairs.

When the acid is found, Faith is shattered by the idea that her father had planned to sink the ship, and Hogan gives her a slow reaction close-up in which she raises her right eyebrow, a mannerism she employed for *The Toast of New York*. Hogan has Frances express tears by moving her face away from the camera, here holding her head in her hands. This emotional moment is capped by Robert pleading, "If only you'd trust me," to which she raises her head and whispers, Garbo-like, "I don't trust anybody." Faith's melancholy is matched by the poignancy of the music on the soundtrack.

The island setting of Kanaki is both exotic and odd. For instance, an English flag flies over the island, even though Attwater is an American. And the incongruity of a statue of Neptune on the beach is balanced by its visual resonance. Said to be warding off strangers, the statue only becomes integral to the narrative when shot at during the climax (ironically, by Attwater). Hogan offers an extreme close-up of Thorbecke, Hulsh and Robert looking through a cane-slatted window at pearl shells, while the crabs and turtles add exoticism to the island. Hulsh sitting on a turtle that walks away inspires the second genuine laugh in the film, and the entrance of Lloyd Nolan as Attwater sixty minutes into the plot is an injection of new energy. He has the criminal glamour that the other three do not, even if Hogan dissipates it as the narrative progresses.

Thorbecke's attempt to shoot Attwater at dinner is badly staged, so that Attwater holding his rifle over his lap appears unrealistic. The phallic rifle pointing towards Thorbecke is more unintended homoeroticism, although Attwater has a female native friend and later ogles Faith. Attwater even gazes at Faith with more intensity than Robert, who is supposed to be in love with her.

Faith's arrival at the island, coming out of the sea in a dripping wet sarong and with her long hair down for the first time, presents her as a goddess, with a sensuality that she had not previously shown in light of the virginal white and blue dresses with lacy collars that she wore. One might ask why Faith has been forced to swim to the island, although we are grateful for the image. (Interestingly, her sarong changes from strapless upon her arrival to having a side strap the next day.)

The climax of the film reads as ineffectual, although we are glad that Hulsh, then Thorbeke, are removed. Hogan zooms in on Robert when he threatens Attwater with a gun, and Thorbecke's death scene is filmed with restraint. It is telling that Hogan uses a shot of the ship as the movie's last image, rather than that of Robert and Faith back onboard for the predictable romantic conclusion. Disappointingly, however, there's no final shot of Attwater left alone on the island; but it is intriguing that Faith is back to dressing as the virgin, with her hair tied up again, when we last see her.

*Ebb Tide* had been previously filmed as a silent short in 1915 for the Selig Polyscope Company, and as a feature for Paramount in 1922. It would subsequently be remade as *Adventure Island* (1947) for Pine-Thomas Productions, with Rhonda Fleming in Frances' part, and as the British made-for-TV movie *The Ebb-Tide* (1988) for the A&E Television Network. The *Hollywood Reporter* announced that Henry Hathaway was originally to direct, but he became unavailable due to his work on Paramount's adventure film *Souls at Sea* (1937), which had been in production since December 1936 and would not be released

Frances in a sarong for a publicity portrait from *Ebb Tide* (1937).

until the following September. Ironically, Frances had been considered for the part of Margaret Tarryton in that production, a role that Frances Dee would play opposite Gary Cooper. According to the Turner Classic Movie Database, tropical vegetation was imported from Hawaii and tropical fish from Tahiti to create the island village of Kanaki for *Ebb Tide*. The filmmakers changed the name of the schooner in the story to accommodate the real name of the 30-year-old schooner used, the *Golden State*. The typhoon scene reportedly cost over $100,000 to create.

Hogan had been directing features since the silent days. He was a talkies contract director for Paramount, and had previously worked with Ray Milland in *Bulldog Drummond Escapes* (1937). Producer Lucien Hubbard had produced the war drama *Wings* (1927) at Paramount and was a prolific B-movie producer at MGM. The uncredited executive producer, William LeBaron, had been working for Paramount since 1926 and was executive producer of *Souls at Sea* and *Easy Living* (1937).

Vienna-born Oscar Homolka fled Europe in 1933 when Adolph Hitler and the Nazi party came to power. Under contract to the Gaumont British Picture Corporation, he had made a memorable impression in his previous film, Alfred Hitchcock's *Sabotage* (1936). *Ebb Tide* was Irishman Barry Fitzgerald's first movie for Paramount, and he would go on to win the Best Supporting Actor Academy Award for another Paramount title, *Going My Way* (1944). Lloyd Nolan had previously co-starred with Frances in *Exclusive*.

Welshman Ray Milland began his film career in Britain. After freelancing at various studios as a supporting player under the name of Raymond Milland, he started at Paramount in the George Raft/Carole Lombard show business drama *Bolero* (1934) and stayed for another sixteen years. His star rose with a featured part in another George Raft title, the crime drama *The Glass Key* (1935), and he played lead in the B-movie *The Jungle Princess* (1936). His prior film had been *Easy Living*. Milland would go on to win the Best Actor Academy Award for Paramount's alcoholic drama *The Lost Weekend* (1945).

## *Release*

November 26, 1937, with the tagline, "The first south seas adventure-romance ever filmed in color!"

## *Reviews*

"A fairly decent transcription of the South Seas

**Unidentified actor and Oscar Homolka in a deleted scene from *Ebb Tide* (1937).**

adventure tale, albeit a shade on the deliberate side in its story-telling.... Frances Farmer has a fine pair of shoulders which, picturesque though they may be, yet were made to bear a weightier dramatic burden.... Coloristically, the picture is almost perfect."—Frank S. Nugent, *The New York Times*, November 19, 1937

"Off-beat adventure.... Fitzgerald steals the show."—Jay Robert Nash and Stanley Ralph Ross, *The Motion Picture Guide, 1927–1983*

"*Ebb Tide* provides several 'firsts': It is Technicolor's first sea story; Viennese Oscar Homolka's first Hollywood vehicle; blonde Frances Farmer's first appearance in a sarong."—*Time* magazine, November 29, 1937

"Beautiful pictures and good acting; but too long...the scenes of a schooner stricken by a hurricane are thrillingly realistic.... Frances Farmer's heroine is uneven—vivid at times, at others merely conventional."—*Film Weekly* (author and date unknown)

"[The] production has guts.... Milland, in his Hollywood debut, and Fitzgerald were excellent, and well supported by Nolan, and Frances Farmer."—John Douglas Eames, *The Paramount Story*

"A moody South Sea adventure by an undistinguished director...a strange and confusing story shot in gaudy Technicolor.... Frances came across magnificently as an almost painfully sumptuous and enigmatic figure."—William Arnold, *Shadowland*

## *Ride a Crooked Mile* (1938)

(aka *Escape from Yesterday*; *The Last Ride*)
Paramount

**Credits:** Adolph Zukor Presents. Director: Alfred E. Green; Producer: Jeff Lazarus; Associate Producer: Dale Van Every; Screenplay: Ferdinand Reyher, John C. Moffitt; Photography: William C. Mellor; Process Photography: Farciot Edouart; Art Direction: Hans Dreier, Robert Usher; Editor: James Smith; Sound: George Dutton, Richard Olson; Interior Decorations: A. E. Freudeman; Music: Gregory Stone; Musical Direction: Boris Morros. Black & White, 70 minutes. Filmed July to September 1938.

**Cast:** Akim Tamiroff (Mike Balan): Leif Erickson (Montgomery "Johnny" Simpkins); Frances Farmer (Trina); Lynne Overman (E. Chester, aka Oklahoma); John Miljan (Lt. Colonel Stuart); J. M. Kerrigan (Sergeant Flynn); Vladimir Sokoloff (Glinka); Genia Nikola (Marie Simpkins); Wade Crosby ("Big" George Rotz); Robert Gleckler (Warden); Nestor Paiva (Leroyd); Archie Twitchell (Byrd); Gaylord Pendleton (Bilke); Fred Kohlen, Jr. (Corporal Bresline). Uncredited: Eddie Acuff (Pilot); Ernie Adams (Visitor); Sam Ash (Secretary to Warden); John Bleifer (Maxie); Eddie Borden (Prisoner); Ethel Clayton; Hal Craig (Officer); Joseph Crehan (Special Agent); James Flavin (Hack); Harry Fleischmann (Leavenworth Guard); Robert Homans (Officer); Charles Anthony Hughes (Federal Agent); T.C. Jack (Prison Guard); Barry Macollum (Spider); George Magrill (Truck Driver); Michael Mark (Foma); William Newell (Kracaw); Eva Novak (Cashier); Dewey Robinson (Bush); Dick Rush (Leavenworth Guard); Ralph Sanford (Officer); Lee Shumway (Deputy Warden); Leonid Snegoff (Ostap); Fred "Snowflake" Toones (Tovarish); Gloria Williams; Alex Woloshin (Misky).

**VHS/DVD:** Not available in either format.

## Synopsis

Russian Cossack Mike Balan is a cattle rustler who causes the death of Big George when confronted at the Liberty Packing Horse Stockyards about stealing some of George's herd. Mike's estranged wife, Marie, visits to reunite him with his twenty-one-year-old son, Montgomery, who has been expelled from a military academy. Mike dubs the boy Johnny and ridicules his surname of Simpkin, so the two fight. Equally matched, they become friends, and both show off their trick horse riding abilities. Johnny is interested in Mike's niece, Trina, who returns the attraction. However, after Mike confesses his life of crime to his son, FBI agents come to arrest Mike. Johnny flees and joins the army as a Westpoint trooper.

Mike is imprisoned at the Leavenworth, Kansas, penitentiary, where his fighting places him in solitary confinement. Johnny, stationed next to the prison, plans to help Mike escape. Johnny also finds that Trina has followed him to Leavenworth and sings at the Rose Pup Café. After Johnny arranges for two horses and army uniforms for Mike and Oklahoma, Johnny has second thoughts about the prison break. He tells Trina his plan to confess, and she goes to Sergeant Flynn, who refuses to implicate his friend. When Johnny is sent to lead the search party, he misdirects the other soldiers and meets with the escapees at a farm silo. When Johnny tells them that he has to take them in, Oklahoma shoots him in the arm. Mike shoots Oklahoma dead to stop him from killing Johnny, then knocks Johnny unconscious so he can escape. The other men chase Mike, who plunges over a cliff to his death. Johnny attends Mike's funeral with Trina.

## Notes

An odd mix of western character study and prison genre, this film quickly loses the promise of its early scenes. But it's not for any lack of trying. In the first of four films he would make with Frances, director Alfred E. Green uses dissolves and some noteworthy montages, and provides an evocative shot of Akim Tamiroff on horseback at night for the climax. However, the narrative reduces Frances to playing a supporting role, and in spite of her delicious Russian accent and her singing, she is generally wasted. Tamiroff probably comes off best, overshadowing Frances' estranged husband of the time, Leif Erickson, in a leading role.

The main obstacle to audience interest comes from the fact that neither Tamiroff nor Erickson have the gravitas to play leading men, and this lack of viewer empathy can't be overcome by a functional but B-level screenplay. Tamiroff's Mike recalls the gruff blowhards enacted by Edward Arnold in his two films with Frances. Unlike Arnold, however, Tamiroff is not positioned as a love interest for her, since the main love story of the narrative is between father and son. Tamiroff lightens his character somewhat by giving him a sense of the ridiculous, but the narrative effectively emasculates him by first presenting him as a man of action, and then imprisoning him and denying him that action until he is able to escape at the climax. Erickson has the distinctive voice of a leading man and some inherent likeability, but he can't match the emotion or technique of Frances for the couple's only screen partnership.

The relationship between Mike and Johnny presents an interesting psychological element, since both men are governed by violent impulses. Mike's estrangement from his son

Windswept Frances, with Akim Tamiroff and Leif Erickson, in a publicity portrait for *Ride a Crooked Mile* (1938).

recalls that of Mark in *Too Many Parents*; and the separation has inflicted damage, since we are told that Johnny has rebelled against his military academy (another association the film has with *Too Many Parents*). Johnny's maturation as a character ironically means having to betray his father—after he has betrayed the trust placed in him by his army superiors. Although their first fight presented them as equally matched, the climactic fight has Mike defeat Johnny, albeit a wounded Johnny. The narrative conclusion remains ambiguous in that Johnny has escaped retribution for his participation in the prison escape, but is left feeling guilty and orphaned by Mike's apparent suicide.

The opening scene is permeated with the adolescent notion of machismo, when Big George accuses Mike of cattle theft and Mike attacks his manhood:

> GEORGE: This is a five-million-dollar business. But it ain't big enough for me and you.
> MIKE: Maybe you're not as big as you think, Big George.
> GEORGE (*grabbing Mike*): I'm bigger, do you understand?!

Unfortunately, the impact of George's death by falling into the path of running cows is lessened by Green's obvious use of rear-screen projection. The father-and-son fight is foreshadowed by the decor of Mike's office, decorated with guns and a bear's head. The bear's head surrounded by pointing guns actually scores a laugh, as does Tamiroff's frustrated grunting during the fight. That Mike repeatedly ridicules the "simp" of Johnny's surname of Simpkon demonstrates his insensitivity and primitive morality (where one's worth is determined by how well one can fight). Mike's acceptance of his son only occurs when he renames him.

Appearing here with braided brunette hair, Frances supplies a new depth to her return to films after her stage experience. It's a pity that Trina is sabotaged by the screenplay and reduced to being the love-struck, long-suffering, decorative girlfriend who's often silenced by abbreviated scenes. Even the initiative she takes in seeking advice from Sergeant Flynn is thwarted by his idea that Johnny's gotta do what a man's gotta do, and the suggestion that Trina has betrayed him by coming to see Flynn rather than trying to help the man she claims to love.

After a light-comedy introduction in which Farmer's and Erickson's ease with each other shows through, and their subsequent song duet at dinner, Frances' best scene is perhaps the couple's first love scene. She shows a new maturity in her acting, no doubt due to her recent stage experience, and while she employs her trademark raised eyebrow mannerism, and Green fails to give her any close-ups, she offers a moment of real inspiration. After Trina tells Johnny, "If I like you I will follow you no matter where you go," she lowers her head in embarrassment before continuing with, "But I think you will come back to me." Trina is wrong in thinking Johnny will pursue her, since she must pursue him instead (though we do wonder how she finds out that he has joined the army).

When Trina sings at the Rose Pup Cafe, she is first viewed by Johnny through a lattice doorway before being revealed as dressed in a traditional Russian costume with headdress. The film only provides Frances one other significant opportunity to emote. When she tries to convince Johnny not to confess, the camera follows her movement from one side of Johnny, who refuses to look at her, to the other as she tries to get his attention. Frances' burst of emotion is soon squelched, but it is startling during the moment when she reveals it.

The arrival of the FBI officers at the bathhouse gives Mike and Johnny another chance to fight, though this time as allies, with the toweled dress of Mike and Johnny adding an

Frances, as Russian singer Trina, performs in traditional costume at the Rose Pup Café in *Ride a Crooked Mile* (1938).

erotic element to the man-play. Green uses the changing date of a desk calendar and a court gavel hammered down to show the passage of time and Mike being convicted. (His time in prison foreshadows Frances' real-life incarceration, especially in his being kept in solitary confinement for misbehaving.) A fight between Mike and Oklahoma, who speaks out of the side of his mouth the way Frances did as Lotta Morgan in *Come and Get It*, presents more homoeroticism when they're cooled off with a firehouse. An exchange between the men after the hosing offers a touch of humor, with Oklahoma's line becoming a running gag:

> MIKE: I feel much better now.
> OKLAHOMA: Let's do it everyday. Relieves the monotony.

The second half of the film's narrative is divided between Mike in prison and Johnny in the army. Johnny's crisis of conscience occurs after the escape has been planned, which would seem a bit late, and Green avoids more conflict by not showing the escape. The phallic-shaped silo is another subconscious homoerotic symbol, with Johnny's fall into the hay prefiguring Mike's jump into the river.

The use of music alerts us to the action of Mike's chase, becoming doubly effective in a film mostly devoid of underscoring (although this absence of music doesn't make it

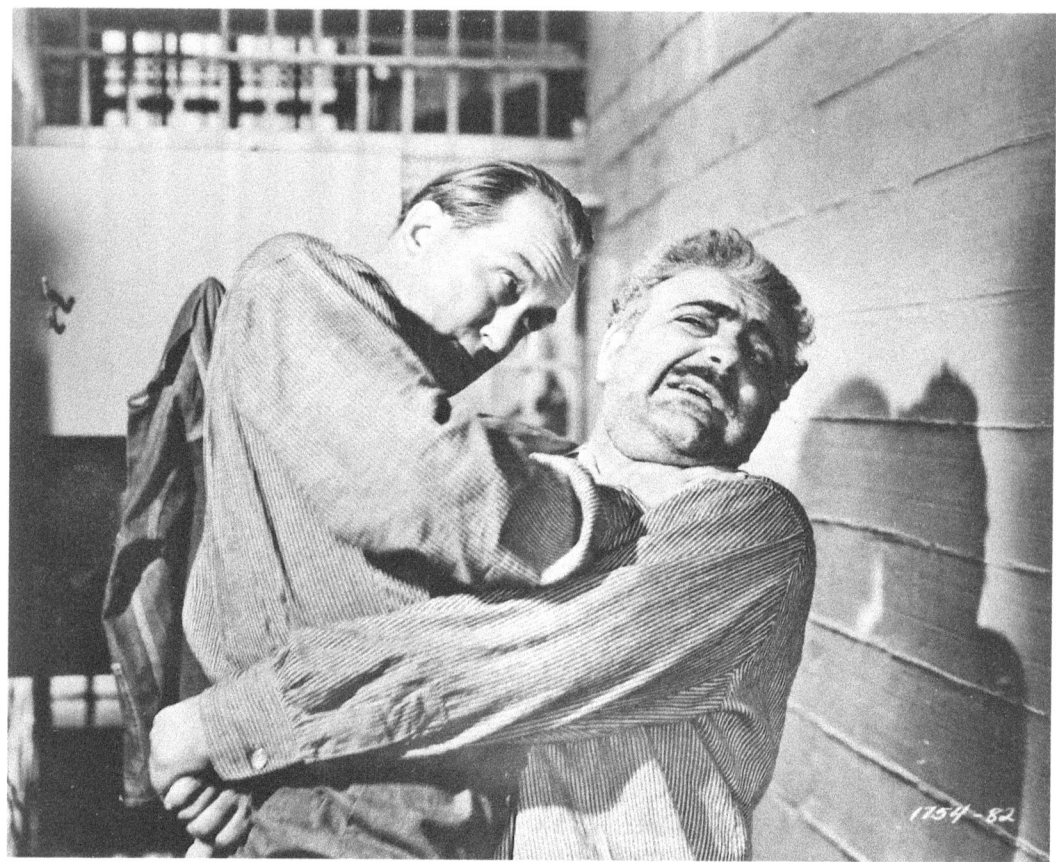

E. Chester, aka "Oklahoma" (Lynne Overman), fights with his prison cellmate Mike Balan (Akim Tamiroff) in *Ride a Crooked Mile* (1938).

as tedious as the equally scoreless *Ebb Tide*). Before his suicide, Mike sits on his horse at the top of the cliff, watching the men chasing him on horseback. This moment of reflection against the beautiful sky underlines Mike's need to die some sort of heroic death (as opposed to being shot or taken back to prison). The final embrace between Johnny and Trina is interesting for the kiss that she offers, which he does not accept, and the way her head is blocked by his as she rests on his shoulder for the closing image.

Notes on the Turner Movie Database say that a set of pistols that Akim Tamiroff used were Russian artifacts that had once belonged to Czar Nicholas II. Regrettably, neither TCM nor the Internet Movie Database identifies the Russian songs sung in the film.

Alfred E. Green was an actor and graduated to directing features in silent films. He had worked for Sam Goldwyn and the Mary Pickford Company in the 1920s. In the 1930s at Warner Bros. Pictures, Green made two notable titles—the provocative Barbara Stanwyck drama *Baby Face* (1932) and the Bette Davis vehicle *Dangerous* (1932), for which she won her first Best Actress Academy Award. To see him go from something like *Baby Face* to B titles illustrates the fall of a once innovative talent.

Green repeatedly worked with Mary Pickford, Colleen Moore, Stanwyck and Davis, and his empathy with actresses would extend to his future work with Frances. Green's prior film had been the MGM musical *Thoroughbreds Don't Cry* (1937), while *Ride a Crooked Mile* was his first title for Paramount. Producer Jeff Lazarus had only previously produced the Paramount comedy *Give Me a Sailor* (1938). Associate producer Dale Van Every had previously produced at Universal Pictures, and was the screenwriter of *Souls at Sea*. William LeBaron served as the uncredited executive producer for *Ride a Crooked Mile*.

Although born in Russia, Akim Tamiroff was of Armenian extraction. He had drawn attention as the servant of John Gilbert in the Greta Garbo MGM vehicle *Queen Christina* (1933), and signed with Paramount in 1936. He was nominated for the Best Supporting Actor Academy Award for *The General Died at Dawn* (1936), and his prior role had been in Paramount's actioner *Spawn of the North* (1938), which also featured Lynne Overman. Leif Erickson had last appeared in Paramount's musical *The Big Broadcast of 1938* (1938).

## Release

December 9, 1938, with the taglines, "BRUTE FORCE AGAINST TRUE LOVE! Which wins? You'll find the amazing answer in this new kind of picture thriller!," "Father and son fighting on opposite sides...for a woman...for honor...for country!"; and, "They chained a rebel heart that was born to be free!"

## Reviews

"A vigorous offering highlighted by a dominating performance by Tamiroff and particularly keen direction by Green.... Business will be handicapped by lack of cast strength and so-so title."—*Variety*, December 1, 1938

"An excellent beginning [but] beyond that all is confusion and muddle...a grand performance by Akim Tamiroff and pleasant supplementary stints by Leif Erikson and Frances Farmer."—Frank S. Nugent, the *New York Times*, December 29, 1938

"An exciting well-made action film. Tamiroff and Erickson give vigorous performances seething with machismo.... Farmer clearly deserved better roles than a small throwaway part like this."—Jay Robert Nash and Stanley Ralph Ross, *The Motion Picture Guide, 1927–1983*

"Only cinemaddicts with phenomenal deductive powers will be able to keep track of the proceedings. Only unusually indulgent cinemaddicts will want to. Typical shot: Akim Tamiroff roaring at Leif Erikson in Cossack dialect while showing him how to take a Cossack Turkish bath."—*Time* magazine, December 26, 1938

"A corny cliché-ridden B picture in which she [Frances] was required to stand on the sidelines and mouth a lot of maudlin dialogue.... The film was her punishment for all the critical remarks she had made about Hollywood."—William Arnold, *Shadowland*

# *South of Pago Pago* (1940)

United Artists

**Credits:** Edward Small Presents. Director: Alfred E. Green; Associate Producer: Erle C. Kenton; Screenplay: George Bruce, Kenneth Gamet; Photography: John Mescall;

Music: Edward Ward; Art Director: John DuCasse Schulze; Costumes: Edward P. Lambert; Makeup: Don Cash; Editors: Ray Curtiss, Fred R. Feitshans, Jr.; Sound: Earl Sitar; Special Effects: Howard A. Anderson; Dance Director: Jack Crosby; Production Manager: Val Paul. B&W, 98 minutes. Filmed March 1940, partly on Balboa Island, California.

**Song:** "South of Pago Pago" (Lew Pollack, Chet Forrest, Bob Wright).

**Cast:** Victor McLaglen (Bucko Larson); Jon Hall (Kehane); Frances Farmer (Ruby Taylor); Olympe Bradna (Malia); Gene Lockhart (Lindsay); Douglas Dumbrille (Williams); Francis Ford (Foster); Ben Welden (Grimes); Abner Biberman (Ferro); Pedro de Cordoba (Chief Moku); Ruby Robles (Luna); Robert Stone (Hono); Nellie Duran (Laulau); James Flavin (Café Customer); Harry Woods (Black Mike Rafferty); Satini Pauola (Native Diver); Ray Mala (Native Diver); Bob Wiley (Native Diver); Julie Carter (Native Girl); Lela Vanti (Native Girl); Al Kikume (High Priest). Uncredited: Nina Compana (Hono's Mother); James B. Leong (Waiter); Robert Wiley (Native Diver).

**VHS/DVD:** Video released by United Home Video on August 11, 1998.

## Synopsis

At the Tingle Tangle Café in Singapore, Bucko Larson, the captain of the ship *La Dessa* drinks with his first mate, Williams. Bucko has heard that Portuguese sailor Ferro supplies virginal pearls to Black Mike Rafferty, and he gets hostess Ruby Taylor to introduce him to Ferro. Bucko offers Ferro a greater cut, and they all sail south of Pago Pago to find the rich pearl beds. After weeks at sea, the island of Manoa is sighted, but Bucko, thinking he no longer needs Ferro, throws him overboard to be eaten by sharks. The Manoan natives see the ship and swarm aboard, led by Kehane, the son of the chief. Kehane is infatuated with the beautiful Ruby, and Bucko gives the islanders presents of clothes so that they will dive for pearls for him.

At a dinner the islanders give for their visitors, Lindsay, a white man who has come to the island to get away from other white men, cautions Bucko and the others about using the islanders. When Bucko learns that the oysters with pearls are only in deep water, he persuades Hono to dive. However, Hono gets diving sickness and dies, which causes Kehane to place a taboo on further diving. To divert Kehane, Ruby marries him, and they sail to the nearby island of Tua Tua for their honeymoon. Bucko gets divers drunk on gin and has them dive for more pearls. When more divers succumb to the sickness, the Chief protests, and Bucko shoots him and Lindsay.

Kehane hears the burial drums and goes back to Manoa to learn what has happened. Ruby pretends she never loved Kehane and rejoins Bucko on the ship. When the natives attack, Ruby is killed when she stands between Bucko and Kehane. Kehane kills Bucko and his crew, and the ship is set adrift as a warning to other white men who would wish to take advantage of Manoa. It is decided, however, to bury Ruby by the waterfall. Kehane and his new bride Malia go to Tua Tua on their honeymoon

## Notes

The second title Alfred E. Green made with Frances is a rather nasty adventure saga, with a treatment that attempts to be politically correct in its presentation of islanders manipulated by white men. Frances is once again cast as the whore with a heart of gold, even if she is playing what amounts to a supporting part (although she is given her one and only death scene in all her films). The set-up is notable for the familiar character triangle it creates, and how this time Victor McLaglen gets to perform the role of plebian father figure previously essayed by Edward Arnold, Oscar Homolka, and Akim Tamiroff in Frances' earlier films.

An opening statement identifies those that travel in search of virginal pearls as "steel-fisted iron jawed adventurers who lived hard, fought hard and died hard." This attempt to ennoble characters that we will see behaving like criminals foreshadows their ultimate fates. Apart from the date on a telegram, period is only indicated by the bustled costume Ruby wears in the café, and the only sense we have of nationality is from the English accents of McLaglen and Douglas Dumbrille. (While McLaglen is British, Dumbrille is from Canada).

Frances' first appearance is handled with some imagination, as the heads of two men sitting with Ruby at a table in the café block our view of her. When the men laugh, their heads are thrown back and she is revealed. Ruby recalls Lotta Morgan of *Come and Get It* (as the café here recalls that film's bar), both in her costume and attitude. Seen as a brunette with sculptured hair worn up, Ruby wears a shimmery, black, low-cut gown and fake jewelry. She talks out of the side of her mouth.

Ruby's humor is expressed by an exchange that occurs when she leaves her original table and guests, which scores its laugh as much from the reaction to her remark as the remark itself:

> PETE: Sit down, have a drink.
> RUBY: No thanks. I never travel steerage (*referring to the two women at the table*).

It's a shame that the character of Black Mike Rafferty is so small a part, given the resonance of his name, and Green uses fast-motion for the fight that breaks out, a technique he will repeat later. Ruby participates in the fight, although her face being hidden suggests that a double was used for Frances.

The ship *La Dessa* recalls the *Golden State* of *Ebb Tide*, although this film makes the rear projection and lack of location shooting more obvious than the earlier picture. Ruby's duplicitous nature is emphasized by the crossed shadow of the masts on her as she talks to Ferro, and also by the fact that her hair being down (as it will be when she seduces Kehane). In this shot Frances' greater fleshiness becomes apparent as Green fails to conceal her double chin. She also wears white pants—perhaps not the most flattering of wardrobe choices.

The suggestion that Bucko is jealous of Ferro talking with Ruby is misleading, since Bucko is not a romantic figure, although he will kiss her late in the film. The effect of the shadowed masts is repeated before Bucko throws Ferro overboard, although Bucko will be shown to be far more duplicitous than Ruby. His murder of Ferro is only the first of the shocking acts he performs, making him a far darker character than those portrayed by Arnold, Homolka, and Tamiroff in Frances' previous pictures.

Jon Hall was cast as Kehane for beefcake purposes, and he's always seen bare-chested and wearing a loincloth. The surprise, however, is that Hall still manages to make Kehane an innocent, despite his lack of apparel. This appealing innocence, however, does not carry over to Malia, whose childish idea of expressing attraction is to throw things at Kehane to get his attention.

**Hunky Manoan Kehane (Jon Hall) is fascinated by Singapore's Tingle Tangle Café hostess Ruby Taylor (Frances) in *South of Pago Pago* (1940). This is Frances' second time in a sarong, and third time playing a cinematic hostess.**

Malia is actually hard-done-by in the narrative, when Kehane rejects her when she dresses as Ruby, with the additional humiliation of her tripping over the dress, which is too long for her. Malia's upswept hairstyle when she attempts to dress as Ruby is also in counterpoint to Ruby being successful in her romance when her hair is loose.

Bucko expresses his attitude toward the islanders when he tells Ruby, "They're just like kids…. You gotta play with them," when he wants her to seduce Kehane. This notion takes a beating in a later exchange Bucko has with Lindsay:

> BUCKO: There's nothing like making folks happy.
> LINDSAY: They were pretty happy before you came.
> BUCKO: They're just like a lot of kids. You know, I've always had a soft spot in my heart for kids.
> LINDSAY: Is there a soft spot in your heart?

Kehane's discovery of Ruby offers another amusing exchange, when she fiddles with her necklace to express both her embarrassment and her attraction. This behavior might also be considered an expression of duplicity, except that at this point she has no reason to be devious in regards to Kehane. Rather, it seems Ruby's reaction is typically of a whore who thinks she is being hit on.

> KEHANE: Your skin is white, like a cloud. And your hair is golden, like the sun at dawn.
> RUBY: Well, it's been described before but not like that.
> KEHANE: I did not expect to find a woman aboard.
> RUBY: You're quite a surprise yourself.

That Kehane should describe Ruby's hair as golden indicates that Frances' hair color does not easily read as blonde in her black and white films. This was apparent in *Too Many Parents, Border Flight, Ride a Crooked Mile,* and even in parts of the Technicolor *Ebb Tide*. While it is probable that Frances wears a wig to play Ruby (given its length), it still seems odd that the "golden hair" line doesn't match the visual evidence.

Ruby's response to Bucko's request that she seduce Kehane is oddly non-sexual: "I get it; you want me to mother him a little." She will not do this, and their love scenes ironically present him as the aggressor, a point highlighted by the fact of Frances often posed lying down by him.

Ruby's response to Kehane in the following exchange suggests low self-esteem and self-hatred, which is hardly surprising for a prostitute. Frances makes it clear when Ruby is being honest and when she is pretending, and Ruby's reluctance to deceive Kehane prefigures the self-sacrifice she will ultimately make for him.

> KEHANE: You are the first white girl I have ever seen. Now I know why my ancestors believed that the first white people that came to Manoa were gods.
> RUBY: Well, if I waited all my life, and then I got me, I'd be kind of disappointed.

Her point of view also hints at the political stance the screenplay takes in terms of the blind trust of the Manoans and the exploitation of white men of what they consider inferior races. That the Manoans have access to the pearls yet do not dive for them is a sign that they are morally superior to the specific white men who have come to use the islanders for their own profit. The cuckoo-clock that the Manoans are frightened by, and the sight of an islander putting on pants back to front, are more examples of presenting the islanders as innocents.

Green uses two montages in the film for pearl diving, the first being shorter than the second. The first one covers the first dive, where only pearl-less oysters are recovered. The second includes shots of the divers bleeding from diving sickness and culminates in a medium shot of Bucko with the dozen pearls that have been harvested. The blood from the sickness adds a pleasing gothic touch, matched by the sign "That other white men will remember Manoa" and the corpses on *La Dessa* at the end. Regrettably, the diving scenes are cheapened by melodramatic music (a trend that continues with a syrupy score underlining the romance between Ruby and Kehane).

Ruby in a sarong recalls Frances in her sarong in *Ebb Tide*. Like Ruby's earlier scene in which she plays with her necklace, here she fiddles with a palm frond. This scene is also notable for Frances' use of the same head-tossing mannerism she had employed for Lotta Bostrom in *Come and Get It*.

Ruby agreeing to Bucko's plan of marrying Kehane has her looking with her eyes down, signifying her shame. This comes after she has recommended that the adventurers leave Manoa with the dozen pearls already acquired, an indicator that she is not as mercenary as Bucko. Frances plays her seduction of Kehane so that we (but not him) can see that it is an act; although, ironically, she grows to love him.

When Ruby looks at herself in a hand mirror while wearing her wedding costume, Frances' expression changes from curiosity to cynicism, topped by her self-mocking, "Queen

Manoan refugee Lindsay (Gene Lockhart) is suspicious of sailors Bucko Larson (Victor McLaglen) and Williams (Douglas Dumbrille) bearing gifts in *South of Pago Pago* (1940).

Ruby the first"—a line she will repeat when she dies. Frances supplies a grimace and a hardness to her face that is new to her acting when she asks Lindsay, "Do I look like a dose of poison?" (a line somewhat prophetic for Frances' private troubles to come). It's a shame that the scene ends with an obvious exchange in which he says, "It's your funeral," and she replies, "Oh no it's not; it is my wedding."

Frances' strangled "Yeah, sure" in response to the High Priest, who asks if "the face of a flower turned up to the sun" and "the gentle whisper of wind through palm trees" are in her heart, is funny and also revealing of Ruby's feelings of guilt. An exchange between Kehane and Ruby at the altar of Tua Tua is also funny.

    RUBY: It's kinda like a church, isn't it?
    KEHANE: I have never seen a church.
    RUBY: It's a new experience for me too.

Green cross-cutting between Kehane and Ruby, and Bucko back on Manoa, sets up the expectation of Kehane finding out about Bucko breaking the diving taboo and also of Ruby admitting the truth—something she never does in spite of her stated feeling of being "clean and new." It is interesting that she suggests that they return to Manoa before they hear the drums that signal the death of Moku, and before Luna turns up to inform on Bucko. Perhaps this is her awareness that she cannot stay on Tua Tua because she cannot escape who she is and what she has done.

Ruby's scene with the dying Lindsay is perhaps Frances' best acting opportunity in the film (although she is very touching during her death scene). Ruby telling Lindsay to stop drinking is ironic in light of Frances' real-life problem with alcoholism, not to mention Ruby's later drinking once she has rejoined Bucko. The scene allows Lindsay to continue the racial slant when he claims that white men "turn paradise into hell." Although the scene allows Frances to move from non-judgmental empathy to righteous anger to quiet comfort, Green withholds a close-up of Frances' reaction to Lindsay's death. Rather, he saves this for the subsequent moment when Ruby sacrifices her marriage by—fully aware that Kehane is eavesdropping—telling Malia that she doesn't love Kehane. Green zooms in on Frances for a close-up as she cries, her face overwhelmed with emotion as she looks out a window and presumably watches Kehane walk away. She turns away from the camera as she sobs—the same technique used for her crying scenes in her earlier pictures. The cane Venetian blinds she lowers are a nice visual representation of her hiding her grief.

Back on *La Dessa*, Ruby is out of sarongs and back to wearing a long black dress, with her hair up. She delivers an amusing insult to Bucko, although her speech is full of warning for the retribution she knows will come:

> RUBY: You boys ever seen 'em try to catch monkeys in Burma? They put something the monkey likes in a jug with a small neck. When the monkey reaches in to grab it he can't get his fist out. And he's too greedy to let it go.
> BUCKO: Well, don't worry about this monkey. When I put my fist in I know how to get it back out again.
> RUBY: Now that you mention it, I can see the resemblance.

The climax features the impressive special effects of bombs going off among the approaching islanders in their canoes, and the knifed Grimes sliding down an angled mast rope, dead. When Ruby is shot, Frances reacts with surprising stillness before she falls into Kehane's arms. Green uses speeded-up photography for the fight between Kehane and Bucko, and some subjective camera shots when Bucko punches, then throws something at, Kehane.

Bucko being pushed into the sea is a payoff for him pushing Ferro, then Luna, overboard, with Kehane's drowning murder of Bucko handled briefly but adroitly. The islanders stripping the crew of their clothes (which is suggested but not shown) is another payoff, since Bucko and Williams had giving them clothes as presents. These last acts being handled with economy, as opposed to the extended length of the fighting, provides some disturbing gruesomeness without wallowing in it. This is necessary for the narrative to maintain the Manoans as morally superior, and a welcome sign of restraint from Green.

Kehane returning to the dying Ruby (recalling Ruby at Lindsay's deathbed) provides her some redemption, a point reinforced by her not being punished with Bucko but rather buried as "one of us." This resolution is important for us to accept Kehane's new marriage to Malia, so that we don't feel that Ruby has been betrayed. Green depriving Frances of a close-up during her death scene seems churlish; however, the film's last moments offer an unusual narrative coda. Malia teaches Kehane to kiss like the white man rather than simply rubbing noses in what we presume is the Manoan tradition. This is odd, since it is an appropriation from those that sought to exploit the islanders. But then again, it's only a kiss. But we have to wonder—how did Malia learn it?!

Notes on the Turner Classic Movies website indicate that other directors were scheduled to make the film before Green was hired. The *Hollywood Reporter* claimed that the first choice was Kurt Neumann, who was under contract to Paramount and refused a loan-

In spite of how it appears in this still, Kehane (Jon Hall) comforts the dying Ruby Taylor (Frances) in *South of Pago Pago* (1940). This is the only death scene Frances would play in her filmography.

out. Neumann had previously made the comedy *All Women Have Secrets*, the crime dramas *Island of Lost Men* and *Ambush*, and the drama *Unmarried* (all 1939) for Paramount. Next was Charles Vidor, who signed in August 1939 but withdrew after production delays. Vidor was a contract director for Columbia Pictures who had directed Edward Small's *My Son, My Son!* (1940). Alfred Werker replaced Vidor but also withdrew after a disagreement over the story. Werker was under contract to 20th Century–Fox and had last made the crime thriller *The Adventures of Sherlock Holmes* (1939).

Since *Ride a Crooked Mile*, Green had made five features. They were the dramas *The Duke of West Point* (1938) and *King of the Turf* (1939) for Edward Small, the action adventure *20,000 Men a Year* (1939), the comedy *The Gracie Allen Murder Case* (1939) for Paramount, and the western *Shooting High* (1940) for 20th Century–Fox. Edward Small had previously produced *The Man in the Iron Mask* (1939) and *My Son, My Son!* (1940), as well as having made Frances' *The Toast of New York*.

Former prizefighter Victor McLaglen had won the Best Actor Academy Award for *The Informer* (1935) and was age 53 when he made *South of Pago Pago*. McLaglen had last played the lead in the crime drama *The Big Guy* for Universal Pictures. Jon Hall, the son of a Tahitian princess, was under contract to Sam Goldwyn and had starred in the action drama *The Hurricane* (1937). His previous film had been the comedy *Sailor's Lady* (1940). Douglas Dumbrille was known as a character villain and the man everyone loved to hate. He had appeared in Green's *Baby Face*, and Dumbrille's prior picture had been the Warner Bros. Western *Virginia City* (1940).

Like Dumbrille, Gene Lockhart was another Canadian; he had been nominated for the Best Supporting Actor Academy Award for *Algiers* (1938). Lockhart's previous movie had been the biographical drama *Edison, the Man* (1940) for MGM. French actress Olympe Bradna was a former Folies-Bergere dancer who had last made the drama *The Night of Nights* (1939) for Paramount.

In *Shadowland*, William Arnold notes that the film was "perhaps the most consistently awful script [Frances] had ever been handed, but this time she didn't object at all. She came to work every day on time, kept very much to herself, and in a quiet way, seemed to enjoy the challenge of creating an interesting character out of nothing." A point of note about the film's title is that although it is never spoken in the film, Pago is pronounced "Pango" in the title song heard under the opening credits.

## Release

July 19, 1940, with the taglines, "Greed and lust threaten a tropical paradise" and "A thousand thundering terrific thrills ... in a fight swept tropic paradise!"

## Reviews

"A good adventure pic. Pictorial settings and backgrounds add much to entertainment values. What story may lack in originality it makes up for in fast-tempoed and vigorous action.... Green's direction is top-notch."—*Variety*, July 17, 1940

"[Green] directs at a snail's pace and the script uses almost every cliché in the catalogue. Under the circumstances the actors are clay figures and Miss Farmer's Ruby Taylor a caricature. The white men stand around in villainous poses; the natives are charming.... Haven't we seen this all before?"—Bosley Crowther, the *New York Times*, August 2, 1940

"Hard-hitting action and first-rate photography makes this story stand out from routine adventure films."—Jay Robert Nash and Stanley Ralph Ross, *The Motion Picture Guide, 1927– 1983*

"With the flavor of *Mutiny on the Bounty* and *Hurricane*, it is exciting enough to interest the most blasé moviegoer. The sort of entertainment the fan is going to pay money to see."—Louella Parsons, Radio City Music Hall ad

"Especially potent for these times, it offers the escapist's paradise of diverting melodrama and picture allure. Considerable name draft with plenty of exploitation possibilities. One of best potential money-makers of the season."—*Daily Variety*, Radio City Music Hall ad (author and date unknown)

"Frances Farmer tosses off wisecracks like a junior Mae West. The opportunity to see the legendary Farmer in a role which, if not exactly typical, she certainly plays to the hilt."—George Aachen, *Popular Films of the Forties*

# *Flowing Gold* (1940)

Warner Bros.

**Credits:** Director: Alfred E. Green; Associate Producer: William Jacobs; Screenplay: Kenneth Gemat, suggested by a story by Rex Beach; Photography: Sid Hickox; Editor: James Gibbon; Art Director: Hugh Reticker; Sound: Stanley Jones; Costumes: Howard Shoup; Makeup: Perc Westmore; Special Effects: Byron Haskin, Willard Van Enger; Music: Adolph Deutsch. B&W, 82 minutes. Filmed June 1940, partly on location on Warner Bros.' Calabasas Ranch.

Cast: John Garfield (Johnny Blake); Frances Farmer (Linda Chalmers); Pat O'Brien (Hap O'Connor); Raymond Walburn (Wildcat Chalmers); Cliff Edwards (Hot Rocks); Tom Kennedy (Petunia); Granville Bates (Charles Hammond); Jody Gilbert (Tillie); Edward Pawley (Collins); Frank Mayo (Mike Branigan); William Marshall (Joe); Sol Gorss (Luke); Virginia Sale (Nurse); John Alexander (Sheriff). Uncredited: Eddie Acuff (Shorty Smith); Erville Alderson (Doctor); Monica Bannister (Girl); Al Bridge (Highway Patrolman); Glen Cavender (Oil Worker); Eddy Chandler (Truck Driver); Cliff Clark (Oil Well Shares Seller); E.E. Clive (Mr. Naismith); G. Pat Collins (Oil Worker); Heinie Conklin (Man Waiting for Job); Robert Elliott (Mac, Highway Patrolman); Phyllis Godfrey (Homely Girl); William Gould (Detective); William Haade (Man Waiting for Job); George Haywood (Chauffeur); Oscar "Dutch" Hendrian (Oil Worker); Stuart Holmes (Man); Eily Malyon (Cashier); Philip Morris (Detective); Jack Mower (Sheriff's Deputy); Frank O'Connor (Detective Taking Johnny); Lee Phelps (Policeman); Cliff Saum (Trainman); Charles Sherlock (Driver); Lee Shumway (Guard); Walter Soderling (Watchman); Harry Strang (Detective Handcuffed to Johnny); Charles Sullivan (Dance Floor Fighter); Sailor Vincent (Man on Dance Floor); Russell Wade (Chalmer's Chauffeur); Dick Wessel (Man on Dance Floor).

VHS/DVD: Not available in either format.

Publicity portrait of Frances as Linda Chalmers in *Flowing Gold* (1940).

## Synopsis

John Alexander is a fugitive from the law after having killed a man in self-defense in Oklahoma. He finds his way to an oil well manned by the crew of foreman Hap O'Connor and asks for a job, identifying himself as John Blake. After John saves Hap from an attack by the drunken Collins, Hap helps him escape from the police. John turns up at the Eagle Neck oil well where Hap and his crew now work for Ellery Q. "Wildcat" Chalmers and his daughter, Linda. John works for the competition, Charles Hammond, until a fight breaks out and John decides to join Hap's team. Hap cannot talk John into staying after John is arrested in a barroom brawl, since he is fearful fingerprints might reveal his true identity to the police.

When Hap's leg is broken by a falling pipe, Linda persuades John to come back as the new foreman. During this time John persuades Linda to fall in love with him—unbeknownst to Hap, who wants to marry her. Oil is discovered the day Hap returns from the hospital, and Hap sees that Linda is now involved with John. John and Linda plan to go to Venezuela to avoid John's impending arrest, although Hap tries to talk them out of a life on the run. The police arrive for John during a thunderstorm in which lightning strikes the well. A fire breaks out. Although Hap tells John and Linda to leave to be married, John returns with a crane and helps put the fire out. The police come for John, who goes back East with Linda, leaving Hap heartbroken but rich.

## *Notes*

This oil drama's star power goes some way to redeem an uninspired treatment and the sluggish pacing of director Alfred E. Green. While he provides the occasional interesting camera shot and some good montage footage, Green indulges in two extended fight sequences for far too long and even subverts the action climax. This film is yet another reminder of how, even when working on an "A" title, Green was unable to match the dramatic heights of his early 1930s work.

The love triangle is similar to those seen in Frances' previous titles, with Pat O'Brien positioned as the older man in between her and John Garfield. Although his character is less of a beast than those played by Edward Arnold, Oscar Homolka, Akim Tamiroff and Victor McLaglen, O'Brien diminishes the equation by incorporating the asexuality of Bing Crosby in *Rhythm on the Range*. Ironically, the treatment's contrivance of antagonistic characters that become lovers, and Garfield's obnoxious persona, allow him to be the beast that O'Brien is not.

Green's third film with Frances is an improvement over *Ride a Crooked Mile* and *South of Pago Pago*, the production seemingly profiting by having been made at Warner Bros. with more substantial character support. Green supplies Frances with better camera coverage, allocating close-ups here that he seemed reluctant to provide in their earlier titles. While Frances' character is pivotal to the narrative, the role's conventionality limits what the actress can do with it. However, she still supplies likeability and presence, accompanied by a simplicity of playing that tones down her previous screen mannerisms.

The oil wipe used for the opening credits is an amusing bit of polish that is soon tarnished by the unnecessary onscreen text explaining the title of the film. The first shot of Garfield's John, partly in shadow, suggests his shady past as an accused murderer on the run; and his fleeing a worksite by climbing over a fence using conveniently placed barrels as steps prefigures the repeated running John does throughout the narrative. John's duplicity by employing an alias runs hand-in-hand with his interest in Linda, as he is fully aware of Hap's similar interest. Hap's passive pursuit of Linda contrasts with John's aggressive approach, highlighted by his repeatedly calling her "Frecklenose" in a misguided attempt at endearment. (That she touches her nose every time he says it is a disappointing directorial decision.)

Green supplies a noteworthy shot—an aerial point of view from the oil derrick platform, looking down toward the ground. This shot will be repeated later when water spouts to the sky. Collin's dropped wrench, falling like a dagger, creates a false expectation of accidental death. The resultant fight between John and Collins comes as a surprise because it is not Hap who fights. After the tussle, in which Collins is knocked unconscious by John, comes a mildly amusing exchange:

Lobby card for *Flowing Gold* (1940).

JOHN: He's okay, isn't he?
HAP: Sure, he's alright
HOT ROCKS: From the way he's sleeping he could have been bitten by a tse tse fly.

John stepping in for Hap induces Hap to protect John from the police, who come searching for him. It's an act of gratitude that typifies the masculine relationship celebrated by Warner Bros., in which a mistrust of police was standard. In one sense, the real romance of the narrative is that between Hap and John, something the music score highlights in some of their scenes together, and which may explain Hap's hesitancy over Linda. This idea has its most provocative expression when John later places a cigarette directly onto Hap's lips.

Green employs vertical wipes and dissolves for transitions, and three montages to indicate the passage of time. The first features a newspaper and sign to indicate Hap and his crew are in Eagle Neck, a pioneer town with mud roads and vast open spaces. The primitiveness of the town allows for some low-brow comedy, with Hot Rocks, Petunia, and Tilly providing alleged comedy relief.

Frances sports a new look for Linda, her thick, wavy, long hair pinned up at the back to give it a shorter appearance, and the color again reading as brunette. Linda's hair being disheveled at the front, and her riding pants, suggest the rejection of feminine self-maintenance rather than presenting any androgyny, and she will wear a dress at the dance, in

Candid photograph taken of the cast enjoying a cake on the set of *Flowing Gold* (1940). From left is Tom Kennedy, Frances, director Alfred E. Green, and John Garfield.

a dinner scene with John, and when Hap confronts her about John. It is John who makes Linda more feminine, although the fact she never releases the back of her hair suggests she is not able to give all of herself over to love. This withholding may be what she saves for the care of her alcoholic father, who speaks in pretentiously florid language.

Linda's femininity will also be contrasted with that of Hot Rocks' girlfriend, Tilly. Tilly's fatness is parodied in the line about her being "the biggest thing in town," although this ostensibly refers to her business acumen. John's romantic aggressiveness is aligned to that of Tilly, who is violently possessiveness, taking a razorblade to Hot Rocks when she believes him unfaithful.

A scene in which Linda's car becomes stuck in the mud was famously referenced in the film *Frances*. The biopic erred in showing the scene being shot on a sound stage, when here it is apparent that the action is taking place on location. Another difference is that in the original, John is seen by the car laughing at her when she falls once forwards and once backwards into the mud. In their book *Hollywood Players: The Thirties*, James Robert Parish and William T. Leonard claim that the studio ordered this scene be repeated fourteen times to purposely humiliate Frances, something which the recreation in *Frances* highlights. However (apart from the fact that this notion is not confirmed in other sources), *Flowing Gold* is a Warner Bros. and not a Paramount title, which makes the idea rather dubious. Linda's mild reaction to being soiled by mud is another expression of her character as down to earth, and, thankfully, her being laughed at receives a payoff in the way she drives away quickly to make John scramble to take up her offer of a lift. John's hostility towards Linda and his sexism is displayed when he comments on her working in the oil industry: "Next thing, they'll be tying bows to the oil pipe."

The second fight scene, the first of two free-for-alls, between the Hammond and Chalmers crews, is instigated by the provocative act of Hap smashing his truck through the fence that Hammond has erected to stop the Chalmers gaining access to their well. Green, at least, leavens the fight with some humor by having Petunia punching air at one point, when there is no one to receive his blows, and Hot Rocks holding his face in shock when punched by John.

While Linda steps in between Hammond and her father to stop their fighting, the antagonism between her and John continues, with her slapping him at the fence, and her response to his being introduced to her by Hap after he has joined the crew. He offers her his hand, calling her "Frecklenose," and she replies, "Too bad you didn't get that swelled head of yours knocked off." John remarks, "She's crazy about me," and the cutesy music on the soundtrack agrees with him.

The idea of the inevitable romance is stated outright when at the dance John remarks, "I've noticed that when two people come out of their corners slugging at each other the way we do they usually end up in a clinch." Although Linda answers this with, "I wouldn't be too sure of that if I were you," she will soon be declaring her love for the man she had previously loathed. The antagonism/attraction relationship gives rise to some amusing dialogue, such as when Linda, in response to John again calling her "Frecklenose," comments, "I've met some wise ones before but that fella'd give even Napoleon an inferiority complex."

The dance begins with the shadowed profile of a dancing couple in front of the sign advertising the shindig, and Linda's plain dress, worn with a pearl necklace, is the attire of a rural girl making a concession to society's notion of femininity. Green scores some small laughs from Linda's exasperated embarrassment in front of John as she dances with the oaf Petunia, but generates a bigger one with the rather bizarre idea of another girl dancing with the unconscious Hot Rocks.

Green's second montage of working on the well includes two matching close-ups of Frances and Garfield, as Linda and John alternately express their admiration for each other. Her scene with John as they sit on steps when she tells him that she is in love with him is arguably Farmer's best sustained scene in the film. It is perhaps no coincidence that Linda wears a dress here, again making the effort to be more feminine. While Green doesn't reward her with a close-up here, Frances' direct and honest playing is no doubt made easier by her history with Garfield, since they had known each other in the Group Theatre, playing together on stage in *Golden Boy*. The camerawork favoring him over her is an indication of Garfield's perceived greater box-office appeal, something which will be confirmed by the last shot of the film. Ironically, while he had been overlooked for the lead in the stage version of *Golden Boy*, a role supposedly written for Garfield, Frances was overlooked for the film version in favor of Barbara Stanwyck when it was made by Columbia Pictures in 1939.

Although Hap's removal from the narrative (via his broken leg) gives John the opportunity to pursue Linda without competition, it is ironic that it is her admission of love that cements the relationship (since he is too hardboiled to do so). Hap's decision to propose to Linda is made when he goes away to the hospital—presumably since absence makes the heart grow fonder—with his gift of a negligee for her symbolic of his new agenda. Green provides an eloquent image of the boxed negligee discarded by Hap to express rejection and also disapproval of John's connection with Linda.

Hap's return also signals the discovery of oil in the well, since it is his expertise that is needed to adjust the pressure of the pumps in order for the Chalmers to strike it. However, his heroics come too late for him to win Linda. Hap's moral superiority over John is highlighted by Hap's insistence that John resolve the murder charge before marrying her. However, the scene in which he confronts Linda only reveals the blind loyalty of a woman in love (wearing a dress), a cliché made palatable by Frances' underplayed defiance.

The prospect of Hap turning John in to the police to stop him from running away with Linda is circumvented by the lightning strike, a narrative convenience which saves Hap from being revealed as morally questionable. While the climax features some impressive second unit work, and the music goes into melodramatic overdrive, the halting of the threat proves anti-climactic. The expectation is created that either John will be killed in a rockslide that accompanies his driving the crane over the collapsing river road, or that one of them will be killed in the fire as Linda looks on. The relatively easy way he gains control of the situation is perhaps a reflection of Hap's character, whose resolve is more whimper than bang. Green doesn't help either, since he can't parallel the power of the oil fire with the passion of John and Linda, or Hap's jealousy.

Petunia (Tom Kennedy), Hot Rocks (Cliff Edwards), Hap O'Connor (Pat O'Brien), Linda Chalmers (Frances), and Johnny Blake (John Garfield) admire a gushing oil tower in *Flowing Gold* (1940).

This makes the narrative conclusion seem a cheat, since although John is arrested and taken away for trial in handcuffs his predicament is lightened by Linda's companionship, with the assumption that he will be found innocent. The handcuffs even get a laugh when they are revealed during his kiss with Linda (with Garfield's face blocking Farmer's reminiscent of Leif Erickson blocking her face during the fade-out of *Ride a Crooked Mile*).

In their review of the film in *The Motion Picture Guide, 1927–1983*, Jay Robert Nash and Stanley Ralph Ross claim that Ann Sheridan was the first choice to play Linda. After she turned it down, Olivia de Havilland was offered the part, but she also declined. Frances was cast after Garfield requested her, knowing the trouble she was having getting film work after she had left the Group Theatre. Nash and Ross also claim that Warners refused to offer Frances a long-term contract because of her bad reputation, and that she and Garfield had an affair during production. William Arnold writes in *Shadowland* how Frances was last-minute casting, and how she allegedly got into arguments on the set. He also claims that Green asked for endless retakes during her falling-into-the-mud scene just to humiliate her, which presumably is the source for the recreation in *Frances*. However, it seems odd that Frances would have agreed to work with Green a fourth time on *Badlands of Dakota* if he had behaved so badly toward her.

John Garfield had signed a contract with Warner Bros. in 1937. He had channeled the anti-hero personas of Warner Bros. tough guys James Cagney, Edward G. Robinson, and George Raft, and mixed it with the Group Theatre's "Method" to add an element of sexuality that none of those stars projected. He had earned a Best Supporting Academy Award nomination for his first film, playing a dying piano player in the romantic drama *Four Daughters* (1938). Garfield's picture prior to *Flowing Gold* had been the romantic drama *Saturday's Children* (1940).

Pat O'Brien had scored a success playing the cynical reporter Hildy Johnson in the 1931 *The Front Page*, and his persona of the sharp, wisecracking con artist in the early 1930s changed to the beneficent man as a result of the roles he was offered after the Production Code crackdown of 1934. Frequently cast opposite James Cagney, O'Brien was used to bantering with tough guys, which would prepare him for playing opposite Garfield. His last film before this one had been the Columbia Pictures drama *Escape to Glory* (1940).

An earlier film adaptation of the Rex Beach novel had been produced under the same title (although utilizing different character names) in 1924 as a silent by Richard Walton Tully Productions, directed by Joseph De Grasse. Having last worked (as an actor) in 1928, De Grasse would die at the age of 67 in May 1940 en route to a hospital after having been found on a street corner.

## *Release*

August 24, 1940, with the tagline, "Even more thrilling than the cry of 'oil' ...The lives of the men who battle for it!"

## *Reviews*

"An action meller of obvious pattern.... Miss Farmer handles the romantic lead without inspiring much audience reaction.... Green accentuates the action to lift it far above basic rating."—*Variety*, August 22, 1940

"[S]hakily written and shakily directed.... Warners have drilled for a gusher and brought up a trickle.... Miss Farmer is a striking lady who is also a good actress when relaxed."—Bosley Crowther, the *New York Times*, September 2, 1940

"Beyond Garfield's dynamic persona, this is just another routine film, with a fairly predictable plot, turned out quickly by Warner Bros. to take advantage of the enormous popularity of MGM's *Boom Town* (1940)."—Jay Robert Nash and Stanley Ralph Ross, *The Motion Picture Guide, 1927–1983*

"Traipsing noisily on the heels of MGM's more pretentious *Boom Town*, *Flowing Gold* indicates that Hollywood has found the U.S. oil industry an acceptable new background for rehashing lusty old melodrama."—*Time* magazine, September 23, 1940

"[P]retty routine stuff."—Clive Hirschhorn, *The Warner Bros. Story*

"[A] generally boring tale of men in the oil fields, well below studio standards, with a meandering script. An effective performance by youngish John Garfield and the presence of Frances Farmer are the film's main attractions."—James Robert Parish, with Gregory W. Mank, *The Hollywood Reliables*

"Frances had never photographed more beautifully."—William Arnold, *Shadowland*

## *World Premiere* (1941)

Paramount

**Credits:** Adolph Zukor Presents. Director: Ted Tetzlaff; Associate Producer: Colbert Clark; Screenplay: Earl Felton, based on a story by Earl Felton and Gordon Kahn; Photography: Daniel L. Fapp; Music: Sigmund Krumgold; Editor: Archie Harshek; Sound: Harry Lindgren, Gene Garvin; Art Direction: Hans Dreier, William E. Flannery. Filmed March to April 1941.

**Cast:** John Barrymore (Duncan DeGrasse); Frances Farmer (Kitty Carr); Eugene Pallette (Gregory Martin); Virginia Dale (Lee Morrison); Ricardo Cortez (Mark Saunders); Sig Rumann (Franz von Bushmaster); Don Castle (Joe Bemis); William Wright (Luther Skinkley); Fritz Feld (Muller); Luis Albernini (Signor Scaletti); Cliff Nazarro (Peters); Andrew Tombes (Nixon). Uncredited: Arthur Aylesworth (Police Chief); Wade Boteler (Conductor); Dick Chandlee (Boy from Bemis' Office); Jack Chapin (Assistant Director); Elizabeth Dow (Bit Role); Ralph Dunn (Pinkerton Guard); Jim Farley (Bit Role); John Hamilton (Bronson); Stanley Mack (Projectionist); Louis Mason (Garfield—Tiger Keeper); Eric Mayne (Important Diplomat); Paul McVey (Information Clerk); Mantan Moreland (Train Porter); Frances Morris (Pauline—DeGrasse's Secretary); William Newell (Fireman); Edward Peil, Sr. (Bob—Studio Guard); Frank Puglia (Dapper Officer); Jack Raymond (Taxi Driver); Francis Sayles (Dining Car Steward); Lee Shumway (Cop); Leonard Sues (Page Boy); Billy Wayne (Mailman); Frank Yaconelli (DeGrasse's Barber); Wolfgang Zilzer (Bushmaster's Aide).

**VHS/DVD:** Not available in either format.

## *Synopsis*

German officer Franz von Bushmaster goes to Hollywood to sabotage the production of a Hollywood propaganda film being made by producer Duncan DeGrasse at his Bengal

John Barrymore in an ad for *World Premiere* (1941).

Studios, entitled "The Earth's on Fire." When he arrives, he is joined by Italian Signor Scaletti, who has also been sent as a spy. Their arrival coincides with DeGrasse's order to hire two actors from Central Casting to play the part of spies in order to generate publicity for his film. Scarletti and Bushmaster are mistaken for actors, hired, and begin their campaign. A threatening note is sent to the lead actor, Mark Saunders; a sandbag is dropped from the catwalk; and the film vault set explodes. The two real spies board the train hired to transport the cast and crew to Washington, D.C., for the film's premiere.

DeGrasse has the film's reels put in a cage with the studio mascot, a tiger, although the spies still plan to destroy the completed film. DeGrasse buys the train to placate the fears of his team, though his co-producer, Gregory Martin, demands that the train be turned back when it reaches Costaville, the home town of the film's star and Mark's wife, Kitty Carr. Kitty is none too happy, since Mark is having an affair with the studio's ingénue, Lee Morrison, who is secretly married to the publicist, Joe Beemis. Field Marshall Muller is sent to supervise the spies and provides a bomb with which to blow up the train. Falsely believing Mark has murdered Kitty, the spies tell Muller that the scandal is enough to ruin the film, but Muller helps them get into the cage and throw the film off the train, replacing it with another.

At the premiere, the film screened is a German propaganda film called "The Land von Peace und Beauty," featuring Muller. The real film arrives, retrieved from the passing train where it landed. Muller locks Bushmaster and Scaletti in a janitor's room with the bomb, but the device falls apart, and "The Earth's on Fire" finally makes its debut.

## Notes

A screwball comedy aided by a good ensemble which lifts it from being a "B" production, this title succeeds because of the fast-paced direction of Ted Tetzlaff in his film debut. If Tetzlaff occasionally falters, and the treatment has a few bad ideas, the casting of comic foils like Eugene Pallette, Sig Rumann, and the scene-stealing Fritz Feld more than compensates. Even John Barrymore earns laughs, in spite of his bloated appearance and occasional unintelligible intonation.

It's a pity that Frances' comic ability is wasted in her one and only farce, playing in another supporting role. The idea of casting Frances as a vain movie star is pure perversity, considering how she despised the falsity of Hollywood. Sporting a black wig (presumably to differentiate her from her blonde co-star and fellow Paramount contract player Virginia Dale), she has little to do except play the cuckolded wife as a monster, although she makes the character funny.

As a title written and produced before America's entry into World War II, the film operates as propaganda against Italy and Germany as "central powers." This is made especially apparent by Feld's character, an obvious parody of Adolph Hitler, complete with matching haircut and abbreviated moustache.

Duncan DeGrasse's Bengal Studios gate looks a lot like the Paramount gate, although a long shot avoids the clarity of comparison, and the title Bengal prefigures the mascot tiger that later figures in the narrative. Our first sight of Frances' Kitty establishes her as a movie star, with accompanying pet monkey and long cigarette holder. The black slinky dress she wears, with diagonal straps at the back over her exposed flesh, presents Kitty as

**Ricardo Cortez and a black-wigged Frances in a publicity portrait for *World Premiere* (1941).**

a femme fatale. However, this expectation is not met since she is not given a love interest, but rather a husband with an interest in another woman.

Frances' expression changes from a smile to annoyance when she sees Mark flirting with Lee, with her telling Lee, "Suppose you mind your own presence and quit poaching on mine." While Lee does not claim to be in love with Mark, but rather loves her husband Joe, Lee still entertains Mark's advances as a means to further her career. The idea of her marriage to Joe being a secret also supports this agenda, since presumably Mark only pursues Lee because he thinks she is single.

Since Lee is the one who insists that the marriage not be revealed, she presents as a manipulative and unlikable character. While those qualities aren't necessarily a hindrance to an actor, Dale's unremarkable performance makes one question why Mark bothers. Conventionally attractive and resembling Carole Lombard (though only in profile), she still is no match for Farmer's beauty, which is deliberately downplayed for her role as Kitty.

An exchange between Kitty and Mark takes place as they both look into a mirror, after she has scared Lee away for the first (but not the last) time:

> MARK: Can I help it if I've got magnetism? All these little butterflies want to dash themselves to pieces against me.
> KITTY: Well, I'll get you a mosquito net.

As DeGrasse John Barrymore's appearance is shocking, his face blotched by his alcoholism, although his introduction shows him being shaved and massaged, as if to rationalize the apparent redness. His technique of slurring words, making odd noises, mugging, and using a faux–Shakespearean flourish are off-putting at first, until one can see that these choices are deliberate for the tone of the piece and not those of an actor past his prime, as was generally believed.

The narrative idea that Bushman and Scaletti are mistaken for actors is an amusing one, and gets a laugh when Bushman tells Joe, "Central Casting? We are from Central Powers." The notion of Central Powers pops up again when the written threat Mark receives warns him not to make fun of same.

The aerial shot looking down from the catwalk at the live set as the sandbag is being cut by Scaletti is the first of two striking visuals in the film, the second being the later fight between Skinkley, Joe and Gregory Martin, with the scuffle obscured behind a tinted glass window. The fire in the vault is pleasingly anarchic, with alarms and smoke and rushing crowds, and DeGrasse at Union Station gets a laugh when his hand is grabbed by Joe during the newsreel interview. After DeGrasse is turned around, he says, "Don't turn my back to the camera," a line that is funny because it reveals that DeGrasse wants to be a star just like his actors.

Farmer's talent for comedy is revealed in the way she delivers a seemingly ordinary line. When she confronts gossip columnist Luther Skinkley (a name clearly meant to conjure "skunk"), the following exchange occurs:

>KITTY: You rat. Where do you get off printing lies about Mark and other women.
>SKINKLEY: I see you read my column.
>KITTY : Strike him, Mark.

Although the subplot of Mark romancing Lee lessens the pace and weakens the narrative, it does offer two pivotal moments. The first (and most conventional) has Mark bad-mouthing Kitty, with the camera revealing her standing behind an opening door, having overheard what he said. The second is much better, when, after Joe has been hiding in Lee's closet, he comes out draped in her clothes. The coda has him walking down the corridor after he leaves her—with her negligee trailing from his back pocket.

A shot of Kitty walking away from the camera, down the aisle, makes her look like a drag queen because of the hulking way Frances walks, her wig, and her padded shoulders. However, her fainting rather than screaming in reaction to the tiger approaching her as she looks in her trunk is both a surprise and a relief. (Interestingly, although editing reveals shots that separate Frances and the tiger, it's not readily apparent whether the filmmakers used rear projection for this sequence.) The tiger being scared back into its cage by the monkey is also a surprise, since the initial setup of the monkey opening the cage creates the expectation that it would get itself eaten.

The narrative notion of characters thinking Kitty has been murdered by Mark is set up by his being overheard to say that he will kill her, and others seeing her unconscious after she has fainted, with Mark bending over her (trying to revive her). This belief allows for a witty exchange between the spies and Muller when the train stops at Costaville:

>MULLER: Your report!
>BUSHMAN: Two words.
>SCALETTI: Suc-cess.

Kitty as murder victim would seem just retribution for her vengefulness in attempting to hand over to Skinkley the love letters Mark has written to Lee. (The tiger's approach

Mark Saunders (Ricardo Cortez), Gregory Martin (Eugene Pallette), Joe Bemis (Don Castle), and Lee Morrison (Virginia Dale) are confronted by an unidentified actor in a deleted scene from *World Premiere* (1941).

is what stops her.) Her intended revenge may paint her as villainess, but it also presents her as a woman willing to humiliate herself by exposing an unsuccessful marriage. The film makes Kitty Mark's antagonist even in the sequence from "The Earth's on Fire" we see being shot. In this scene Frances employs a Russian accent, recalling her Trina from *Ride a Crooked Mile* (though here playing a torturer).

Frances has another rare good moment after Kitty awakes to the sound of the Costaville crowd chanting "We want Kitty Carr." She regains consciousness and says to herself, "Oh, my public," to motivate herself to go to them. Again this is ironic for Frances, who was contemptuous of her fame as a film actress, so that Kitty's waving and blowing kisses at the crowd is hilarious. Thankfully, Tetzlaff shows restraint here by having her doing it as the train retreats from the camera.

Tetzlaff uses the train whistle for a sound gag when we see Lee go to Joe's compartment, and it changes to a wolf whistle; while Barrymore has a moment of physical comedy when he falls backwards into his chair at the premiere screening. The winding down of a lullaby, and the ticking sound, generate suspense in the climactic bomb scene, with the final gag arising from the "Made in Japan" sign that reveals the bomb to be a dud. The soundtrack again comes into play at film's end, when Peter's chatter is sped up and then mouthed by the monkey, although its "That's All Folks" is an unnecessary appropriation from the Warner Bros. Porky Pig cartoons.

Frances has no individual scenes with Barrymore; nevertheless, *Will There Really Be a Morning?* comments that she considered him a dead man. "He was so dissipated at the time that he moved and spoke by rote. He would reel up to me and try to say something, then his pale watery eyes would go blank and he would stumble off to his dressing room muttering to himself.... His career had become a mockery, and there was nothing left of him as an actor."

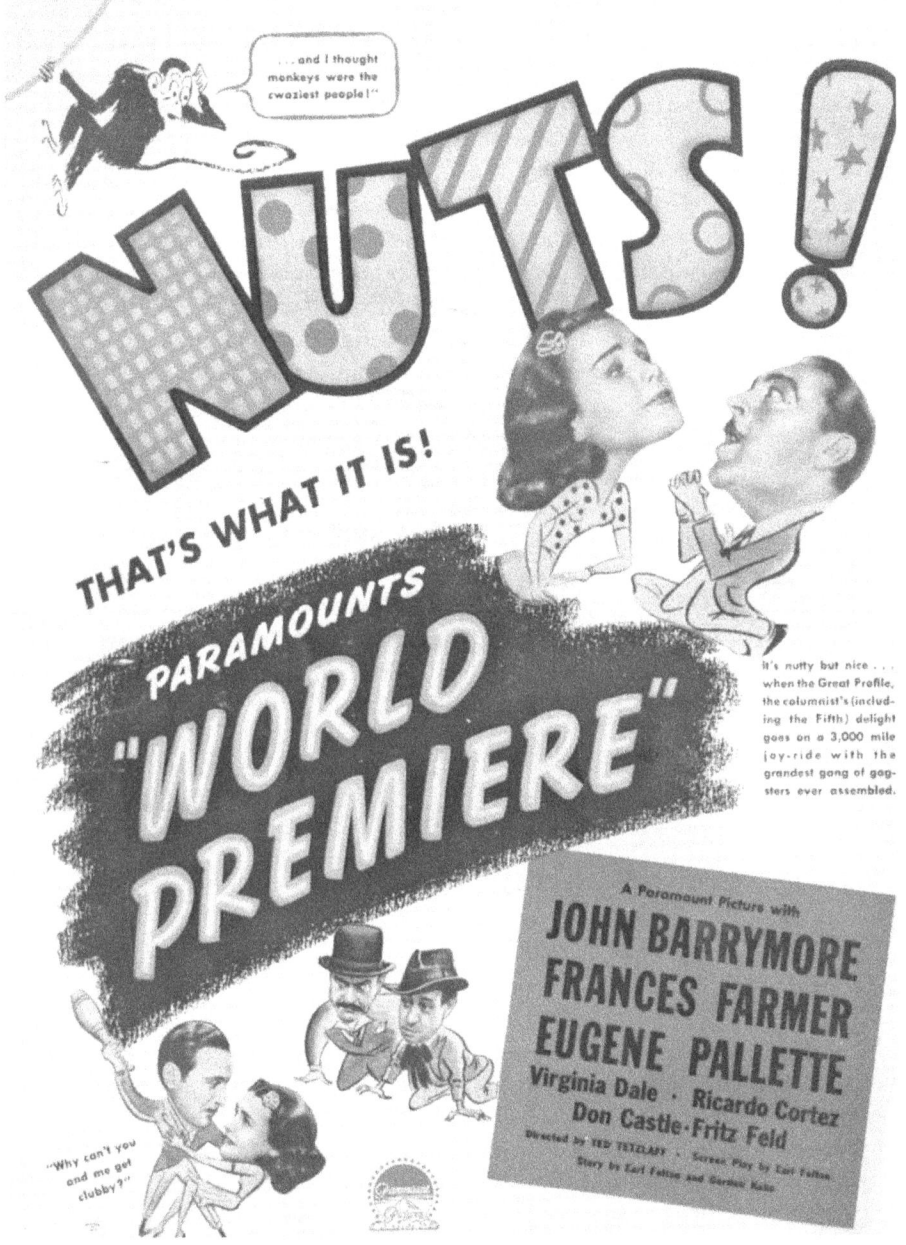

Although the poster for *World Premiere* (1941) suggests otherwise, Frances and John Barrymore, regrettably, do not have a scene together in the film.

Edith Farmer says in *Look Back in Love* that the once fine actor was "sick and alcoholic to the point where he could barely remember his lines from one minute to the next," which engendered Frances' pity. Edith also says that Frances hated the exploitation factor of Barrymore playing a caricature of himself, and that she was aware of the "implication of what lay ahead for performers who outlive their talents and good looks."

Barrymore was known as "the Great Profile," which is also the title of a 1940 show business comedy in which he played a famous actor given over to drink. A matinee idol in silent films, with an unforgettable voice and grand theatrical manner, he was a fine Shakespearean actor and light comedian. His addiction to drink began to take its toll soon after his self-parody role in *Dinner at Eight* (1933), and time away from films in 1934 did not help him recover. Barrymore's previous outing before *World Premiere* was the Universal science fiction comedy *The Invisible Woman* (1940). *World Premiere* would be his penultimate screen work; he died penniless in May 1942.

*The Hollywood Reporter* originally announced that Rudy Vallee had been cast as Mark, although it seems he made *Too Many Blondes* (1941) for Universal Pictures instead. *The Hollywood Reporter* also said that Otis Garrett was scheduled to direct but was replaced when he had to undergo a major operation. Garrett, aka Paul Gerard Smith Otis Garrett, was a screenwriter and editor who had started directing in 1938 but would only do so up to 1940, making ten titles. He had last made the romantic comedy *Margie* (1940) for Universal.

*World Premiere* director Ted Tetzlaff had been a director of photography, signing with Paramount in 1938. He enjoyed a close working relationship with Carole Lombard, whom he met at Columbia Pictures when she was on loan out. Tetzlaff would lens ten titles for Lombard. His most notable directing assignment would be in the future—the RKO suspense drama *The Window* (1949, which starred Bobby Driscoll, who would go on to co-star with Frances in 1958's *The Party Crashers*. Producer Colbert Clark was the associate producer on the Paramount comedy *West Point Widow* (1941), and would serve in the same capacity on Frances' *Among the Living* (1941). Uncredited producer Sol C. Seigel had also produced *West Point Widow*.

## *Release*

August 15, 1941, with the tagline, "The Great Profile kids the panzers off the Nazis."

## *Reviews*

"An entertaining good grade ... entire thing is treated frothily and with tongue-in-cheek, but this type of farce requires a peculiar talent which Tetzlaff evidently does not possess."—*Variety*, August 27, 1941

"An utterly mad buffoonery...pops with impulsive fun and occasionally works itself into tangles which generate some side-splitting mirth."—Bosley Crowther, the *New York Times*, August 21, 1941

"A silly and occasionally uproarious comedy...as masterful as Barrymore can be, [the film] is a success chiefly because of the comic scene-stealing by Rumann, Feld, and Albernini."—Jay Robert Nash and Stanley Ralph Ross, *The Motion Picture Guide, 1927–1983*

"Atrocious would-be comedy.... [Frances] hated the black-wigged mock-glamour role she played."—Edith Farmer Elliot, *Look Back in Love*

"Frances looked stunning and turned in an excellent movie-star performance."—William Arnold, *Shadowland*

"A mad satire on movie moguls, with another frenetic performance by Barrymore, replete with much mugging."—Tony Thomas, *Cads and Cavaliers: The Film Adventurers*

"An almost forgotten comic masterpiece.... Feld, diminutive with toothbrush moustache, and Rumann, a ludicrously fumbling giant, deserved on this showing to become as famous a team as Laurel and Hardy, but alas they never did.... Feld's scenes had an inspired zaniness."—Charles Higham and Joel Greenberg, *Hollywood in the Forties*

"A meaningless jumble of spies, vamps, bombs, and lions on the loose through which Jack [Barrymore] plodded wearily."—Margot Peters, *The House of Barrymore*

"The movie has no sense of timing or pace...there is no enthusiasm or sense of fun."—Joseph W. Garton, *The Film Acting of John Barrymore*

"[Not] of much artistic merit, but an opportunity to portray a character other than a caricature of himself, for which he undoubtedly was grateful."—Michael A. Morrison, *John Barrymore, Shakespearean Actor*

# *Badlands of Dakota* (1941)

## Universal

**Credits:** Director: Alfred E. Green; Associate Producer: George Waggner; Screenplay: Gerald Geraghty, based on an original story by Harold Shumate; Additional Comedy Sequences: Victor McLeod; Photography: Stanley Cortez; Art Director: Jack Otterson; Film Editor: Frank Gross; Musical Director: H. J. Salter; Sound: Robert Pritchard; Costumes: Vera West; Set Decoration: R. A. Gausman; Location Sequences Director: Ray Taylor; Location Sequences Photography: William Sickner; B&W, 74 minutes. Filmed July 1941 at Red Rock Canyon, California.

**Songs:** "Goin' to Have a Big Time Tonight" (Carson Robison), sung by the Jesters; "No One to Love" (Carson Robison), sung by the Jesters; "McNamara's Band" (Shamus O'Connor, John J. Stamford), sung by the Jesters.

**Cast:** Robert Stack (Jim Holliday); Anne Rutherford (Anne Grayson); Richard Dix (James Butler "Wild Bill" Hickok); Frances Farmer (Jane); Broderick Crawford (Bob Holliday); Hugh Herbert (Rocky); Andy Devine (Spearfish); Lon Chaney, Jr. (Jack McCall); Fuzzy Knight (Hurricane Harry); Dwight Latham, Walter Carlson, Guy Bonham (the Jesters); Addison Richards (General Custer). Uncredited: Bradley Page (Jesse Chapman); Samuel S. Hinds (Uncle Wilbur Grayson); Richard Alexander (Henchman); Don Barclay (Joe, the Drunk); Robert Barron (Gambler); Hank Bell (Townsman); Al Bridge (Plainview Lawman); Jean Brooks (Bella Union Girl); Paul Bryar (Barfly); John L. Cason (Townsman); Harry Cording (Jackson, Riverboat Gambler); Rube Dalroy (Townsman); Eddie Drew (Henchman); Jim Farley (Councilman); Edward Fielding (Councilman); Willie Fung (Wong Lee); Charles King (Plainview Gunman); Joe King (Ship's Captain); Ethan Laidlaw (Gambler); Kermit Maynard (Poker Player); Chuck Morrison (Henchman); Clinton Rosemond (Grayson's Butler); William Ruhl (Ship's Officer); Carl Sepulveda (Barfly); Glenn Strange (Bob Russell); Emmett Vogan (Ransome); Nolan Willis (Plainview Gunman); Carleton Young (Ben Mercer).

VHS/DVD: Not available in either format.

## Synopsis

In 1876, Deadwood, South Dakota, is the latest gold mining boom town. The owner of the saloon The Bella Union, Bob Holliday, sends his younger brother Jim to St. Louis to collect Bob's fiancée, Anne Grayson. Anne and Jim fall in love and marry, but are stopped from telling Bob since he has arranged a huge celebration. Bob's former sweetheart, Jane, comes to the house that Bob has purchased for his bride, where Anne tells her of the secret marriage. Jane tells Bob, who confronts Jim and Anne. Angry at being deceived, Bob joins with Jack McCall, masquerading as Indians to hold up the stagecoach. General George Armstrong Custer urges the town to elect a marshal for protection against more Indian attacks. Bob declines the job but suggests Jim, who has moved out of town with Anne to mine for gold.

Jim accepts but is made to look like a fool during a fire; Anne plans their return to St. Louis. When Jim sees McCall shooting up the Union, he arrests him and sets up a fake stagecoach run to catch the faux Indians. During the chase, Jim finds Bob's fob. McCall escapes from jail and murders "Wild Bill" Hickok. Jim deputizes a posse to go after him, until Jane warns of an impending attack by real Sioux. During the attack, McCall and Bob again dress as Indians and rob the bank. Jane shoots Bob to save Jim, and Bob shoots McCall to save Jane. Custer's army arrives and drives away the Indians.

## Notes

Alfred E. Green's fourth and final film with Frances is a forgettable Western overloaded with plot and coated in an unrelenting stock music score. The narrative repeats the romantic triangle featured in all of Frances' prior titles, but this time she isn't even at the center. While Green can be praised for creating a believable mining town milieu, it's a pity that the screenplay equates small-town with lowbrow comedy, though greed and lawbreaking are acceptable sources of conflict.

The triangle is interesting here since the older man is rejected early in the story, and, as a result, his character changes from protagonist to antagonist. Not even the love of a second woman (though one who had loved him first) is enough to stop him from pursuing a life of crime as retribution. This moral ambiguity is enhanced by the emotional depth that Broderick Crawford brings to his performance, although Robert Stack and Ann Rutherford are equally fine in their respective roles.

As the fourth wheel, Frances again plays a supporting role. The androgyny that her Linda from *Flowing Gold* hinted at is here made overt, since her Jane dresses in men's clothes, including fringed cowboy leathers and spurs, and hides her long hair under a cowboy hat. Frances uses a masculine swagger and loud voice to butch up her already seemingly masculine qualities, with Jane presented as a better shot than any man in town (as well as possessing the strength to serve as a scout for General Custer).

Since Jane initially presents as such a memorable character, it's a great disappointment that her role is secondary. Additionally, while Green rewards Frances with an occasionally flattering close-up, she has trouble varying her performance, so that her pitch becomes

Publicity portrait of Frances in costume as Jane in *Badlands of Dakota* (1941).

monotonous. And Green fails to add any kind of visual point to Jane's important scene when she changes into a frilly dress.

The film begins with an unnecessary title card, recalling those used in *Flowing Gold* and *South of Pago Pago*. A montage of wagons, gold panning, and house building establishes the origins of Deadwood.

Jane gets an erotic and perverse introduction when she's seen whipping the bottom of a man leaning over a wagon, with Frances' hair here looking more blonde than brunette. Jane's androgyny is commented on in an exchange between her and Bob, which Frances makes funny by the way she pronounces "effeminate":

> BOB: Don't you ever wear a dress anymore?
> JANE: Not unless I have to. Makes me feel too darn effeminate.

A romance between Anne and Jim becomes almost inevitable given their young ages, as opposed to the much-older Bob, not to mention such contrivances as Anne clinging to Jim in reaction to the whistle of the riverboat. Another factor is that both of them are outsiders to Deadwood, which the narrative emphasizes when they move out of town to mine independently before Jim is made marshall. This is in opposition to Bob and Jane, who have helped found Deadwood together, something she refers to in her speech to Anne.

An exchange between Anne and Jim shows a slightly more adult attempt at wit, after Anne refers to Deadwood as "life in the raw":

> ANNE: Tell me about the social life in Deadwood. I suppose they have dances every Saturday night.
> JIM: I've even seen men dancing Friday afternoon—at the end of a rope.

The screenplay introduces the infamous historical gunfighter Wild Bill Hickok as a figure of foreboding, so it's odd that he will only be used as a periphery character, as someone to be murdered. Hickok had received biopic attention three times before—as played by William S. Hart in the silent title of 1923, Gary Cooper in *The Plainsmen* (1936), and Roy Rogers in *Young Bill Hickok* (1940). Jane, on the other hand, is not referred to as "Calamity" Jane, although clearly she is meant to be the famous sharp-shooter who was played by Jean Arthur in *The Plainsmen* and would get her own movie, starring Doris Day, in 1953 (with Howard Keel as Hickok).

Director Green cleverly uses the paddles of the riverboat to portray the passage of time, with the transition shot after Anne and Jim kiss earning a laugh with its implication of sex. When the boat stops at Plainview, Jim and Anne fall into the mud of its unpaved street, recalling *Flowing Gold*. (Deadwood's roads being paved positions Plainview as an even more primitive pioneer town than Deadwood.)

Apart from her later desire to leave Deadwood when she believes Jim to be an impotent marshal, Anne isn't the silly woman that Jane considers her to be. Rather, Anne is far luckier in love than Jane, and at the same time she doesn't use her femininity to manipulate.

Jane slapping the drink out of the hand of the barman who toasts, "Here's to the bride," is evidence of her impulsivity, with Jane's jealousy of Anne partly based on Anne being described as a "lady." The implication is that Jane is *not* a lady—i.e., not a real woman—although the speech she will give mentions nurturing Bob. Jane delivers her speech after walking into Anne's house without knocking (for which she apologizes). Jane circles Anne, sizing her up:

> Me and Bob helped settle this town. We tracked for food before the wagon trains come. And we fought injuns before there was soldiers. And when the small pox hit us I nursed him through it. Could you have done that with your pretty face and your fine clothes? No frizzly-haired hoity toity petticoat rustler's gonna beat my time.

Apart from Jane's bad grammar (to indicate her lack of education), it is interesting that she calls Anne pretty as a patronizing insult. It is apparent that Jane does not consider herself pretty, an idea made somewhat unbelievable if one compares Farmer's great beauty to the conventional prettiness of Anne Rutherford. It is also apparent that any notion of romantic feeling Jane has felt towards Bob has been one-sided, which is also remarkable.

A clue to why Bob would have preferred Anne to Jane is Jane's lack of emotion, since the way she reveals Jim's marriage to Anne is done in ridicule rather than as an expression of opportunity for her and Bob to get together. Green provides Frances with a close-up

Jim Holliday (Robert Stack) enjoys a romantic moment with his sweetheart, Anne Grayson (Anne Rutherford), in *Badlands of Dakota* (1941).

when Jane looks at Anne after the speech, in which Frances uses stillness to convey Jane's wounded pride.

Bob slapping rather than punching Jim's face in reaction to the marriage betrayal is an intriguing choice for an act of violence, though perhaps suitable given that they are brothers. Bob's later slap of Jane suggests, however, that he is more a slapper than a puncher, since we never see Bob throw a punch (he uses a gun at the climax).

Jane copes with Bob's rejection by having the Jesters sing "No One to Love"—a song of heartbreak—*fifteen* times to her (we only have to hear it twice) at gunpoint. Regrettably, Green doesn't linger on the sight of the depressed Jane, and cuts away to a funny line delivered by a drunk at the bar: "Beautiful sentiment. Makes me want to reform. From now on I'll never touch another bottle of whisky. Get me a dry martini."

Jane's depression deepens after she finds the beaten up Bob. After she scares away his attacker by shooting at him, she wipes the blood from Bob's face, and he says Anne's name, thinking she is Anne. Jane's compassion and love is rewarded with Bob failing to recognize her, consumed with feeling for a woman that does not want him. That Jane is consumed with feeling for a man that does not want *her* is sad irony.

Green uses obvious rear projection for the runaway wagon sequence, with the cutaways to the drunk sleeping in the carriage receiving a payoff after the wagon crashes into Wong Lee's laundry. Against the animated chatter of Wong Lee, the drunk gets out of the carriage and says to Spearfish, "Hey, you look like the big fat blubber head that drummed me out of Deadwood." When Wong Lee's laundry is later on fire, Green features an aerial shot of the fire bell being rung, one of only two arresting visual touches in the film; the other being a pan back to the approaching army soldiers at the climax.

Bad guys dressed and painted as Indians is a seemingly new twist on the Western, but the arrival of the real Indians for the climax is troubling for the narrative. The raid comes out of left field and reads as a contrivance to hype up the climax (the murder of Hickok and the pursuit of Bob and McCall apparently being insufficient). The Indian raid does, however, draw parallels between Anne, who is left to watch over the town's children (as a real woman), and Jane, who shoots with the men (as a real man). While the attack of the Indians allows for lots of gun-tootin', injun screamin' action, the narrative thankfully focuses on the Cain-and-Abel conflict between Jim and Bob, with McCall's shooting allowing Bob one last act of decency by saving Jane's life.

Bob's death scene again displays Frances' difficulty with tears, as Jane's sobs are obscured by a comforting hug from Anne (who one might think an unlikely source of said comfort). However, Frances does provide an emotional "Bob!" after she shoots him, perhaps as an awareness of the horror of having to shoot the man she loves in order to stop him from killing his brother.

The end of the film includes an ironic narrative touch when the victory over the Indians is capped by Custer announcing his soldiers will be leaving for the Little Big Horn, a journey that we know will result in their massacre. Additionally, Jane is given an ambiguous moment with Rocky, with the rather pathetic suggestion of a romance blossoming between them. She sees him looking at her as she looks at him, and comments, "What are you staring at?! Don't you know when a lady needs a drink?" Jane labeling herself a lady is an embrace of her formerly rejected femininity, though it is depressingly attached to alcohol.

In *The Rise and Fall of the Love Goddesses*, Patrick Agan reports that Frances caused trouble by demanding that Jane be presented as less glamorous and more truthfully gritty. The claim seems odd, since it is hard to consider Jane's look in the film as glamorous. True, she looks very clean, which may imply that gritty meant unkempt, so perhaps Frances was partly successful in her quest.

The *Hollywood Reporter* had announced on June 24, 1941, that Miriam Hopkins had agreed to star in the picture, presumably as Jane, but that she left the planned production two days later because she was unhappy with her role in the final draft of the script. Since *Flowing Gold*, Alfred E. Green had stayed at Warner Bros. to make the John Garfield drama *East of the River* (1940), and then moved to Columbia Pictures for *Adventure in Washington* (1941). Associate producer George Waggner was a screenwriter and director of Universal Westerns and horror titles, and *Badlands of Dakota* was his first film as producer.

Robert Stack was a Universal contract player who had last made the Deanne Durbin vehicle *Nice Girl* (1941). He would go on to be nominated for the Best Supporting Actor Academy Award for *Written on the Wind* (1956). Anne Rutherford was an MGM contract player who had found fame as Polly Benedict in the Andy Hardy series, and had played Scarlett's sister, Careen O'Hara, in *Gone with the Wind* (1939). Her prior title had been *Life Begins for Andy Hardy* (1941). Lon Chaney, Jr. had acquired the screen role of Lenny in *Of Mice and Men* (1939), which Broderick Crawford had originated on Broadway. Substantial leading roles in film would allude the large and burly Crawford until *All the Kings*

Spearfish (Andy Devine) watches as Jim Holliday (Robert Stack) is confronted by his brother, Bob Holliday (Broderick Crawford), in *Badlands of Dakota* (1941).

*Men* (1949), for which he would win the Best Actor Academy Award. Crawford's prior title had been the comedy *Tight Shoes* (1941).

## *Release*

September 5, 1941, with the taglines, "THE LAND OF LAWLESSNESS!," "Deadwood City—where a slow draw meant a fast death!," and "Thundering Down from the Black Hills…Come the Boldest, Blackest Days of the West! Deadwood City—a Roaring Capitol of an Empire of Lawlessness—Where Life Was Cheap—Love Priceless!"

## *Reviews*

"A surprise entertainment entry … moving melodrama.… Miss Farmer turns in an outstanding performance."—*Variety*, September 10, 1941

"[P]lenty wild and confused. Presumably the boys [at Universal] couldn't quite make up their minds whether the emphasis was to be upon a conventional Western fable about two brothers who have a feud over a girl or upon certain comic digressions, so they generously provide both.… The consequence is that a balance somewhere near neutral is hit."—Bosley Crowther, the *New York Times*, September 9, 1941

"A great programmer with an incredibly good cast. Farmer is a standout."—Jay Robert Nash and Stanley Ralph Ross, *The Motion Picture Guide, 1927–1983*

"An 'A' grade western with a 'C' grade storyline offers action in lieu of a decent plot."—Clive Hirschhorn, *The Universal Story*

"Slickly directed by Green and capably acted by a strong cast, this is a better than average Western."—Phil Hardy, *The Western*

"A very enjoyable minor 'A' Western. The acting is first rate.... Farmer shows a great range of honest emotions, depicting tenderness and toughness, happiness and despair as the story calls.... Green's direction is on target."—Gene Blottner, *Universal Sound Westerns, 1929–1946*

"The comedy is crude but the pace is quick. Farmer is wonderful. Dated and confused, but fun."—Brian Garfield, *Western Films, a Complete Guide*

## *Among the Living* (1941)

Paramount

**Credits:** Director: Stuart Heisler; Associate Producer: Colbert Clark; Screenplay: Lester Cole, Garrett Fort, based on a story by Brian Marlow and Lester Cole; Photography: Theodor Sparkuhl; Music: Gerard Carbonara; Art Direction: Hans Dreier, Haldane Douglas; Editor: Everett Douglas; Sound: Hugo Grenzback, Gene Garvin. B&W, 68 minutes. Filmed April to June 1941.

**Cast:** Albert Dekker (John Raden/Paul Raden); Susan Hayward (Millie Pickens); Harry Carey (Doctor Ben Saunders); Frances Farmer (Elaine Raden); Gordon Jones (Bill Oakley); Jean Phillips (Peggy Nolan); Ernest Whitman (Pompey); Maude Eburne (Mrs. Pickens); Frank M. Thomas (Sheriff); Harlan Briggs (Judge); Archie Twitchell (Tom Reilly); Dorothy Sebastian (Woman in Café); William Stack (Minister). Uncredited: Len Hendry (Clerk); Ella Neal (1st Mill Girl); Catherine Craig (2nd Mill Girl); George Turner (Mill Worker); Harry Tenbrook (Mill Worker); Patti Lacey (Jitterbug Dancer); Roy Lester (Jitterbug Dancer); Ray Hirsch (Jitterbug Dancer); Jane Allen (Jitterbug Dancer); Delmar Watson (Newsboy); Eddy Chandler (Motorcycle Cop); Richard Webb (Hotel Clerk); Mimi Doyle (Telephone Operator); John Kellog (Reporter); Blanche Payson (Woman at Trial); Ethan Laidlaw (Guard); Charles Hamilton (Guard); Frank S. Hagney (Neighbor); Lane Chandler (Neighbor); Lee Shumway (Scissors Grinder); Clarence Muse (Waiter); Rod Cameron (Eddie, Man in Café); Jack Curtis; Abe Dinovitch; Jim Farley; Christian J. Frank; Kit Guard (Mill Worker); James Millican (Townsman); Keith Richards; Bess Wade; Jack Weston.

**VHS/DVD:** Not available in either format.

## Synopsis

The founder of Radentown, Maxim Raden, has died, and his son John returns home with his bride Elaine after an absence of twenty-five years. After Maxim's other son, Paul, escapes from the room where he has been hidden since he was ten, Dr. Ben Saunders reveals the secret of Paul's falsified death certificate to John. Paul comes to Dr. Saunders' office after having strangled Pompey, his keeper, but the doctor is unable to sedate him.

Paul goes to the city and rents a boardinghouse room, and visits John in his hotel room. The brothers fight, and Paul wanders into the River Bottom Café, where he chats with a hostess, Peggy Nolan. Rejected by Peggy, who is jealous of Paul's expressed interest in Millie, who works at the boardinghouse, Paul leaves and waits outside until the café closes. He follows Peggy, then strangles her.

Dr. Saunders talks John into offering a reward for Paul's capture, which excites the townspeople, including Millie. She persuades Paul to go with her back to the Raden house, armed with a pistol. Paul becomes upset when Millie enters his mother's bedroom, and Millie is rescued by Bill Oakley, another boarder. Paul is shot in the scuffle and escapes, but not before knocking out John, who Elaine has convinced to return to Raden house to find evidence of Paul's existence. John is mistaken for his brother and put on trial by the mob at the courthouse. Elaine convinces Saunders to come and confirm John's story of his twin brother, but John runs away. He is followed by the mob, who finds him at his mother's grave, along with the dead body of Paul.

Poster for *Among the Living* (1941).

## Notes

Made before *Badlands of Dakota* but released after it, this well-directed mix of horror and film noir by Stuart Heisler is fascinating when one considers, with hindsight, the private lives of Frances and its star, Albert Dekker. After the mediocrity of direction offered by Alfred E. Green's four titles, it's a relief to see Frances in a film by a director still willing to be innovative, even though she is reduced to playing a supporting and practically mute character. The film is better for Dekker, and particularly as a showcase for newcomer Susan

Hayward, who impresses in the role of a femme fatale—a duplicitous manipulator who betrays friendship for money. While clearly working within a low budget, Heisler offers some trick photography, a point-of-view sequence of panic, angled camerawork, and two whip-pan edits to heighten this tale of twin brothers and murder.

The story begins and ends in a graveyard, the former in daylight and the latter at night. The crowds behind gates and their insensitive commentary are the first expression of the ignorance of the mob, an important component of the narrative, rationalized as it is by the idea that Raden's closing of the town's mill has created social misery.

A storm after the funeral makes an evocative backdrop for the introduction of Paul; and the design of the house, the cellar, and the swamp on the grounds all prefigure similar elements later seen in *Psycho* (1960). Paul in a strait-jacket echoes what will happen to Frances in real life, though his character is presented as a child-like innocent. The one aspect of the scheme devised to hide Paul that remains unexplained is the fact that Dr. Saunders buried another ten-year-old boy in the grave that was said to be Paul's.

Paul's murder of Pompey, though atmospherically shot, presents a moment of incongruity. Heisler employs a torch-lit close-up to show Pompey holding his hands up to his ears as Paul strangles him. Surely one would try to pull the strangling hands away from oneself rather than simply holding one's hands to one's head in dismay?

The exposition of Paul's back story includes two interesting points. First, Paul's father had thrown him across the room when Paul had intervened in a fight between his parents, which might explain Paul's mental illness. Second, Paul continues to hear his mother's screaming in his head, something that will play a pivotal role in the Café scene.

Heisler employs both sight and sound to good effect. The camera reveals visual cues leading to the discovery of Paul at Saunders' office: a broken window; glass on the carpet; a bloodied, extended arm; and Paul asleep on the sofa. Heisler's use of silence when Saunders attempts to drug Paul displays admirable restraint, with Paul's line "It's good outside" generating empathy for Paul as an imprisoned victim (in spite of his murdering Pompey). Paul is like the misunderstood monster in *Frankenstein*, though *Among the Living* avoids that earlier film's climactic mob attack.

Mrs. Pickens is amusingly played by Maude Eburne, leavening the suspense with some much needed comedy relief. The landlady's humor and pretentiousness is demonstrated by what she tells Paul about her previous border, a Frenchman who would kiss her hand. "I always admired a gentleman. But if there's something I hate it's to have somebody slobbering all over me." She also gets a laugh in regards to her house rule of no foul language: "I didn't always tell my roomers this but I had a man here last month, and honest to goodness, the language that that man used would have melted your gold teeth."

Heisler uses both low- and high-angled camerawork for our first sight of Millie at the top of the stairway, as well as Paul's ascent upstairs, and their talking back to Mrs. Pickens from upstairs. Hayward smiles to try to hide Millie's deviousness, but the flick of her hair and its curls on the right side of her forehead attest to her true nature. Millie concealing the money Paul gives her is more evidence of her deceitfulness; however, she scores one good point for trying to direct Paul to a cheaper priced room. It is to her credit that Hayward's likeability makes us warm to Millie, despite her duplicity.

The hotel scene in which Paul visits John features a beautiful close-up of Frances as she stares at Paul, dressed in a negligee and billowy white robe. As in most of her films, Frances' blonde hair here reads as brunette. Her performance is hurt, however, by the dubbed sound of her scream (with the same scream used for Millie at Raden house).

## *Among the Living* (1941)

The scenes of confrontation between the brothers uses trick photography for shots of the twins facing each other, while body doubles are employed for over-the-shoulder shots, with the double's back to the camera. These scenes demonstrate how Dekker believably differentiates the personalities of the brothers, which the screenplay will play with later when Paul's change of clothes and shaving allow for confusion and mistaken identity.

The legless man who drags himself around on a rolling cart selling puppies in the street is an element of gothic guignol that makes for a nice complement to the mentally unbalanced Paul, who conveys his gentle spirit by returning an escaped puppy to the man. The legless man also introduces the debauchery of the River Bottom Café, which is epitomized by the character of Peggy. Platinum blonde, chewing gum, and wearing the same belt and tight skirt as Millie, Peggy also has curls on the right side of her forehead. It helps that Jean Phillips resembles a cheap Jean Harlow. Peggy is a soul sister to Millie, if perhaps not as bright.

The climax of the café scene is a point-of-view anxiety attack in which Paul is overwhelmed by the music, and the sight of customers laughing and wildly jitterbugging. Intercutting shots of Paul holding his hands to his ears—like the strangling victims, Heisler builds this sequence to the climax with fast editing, until Paul runs out. The abandon of

Albert Dekker and a mismatched body double with Frances in *Among the Living* (1941). This posed shot provides a rather poor demonstration of the twin roles Dekker plays in the film.

the crowd is heightened so that they seem a mob, a foreshadowing of their later mass riot and hunt for Paul. Heisler demonstrates further artistry for Paul's chase after Peggy through the streets. The director uses high-angle camerawork and stops the accompanying music when she screams, so that the struggle occurs in silence and is seen in long-shot, far from the camera.

Mrs. Pickens scores another laugh when she compares Bill Oakley, another of her boarders who is interested in Millie, with Paul: "Us Pickens has always had a weakness for refinement." This moment's comedy is underscored by the way Mrs. Pickens gets up and straightens her dress as she walks up the stoop, bent over in pain from her lumbago.

Elaine Raden (Frances) implores Dr. Ben Saunders (Harry Carey) to help her husband John (Albert Dekker) in *Among the Living* (1941).

Another laugh comes from an exchange between John and Saunders over the $5,000 reward to find the killer:

> JOHN: Are you insane?!
> SAUNDERS: Not entirely.

Millie gets a revealing moment when Hayward uses her lower register to seduce Paul into going to Raden house. Heisler provides her a close-up when she asks him, "Don't you like me? Won't you do what I want?" Millie's determination to get the reward comes with her admission, "For five thousand dollars, I'm not afraid of anything. Not even death." It's an ironic statement, as she is unaware that she is being accompanied by the same man the mob is searching for.

Heisler shows the mob's search in small scenes, where any outsider is questionable and logic is jettisoned in favor of impulsivity. This mob mentality is represented by the character of Bill, as leader of the vigilantes, who himself is slugged at one point.

Frances' best scene in the film occurs when Elaine convinces John to go back to the Raden house. Elaine's reasoning is rather flimsy—hoping that Saunders has been careless in leaving behind some evidence of Paul's existence in the cellar room; however, it is enough that John agrees to do as Elaine suggests. Although the scene only gives her a few lines, Frances is direct and truthful in her readings.

While scenes of Millie and Paul walking through the Raden house slows down the film's pacing, and the score makes obvious the contrivance of Millie as a Woman in Peril, the narrative twist of Paul's exposure as a Raden and as the killer redeems the sequence. Her quickness to turn on Paul when he is exposed is the mark of her character, although we do not know whether it is she or Bill who shoots Paul. Heisler's second use of panning transitions connects John's capture with his being taken to the courthouse, punctuated by a series of short reaction shots, including Elaine's. Her beseeching Saunders to rescue John reveals Frances in a rare moment of overacting, as she spits her lines "You're cold, you're heartless" and "You're deliberately committing a murder and all you can say is you're sorry."

The Turner Classic Movie Database reports that the New York Board of Review disapproved the film for general export because it portrayed a lawless lynch mob trying John Raden without proper court proceedings, and it was felt that it could be misused by propagandists in other countries. However, the narrative allows for John to be punished even though he runs away when the attention is on Saunders and not him. This scene also features a comic moment when first, Bill puts his hand on Millie's knee; second, Millie puts her hand on his to show their united front against John; and third, Mrs. Pickens pulls Millie's skirt over her daughter's exposed knee.

The end of the film has John tripping over Paul at their mother's gravesite, with Paul presumably dead from the gunshot. Although no words are spoken, it is the sight of Paul that frees John from the mob. Paul's death this way circumvents justice for Pompey and Peggy, since he cannot be prosecuted for their murders, but it also deprives Millie, Bill, and the mob of the reward money. However, what Paul's death means to John remains unknown, since twins are known to have a psychic bond. He is left comforted by Elaine, but one wonders whether Saunders' comment about insanity running in the family will eventually ring true for John. The film's title implies that Paul's imprisonment had been a form of death, and that his freedom had placed him among the living—with his real death inevitable, given the town's mob rule. However, John can also be considered one among the living, with his inherited potential for violence. John, then, could be a new threat among those around him, with the urge to violence now blossoming within him.

The casting of twenty-seven-year-old Frances in a thankless role, and the twenty-four-year-old Hayward in the larger female role, a role that Frances could have played, is indicative of Paramount's agenda. By promoting a less experienced and younger actress over a celebrated but older actress with a bad reputation, the studio showed who it thought had more of a future with them. Ironically, in spite of the good notices Hayward's performance earned her, Paramount would only cast her in supporting parts as follow-up, and she would have to go elsewhere to obtain leading roles. She would go on to work two more times with Stuart Heisler. Heisler was a former editor who had begun directing for Paramount in 1936. His prior title had been the horror film *The Monster and the Girl* (1941). Associate producer Colbert Clark had also been associate producer on *World Premiere*, which was also produced by this film's uncredited producer, Sol C. Seigel. Seigel's prior title had been the Paramount comedy *Glamour Boy* (1941).

Albert Dekker was best known for playing the mad scientist title role in Paramount's horror film *Dr. Cyclops* (1940), and he had last been seen in a supporting role in the MGM western *Honky Tonk* (1941). Although he would go on acting in films until *The Wild Bunch* (1969), Dekker's bizarre death the year before that picture's release became notorious via the coverage it received in Kenneth Anger's book *Hollywood Babylon*. The Turner Classic Movie Database says that he died by accidentally asphyxiating himself while attempting autoerotic asphyxia, and that he was found nude, with sexually explicit writings lipsticked on his body. Anger, who calls Dekker "Mr. Kink of All Time," reports that he was dressed in women's silk lingerie and had carefully printed his final unfavorable notice on his body in crimson lipstick. On his *Find a Death* website, Scott Michaels lists the words that were found on Dekker's body. In opposition to Anger's claim, Michaels says the words were not a review but sexually explicit terms written in red lipstick. Dekker had played the head doctor of a hospital in *Suddenly, Last Summer* (1959), which appears to be the closest he ever came to a real asylum. The nature of his death led to rumors that he was a closet homosexual leading a double life, in spite of the fact that he was engaged to be married when he died.

Brooklyn-born Susan Hayward was a former model who had come to Hollywood to test for Scarlett O'Hara in *Gone with the Wind* under her real name Edythe Marriner.

Susan Hayward in a publicity portrait for *Among the Living* (1941).

After playing bit parts at Warner Bros., she moved to Paramount to play supporting roles, including a prominent one in *Beau Geste* (1939). Her role prior to *Among the Living* had been in support of Judy Canova in the musical comedy *Sis Hopkins* (1941) for Republic Pictures. Hayward would go on to win the Best Actress Academy Award for *I Want to Live!* (1958).

## Release

December 19, 1941, with the tagline, "Monster in human guise! What weird fascination has this maniac for women?"

## Reviews

"A good B.... Heisler kept the story moving at a good pace and didn't inject any unnecessary hokum.... Farmer has extremely little to do and is wasted."—*Variety*, September 3, 1941

"One of the dreariest films of the year [featuring] an outstandingly bad performance by Albert Dekker.... Susan Hayward, Frances Farmer and Harry Carey all look equally unhappy in it."—*The New York Times*, December 13, 1941

"Decker does very well with the dual role in this moody, unusual B picture, but the real interest is generated by the presence of Hayward and Farmer. The brilliant photography by Theodor Sparkuhl is a very early example of the film noir chiaroscuro style."—Jay Robert Nash and Stanley Ralph Ross, *The Motion Picture Guide, 1927–1983*

"[W]avers between the noir tradition and Southern Gothic ... an indication of the noir film's debt to German Expressionism and French poetic realism."—Alain Silver and Elizabeth Ward, *Film Noir*

"A collector's item for connoisseurs of off-beat thrillers ... a low-budget item which achieved quite a reputation in its day for unusual suspense elements.... Susan Hayward show[s] vivid dramatic quality for the first time."—John Douglas Eames, *The Paramount Story*

"A grim little B picture which [Frances] made to fulfill the final obligation of her Paramount contract."—William Arnold, *Shadowland*

"A superior psychological melodrama—head and shoulders above most of the filler shows ground out by Hollywood.... Susan Hayward is especially good."—*Los Angeles Herald Tribune* (date unknown)

# *Son of Fury: The Story of Benjamin Blake* (1942)

(aka *Benjamin Blake*)
Twentieth Century–Fox

**Credits:** Director: John Cromwell; Producer: Darryl F. Zanuck; Associate Producer: William Perlberg; Screenplay: Philip Dunne, based on the novel *Benjamin Blake* by Edison Marshall; Photography: Arthur Miller; Music: Alfred Newman; Art Direction: Richard Day, James Basevi; Set Decorations: Thomas Little; Editor: Walter Thompson; Costumes: Gwen Wakeling; Makeup: Guy Pearce; Sound: Eugene Grossman, Roger Heman. B&W, 98 minutes. Filmed September 4 to November 15, 1941, in Busch Gardens, Pasadena, California.

**Cast:** Tyrone Power (Benjamin Blake); Gene Tierney (Eve); George Sanders (Sir Arthur Blake); Frances Farmer (Isabel); Elsa Lanchester (Bristol Isabel); Kay Johnson (Helena); John Carradine (Caleb Green); Harry Davenport (Amos Kidder); Dudley Digges (Pratt); Master Roddy McDowall (Benjamin as a Boy); Halliwell Hobbes (Purdy); Marten Lamont (Kenneth Hobart); Arthur Hohl (Captain Greenough); Pedro De Cordoba (Feenou); Heather Thatcher (Maggie Martin); Lester Matthews (Prosecutor); Charles Irwin (Captain); Dennis Hoey (Lord Tarrant); Robert Greig (Judge); Ray Mala (Marnoa); Clifford Severn (Paddy). Uncredited: Besmark Auelua (Native); Louis Bacigalupi (Fighter); Elena Beattie (Native); Matthew Boulton (Jury Foreman); Odetta Bray (Native); Billy Bunkley (Native); Leonard Carey (Pale Tom); Sonny Chore (Native); David Clyde (Shellback); Harry Cording (Turnkey); James Craven (Guard); Romere Darling (Native); Rosita Delva (Native); Ethel Griffies (Matron); Vic Groves (Native); Keith Hitchcock (Crier); Olaf Hytten (Court Clerk); Charles Irwin (Captain); Mailoa Kalili (Native); Billie Lane (Native); Thomas Louden (Court Clerk); Mae Marsh (Mrs. Purdy); Tani Marsh (Native); Cyril McLaglen (Grimes); Clive Morgan (Lord St. George); Agnes O'Laughlin (Native); Patsy Perrin (Native); George Piltz (Native); Lucille Porcett (Native); Marjorie Raymond (Native); Rodd Redwing (Native); Leina Ala Reid (Native); Ignacio Saenz (Native Boy); Kay Adell Stork (Native/Gene Tierney Stunt Double); Harry Tauvera (Native); Cyril Thornton; David Thursby (Wardman); George Urchell (Native); Vanita Wade (Native); Dorothy Ward (Native); Sethma Williams (Native); Rosemary Wilson (Native).

**VHS/DVD:** DVD released by 20th Century–Fox on May 1, 2007.

## *Synopsis*

In Bristol, England, during the reign of King George III, Sir Arthur Blake of Bleetholm Manor learns he has a nephew, Benjamin, being raised by the gunsmith Amos Kidder. The boy is the son of Arthur's brother, Sir Godfrey, who was the manor's baronet but died in India. It is believed that Benjamin is illegitimate since Godfrey did not marry the boy's mother—Amos' daughter, Bessie Kidder. Arthur takes Benjamin and makes him a bonded servant, mistreating him and causing the boy to hate his uncle. The boy grows into manhood as a groomsman and falls in love with Arthur's daughter (and his own cousin), Isabel. When Arthur overhears Benjamin propose to Isabel, he beats him. Benjamin comes back later but is caught by his uncle; he escapes, stowing away onboard the ship *Tropic Star*.

Benjamin is befriended by a sailor, Caleb Green, who tells him about a tropical island where they can find a fortune in pearls. Altering the ship's course, the pair desert and swim to the island, befriending the natives. Benjamin lives with the native girl Eve but yearns to go back to England to claim his birthright. When a Dutch ship appears, Benjamin returns to Britain and employs the solicitor Bartholomew Pratt, paying him with pearls. Benjamin visits Isabel and tells her where he is staying while awaiting the results of Pratt's investigation. Arthur arrives with the king's soldiers, and Benjamin is brought to trial for breaking bondage and assault with intent to kill his master. Found guilty, the sentencing is interrupted by Pratt, who reveals that Godfrey and Bessie actually were married, which makes Benjamin the rightful heir of Bleetholm and therefore not guilty of any crime. Released, he goes to the manor house, where he learns of Isabel's treachery. Benjamin evicts his relatives, deeds the manor house to Amos, and orders that the land be divided among the tenant farmers. He then returns to Eve's island to be with her.

## Notes

Since it features Frances' last appearance in an "A"-budgeted picture before her troubles with the law began, it's a pity that this historical adventure is routine, and that she once again plays merely a supporting role. And director John Cromwell provides far more favorable coverage to Gene Tierney and even Elsa Lanchester (in her one scene) than to Frances.

Even so, Frances delivers an arch performance, using breathy intonation to portray the vanity and duplicity of her character. Although she and Tyrone Power would seem to be the perfect match of physical beauty, Cromwell undercuts their romance with shadowy lighting and by emphasizing Farmer's lack of height (at five-foot-six, compared to the five-foot-eleven Power, and especially the six-foot-three George Sanders). By contrast, Tierney and Power are presented as the more idealized partnership (the fact of both Power and Tierney being Fox contract players perhaps was a factor). However, even photographed by a director who favors less attractive women, the twenty-eight-year-old Frances still remains a stunning visual subject.

The opening scene is notable for seeing George Sanders stripped to the waist as Arthur fights him and wins. Unlike Howard Hawks in *Come and Get It*, and Alfred E. Green in *Ride a Crooked Mile*, *South of Pago Pago* and *Flowing Gold*, Cromwell doesn't linger over this pugilistic display, nor does he include a second fighting sequence—until the climax.

The young Benjamin fighting Paddy, a boy older and bigger than he, indicates Benjamin's bravery and pride, and also prefigures his adult battle with Arthur, who is taller than he. Benjamin's claim to "never submit" demonstrates stubbornness and determination, for which he will be ultimately rewarded. Paddy hitting Benjamin for accidentally dropping the horses' saddle into the mud is unreasonable but evidence of the cruelty and humiliation of Benjamin's station.

Frances' first scene as Isabel shows her laughing with Hobart, with her face revealed in a similar manner to her introduction in *South of Pago Pago*. In her subsequent scene with Power's Benjamin she employs archness for both flirtation and haughtiness, capped by an English accent. Her hair color here is more blonde than brunette, with her long tresses done up in ringlets. The sequence features an amusing exchange in which Isabel tries to make Benjamin jealous over her friendship with Hobart:

> ISABEL: He's asked for my hand.
> BENJAMIN: Well, it's only to be expected. I've noticed him handling it at every opportunity.

His failing to rise to the bait inflames her anger, and she throws down the jacket he reaches for. She then stands on it to stop him from retrieving it, and pulls his hair to get his attention. But he simply pushes her off it. Farmer makes Isabel's anger funny with her delivery of "You lout—you impertinent, unruly clod." Her attempt to strike him with her riding crop, however, shows how vicious and dangerous Isabel can be, and his forcing her hand

Benjamin Blake (Tyrone Power) stops Isabel (Frances) from striking him with a riding crop in *Son of Fury* (1942).

down shows his greater physical and moral strength. These acts of violence leading to an embrace show how unhealthy their relationship is, and also introduces the perversity that is prevalent in the narrative. (Benjamin and his cousin having a romantic relationship is only perverse by modern standards, since this kind of union was more acceptable for the period).

The masked ball furthers this element of perversity, since the eye masks conceal the beautiful faces of Frances and Tyrone Power. Benjamin posing as a gentleman is believable because Power looks so natural in gentlemen's clothes (though Isabel failing to recognize him behind his mask is less believable).

The masked ball sequence, particularly with its opening musical cue, recalls an incident recounted in William Arnold's book *Shadowland*. At Christmas 1946-1947, during Frances' commitment, she was taken out of her ward and led to the main dining hall where *Son of Fury* was screened. Allegedly, upon seeing herself, Frances began screaming and was put under restraint and carried back to the violent ward. Arnold relays the grotesque detail of the staff and patients "grinning and holding back giggles" as Frances arrived, presumably complicit in their anticipation of her humiliation. This anecdote is not mentioned in the autobiography *Will There Really Be a Morning?*, though the made-for-TV movie included it (but replaced the title with *Come and Get It*, with the same effect).

Isabel's high-waisted and shimmery gown may have been designed for period accuracy—or to conceal Farmer's weight, since all her subsequent gowns are equally high-waisted. The love scene between Isabel and Benjamin employs odd lighting and staging, with Frances laying down at an unflattering angle and Power's face in profile, almost in darkness. However, Cromwell gives her a beautiful reaction shot upon Arthur's entrance.

The subsequent fight between Arthur and Benjamin demonstrates Arthur's underhandedness, as he takes Benjamin unawares when Benjamin is still removing his clothes. This will make Arthur deserving of his downfall, much as Benjamin will be worthy of his reward.

Elsa Lanchester's scene with Power, as a maiden at the Bulls Head Grog Shop who hides him, is a fascinating one in terms of the remarkable range it allows the actress to express. It is also one of the few sequences in the film where the music score actually adds to the atmosphere rather than upstaging and overwhelming it. In this scene, Lanchester conveys quirkiness, humor, vulnerability and strength, as well as being photographed as a beauty. That the character's name is also Isabel is ironic, given that in this one scene the actress has more to play than in Frances' four scenes. The scene also has a funny cap when this Isabel is seen walking in the street with Benjamin by Isabel's neighbor Maggie Martin. To Maggie's "Who were he?" Isabel replies, "The Duke of Roehampton," and Maggie's arm, which had been resting on the windowsill, slips off in shocked reaction.

The ship *Tropic Star* recalls the ships from *Ebb Tide* and *South of Pago Pago*, although the shots of it, and those of swimming whales and dolphins, are clearly stock footage. Medium shots of the ship employed during dialogue scenes are clearly studio-set, using rear projection. And Cromwell's use of a map to show the ship's movement is a conventional technique.

The debtor's brand worn by Caleb creates an expectation of Caleb being a duplicitous criminal. Rather, Caleb turns out to be a softie who informs Benjamin about the pearls on the island in order to share the wealth (although he does need help to dive for them). And Caleb ultimately stays on the island when Benjamin leaves to return to England.

The plot point of pearl diving recalls the similar scenario of *South of Pago Pago*, and the island locale was apparently the aspect that appealed to producer Darryl F. Zanuck. The *Hollywood Reporter* noted that these sequences in the film had been expanded at the request of Zanuck to satisfy the public's supposed "increasing penchant for films with a South Seas locale."

Cromwell creates tension during the arrival of Benjamin and Caleb on the beach via the observing natives, although this is dissipated somewhat by Cromwell repeating the same shot of an approaching native three times to indicate three different natives. However, Benjamin's whip scars help form a bond with the natives, since presumably the natives had been whipped by the Spaniards who previously colonized the island.

Gene Tierney's native dance, aided by a throbbing drumbeat, is an evocative and seductive introduction to the native girl that Benjamin will fall in love with. Benjamin living with Eve after he kisses her adds a rather racy element, although the Turner Classic Movie database provides another take on it. Apparently, the Hays Office objected to the relationship, considering it was one of "illicit sex," and demanded that it be firmly established that Benjamin and Eve considered themselves officially married according to native customs. This notion invalidates Benjamin's engagement to Isabel, which the narrative will conveniently nullify when he learns of her treachery. One can consider Benjamin an opportunist, since he "marries" Eve when he thinks he will not leave the island, and then resumes his engagement to Isabel when he returns to England.

While we can rationalize Benjamin's need for Eve to learn English (rather than he

Native girl Eve (Gene Tierney) intrigues British refugee Benjamin Blake (Tyrone Power) in *Son of Fury* (1942).

learning her language) as a convenience for the viewer (so we can understand what they are saying), Caleb learning the island language casts him in a more accommodating light. We do hear Benjamin speak some native words when he leaves the island, although he is still not as fluent as Caleb. Benjamin making knives and forks for the natives is his own attempt at colonization, but results in Eve considering herself "stupid" for not being able to use them (and for her difficulty learning English). Eve's repeated self-description as stupid is indicative of her as an idealized woman, since she tells Benjamin, "I can only be happy if you are happy," when she sees his sadness about having to stay on the island. Eve (that name is no coincidence) is also self-sacrificing, willing to let Benjamin leave and not wanting him to stay with her out of pity—an advanced concept for someone presented as a simple native girl. Eve is both childlike innocent and wise, with a mystical touch thrown in (since the Dutch ship arrives after she has asked the sea to bring Benjamin a way off the island). She is also positioned as the moral opposite of Isabel, which makes his return to her inevitable.

The TCM notes point out that the film altered the original ending of the novel on which the screenplay was based. The book had Eve committing suicide and Benjamin staying in England with Isabel. Twentieth Century–Fox changed this supposedly to please the public, which would not want Benjamin to desert Eve. A *New York Times* article dated

October 19, 1941, also reported on this change. It stated that the alteration had been made in response to public outcry over the death of Tyrone Power's character in *Blood and Sand* (1941), after which Darryl F. Zanuck had declared that no other 20th Century–Fox films in 1941-42 would have sad endings. It is interesting that Zanuck would consider Benjamin staying with Isabel as a sad ending, though presumably this idea alludes to the narrative positioning her as the bad woman compared to Eve's good one.

Cromwell attempts to give Benjamin's leaving the island a visual metaphor in Eve dropping the flower she had worn in her hair into the sea, with the flower floating away. However, the image lacks the lasting coverage to create resonance. Benjamin's appearance with a beard suggests the passage of time during the voyage, and it is unusual to see Power wearing a beard, which seemingly distracts from his face.

The scene between Isabel and Arthur includes a perverse touch in the way he fingers the pearl necklace she wears, with the suggestion of incest between them. Isabel's speech to him is Frances' only sustained piece of dialogue, and she delivers it with faultless conviction, devoid of her previous archness. In response to Arthur's threat to tell Benjamin that it was she who told where to find him, she replies:

> Why do you think he came back? For revenge? No. For me. He loves me. All his life he's worshipped me. He'll do anything I ask him. Believe anything I tell him. Even if you were to swear to him on a Bible—

Her last line dies on her lips when she looks into the mirror and sees the eavesdropping Benjamin.

The length of the fight between Benjamin and Arthur is a surprise, if a disappointing one, and creates an expectation that one of them will be killed. This is because Benjamin is prepared to walk away from Arthur after having knocked him down, but Arthur returns to fight a second time. (This recalls Benjamin returning to fight Arthur a second time in the first half of the film.) The expectation of death is not met, as Arthur is knocked unconscious. Additionally, after all the effort Benjamin has made to claim his birthright, it seems odd that he ultimately abandons it to return to the island and Eve. However, as stated, this was the ending Zanuck asked for.

Producer Zanuck was the chief of production at 20th Century–Fox since 1935 and would continue to be so until 1956, when he became an independent producer. He was known as a populist studio head who knew what audiences wanted; and although he concentrated on profit and entertainment, he would also make pictures with ethical concerns.

Associate producer William Perlberg had been producing at Columbia Pictures, and joined Fox to make the comedy *Charley's Aunt* (1941). His prior title was the romance *Remember the Day* (1942).

The TCM notes state that the film's time period was set later than in the book in order to avoid the historically accurate need for wigs, since Zanuck thought they had proved to be a detriment to every picture in which they had been used. In his book on the films on John Carradine, Tom Weaver lists the film's budget as two million dollars.

Frances, borrowed from Paramount, was fourth choice for the part of Isabel. Ida Lupino was the studio's first choice, but she was cast in Fox's *Moontide* (1942) instead. Maureen O'Hara was chosen next, but she fell ill after requiring an emergency appendectomy. Twenty-year-old Fox ingénue Cobina Wright, Jr., was then cast and supposedly began filming. Both Jay Robert Nash and Stanley Ralph Ross, in *The Motion Picture Guild, 1927–1983*, and Weaver claim that Wright can be seen in some long shots, but she withdrew from production after contracting a throat infection.

**Sir Arthur Blake (George Sanders), with his wife Helena (Kay Johnson), in *Son of Fury* (1942).**

Nash and Ross also report that Virginia Gilmore, who was first cast as Helena Blake, can also be seen in some long shots. Gilmore was replaced by Kay Johnson, who was married to the director. While it is not known why Gilmore was replaced, the fact that she had parts in six other films released in 1942 is evidence that she was not devoid of work opportunities.

In her autobiography *Self-Portrait*, Gene Tierney commented on Frances, although Tierney relies on inaccurate hearsay rather than first-hand observation: "It was during the making of *Son of Fury* that I had my first exposure to mental illness—someone else's.... Frances had thrown a brush at one of the hairdressers, had a tantrum on the set, and literally snarled at people." Tierney would herself be repeatedly institutionalized in the 1950s for her own mental illness, receiving shock treatment like Frances. Her daughter Daria being born with mental retardation after the pregnant Tierney had contracted measles from a fan is said to be the source of her depression.

In the WRTV special on Frances, *Indiana Epilogue*, Conrad Lane speaks of her performance in *Son of Fury*, stating that watching Frances in it enables one to see her troubles ahead. While this claim may seem reasonable in hindsight, it remains a spurious one, given that Frances is playing a character and not herself. In the special, Lane says, "All the tensions really show up. All the nervousness. Sometimes on camera she appears as though she's going to fly to pieces almost any minute, so it's not too hard to see that in the months ahead that she's going to explode, which is what she did."

John Cromwell had directed Bette Davis in her break-out role *Of Human Bondage* (1934), and the romantic adventures *The Prisoner of Zenda* (1937) and *Algiers* (1938). Having come from Broadway, Cromwell's work with actors would earn various thespians ten Academy Award nominations. His prior picture to *Son of Fury* had been the United Artists World War II drama *So Ends Our Night* (1941). Cromwell would go on to direct the film Frances might have made, *The Enchanted Cottage* (1945). After being blacklisted in the early 1950s, he came back to make *The Goddess* (1958), the tale of a Marilyn Monroe type who suffered a mental breakdown.

After playing minor roles, Tyrone Power emerged as a star in Fox's drama *Lloyds of London* (1936) and was signed to a contract with the studio that would last for twenty years. He had the romantic appeal of both lover and dashing action hero, and was comfortable in both period and contemporary roles. Power's prior film had been the aviation drama *A Yank in the R.A.F.* (1941). He would soon begin to seek out acting challenges so as to be seen as more than just a beautiful man, and enjoy an extended career on Broadway. However, Power would die after filming a dueling scene (coincidently, with his *Son of Fury* antagonist George Sanders) in the Biblical epic *Solomon and Sheba* (1959).

Gene Tierney had signed with Fox in 1940 but wouldn't achieve screen immortality until she made the film noir classics *Laura* (1944) and *Leave Her to Heaven* (1946), for which she would be nominated for the Best Actress Academy Award. Her exotic looks saw her cast as an African mystery woman in *Sundown* (1941), her prior title to *Son of Fury*.

George Sanders had played supporting roles (usually as a suave English scoundrel) in titles like Alfred Hitchcock's *Rebecca* (1940), and leading roles in the Falcon and the Saint film series. He would go on to win the Best Supporting Actor Academy Award for *All About Eve* (1950).

*Son of Fury* would be remade by Fox as *Treasure of the Golden Condor* (1953). It would be directed by Delmer Daves and star Cornel Wilde, Constance Smith, George Macready, and Anne Bancroft in the Isabel role.

## Release

January 29, 1942, with the tagline, "Blood Swooping Tremendous Adventure!"

## Reviews

"Sound, compelling entertainment.... Farmer suits her role well and gives it as much warmth as could be permitted."—*Variety*, January 7, 1942

"Another juvenile charmer with a great deal more brawn than brain.... Farmer appears in a lesser role."—Bosley Crowther, the *New York Times*, January 30, 1942

"Employing all the usual island romance clichés, [the film] is a solid escapist adventure. Adroit direction of Cromwell, and the all-star cast never fails to hold one's attention."—Jay Robert Nash and Stanley Ralph Ross, *The Motion Picture Guide, 1927–1983*

"[A]n almost perfect screen entertainment, with something going for it in every department.... [Frances] turned in a mature and masterfully restrained performance."—William Arnold, *Shadowland*

"One of the richer more robust adventure-dramas from Fox's golden age." — Tom Weaver, *John Carradine: The Films*

"An almost perfect entertainment, with everyone giving their best.... Cromwell's direction discreet yet never showy keeping the narrative flowing beautifully." — Charles Higham and Joel Greenberg, *Hollywood in the Forties*

"Produced on a lavish scale, this is a romantic adventure-drama of box office merit." — *Variety*

"Well-written and played, a top-notch adventure story." — Tony Thomas and Aubrey Solomon, *The Films of 20th Century–Fox: A Pictorial History*

# *No Escape* (1943)

(aka *I Escaped from the Gestapo*; *The Escape*)
Monogram

**Credits:** Director: Harold Young; Producer: Maurice King; Associate Producer: Franklin King; Screenplay: Henry Blankfort and Wallace Sullivan, based on an original story by Henry Blankfort; Photography: Ira H. Morgan; Production Manager: George Moskov; Editor: S. K. Winston; Sound: Tom Lambert; Art Director: Dave Milton; Set Dresser: Vin Taylor; Music: W. Franke Harling. B&W, 75 minutes. Filmed January 1943.

**Song:** "The Spring Song" (Felix Mendelssohn).

**Cast:** Dean Jagger (Torgut Lane); John Carradine (Martin); Mary Brian (Helen); Bill Henry (Gordon); Sidney Blackmer (Bergen); Ian Keith (Gerard); Anthony Ward (Lokin); Billy Marshall (Lunt); Ed Keane (Domack); Norman Willis (FBI Chief Rodt); Peter Dunne (Olin); Spanky McFarland (Billy); Charles Waggenheim (Hart). Uncredited: Frances Farmer; Arthur Gardner (FBI Man); Greta Granstedt (Hilda); Jack Mulhall (Police Dispatcher); "Snub" Pollard (Thief on Train); Billy Vine (One-Armed Sailor); Charles Williams (Secretary).

**VHS/DVD:** Not available in either format.

## Synopsis

Counterfeiter Torgen Lane is rescued from prison by German saboteurs and kept in locked quarters at the Los Angeles Joyland Arcade amusement park. Lane agrees to make counterfeit bills and gold bonds, which will disrupt the Allied war effort, since the Germans hold his mother hostage. Lane becomes intrigued by the automaton voice recorder Helen, who works at a booth in the arcade but is not involved with the spies. A young German, Gordon, joins the group and is assigned the job of guarding Lane. Gordon is also interested in Helen, and Lane arranges a date between the two, encouraging the boy to go after Helen, who has left her job to go to Seattle. Gordon goes, taking some of the counterfeit money, but is killed on the train on the way.

A passenger takes Gordon's money but is caught by the FBI, who recognizes the bills as fake. Lane has engraved the location of the spies on the bills, which leads the FBI to

John Carradine stands, second from left, among a group of conspirators that include Ed Keane (second from right) and other unidentified actors in this lobby card for *No Escape*, aka *I Escaped from the Gestapo* (1943).

their hideaway, saving Lane and his mother. Helen is also saved, since she had returned to find Lane to tell him that she loves him. Lane eludes his rescuers and goes to an oil refinery, which is to be blown up by the saboteurs. With the FBI's help, Lane thwarts the plan. He is taken back to prison by the FBI, although it is intimated that his actions in capturing the spies will shorten his sentence. Helen promises to wait for him.

## Notes

While the low budget of this World War II espionage drama is readily apparent, director Harold Young employs economic technique, innovative visuals and a judicious use of music to alleviate its shortcomings. Though pacing flags when the narrative focuses on the secondary love triangle, the screenplay admirably conceals the Nazi connection until halfway into the film.

Reportedly completing only one day of shooting before walking out, Frances is seen only in a montage, although even then it is hard to tell if the woman is really her. Looking beautiful in her final screen appearance for fifteen years, it is impossible to judge her performance based on a one-second shot. However, the role she might have played, as enacted by Mary Brian, was yet another supporting part.

Director Young frequently circumvents his budgetary restrictions with clever visuals. The swastika under the opening credits suggests either locale or political agenda, while an animated octopus sitting over Europe has tentacles reaching out to the United States. Lane's prison breakout is suggested with minimal effects and darkness to conceal the lack of extras in the cast: a siren, a smoking whistle, and gunfire. (The prison locale, and the escape, prefigure Frances' own experience with imprisonment.)

Gerard toying with a baby turtle, turning it over onto its back so it is helpless, is a sign of his perversity, his need for control, and presumably what he hopes to do with the country. Thankfully, the turtle escapes any real harm (as does Lane's kitten later), with the animals' presence adding narrative interest. The turtle torture is commented on by Lane when he says, "Why don't you pick on someone your own size?"

Lane's exit from the house is presented with a man in profile in darkness exhaling the smoke of a cigarette in the foreground, which confirms Lane as a man under guard. While it is unclear who it is that is left unconscious on a train track, the act of being run over is suggested by the light of the approaching train. Lane comments on this murder with a clever line when he says, "What do you fellas use for a heart? I remember. Brains."

The spies allow Lane to take in a kitten that he finds. The kitten will provide an excuse for Lane to talk aloud, before Gordon arrives, and also presents Lane as a soft character. This softness contrasts with the aggressive advances he makes towards Helen, but remains in keeping with Lane's ineffectualness during the climactic fights.

Frances' replacement as Helen, Mary Brian, was thirty-six at the time of filming, as opposed to Frances' age of twenty-nine. Helen, while working in the seedy arcade (meeting young soldiers who make voice recordings), also studies to become a ship welder, a sign of the wartime necessity for females to take on male jobs while the men are away fighting. Helen as a potential welder adds an element of masculinity to her character, which matches Brian's persona. Frances' voice and personality also possessed a masculine character, a factor utilized in some of her roles, although her great beauty counterbalanced it.

For the arrival of Gordon, Young intercuts between Martin and Bergen on the beach, the submarine that drops Gordon off, and Lane searching the hideout's office. This crosscutting creates suspense in regards to whether Lane will be caught as he snoops, with the horror movie device of the slowly opening door thrown in as a kicker. The cliché earns a laugh when the kitten strolls across the threshold. The oil refinery blueprint that Lane finds in the office is a plot point that doesn't come to full fruition until the climax, with the spies' major plan seemingly being to flood the American market with fake money to cause inflation and replicate the economic conditions that allowed the Nazis to rise to power the way they did in Germany. Mist mixes with the darkness to add mystery to the scene of the emerging submarine, with Gordon and two other men stripping down to their underpants giving the sequence an odd—and homoerotic—touch.

Lane calling Gordon a "fascist" and making reference to Goerring is the narrative's first overt connection to Nazis, with Gordon's formal mode of speech indicating someone whose native language is not English. When Gordon tells Lane, "I'll not talk with you," Lane replies, "That's alright with me, I'm used to talking to myself." This references Lane doing exactly that, which is also the mark of an unimaginative screenwriter struggling to create interactive dialogue.

Lane attempts to alert Helen about the spies by using the old distraction ploy, in which he drops something that she and Gordon pick up, allowing him time to write "Spies here" on a note for her. However, this ploy doesn't play out as expected, when she fails to take the note because he overplays his romantic advance by touching her face as he tells her, "This is for your scrapbook." Her reply of "I'm afraid my scrapbook is too small—the size of your head, you know" is a rejection of his advance. Lane rips up the note when the men arrive to take him back, and even Lane subsequently passing the pieces to Helen doesn't work, since she throws them away out of hand.

Helen's plan to go to Seattle seems a deliberate reference to Frances' casting, since we know Seattle to be her home town. It's also hard to overlook the parallel of Helen not staying in Seattle with Frances' own experiences there; Frances probably shouldn't have stayed after she left Hollywood, since it was the Seattle connection with her mother that would result in her commitment. This isn't to say that Helen has it easy, either, when she returns for Lane, since she is caught with the spies alongside him and threatened with murder. Even the final remark Lane makes to her at the end of the film suggests that life with Lane is not going to be an idealized one, with the additional implication made that she is prepared to sacrifice her new career for him.

Mendelssohn's "The Spring Song" is heard on the arcade jukebox and identified by Gordon as forbidden music (since the German Mendelssohn was Jewish), although his liking it prefigures his abandonment of his duties, which will be punished by death. The music is used to soften Helen when Gordon romances her.

Lane arranging for the date between Gordon and Helen can be interpreted as part of a bigger scheme to manipulate the German, but on face value it reads as a way for him to deflect his own supposed feelings for her. Young includes a montage of Gordon and Helen dancing to the Mendelson song, with shadowed violin players and a pianist, and perhaps the funniest line in the film comes when Gordon tells Lane after the date, "For the first time in ten years I forgot about the New Order."

The deflected romance of Helen and Lane continues with Gordon's confession to Lane that "all she did was ask questions about you," with Lane replying, "That was to make you jealous." Although Gordon doesn't tell Lane how he and Helen danced (which makes the "all she did" part a white lie), if we believe Lane's rationalization for Helen's attitude, it makes her appear as self-denying as Lane. Presumably the hostility between Helen and Lane is supposed to be that of the squabbling couple who fight to hide their true romantic feelings and who will inevitably fall into a clinch, an idea earlier encapsulated by Frances and John Garfield in *Flowing Gold*. However, the casting of Brian as Helen and Dean Jagger as Lane, who is more uncle than husband material, works against this notion.

Gordon's death scene provides the montage in which Frances purportedly appears. The setup for his death is interesting, since although Gordon has run away with some of the fake money, the guilt over his past is what entraps him. The one-armed sailor on the train gives a speech that Gordon overhears: "One of these days I'll run into one of these Nazis. I'll know him. I'd give my other arm right now to meet one. Butchers, that's what they are." Young then lays the groundwork for the thief sitting next to Gordon to see the bag of money in order for him to take it later.

The Sailor's speech makes Gordon retreat to the observation deck at the end of the train, prefiguring the faked suicide in *Double Indemnity* (1944), with Young combining newsreel footage of Hitler and war bombing with staged vignettes for the montage. Again, minimalist action conveys suggested violence, with a Nazi smashing the window of a Jewish shop and people being attacked by soldiers. A peasant woman wearing a shawl (clearly not Frances) reacts to a soldier thrusting a bayonet, and then Frances is seen lying on the ground with the shawl fallen aside. Presumably we are supposed to associate her with the peasant woman, although she does not resemble her, and Frances' scream is heard as we see the soldier aiming his bayonet at her.

What makes this footage so perplexing is the idea that she would have filmed it while she was playing Helen. We know that she wasn't brought back to shoot it after she had been replaced by Brian, so it is apparent that there is supposed to be a connection between this persecuted peasant woman and the character of Helen. Clearly, with Brian's casting, Frances is not playing Helen, so perhaps we are meant to think that this is Gordon's projected fear of Helen's murder. If so, then this dilutes his guilt.

Young repeats the word "butcher" on the soundtrack, which becomes a repeated "You're a butcher," with the image of the sailor walking towards Gordon. This approaching figure makes Gordon fall back from the deck and into the path of another train. Young uses shots of hands exchanging money to introduce the thief paying for a drink at a bar, with the barman looking questioningly at the note and nodding to someone off-camera, and then a policeman placing his hand on the thief's shoulder.

The narrative moves to San Francisco, where Gordon was supposedly headed with the counterfeited money. Whether or not he intended to continue to Seattle to follow Helen is unclear, although the spies' new plan to hold down production at the Western Utilities refinery in order to send a formula to Germany is more plot obtuseness. This scene ends with a clever visual transition when Domack lights a cigar, saying, "I'm not worried about the FBI, not worried at all." Next we see the thief from the train lighting a cigarette as he is questioned by the FBI.

Lane's final line to Helen, in response to her "I'll be waiting," is, "If you're even thinking of standing me up, I'll break your neck." This strange comment continues Lane's series of inappropriately aggressive romantic overtures, which had previously put Helen off, and should be a warning not to wait for this abusive jerk. However, the music cues indicate that we are supposed to find such a remark charming. We can only hope that his successful mission to sabotage the saboteurs didn't abbreviate his prison sentence as much as the narrative implies.

In his book on John Carradine, Tom Weaver says that the film's budget was between $20,000 and $25,000, and quotes from assistant director Arthur Gardner and Carradine himself about Frances. Gardner tells how he went to get her one day, as she was not on the set at 6:30 A.M. for make-up, and had to get her out of bed and dressed. Gardner concludes that Frances might have been an early user of "something or other." Carradine remembers shooting a scene with her when she started singing dirty songs and refused to stop. The studio wanted to call

Publicity portrait of Dean Jagger, the protagonist of *No Escape* (1943).

the police, but Carradine said what Frances needed was a doctor. The next morning she had been replaced. In the *A&E Biography* episode on Frances, "Paradise Lost," Jeffrey Kauffman says that on the set she "sees imaginary people. An imaginary dog which she keeps shooing away. She keeps breaking out in singing at inappropriate moments."

In the film *Frances*, a swastika flag and portrait of Hitler is displayed on a wall for the supposed set of the film, although these items are not in the original. Additionally, the painted backdrop of the exterior of the arcade, with rollercoaster and sky, is misleading, since the film features stock location footage of same, with a sizable set for the arcade's interior. Also in *Frances*, Farmer arrives four hours late for her call, rather than being rousted from bed by the assistant director, as detailed in Gardner's anecdote. However, her name simply taped on her dressing room door wittily demonstrates the impermanence of her situation.

The autobiography *Will There Really Be a Morning?* refers to the film as *There Is No Escape* (as does Edith Farmer Elliott's biography *Look Back in Love*), with the only production information supplied being that she had called a halt to shooting on a particularly difficult day. This "particularly difficult day" goes against the idea that Frances only worked on the film for one day, with the difficulty said to have been due to *her* more than the filmmakers, since the autobiography details Frances' emotional problems of the time. She heard herself talking in a voice that was not hers. She suffered severe head pain and developed a nervous twitch in one eye. She knew she was behaving in a peculiar manner, but was aware of the money that was riding on her to make another film. The only allusion to the attack she would make on the film's hairdresser is her comment that her head hurt so badly that she could hardly bear to have her hair combed—a portent of things to come.

The fact that Frances had gone from Paramount contract star to Monogram supporting player in only seven years demonstrates her fall from grace. Monogram Pictures was one of the small studios, like Republic, that were collectively known as "Poverty Row" because they made "B" titles. Unable to afford big-name stars, they generally employed up-and-comers, or stars that were idle and not contracted to another studio (or were on the way down).

Harold Young was a former editor who had been directing consistently since his debut, the Warner Bros. comedy *Leave It to Blanche* (1934). He had made the adventure *The Scarlet Pimpernel* the same year for London Film Productions and had subsequently moved from Paramount to Universal Pictures. His film prior to *No Escape* had been the Universal musical *Hi, Buddy* (1943).

The King Brothers had previously made the murder mystery *I Killed That Man* (1941) and the drama *Klondike Fury* (1942). Producer Maurice King had also produced the Monogram crime drama *Rubber Racketeers* (1942), which Young had directed, and Frank King had associate produced.

Like Frances, Dean Jagger had been briefly under contract to Paramount and had previously worked with Young on the crime drama *Woman Trap* (1936). He had played the title character in Fox's romantic drama *Brigham Young* (1940) and had appeared with John Carradine in the Western *Western Union* (1941). Jagger's prior title was the MGM Western *The Omaha Trail* (1942). He would go on to win the Best Supporting Academy Award for *Twelve O'Clock High* (1949).

Mary Brian had been a leading lady in silent films and the 1930s, ending up at Republic. After having been off the screen for five years, she reappeared in a Hal Roach short, *Calaboose* (1943), which was her last screen work prior to *No Escape*. After playing uncredited bit parts for six years, John Carradine signed with 20th Century–Fox in 1935 and began playing memorable character roles. He had previously appeared in *Son of Fury* (although he had no scenes with Frances), and his last film before *No Escape* was the MGM Joan Crawford war drama *Reunion in France* (1942), in which he played another Nazi.

## Release

May 14, 1943

## Reviews

"A satisfactory spy melodrama grooved for dual support in the secondary houses.... Direction is adequate in concentrating on the suspense provided by the script."—*Variety*, April 11, 1943

"Low budget World War II thriller; the title tells the story."—*Leonard Maltin Movie and Video Guide*

"A well-cast but typically undernourished Monogram potboiler."—Tom Weaver, *John Carradine: The Films*

"Well cast with strong feature names and well directed."—*Motion Picture Exhibitor*

# *The Party Crashers* (1958)

### Paramount

**Credits:** A William Alland Production. Director: Bernard Girard; Producer: William Alland; Screenplay: Bernard Girard and Dan Lundenberg, from a story by William Alland and Dan Lundenberg; Photography: Edward Fitzgerald; Art Direction: Hal Periera, Lamby Larson; Special Photographic Effects: John A. Fulton; Process Photography: Farcot Edouart; Set Decorations: Sam Comer, Grace Gregory; Costumes: Edith Head; Editor: Everett Douglas; Makeup: Wally Westmore; Hair: Nellie Manley; Sound: Lyle Figland, Winston Leverett. B&W, 78 minutes. Filmed April to May 1958.

**Cast:** Connie Stevens (Barbara Nickersor); Robert Driscoll (Josh Bickford); Mark Damon (Twig Webster); Frances Farmer (Mrs. Bickford); Doris Dowling (Hazel Webster); Walter Brooke (Mr. Webster); Cathy Lewis (Mrs. Nickersor); Denver Pyle (Ted Bickford); Theodora Davitt (Sharon Lee); Bob Padgett (Mumps Thomberg); Gary Gray (Don Hartlow); Onslow Stevens (Jim Nickersor); Joseph Sonessa (Larry Bronsen); Gene Persson (Stan Osgood); Skip Jorgerson (Bill Leeds). *Uncredited*: Jeremy Hunt (Boy at Party); Michael Ross (Ed); George Cisar (Willy); Jean Engstrom (May); Greta Granstedt (Phyllis); Sid Chute (Motel Clancy); Baynes Barron (Garage Clancy); Hugh Lawrence (Police Captain); Dick Davies (Police Lieutenant); Robin Morse (Crane); Wilma Ewell (Mildred); James Cross (Frank); Brandy Bryan, Shirley Edgcomb, Cari Stevens, Harriet Taylor (Girls in Motel); Phyllis Cole, Delia Salvi (Women in Motel); Rudy Germaine, Victor Paul, Max Power, Jeffrey Sayre, Carl Saxe (Policemen); Al Paige (Prisoner); Courtland Shepard (Desk Sergeant); Robert Moechel (Boy in Court); Mike Mahoney, Bill Meader (Detectives); Lee Anthony,

Tim Johnson, Titus Moede, Robert Whitesides (Boys at Stan's Party); Judy Brand, Delores De Martin, Kevin Kelly, Cecile Rogers, Steffi Sidney (Girls at Stan's Party); Joe Kelsey (Jake); Lowell Brown (Ted); Alan Aaronson (Ted Nickerson); Jim Johnson (Boy); Don Lyon (Billy); William Bloom, Al Cavens (Waiters); Jill Marlyn (Girl at Motel Party).

**VHS/DVD:** Not available in either format.

## Synopsis

Teenager Twig Webster and his friends decide to crash a party being held by Stan Osgood at his parents' home. Twig ignores Stan's request for them to leave and entertains the group with his bullfighting game. However, a fight breaks out when he is tripped by Josh Bickford, who is jealous of Twig's interest in his girlfriend Barbara Nickersor. Barbara tells Stan to call the police to stop the fight; they arrive in minutes. Josh is disturbed when Barbara confesses her attraction to bad-boy Twig. Twig returns home to find his father drunk again and witness his mother Hazel beat her husband. The next morning Twig comes to Barbara's house, invited by Barbara's father, when Josh is there, and the two boys are encouraged to shake hands in forgiveness.

Twig invites Josh and Barbara to go with him to "The Shack"; although Josh is unsure, he agrees to go because Barbara wants to. When Twig goes home to get gas money, his father tells him that he has heard of a party to be held that night at The Lodge motel and warns his son not to crash it. Twig tells the others about the party, although Josh doesn't want to go. Clancey stops Twig from fighting with Stan at the gas station, where the teenagers meet before the party, and Twig is pleased that Barbara has come, driven by Josh (who has changed his mind). They gain entry to The Lodge but are shocked to discover that it is peopled by adults, who decide to lock the teenagers in to teach them a lesson about party crashers.

Josh starts a fight with a man who dances with Barbara—as a diversion to allow Twig to find a way out. However, Twig finds Hazel in a room with a man. Twig forces her to leave with him, but she falls down a flight of stairs in the struggle. The police arrive to break up the party. Twig beats Barbara, demanding that she give him the keys to her car, and fights off Josh when he comes to her rescue. Later, at the police station, Josh is released from custody and greeted by his parents. He tells them he wants to visit the hospitalized Barbara before coming home to talk about what has happened to them. The two teens reconcile, with Barbara admitting that she was wrong about Twig. Twig is brought to the hospital by police, where his father tells him that his mother has died. They all go back to the police station, where father and son are finally united in a new commitment to each other.

## Notes

A teenage drama with a romantic triangle at the center, this effort by director Bernard Girard features some well-directed scenes, contextual hand-held camerawork, and a pleasing use of silence. The narrative presents amusing bad boy behavior, with the parents of teenagers portrayed as being just as troubled as their children. There are also some queasy incest inferences. The pacing flags when the treatment dwells on the banal teenage concerns of getting a car and threatened allowances; however, the screenplay does offer a few unexpected twists and the occasional funny dialogue exchange.

Frances' return to films after an absence of fifteen years casts her, disappointingly, once again in a supporting role, though given her age of forty-four this is hardly a surprise. What is more disappointing is that Girard doesn't give her one close-up. Though her head-tossing mannerism is back, her performance is focused and sensitive.

A pre-credit sequence features revving car engines as the first of many sound effect motifs that Girard will employ. Naturally, the revving can be aligned with the heightened testosterone of teenage boys, which is exemplified by Twig's bullfighting game, with Larry's car as the bull and Twig's coat as his cape. This action also suggests the homoeroticism of Twig's behavior, something which is supported by the beauty of Mark Damon's Twig. The clothes of these supposed bad boys—buttoned-up shirts but no tie—contrasts with the suits and ties of the boys at Stan's party.

Barbara looking for Josh allows the camera to take in all the activities and guests at the party, with her reason revealed to be that she wishes to leave because she is bored. Given Barbara's dissatisfaction with her life and her relationship with Josh, the narrative can be viewed as a life lesson for her, since she will learn that Twig's perceived excitement will turn out to be physical and criminal threat and betrayal.

The throwing of bottles among the crowd leads to the inevitable breaking of one of them, and director Bernard Girard utilizes a handheld camera, quick cuts, and girls screaming in

Poster for *The Party Crashers* (1958).

delight to emphasize the growing mayhem. Twig uses the jagged-edged broken pieces of the bottle as his horns for the bullfighting game, with himself as the bull this time—an expression of how dangerous he is. Girard again employs the hand-held camera for the fight, with one face so close to the camera that it appears half in shadow.

An exchange between Barbara and Josh after they leave the party expresses the difference in their feelings about Twig, and further differentiates between the behavior of the good boy and the bad:

> BARBARA: He's like an animal *(meant as a compliment)*.
> JOSH: He *is* an animal.
> BARBARA: Don't knock it!

As Mrs. Bickford, Frances' first scene has her walk down a flight of stairs, and the pleasure of her introduction isn't diluted by the long shot or the cutaway to Josh. Her smoking in the next scene is a bit of a shock, although presumably it's meant as a way to reduce the stress of her concern about her son. In spite of Mrs. Bickford (her first name is never said) later complaining about her husband Ted working so many hours, Josh's parents are presented as the preferred ones—in comparison to the Nickersors and the Websters—though they are responsible for Josh's sexual inhibition. Along similar lines, Mr. Webster's alcoholism and Hazel's adultery can be seen as the reason for Twig's acting out as a bad boy.

Hazel's character is perhaps the most interesting; she is certainly the most perverse in the screenplay. She berates her husband for thinking her a tramp—something he actually calls her—and thinks he likes the idea of her seeing other men. When Hazel comes home from a date "at the movies," she greets Twig with "Give me a kiss; I don't get many, you know," and her lingering after he kisses her on the cheek expresses the sexual tension between mother and son. This moment will be echoed in the climactic Lodge sequence when she attempts to use her awareness of her son's attraction to her to free herself from his entrapment.

It's hard to know what came first—Hazel's adultery or her husband's drinking—and whether each behavior is a reaction to the other. It is surely a sadomasochistic relationship, with her repeatedly beating him with her handbag and him not fighting back. This act of violence is a mirror of Twig later shoving a sandwich into Stan's mouth. Although the handbag beating can be seen as funny, her overkill drains the humor from it. The attack is also a demonstration of Hazel's cruelty, although her husband is equally cruel in his selfishness in regards to his drinking.

Girard utilizes the sound of a typewriter on the soundtrack when the Nickersor family is introduced, with it stopping at the moment when Josh and Twig shake hands in reconciliation. The husband, Jim, is established in the female role by preparing breakfast, while Mrs. Nickersor fulfills the male role as the worker, typing up a speech on teenagers she is to make. This scene includes another incestuously perverse touch in the ardent way Barbara's father admires her in her dress, and Barbara winking back at him. Mrs. Nickersor's lingering look when greeting the attractive Twig recalls the same interest shown by Hazel, with Mrs. Nickersor also perhaps demonstrating some sexual frustration. Her disdain for her husband is expressed when she tells him, "Your waffles are burning," to stop him talking. Mrs. Nickersor's recited speech about how their fear of the atom bomb has made teenagers afraid to marry and become parents, entitled "The Natural Grain of Life," ties in to the nihilistic mentality of the party-crashing Twig and his friends.

Twig Webster (Mark Damon) is entrapped by his mother, Hazel (Doris Dowling), in perhaps the film's most provocative moment, as seen in this lobby card for *The Party Crashers* (1958).

Twig inviting Barbara and Josh to The Shack, and even his crashing Stan's party, is his attempt to join Barbara and Josh's group, a point his father highlights when he tells Twig, "Maybe if you learned to act like a gentleman they'd invite you." Even though we can see that part of Twig's agenda is to pursue Barbara, the subtext of his character indicates that he is a lonely rebel in spite of his beauty. However, the idea that he wants to pursue a girl he knows to be involved with another boy also shows his selfish opportunism, a quality that will be exposed at the film's climax.

Twig wanting to crash The Lodge party, in spite of his father's warning, is an indication that Twig's impulse to rebel is stronger than his common sense. It's interesting that Mr. Webster's threat to take Twig's car and cut off his allowance if his son party-crashes again presents him as a figure of authority, in spite of the perceived impotence of his alcoholism. However, this stance suggests that Mr. Webster is not totally lost to his addiction, and rationalizes his later ability to sober up and face Twig at the police station. This scene also reveals the information that Hazel does not cook at home, which further stamps her as being a failed 1950s housewife and not a real woman. This failing parallels that of Mrs. Nickersor, who also does not cook, with the fact that Mrs. Nickersor also has a maid being another sign of her failing as a real woman. Although we don't see Mrs. Bickford cook, we assume that she does because there is no cook/maid visible at her house.

The comparative badness of Twig and his friends to Josh and Stan is commented on by one of the boys at The Shack when he jokes that they "don't wear a leather jacket and have switchblades in every pocket." These kind of extreme bad boys were presented as motorbike-riding delinquents in *The Wild One* (1953), who came to a small town to cause havoc and steal their virginal daughters. Twig and his friends are mild in comparison to the hoods of that film, with the difference being that they are not outsiders who come into the community but rather insiders who feel they don't fit into the status quo. The narrative makes Twig a bad influence on the good boys (and girls), leading them to The Lodge, where a delicious irony reveals the adults they find there to be more radical than they are.

Barbara's sexual frustration is expressed when she and Josh dance, and the following exchange occurs:

>BARBARA: Stop fighting it.
>[*He presses his face to hers.*]
>BARBARA: Was that so bad?
>JOSH: You know how I feel.
>BARBARA : Show it then.

Josh's inhibition contributes to Barbara's frustration and her interest in Twig as a romantic alternative, although, thankfully, the narrative allows Barbara to be ambivalent and therefore proceed cautiously.

Mrs. Bickford worrying about Josh more than Ted demonstrates both her greater sensitivity and his preoccupation with work, which is shown in a telephone conversation they have that we witness from her side. Frances makes her lines funny when Mrs. Bickford tells Ted, "Frankly, darling, I could do with a lot less. I don't want to be the richest widow on the block." The idea that Ted might work himself to death suggests his interest is more obsessive than healthy, although Ted presents as more stoic than neurotic. Rather, this focuses on his wife's projected fear of abandonment, particularly in the face of her intuition about Josh's troubles. But it also shows a generosity of spirit and concern for a spouse that we don't see with the Websters or Nickersors. Mrs. Bickford's scene with Josh, trying to get him to open up about what is happening with him, is as abbreviated as all of Frances' scenes; however, she plays it simply and with gentleness. Her voice expresses maternal concern without judgment, and her offering her car to Josh is an act of empathy.

Barbara's initial refusal to get into Mrs. Bickford's car shows her to be more concerned about peer pressure and appearances than he, since the vehicle is not the racing car that the other teenagers favor. Josh will be ridiculed for driving such a car when they get to Clancey's, though only in a small way. Girard adds another sound effect, the repeated ring of the petrol bowser, under the flirtatious dialogue between Twig and Barbara. These rings indicate the rising excitement between the two, and Twig's perceived victory and Josh's loss. The image of the cars all leaving Clancey's as they head to The Lodge is a portentous one.

As they survey The Lodge from the grounds outside, Twig takes a cigarette from Barbara's packet, but it is lit by Josh. While this act demonstrates Josh's propriety over Barbara, it can also be read as another homoerotic act, especially in the smirk Twig provides in response. Girard uses his hand-held camera again for more mayhem when the teenagers are locked into the adult party; the adults are presented as horror movie monsters from the teenager's perspective, in spite of the fact that they are only drinking and dancing. The one man who wears a woman's shiny earring is both a sign of drunken silliness and a suggestion of kinky adult sexuality, something reinforced by the adult women coming on to the teenage boys. Twig is the only one who isn't repelled by the older women's sexual advances, and, interestingly, Josh remains the only boy not chosen for a dancing partner. This factor also conveniently allows him the freedom to pick a fight with the man who dances with Barbara, as a ruse for Twig to find them an avenue of escape.

When the adult man refrains from fighting Josh and merely laughs at the boy's bravado, it is both a pleasing undercutting of the potential violence of the situation and another indictment of Josh's perceived masculine threat. A fight will eventually break out, but even then Girard conceals it from the camera; and its potency is quickly diluted by the arrival of the police.

The appearance of the robed neighbors to stop the running teenagers in the street aids the police roundup, and Twig striking Barbara to get her car keys displays a fight or flight panic as much as his selfishness. While her crying helplessly as Twig and Josh fight, and Twig overpowering Josh remain disappointing, Twig apparently eluding the police does not. The narrative doesn't show Twig being arrested, creating the impression that he escapes capture, something which remains ambiguous during the police station scene. Josh has been idealized as the moral good boy, so Twig's badness needs to be punished, with Twig turning against Barbara costing him any redeeming audience empathy Twig may have had.

The police station scene has a real-life parallel for Frances, in light of her 1940s arrests, and we imagine that the reminder must have been painful for her, even when contained within a Hollywood soundstage. Frances brings emotion, as well a hushed tone of embarrassment, to Mrs. Bickford's exchange with Ted:

> TED: He'll [Josh] be alright.
> MRS. BICKFORD: How can you be so sure?!

Ted attempts to rationalize his guilt over being in the police station and the perceived neglect of his son, and also expresses the dreariness and demands of his life:

> There's just not enough time. It's an hour to get to work. You work all day. And it takes an hour to get home. You get home. There's always something to be fixed. Someone on the phone. Something to see on television.

Twig Webster (Mark Damon, at left), and Larry Bronsen (Joseph Sonessa, at right) look through the window of the party that they plan to crash in a lobby card for *The Party Crashers* (1958). The actors dancing inside are unidentified.

Mrs. Bickford responds to this with, "We're not like the parents of some of those other poor kids; we'll find the time."

The Bickfords' concern over their son is contrasted with Mr. Webster not wanting to see Hazel in the hospital, and the Nickersors coming to the station rather than being at the hospital with Barbara. (Barbara must have been hospitalized for shock, since the slaps she received from Twig hardly justify medical attention.) Mr. Webster being sober marks a change in his character, and his sobbing releases the emotion that his drinking had been suppressing. However, we assume he cries over the missing Twig rather than his injured wife. Perhaps we feel that Hazel being caught with another man makes her death morally justifiable, but it's a hard lesson that she has to die in order to obtain father and son reconciliation.

When Josh is released, the Bickfords are happy and relieved to see him rather than angry, with Ted's "an awful lot to be said but it's a cinch that this isn't the place to be saying it" demonstrating a consciousness of environment and sensitivity to the moment. Josh's request to see Barbara before he comes home is reasonable given that the hospital is next door to the station, but still, it is generous of his parents to allow him to do so. Josh at the hospital also lets us see that Mr. Webster has relented and gone there too, to find out about his wife. That he is told she has died is perhaps punishment for his delay, and Twig's appearance as the prisoner of two policemen makes his capture apparent.

There is a momentary doubt about whether Mr. Webster will go with Twig back to the station, and perhaps the decision to accompany his son is made to avoid the consequence of another delay. Unlike coming to the hospital for Hazel, this new decision is a pro-active one—a step forward from the indulgence he might have chosen by not going. It doesn't read as a pat happy ending in the face of Twig's presumed prosecution for the assault on Barbara and the party crashing that has led to his future being compromised. However, it does restore the moral balance of the families we have seen and the community they live in. We doubt that there will be any more party crashing soon, at least by these teenagers.

The Turner Classic Movies Notes cite a synopsis found in Paramount press materials that indicate the film's original ending had Twig escape the police, then return to Clancey's, where Twig is shot and killed by Clancey after he tries to rob the cash register and steal a car. This would have nullified the coming together of what remains of the three families at the police station. With Hazel's death, this also would have been two losses for Mr. Webster, and would possibly have led him back to drinking, which the current ending implies he will avoid.

In *Shadowland*, William Arnold calls *The Party Crashers* a "grade-B teen-age exploitation picture." He says that Frances could not memorize lines, did not respond to cues, and often appeared on the set drunk. Arnold claims that this affected her performance, which he says lacked "all the old drive, the mystical beauty, and the exciting sense of timing. What had made her a great star was completely burned out, and there was not even enough left to make a credible character actress." The fact that Frances did not make another film does not necessarily support Arnold's view, especially as she was more interested in working in the theater, as per her original goal. Additionally, his view would seem necessary to support his book's claim that Frances had had a lobotomy. This author does not agree with Arnold's judgment of Frances' performance in *The Party Crashers*, and it's noteworthy that neither the autobiography nor Edith Farmer mentions any difficulties experienced by Frances during production. The *A&E Biography* episode on Frances, "Paradise Lost," described the filming experience as disappointing and unsatisfying [for her]. In the *E! Mysteries and Scandals* television episode on Frances, Connie Stevens comments on her co-star (keep in mind that they did not work together directly, as they shared no scenes):

> It was very tragic in a career sense because she was rather brilliant.... [During the production] she isolated herself. She did not talk to the crew. She did not talk to anybody. She seemed to be far away all the time. Something was in her that was far, far away. Almost too far away to come back.

Connie Stevens and Mark Damon in the foreground on the set of *The Party Crashers* (1958). The identity of the crew members in the background is unknown.

Screenwriter Bernard Girard had made his directing debut with the independent comedy *As You Were* (1951), and his films prior to *The Party Crashers* had been the Western *Ride Out for Revenge* and the drama *The Green-Eyed Blonde* (both 1957). Producer William Alland had previously made science fiction films and Westerns at Universal Pictures, including *It Came from Outer Space* (1953), *Creature from the Black Lagoon* (1954), *This*

*Island Earth*, and *Tarantula* (both 1955). His prior title was the Esther Williams vehicle *Raw Wind in Eden* (1958).

Mark Damon had made his film debut in a supporting role in the crime drama *Inside Detroit* (1956), and had subsequently been seen in the war dramas *Screaming Eagles* and *Between Heaven and Hell* (both 1956). He scored his first leading role in the gang drama *Young and Dangerous* (1957), and followed it with another teen drama, *Life Begins at 17* (1958), his film prior to *The Party Crashers*. Ingénue Connie Stevens had made her film debut, unbilled, in *Eighteen and Anxious* (1957), and played supporting roles in *Young and Dangerous*, *Dragstrip Riot*, and the Jerry Lewis comedy *Rock-a-Bye Baby* (both 1958), her prior title. *The Party Crashers* would be Stevens' first leading role.

Robert "Bobby" Driscoll had been a child star who had won a special Academy Award as the Outstanding Juvenile Actor of 1949 for his performance in the RKO film noir *The Window* (1949). After a troubled adolescence, during which he retreated from films because his face was scarred by acne, Driscoll returned in a supporting role in the MGM adventure drama *The Scarlet Coat* (1955). *The Party Crashers* was his first title in three years, and it would be his last feature. Driscoll's future was a sad one, as he became a drug addict unable to obtain work, then a vagrant, and was finally found dead in 1968 at the age of thirty-one.

## *Release*

September 1958 with the tagline, "Who are the delinquents—kids or their 'respectable' parents?"

## *Reviews*

"Modest programmer ... entry comes up with novel approaches.... Farmer does well as a distraught parent."—*Variety*, September 17, 1958

"Melodramatic trash."—Jay Robert Nash and Stanley Ralph Ross, *The Motion Picture Guide, 1927–1983*

"Nasty."—John Douglas Eames, *The Paramount Story*

"Cut-rate exploiter in which the usual pubescent gangs run riot."—Robin Cross, *2000 Movies The 1950s*

# TELEVISION

## *Toast of the Town/ The Ed Sullivan Show* (1957)

Season 10, Episode 40
CBS

**Credits:** Director: Kenneth Whelan; Producers: Chester Feldman, Bob Precht; Executive Producer: Ed Sullivan; Writers: Jerry Bresler, Lyn Duddy, Jerry Juhl; Music: Buddy Arnold, Ray Bloch; Orchestrator: Will Schaefer. B&W, 60 minutes.

**Songs:** "Bye, Bye Love," sung by the Everly Brothers; "Aura Lea," sung by Frances Farmer; "Freight Train," sung by Nancy Whiskey & the Charles McDevitt Skiffle Group; "Dark Moon," sung by Bonnie Guitar; "June Is Bustin' Out All Over," "Hand Holdin' Music," "If I Loved You" and "The Georgia School Song," sung by the University of Georgia Glee Club.

**Cast:** Ed Sullivan (Host); Kaye Ballard, Barber and Manselle, Donald Campbell, Davis and Reese, the Everly Brothers (Don and Phil Everly), Frances Farmer, Hank Garland, Bonnie Guitar, Jo Jac and Joni, the Kirby Stone Four, Michael Mark, Charles McDevitt and His Skiffle Group, Jackie Pung, Rex Smith, the University of Georgia Glee Club, Nancy Whiskey (Guests).

**VHS/DVD:** Not available in either format.

## Notes

Frances' first appearance on *The Ed Sullivan Show* gives her a touching vulnerability in light of our knowledge of what she had lived through in her private life. She is first seen in the show's "backstage" introduction, standing with Michael Marks, Jackie Pung, and Donald Campbell. The last to be introduced, the silent Frances is welcomed by Sullivan with, "Making her comeback to show business on our stage, the movie star Frances Farmer." Edith Farmer reports that Frances was positioned as the second spot on the show, a fact that this author was unable to verify because only Frances' footage of both of the Sullivan programs was available (material provided by Jeffrey Kauffman, with the remainder of the shows commercially unavailable). Reportedly, Sullivan asked Frances to sing "Aura Lee," the song she had sung in *Come and Get It*; this song had been revived by Elvis Presley with the title "Love Me Tender." Sullivan's introduction:

We're very thrilled because returning to show business she picked our show. Here's the girl who, in *Come and Get It* some years back—the movie star—sang a song written by Stephen

Foster. The song this year came out as Elvis Presley's "Love Me Tender." Here is Frances Farmer.

We can forgive Sullivan's claim that Frances chose him rather than he admitting he invited *her* onto his show after the publicity of her April press conference. Standing in a doorway, she walks over a white line to hit her mark in a medium shot as she sings. Wearing a simple, belted, knee-length dress, Frances appears relaxed, although her vocal vibrato may be an indication of nervousness. She is never given a close-up, although dissolves are used to vary the medium shot, and she looks to the right of the camera. The fronds of a plant on the set upstage her, and she bows after finishing the song.

In *Will There Really Be a Morning?* Frances recounted:

> My voice faltered as I began the song, but then something inside me, that other person, saw past the cameras and technicians, on into the audience that filled the darkened theater. Contact was made, and I drew strength from the power that I was once more standing in my rightful place, giving the only part of myself that was still alive. Giving, to the millions beyond. I had never been an exceptional singer, and I would have preferred to appear as an actress, but the effect was satisfactory.

After her performance, Frances comes to the front of the stage to meet Sullivan, who hugs her. She does not make direct eye contact with him until he comments that she will be back because he has signed her up exclusively. Frances' feigned surprise at the idea reads as genuine, although we assume she knew of her second scheduled appearance prior to this moment.

Edith Farmer alludes to the synchronicity of the idea of Frances being on the same episode as Jackie Pung. Pung was a Hawaiian golfer who had lost the 1957 U.S. Open on a technicality, and who was making her own comeback after a nervous breakdown. Edith would write of Frances' performance in *Look Back in Love*:

> I was amazed at the mellow richness of her voice after all these years without practice or training. She sang and acted quite naturally—without pose or artifice—and got excellent applause both when she was first introduced and after the song.

In the *A&E Biography* episode on Frances, "Paradise Lost," Jeffrey Kauffman would say, "She was obviously terrified and very nervous, but again that inner strength and reserve just rose up again and she made it through the song beautifully and she brought down the house.

In *Shadowland*, William Arnold makes the incorrect statement that "after a long and patronizing speech about how this pathetic woman had triumphed over nearly two decades of mental illness, he let her sing two folk songs to the accompaniment of an acoustic guitar." The latter reference to two songs mistakenly includes Frances' second appearance on the Sullivan show.

Former actor, screenwriter and radio columnist Ed Sullivan was known as "the Great Stone Face" because of his supposed nervousness on camera, which made him appear stilted (although this is not apparent in this episode). *Toast of the Town* was the first television show produced by Chester Feldman and Bob Precht, who was Sullivan's son-in-law.

## *Release*

Broadcast June 30, 1957

•••••••••••••••••••••••••••••••••••••••••••••••••••••••••••••••

# Toast of the Town/
# The Ed Sullivan Show (1957)

Season 11, Episode 5
CBS

**Credits:** Same as previous episode.

**Songs:** "The Great Pretender," sung by the Platters; "Down in the Valley," sung by Frances Farmer; "Fascination," sung by Jane Morgan; "Rock-a-Boogie," sung by Andy Quinn; "You" and "The Night and the Music," sung by Constance Towers; "Hello My Baby" and "Goodbye My Lady Love," sung by Joe Howard; medley: "Lonesome Road," "How Come You Do Me Like You Do," "When My Sugar Walks Down the Street All the Birdies Go Tweet-Tweet," "Melancholy Baby" and "Blue Heaven," sung by Gene Austin; "Teasin' Rag" and "Somebody Loves Me Rag," sung by Blossom Seeley; "Catch," sung by T.C. Jones; "Thine Alone" (Victor Herbert), sung by Dario Cassini; "Bring Back My Summer Love," sung by Don Rondo; "Some Enchanted Evening" and "I'm So in Love with Me," sung (in satire) by Frank Faye.

**Cast:** Ed Sullivan (Host); Gene Austin, Dario Cassini, Maurice Chevalier, Frances Farmer, Frank Fay, Rudolf Friml, Whoopi Gilbert, W.C. Handy, Joseph E. Howard, T.C. Jones, Grace Kahn, Johnny Mize, Jane Morgan, the Platters, Andy Quinn, Don Rondo, Blossom Seely, General Oscar Silber, Constance Towers (Guests).

## Notes

This episode was an ASCAP show, celebrating the American Society for Composers, Authors and Publishers. Again, this author has only been able to view Frances' segment (thanks again to Jeffrey Kauffman), since the whole show is not commercially available. Frances apparently appeared towards the end of the show to sing "Down in the Valley," which Ed Sullivan says is a folk song by Carl Sandburg. Sitting on a chair, wearing a striped crepe de chine full skirt and black sweater, Frances strums a guitar (though does not do the chord fingering). The spotlight on her makes Frances' hair look blonder than it did in the first episode. Again filmed in medium shot, this time she is upstaged by a stuffed rooster placed next to her head. Looking happier, Frances appears less vulnerable than in her prior appearance, with perhaps the added confidence of being a previous performer on the show. However, her performance is shorter and less memorable, perhaps lacking the resonance of her first (*because* it was her first). In Patrick Agan's *The Decline and Fall of the Love Goddesses*, he writes incorrectly of her second appearance as being her first, even mistakenly captioning a still of Frances from this episode with, "It was the first time the public had seen her in fifteen years."

## Release

Broadcast October 27, 1957

## *Playhouse 90*—"Reunion" (1958)

### CBS

**Credits:** Director: Unknown; Producers: Mildred Freed Alberg, Ralph Levy; Associate Producers: Anthony Barr, Joe Scully; Writer: Merle Miller. B&W, 90 minutes. Filmed in December 1957 in Hollywood.

**Cast:** Patricia Barry (Lucille); Dane Clark (Saul Levanthal); Charles Drake (Guy Schmitt); Frances Farmer (Val Schmitt); Martha Hyer (Louise Merrick); Jack Lord (Homer Aswell); Hugh O'Brian (Jason Merrick); Robert Paget (Bell Boy); Neva Patterson (Elizabeth Murray).

**VHS/DVD:** Not available in either format.

### *Synopsis*

A World War II veteran hosts a reunion party for three wartime comrades. At the party each of the four reveals a secret about his life.

### *Notes*

In *Shadowland* William Arnold claims that it took Frances many weeks to learn her part, a delay that "infuriated" the rest of the cast. However, he reports, "Remarkably, under the circumstances, her performance was credible and she received polite notices."

*Playhouse 90* was the first television producing job for writer Mildred Freed Alberg. Producer Ralph Levy had directed television comedy and the Jack Benny family drama series *Shower of Stars*. Associate Producer Anthony Barr had also directed for the series, as well for *Studio One*, *Climax*, and *General Electric Theater*. Associate producer Joe Scully was also a writer and casting director, with *Playhouse 90* being his first television producing job.

### *Release*

Broadcast January 2, 1958, by CBS as episode 17 of *Playhouse 90*, season 2.

## *Matinee Theatre*—"Something Stolen, Something Blue" (1958)

### NBC

**Credits:** Director: Unknown. Producers: George M. Cahan, Frank Price; Executive Producer: Albert McCleery; Writer: William Mourne. Color, 60 minutes.

**Cast:** John Conte (Host); Frances Farmer (part unknown); Dolores Hart (Corrine March).

**VHS/DVD:** Not available in either format.

## Synopsis

When her bridegroom-to-be doesn't show up for the wedding, Corinne March's family is certain she has been jilted. But Corinne is equally certain that Johnny has fallen victim to foul play and decides to investigate.

## Notes

There is no information about this show in the autobiography, or in Edith Farmer's or Patrick Agan's books, and Frances is not credited in David M. Inman's *Performers Television Credits, 1942–2000, Volume 1: A–F*. However, it will be mentioned by Ralph Edwards as having been made before the *This Is Your Life* television show appearance.

*Matinee Theatre* was the first television producing jobs for George M. Cahan and Frank Price. Screenwriter and executive producer Albert McCleery also produced and directed other episodes for the series, as he had previously done for the television dramas *The Philco Television Playhouse, Masterpiece Playhouse, Fireside Arena Theatre, Hallmark Summer Theatre, Hallmark Hall of Fame,* and *Cameo Theatre*. Dolores Hart would enjoy a brief leading lady career in films after this show and then retire from show business in 1963 to become a nun.

## Release

Broadcast January 16, 1958, by NBC as episode 79 of *Matinee Theatre*, season 3.

•••••••••••••••••••••••••••••••••••••••••••••••••••••••••••

# *This Is Your Life* (1958)

### Ralph Edwards Productions/NBC

**Credits:** Director: Richard Gottlieb; Producer/Writer: Axel Gruenberg; Executive Producer: Ralph Edwards; Researchers: Jan Boehme Miller, Don Malmberg, Alice Keyser Armbruster; Music: Von Dexter. Black & White, 28 minutes.

**Cast:** Ralph Edwards (Host); Frances Farmer (Subject); Edith "Dede" Farmer, Belle McKenzie, Professor Glenn Hughes, Jane Finn Rose, Rita "Mrs. James" Hill, Lee Mikesell, Harry Haste, Mabel Haste (Guests).

**VHS/DVD:** Video *This Is Your Life: The Classics* was released by Ralph Edwards Productions, copyrighted 1990, but appears to be out of print.

## Notes

Confirmed by host Ralph Edwards during his introduction to the video of Frances' episode is the fact that she was intentionally warned in advance about her appearance on

*This Is Your Life* on January 29, 1958. This prior notification was an exception to the general rule of subjects being unaware of the tribute to come. In *Look Back in Love*, Edith Farmer describes how the show had a rehearsal the day before, with a director, so that guests could memorize their lines, although Frances was represented by a stand-in so that her surprise at seeing the attendees could be genuine. Edith also says that Frances had script approval as part of the deal, which tends to dilute the idea of her being angry or upset about what was said about her. In *Shadowland*, William Arnold says that Edwards had asked for a guarantee from her manager, Lee Mikesell, that Frances was stable enough to do the show live. This concern, although indelicate, is perhaps justifiable for live television and also an indication that Edwards' treatment of her would not be as sensitive as one might have hoped.

While a viewing of the show provides a sense of déjà vu, due to the material being recreated in the film *Frances*, it is nonetheless a fascinating document because it allows us to see Frances as a real person (as opposed to her in performance mode). Naturally, at the age of 44 she no longer has a youthful beauty, but she presents a look of a maintained glamour and elegance. Wearing a black dress suit, white gloves, white ascot, and sparkly earrings, she is likable and seemingly honest with Edwards; and, unlike with Ed Sullivan, Frances makes direct eye contact with Edwards. Emotionally distant at first, Frances relaxes more with the show's guests, and presents as articulate and impressive. Using the acting mannerisms of raised eyebrow and head-tossing, she also displays humor, surprise, and moments of what appear to be repressed anger—expressed by a twist to her mouth and biting her lip, and a distorted look on her face.

Edwards alludes to Frances' past in his introduction: "A beautiful lady whose life might well have served as the model for a play by Eugene O'Neill or a novel by Theodore Dreiser. Talented, star of Broadway and Hollywood, Miss Frances Farmer." When Frances joins him, he asks what prompted her to accept the invitation to relive her life. She replies as follows:

> In the first place, I wanted to tell something of my own experiences to help people I know have been in the same kind of predicament. I receive so many letters. People who want hope or advice even, and perhaps I can suggest where they can find it. For myself I would very much like to correct some impressions that arose out of a lot of stories that were written about me, I guess, but they weren't about me, suggesting things that I could have possibly been doing which I never did. I wasn't in a position to defend myself at the time these stories were published. I'm very happy to be here tonight to let people see that I am the kind of person I am and not a legend that arose.

The intention to correct impressions allows Frances to speak apparently spontaneously in answer to specific questions, although we presume that her having script approval also meant that she knew the questions in advance. However, such stated intention seems somewhat disingenuous since she presents as a more reactive, if not outright passive, figure to Edwards. Frances repeatedly saying "Ralph" before each response is another element that undercuts the notion of the encounter's spontaneity, although this way of speaking may be both a period and show business convention. (The film *Frances* will create the impression that this is the result of her lobotomized brain.) Frances denies being an alcoholic and dope user (this denial offers some humor in her reaction to such a suggestion), and Edwards asks her what it was that interrupted her career and brought her to the brink of disaster. Though purplish, such phrasing is acceptable given the gothic reality of Frances' past ordeals. She answers:

It was a combination of quite a few things. So much had happened to me when I became first successful as an actress. Many agonizing decisions arose that I had to make, and I just wasn't mature enough and didn't have enough time to make them, without time and peace to think, and I had a nervous breakdown.

Although her categorizing her condition as a nervous breakdown is interesting, she also avoids giving any specifics about the "many agonizing decisions." Edwards continues with, "As a result, you spent nearly ten years in and out of mental institutions" (a fact she doesn't correct him on). A still from *Come and Get It* is followed by one of the arrest photographs. Edwards ends this introduction with, "The curtain comes down on a kind of oblivion," at which point Frances' twisted mouth and raised eyebrow are seen.

Frances with Ralph Edwards, the host of the television show *This Is Your Life*, on which she appeared on January 29, 1958.

The guest segments are divided by the chaptered "1931," "1936," and "1951" seen as figures onscreen to show the progress of time. It's pleasing to see Edith Farmer Elliot live, as the first guest in the first chapter, since she is otherwise known as the author of *Look Back in Love*. Edith looks smaller than Frances, and one can see a faint facial resemblance, although Edith lacks her sister's blondness and beauty. Schoolteacher Belle McKenzie's appearance causes a shocked, funny and defensive reaction in Frances when Edwards reads aloud the beginning of Frances' "God Dies" essay. College professor Glenn Hughes describes Frances as having "an intellectual chip on her shoulder." He says at college she was lovely, but her dramatic talent was slow in developing, so that she wasn't cast in a play until her third year when a suitable vehicle was found (*Alien Corn*). Hughes also tells that the trip to Russia interrupted Frances' course, and that she never finished. This segment also features stills from *Rhythm on the Range*, *Ebb Tide*, and *The Toast of New York*, with Jane Rose commenting that Frances' decision to leave Hollywood for New York was made to give herself "training."

The "1936" segment shows Frances with a disturbed look on her face as Edwards speaks of her "mounting tensions." A solo still from *Golden Boy* is displayed, and Edwards asks her why her marriage to Leif Erickson failed. After an emotional gulp, she replies with faltering words (interestingly, she doesn't call Leif by name):

I guess neither one of us should have married each. He wasn't to blame and neither was I. We had different goals and different directions, and we realized that it was better to just let the marriage go and go our separate ways. It was a very difficult emotional decision for both of us.

Edwards says, "On the soundstages your brilliant mind fails you now and you become more and more uncooperative, less and less competent. Resentment against you mounts in all quarters until no more parts are offered to you." Hearing this, Frances raises her eyebrow, and a faraway look comes over her face. Is she remembering? Or is she angry at the way she is being spoken about by Edwards? Edwards continues with, "In loneliness and despair you turn to drink to blot out the raging conflicts of your mind." Frances bites her lip, and again her face is distorted, as Edwards says, "Psychological tests indicate that you're suffering from schizophrenia—hallucinations, fantastic delusions, disorganized emotions." The appearance of her sister Rita allows Frances to defend herself against the charge of being mentally ill:

> I didn't think then and I still don't that I was actually sick, but there were so many people who seemed to think I was mentally ill that I just had to find out why and find out whether it was my fault what was happening. You know, if you get treated like a patient, why, you're apt to act like one, and these things just pushed me a little too far and it led to conflicts and strife with my mother. She thought I needed more care so she had me committed to the Western State Hospital in Washington.

Frances' denial of ever being sick is either a sign of the strength of her self-awareness and independent spirit, or a refusal to acknowledge the reasons for her behavior, at least in this forum. Her "I just had to find out why" implies she had an active role in overcoming the situation, which is revisionist fantasy. It is interesting that she names her mother as the one to blame for having her committed. Although we know it to be true, and Lillian admitted to this in press interviews, it still reads as an exposure of the private self by a public figure. Perhaps it helped that by this time her mother was deceased and not able to be affected by the public shame. "If you get treated like a patient, why, you're apt to act like one" sounds like a platitude, and also like the psychobabble that she must have needed to spout to obtain her release. To Edwards' enquiry about life at Washington State Hospital, Frances says the following:

> It was very much like anyone else who is admitted to a public institution. They don't have means for individual psychiatric care. There's only so many beds available. I stood in line with fifteen or twenty girls who, like myself, were in the hospital for one reason or another. We received shots or hydrotherapy baths or electric shock treatment, and this was supposed to relax the tensions and keep you quiet, which it did. I don't blame the hospital at all. I think they did everything in their power to take care of the enormous number of people they had, but I really don't think it helped me much.

Edwards then asks Frances if she has any thoughts on how her cure came about, her recovery, to which she replies:

> Well, it took me a long time going this way, and finally I realized that I would have to do it for myself because, first of all, any cure to be effective has to be based on faith in oneself, which means faith in God. If you don't have that, why, all the tensions that are relaxed to the end of the world won't solve your problems for you. The reason why you are emotionally disturbed. I was able, in a kind of grim and very lonely battle, to find this faith for myself or re-find it and hang onto it, and it eventually led me out of the hospital and back to church, which I think is the only place where you can find a really potent answer to the problems of the spirit in this world that we live in now.

This idea of having to cure herself parallels a similar notion in the autobiography that says it was Frances' change of attitude that enabled those in charge of her to see that her behavior had changed and for them to interpret this as her being cured. However, Frances' description here lacks the implication that it was a pretence—which is apparent in the autobiography—since she always thought the change had to come from the perception of her.

The "1951" segment introduces Frances' manager, Lee Mikesell, whose hair ends in a widow's peak that gives him an unfortunate resemblance to Bela Lugosi's Dracula.

Edwards tells Frances that one-hundred-and-twenty-five Hollywood producers have been wired, urging them to look in on the show tonight and keep her in mind for important dramatic roles. He also announces that she has been offered the lead in an upcoming Broadway production of *The Passions of the Women of Glynn*. Edwards says the production is to be staged by Eddie Dowling, who was a Broadway actor, producer, and director. The author of the play is unknown, and while it is known that Frances did not take the part, it also seems the play was never produced.

The coup de grace comes with the show's gift of a free car—a two-door Edsel Pacer—since Edwards states that Frances has been depending on friends for transportation. Apparently, as part of the deal to do the show, Mikesell had insisted upon Frances receiving the car, rather than just the usual memory book and charm bracelet. Although not intended to be an insult at the time, the Edsel would become famous in the future as one of the biggest commercial failures in the history of American business.

Edith Farmer believes that the show went smoothly, and that Frances took her part in stride, seemingly touched by the reunions. Patrick Agan and William Arnold both consider her appearance on the show an embarrassment in light of the way she was questioned by Edwards. Matters were made worse, Agan claims, by the fact that none of Frances' old friends or co-workers would consent to appear on the show with her because of the ill will she had created so many years before. Jeffrey Kauffman contends that the only embarrassment was Edwards and his "smarminess," and says that Frances was "in complete control of her faculties, responding at length and with great intelligence to all questions put to her." This is in opposition to Arnold's claim that she barely uttered a word, was near-catatonic, and responded to questions with a blank stare. Kauffman also says that Frances "sometimes seemed to be on the verge of tears or suppressing rage at the indignity of being asked such crude questions," and there *are* several flashes of her temperament throughout the episode. In the *A&E Biography* episode on Frances, "Paradise Lost," Kauffman observes, "If you watch closely you can see the tears well up in her eye. She bites her lip heavily. You can see the torment she's going through."

David Farmer, in the same *A&E Biography* episode, says, "You can see the painful memories it dredges up, and you can see some tremendous anger flitter across her face, but it seemed very exploitive, which it was." In the making of the documentary *A Hollywood Life: Remembering Frances*, Jessica Lange would comment on the *This Is Your Life* show. "Of all the great tragedies of Frances' life, I think that was probably one of the worst, her appearance on that program.... It was so horrible the way he talked to her, and you just know if she had been in her right mind she could have cut him to the quick." Again, this idea of Frances not being "in her right mind" follows the notion, maintained in the film, that she had been lobotomized and her mind thereby affected. On the *E! Mysteries and Scandals* documentary, film historian Dr. Conrad Lane says, "It is excruciating to see how this man [Edwards] grills her ... and knowing what all the girl had been through, watching her sitting here calmly field his questions is almost more than you can take." Edith would quote from a letter to her from Frances herself, dated March 30, 1963, in which she referred to the show as a harrowing travesty.

Ralph Edwards was a former radio announcer and actor who had previously produced the television game shows *Truth or Consequences, Funny Boners,* and *It Could Be You.* He played himself in the recreation done of *This Is Your Life* for the film *I'll Cry Tomorrow* (1955), and would continue to host *This Is Your Life* until 1961, and then in a syndicated revival from 1971 to 1973. Director Richard Gottlieb had worked with Edwards on *Truth* or *Consequences*, and would also write for *This Is Your Life*. Producer Axel Gruenberg had written for the television drama series *Greun Guild Playhouse* and also directed for *This Is Your Life*. This show was the only one on which he served as producer.

## Release

Broadcast January 29, 1958

# *Studio One*—"Tongues of Angels" (1958)

### CBS

**Credits:** Director: Herbert Hirschman; Producer: Norman Felton; Associate Producer: Anthony Barr. Teleplay: John Vlahos; Music: Jerry Goldsmith. B&W, 60 minutes. Filmed in Hollywood.

**Cast:** Leon Ames (Cyrus Walker); Frances Farmer (Sarah Walker); James MacArthur (Ben Adams); Margaret O'Brien (Jenny Walker); Olan Soule (Doctor).

**VHS/DVD:** Not available in either format.

## Synopsis

"Though I speak with the tongues of men and of angels and have not charity, I am become as sounding brass or a tinkling cymbal ..." Ben Adams appears at the front door of the Walker house looking for work on their farm. He uses crude signs and written notes to communicate, as an indication that he is deaf and dumb. Although initially reluctant, Cyrus Walker eventually succumbs to the will of his wife Sarah and his daughter Jenny and agrees to hire the boy. Jenny comes to realize that Ben can hear just fine and that he is not dumb, but suffers from a stuttering affliction so severe that he would rather not speak at all than reveal it. With patience and love, Jenny eventually helps Ben overcome his fears and begin to conquer his affliction.

## Notes

On his internet website www.jamesmacarthur.com, James MacArthur reports that he came by the role of the stutterer because his mother, Helen Hayes, and playwright John Vlahos had the same agent, who asked Hayes to read the script to evaluate it. When she learned that *Studio One* planned to produce it, she urged James to come back from his vacation in Mexico to audition for it. After being cast, MacArthur visited a class of stutterers to gain insight into the affliction that his character suffered from. To do the show, he decided to use tortured facial expressions and sounds outside of normal speech that he had seen and heard in the class, rather than the stereotypical repeating consonants of previous portrayals. MacArthur says that his performance has been widely credited by stutterers as one of the most realistic ever seen on television or film.

Jeffrey Kauffman writes that the show

> boasts impressive performances by both Margaret O'Brien and Frances Farmer.... O'Brien, in a relatively rare late-teen role, shines.... Farmer is simply perfect as a down-home, church-going farmer's wife. Farmer fans will also delight to see and hear her playing the piano and singing live with Leon Ames.

Herbert Hirschman was a producer of *Playhouse 90* and had previously directed for the television anthology dramas *The Philco Television Playhouse*, *The Alcoa Hour*, *Goodyear Television Playhouse*, *Studio One*, and *Pursuit*. Producer Norman Felton had written for and directed episodes of the television anthology drama *Robert Montgomery Presents*, and produced *Studio One*.

## Release

Broadcast March 17, 1958, by CBS as episode 24 of season 10 of *Studio One*.

## Reviews

"MacArthur gave a striking performance as a frightened, brooding stutterer.... Although Miss O'Brien was at all times a bit shrill, the scenes with MacArthur were often deeply touching. Vlahos' drama was moving and believable ... excellent supporting performances from Miss Farmer and Ames."—Bob Williams, *The Evening Bulletin*, March 18, 1958

"Primarily a very gentle and moving love story, it deals with tenderness and perception on an emotional crisis in the lives of two likeable people in a commonplace setting.... Herbert Hirschman caught the spirit of the script, and James MacArthur gave a sensitive and accurate portrayal of the troubled youth."—Donald Kirkley, *The Baltimore Sun*, March 20, 1958

"Some of the harrowing explanation of [the farmhand's] difficulties seemed a bit excessive, but the play and its people were always warm and endearing.... Margaret O'Brien was splendid, and James MacArthur conveyed movingly Ben's torment.... Frances Farmer and Leon Ames rounded out the first rate cast skillfully directed by Herbert Hirschman."—Harry Harris, *The Philadelphia Enquirer*, March 18, 1958

# *Frances Farmer Presents* (1958–1964)

## WFBM-TV

**Credits:** Producer: Fletcher Markle; Theme Music: "Thus Spake Zarathustra" (Richard Wagner). B&W and Color, 120 minutes. Filmed in Indianapolis, Indiana.

**Cast:** Frances Farmer (Hostess); Carolyn Churchman (Commercials), Jim Gerard (Fill-in Host).

**VHS/DVD:** Not available in either format.

## Synopsis

Hollywood actress Frances Farmer introduces the afternoon movie, and interviews celebrities and politicians visiting Indianapolis.

## Notes

Following on from Frances' television appearances on *The Ed Sullivan Show* and *This Is Your Life*, and her supporting role in the film *The Party Crashers*, was Frances' live hosting of this afternoon movie program. It is suggested that Frances was approached about doing it when she came to Indianapolis to appear on stage in *The Chalk Garden*. The show's opening Wagnerian music would become more famous when used in the feature film *2001: A Space Odyssey* (1968). During the six years of the show's run, Frances would interview, among others, Ginger Rogers, Barbra Streisand, Sophie Tucker, Kathy Crosby, Rory Calhoun, Hildegarde, Sylvia Sydney, Helen Hayes, and her ex-husband Leif Erickson. The show was a consistent ratings winner, and varied from its live format for two weeks during February and March 1963 when Frances filmed her segments at Purdue University, where she was also performing in *The Sea Gull*. After Frances left the television show, hosting was taken over by the morning movie host Bernie Herman.

In *Shadowland*, William Arnold says that the video footage he saw of the series showed "a reasonably intelligent woman who seems never quite in control of the situation." He says her sentences were punctuated with long pauses, and it was a "depressing spectacle to see someone who had once been such an artist trying so hard to drum up enthusiasm for trashy movies with which she formerly would not have even considered associating herself, putting up with the whims of semi-celebrities without a tenth of her former talent, and humoring right-wing political figures whose very presence once would have deeply offended her." Jeffrey Kauffman, on the other hand, says that the material he has viewed shows a "warm and congenial hostess, laughing and interacting beautifully with her on-air guests."

In his *Frances* DVD audio commentary, director Graeme Clifford comments that he found Frances "wooden" in the appearances he saw of her on the show. In the *E! Mysteries and Scandals* television episode on Frances, Dr. Conrad Lane comments, "I would sit there and think, at the end of the show, you made it through another day," implying that she had difficulty doing so. In the *A&E Biography* episode on Frances, David Farmer says of the show:

> It was an ideal world for her because she was a hometown celebrity. They were respectful of her privacy and she was working regularly. She had a great amount of self-esteem. Those were good years for her.

Producer Fletcher Markle was an actor, writer, and director who had previously produced the family comedy television series *Life with Father* (1953), the television drama *Front Row Center* (1955), and episodes for the television anthology series *The Ford Television Theater* (1952), *Studio One* (1953), *The George Sanders Mystery Theater* (1957), and *Colgate Theater* (1958).

In 1982 WFBM was known as Channel 6 WRTV, and their news show broadcast a twenty-eight minute, five-part special report on Frances entitled *Indiana Epilogue*. The special was produced Lyn Letsinger-Miller, with photography and editing by Leo Miller, and was hosted by Howard Caldwell, sitting in the same studio where Frances had filmed her show (although it was now empty of the set, naturally). The report covered Frances' history leading up to the television show, her "stormy" relationship during its production, the issue of her being mentally ill and whether or not she received a lobotomy, and her life after the show ended. The program incorporated photographs of her homes, businesses, and one of Jean Ratcliffe with Frances. Caldwell also conducted interviews with Conrad Lane, former Channel 6 general manager Eldon Campbell, co-worker and replacement host Jim Gerard, former Channel 8 executive Dave Smith, friends Marge Tissot, Rosilee Dilts, Charles Barnes, Lee Howery, and Mozelle Schaffer, Wishard Neurology director Shirley Mueller, and psychiatrist Dr. John Nurnberger.

Chapter one covers Frances' years in Hollywood, displaying stills, a poster and lobby card from *Too Many Parents*; stills and footage from *Rhythm on the Range*; a still from *Come and Get It*; pictures from the *Life* magazine article on *Golden Boy*; and a lobby card for *Ride a Crooked Mile*. Conrad Lane comments that Frances' career failure was due to the material she was offered, her attitude, and the directors she worked with (according to Lane, Howard Hawks was the only director worthy of her). Some of the famous 1943 arrest photographs are shown, as is the 1938 picture taken of Frances with her parents seen in Edith Farmer's book *Look Back in Love*, when Lillian is spoken of as the one who had her daughter committed to Steilacoom. A photograph of Frances with Lee Mikesell is also included.

The second chapter concentrates on the six years of Frances' employment on the show. Three excerpts are shown. One is dated 1963 and shot at Purdue University where she was concurrently appearing on stage in *The Sea Gull*. In this clip she talks to the camera and presents as articulate and composed, confident and friendly. In another excerpt, shot around the same time, Frances interviews the head of the university and laughs when he tells her how he enjoys talking to beautiful women. However, the third clip shows Frances to be nervous as she talks to the camera, with faltering speech, and it is used to highlight Caldwell's claim that she was "ill at ease in front of the camera." Lobby cards for *Flowing Gold* and *Ebb Tide* are shown as evidence that Frances introduced some of her own movies on the show. Caldwell says that by 1962 Frances was becoming angry and would leave the set on occasion, something which Jim Gerard says was due to a misunderstanding only "in her mind." The report also contends that Frances' use of alcohol is what led to the end of her run on the show, with Eldon Campbell acknowledging that her badly handled appearance on *The Today Show* in the spring of 1964 was the beginning of the end, and the "trigger" to her deterioration.

In the third segment of the report, Campbell states that in the first four years of her TV show Frances was "malleable and directable," but thinks she had moments when she "flashbacked to her big time days," which "bothered" her. He says that her last two years were "one descent after another." The episode offers footage of Frances' North Park home and her cabin in Brown County. Caldwell says that Jean Ratcliffe refused to grant an on-camera interview, and also denied altering Frances' copy of the alleged autobiography *Will There Really Be a Morning?*, as was claimed by Edith Farmer. This segment also reveals some of Frances' Brown County friends, who gather at the Old Hickory Tavern to speak about her. Marge Tissot comments on the financial failure of the gift shop that Frances opened in 1966, with footage of the old bank building in Nashville that housed the shop. "She had a very artistic talent and had a way of talking to people," observed Tissot, "but when it came down to the nitty gritty of the gruesome details of book keeping and so forth, that's where she was long gone." Interestingly, Caldwell states that Frances had known Marge in Hollywood, since she had been a technicolor engineer. Antiques dealer Lee Howery, who is shown in a photograph with Frances, also comments that he never saw her inebriated, countering the claim that alcohol remained a problem for her.

Episode four explores the questions of whether or not Frances was "insane," and whether the lobotomy occurred. After another 1943 arrest photograph and the 1944 Antioch arrest photo seen in William Arnold's book *Shadowland* are shown, we get dramatizations of the insulin, electric shock, and hydrotherapy treatments Frances received at Steilacoom. These dramatizations are filmed either in yellow or blue light, and are accompanied by horror movie music. The "possible" lobotomy receives a similar presentation, although it is not as graphic as that seen in the later documentary on Walter Freeman, *The Lobotomist*. Caldwell acknowledges that Steilacoom has no record of Frances being lobotomized, though the institution does confirm the other treatments. Expert testimony from Shirley Mueller does not support the lobotomy conjecture, yet remains inconclusive. After viewing footage of Frances on her show, Mueller concludes, "She initiates conversations with her guests and carries it off nicely. And is able to talk in a conversational manner with her guests, but it would be impossible to tell from the tapes whether she had a transorbital." Close friend Mozelle Schaffer believes Frances never had the lobotomy because, she says, "She [Frances] told me so."

As to the question of whether Frances was "insane," Dr. John Nurnberger disagrees with the hospital's diagnosis of Frances as a paranoid schizophrenic. He says, "Paranoid schizophrenics are very, very sick people, but they are sick in very special ways. They are not necessarily agitated at all or over-active, as she [Frances] apparently was many times during her hospitalizations."

Caldwell claims that Frances' sporadic use of alcohol could be evidence of her mental disturbance. Schaffer adds:

> I think Frances was always worried about maybe being sent back to an institution, even though she was not insane. And when she saw her hospital records—it was only maybe a couple of years before she died—at that point she said to a doctor who went over with her, "Do you think I was ever insane?" And he said no. And she said, "Neither did I."

None of the biographical source materials mention Frances returning to Steilacoom for this viewing of her medical records at the time that Schaffer attests; although that doesn't mean that it didn't happen. Perhaps at the time it was possible to view them without having to return to the Washington hospital, since one imagines that the prospect of going back there, if only to visit the administration section, would have been traumatic and therefore unlikely.

After showing footage from Frances' episode of *This Is Your Life*, the final segment has Mozelle Schaffer, Eldon Campbell, Jim Gerard, and Caldwell giving an assessment of Frances. Asked to use five or six words to describe her, Schaffer replies, "Intelligent, extremely so, marvelous sense of humor, total integrity, extremely direct, honest, great fun to be with, relaxed, reserved." Campbell says of Frances:

> First of all, one of the most beautiful women I ever saw in my life. When she was on, she was really on. And she was gracious. She was very sensitively kind at heart. She was cooperative. She was well-read and informed.

Gerard responds with, "She was an elegant, elegant woman. And unfortunately, when she drank, she was a Jekyll and Hyde and she changed dramatically. But I like to focus on the style, the caring elegance which was Frances Farmer." Caldwell comments, "There are those who call her life a disaster, but many who knew her best wouldn't agree. They only remember a talented outspoken beauty who battled back to find a great deal of happiness." The program ends with a montage of footage and photos from *Rhythm on the Range*, *Ride a Crooked Mile*, *Ebb Tide*, *Exclusive*, studio portraits of Frances, and stills from *Frances Farmer Presents*. The montage is accompanied by Elaine Paige's recording of the song "Memory" from the stage musical *Cats*.

## *Release*

Broadcast October 13, 1958—September 4, 1964.

# BIOPICS AND DOCUMENTARIES

## *Frances* (1982)

Brooksfilms

**Credits:** A Brooksfilms Production. Director: Graeme Clifford; Producer: Jonathan Sanger; Co-Producer: Marie Yates; Associate Producer/Unit Production Manager: Charles Mulvehill; Screenplay: Eric Bergren, Christopher Devore, Nicholas Kazan; Photography: Laszlo Kovacs; Costumes: Patricia Norris; Music: John Barry; Editor: John Wright; Production Design: Richard Sylbert; Art Director: Ida Random; Set Decorator: George Gaines; Set Designer: Emad Helmey; Sound: Kay Rose; Makeup: Dorothy Pearl; Hair: Toni Walker; Script Consultants: Stewart O. Jacobson, Lois Kibbee. Color, 140 minutes. Filmed on location in New York, Seattle, Malibu, and Hollywood, California.

**Songs:** "Piano Sonata in A Major, K331" (Wolfgang Amadeus Mozart), performed by Chet Swiatkowski; "It Don't Mean a Thing" (Duke Ellington, Irving Mills), "Jeepers Creepers" (Harry Warren, Johnny Mercer), "Million Dollar Baby" (Harry Warren, Mort Dixon, Billy Rose), performed by Mood Indigo; "Symphony No. 7, Opus 92, 2nd Movement in A Major" (Ludwig van Beethoven), performed by the Berlin Philharmonic Orchestra; "Flow Gently Sweet Afton" (Robert Burns), performed by Jessica Lange; "Love Is So Terrific" (Sunny Skylar, Arthur Shaftel), performed by Bing Crosby and the Rhythmaires.

**Cast:** Jessica Lange (Frances Farmer); Sam Shepard (Harry York); Kim Stanley (Lillian Farmer); Bart Burns (Ernest Farmer); Christopher Pennock (Dick Steele, aka Dwayne Steel); James Karen (Judge Hillier); Gerald S. O'Loughlin (Lobotomy Doctor); Sarah Cunningham (Alma Styles); Allan Rich (Mr. Bebe); Woodrow Parfrey (Dr. Doyle); Jack Riley (Bob Barnes); Darrell Larson (Louella's Spy); Jordan Charney (Harold Clurman); John Randolph (Kindly Judge); Keone Young (Chinese Doctor); Bonnie Bartlett (Studio Stylist); Jeffrey DeMunn (Clifford Odets); Lane Smith (Dr. Symington); Jonathan Banks (Hitchhiker); James Brodhead (Desk Sergeant); J. J. Chaback (Lady at Roosevelt Hotel); Daniel Chodos ("No Escape" Director); Rod Colbin (Sentencing Judge); Donald Craig (Ralph Edwards); Lee De Broux ("Flowing Gold" Director); Jack Fitzgerald (Clapper Man); Nancy Foy (Autograph Girl); Anne Haney (Hairdresser); Richard Hawkins (Bum on Street); Patricia Larson (Mrs. Hillier); Albert Lord (*Flowing Gold* A.D.); Vincent Lucchesi (Arresting Sergeant); Jack Manning (Studio Photographer); Rob Pilloud (Martoni Kaminski); Larry Pines (Man on Phone/Bookie Joint); David V. Schroeder (Studio Lawyer); Helen Schustack (Wardrobe Mistress); Sandra Seacat (Drama Teacher); Charles Seaverns (Real Estate Man); Karen Strandjord (Connie); Vern Taylor (Studio Executive); Andrew Winner (Firechief); Biff Yaeger (Motorcycle Cop); Alexander Zale (Man in Screening Room); Paul Fleming, M. C. Gainey, Roger Galloway, Matthew Goldsby, Paul

Keith, F. William Parker, Charles Shull (Reporters, Publicists, Photographers); Teda Bracci, Jan Burrell, Flo di Re, Dodds Frank, Patricia Gaul, Robin Ginsburg, Pamela Gordon, Angelica Huston, Jamie Johnston, Ola Kaufman, Donna LaMana, Sharmagne Leland-St. John, Jane Lillig, Alexandra Melchi, Patricia Post, Zelda Rubenstein, Nina Schneider, Marlene Silvers, Vicki Williams, Susan Wolf (Hospital Sequence Mental Patients); Tom Amundsen, Anne Haslett, Barry Jamesby, Len Lookabaugh, Oceana Marr, Vahan Moosekian, Tom Pletts, Eileen T'Kaye, Lila Waters (Doctors, Nurses, and Orderlies); Charles Prior, Carl Kraines (Soldiers). Uncredited: Kevin Costner (Luther Adler).

**VHS/DVD:** DVD released June 22, 1999, by Republic Pictures, and February 19, 2002, by Starz/Anchor Bay.

## Synopsis

After winning an essay writing contest in school at sixteen, Frances Farmer has her first taste of notoriety, which continues when, at twenty-one, she travels to Russia to see the Moscow Art Theater. Back in New York, she is unable to find work as an actress on Broadway so accepts a Paramount movie contract. Having made a few movies but unhappy in Hollywood, Frances jumps at the chance to star on Broadway in the Group Theater production *Golden Boy*. She begins an affair with the playwright Clifford Odets, but he ends it when the play's run finishes. Heartbroken, Frances returns to Hollywood but with a drinking problem. During World War II she is arrested for drunk driving and later charged for parole violation and assaulting a hairdresser on the set of a movie. Frances' mother, Lillian, allows Frances to avoid prison by transferring her to the Meadow Wood Convalescent Home, since she believes that her daughter is crazy. When Frances' friend Harry York visits, he helps her escape. After Frances returns home, Lillian is made her daughter's legal guardian. Frances realizes she is not suited to a Hollywood career, but her mother cannot accept this decision and, after the women fight, has Frances committed to a state hospital.

Harry colludes with a Chinese hospital doctor to give Frances a drug to help her successfully get through a review hearing, and she is released, thought to be cured of mental illness. Running away from home the night she is returned, Frances rejects Harry's marriage proposal. Found as a vagrant by the police, Frances is brought back home, but Lillian again has her taken back to the hospital, where she remains—in the violent ward—for the next five years. During this time she is given a lobotomy by Dr. Walter Freeman. In 1958 Harry watches Frances on the television show *This Is Your Life* and goes to the Roosevelt Hotel to meet her. Harry sees how the lobotomy has robbed her of her once vibrant personality, and walks with her. An end title tells us that Harry does not stay with Frances, who, after starting a family and hosting her own television show in Indianapolis in the 1960s, dies alone.

## Notes

This first and perhaps best-known biopic of Frances stars Jessica Lange in a heartbreaking (and Academy Award–nominated) performance. The sensationalistic treatment (in its inclusion of a lobotomy) presents Frances as a classically tragic rather than pathetic figure. Unlike the made-for-TV movie *Will There Really Be a Morning?* the screenplay does not position Frances as being mentally ill; rather, she is the victim of her mother. While the pacing of director Graeme Clifford slows down for the dramatic scenes after the smooth and rapid first sixty minutes, he can be congratulated for drawing out good supporting performances, and balancing emotionalism and restraint in a scenario that could easily invite gothic excess. Additionally, the music score by John Barry, featuring a mournful harmonica (recalling the use of the same instrument in his score for the film *Midnight Cowboy* [1969], infers the lonely sadness of Frances' life. Acceptable production values allow for solid recreations of imagery and scenarios from Frances' career and life, even though purists will balk at some historical inaccuracies.

French movie card for *Frances* (1982).

The film opens with a title that says it is "based on the true life story of Frances Farmer," although the material used will be a mix of that available in the autobiography and William Arnold's book *Shadowland*, as well as composites and fictionalizations. One example is the character of "Dick 'Dwayne' Steele"—clearly modeled on Leif Erickson, and named as such presumably to avoid a possible libel suit, since Erickson was still alive at the time of filming (Erickson died in 1986).

Frances' "God Dies" essay is showcased during the opening credits, from her writing it, to reading it to Lillian, and then reciting it to a community audience. Our first sight of Frances comes via the reflection of a mirror, with her being seen in mirrors becoming a recurring motif.

The classical music played in Frances' home suggests it is a place of intellectualism (as opposed to the more plebian mentality of popular period music). Ironically, this intellectual stance will not stop Lillian's anti-intellectual attack on her daughter, which will be realized in the most extreme reaction of curtailing her freedom. Lillian's blindness in this regard will extend to her idolatry of Hollywood, and Frances' polar opposite contempt for it.

More than the voices of Susan Blakely and Sheila McLaughlin in *their* biopic efforts, Lange's huskiness is closer to Frances' own voice; and although Lange is slightly taller (at five-foot-eight) than Frances, Lange's sturdy, Midwestern body shape also matches Farmer's. Additionally, Lange's natural dirty blonde hair color is made blonder for Frances' Hollywood period. The only disappointment regarding Lange's appearance is that she has brown eyes, while Frances had blue eyes. Even when portraying Frances as a teenager, Lange's performance suggests both Frances' intelligence and sensitivity, with a touch of eccentricity. While Lange may not possess Farmer's stunning beauty, she is beautiful in her own way. Lange brings Frances' sense of humor to the fore in the scene in which Frances laughs during an awkward screen test kiss, which makes her likeable and creates audience empathy (something vital for the trauma to come). In a film in which we don't see any of evidence of Frances' acting ability, this screen test sequence suggests that her performances are as natural as she is. Although Lange was around the same age as Susan Blakely when Blakely starred as Frances in *Will There Really Be a Morning?*, Lange passes as a teenager (and a woman in her twenties) better than Blakely will, although Lange's greater ability as an actor also helps.

The newsreel that features the congressional candidate Martoni Kaminski is only used to introduce the Harry York character, although it is feasible to compare Kaminski to Marion Zioncheck from Arnold's book. Arnold had used the case of Zioncheck, a Washington congressman of the 1930s who was admitted to the Washington State Hospital and is said to have committed suicide soon after, as part of his conspiracy theory that claimed Frances was committed in order to silence her political activism. Arnold states that Zioncheck's bodyguard had been a man named Stewart Jacobson, who is clearly the inspiration for the Harry York character. (Jacobson serves as one of two script consultants on *Frances*, the other being Lois Kibbee, who had attempted to write Frances' autobiography.)

The Kaminksi affair is absent from the filmed screenplay, although on the DVD audio commentary, Graeme Clifford advises that the original screenplay by Eric Bergren and Christopher Devore split the narrative between the stories of Zioncheck and Frances. Clifford says that, apart from the Harry York character, the Zioncheck connection to Frances is that her father Ernest had done some legal work for Zioncheck. The film's Harry York exists as narrator and convenient Frances savior. Thankfully, this narrative conceit is redeemed by the obvious rapport between Lange and Sam Shepard, who would become a real-life couple after making the movie.

When Frances tells Lillian of her winning the trip to Russia as a way to get to New York, she speaks lines that prefigure both her independence and Lillian's vindictiveness: "I learned your lesson. Do what you think is right. Everyone else be damned." The screenplay jumps over Russia and New York and lands Frances in Hollywood, recreating a photo shoot of her in front of a wall of white flowers.

The character of Mr. Bebe becomes the Paramount production head, although no one by this name is mentioned in the studio history provided by John Douglas Eames in his book *The Paramount Story*. Bebe is shown to be sexist when he comments on Frances' "good tits" and calls her "tootsie" (which is ironic, given the name of Lange's next film). Bebe's "toots" comment is made during shooting of *Rhythm on the Range*, after he tells Frances that he plans to make a great deal of money off her.

Frances' honesty and troublesomeness is indicated by her refusal to change her name and her resistance to the unreal neatness of the suit she wears. Frances' resistant spirit is seen in Lange's eyes and mirrored by the men demonstrating at the studio gate in her line of vision. Clifford says on the DVD audio commentary that this protest was by union men over Paramount hiring non-union people when the studio found the union too difficult to deal with.

Even though Clifford overplays the Depression-era milieu of Seattle, Frances making a scene at

*Right:* The real Frances in an original Paramount publicity portrait, circa 1936. *Below:* A still for *Frances* (1982) that shows the film's attempt to recreate the original portrait session, although Jessica Lange as Frances is costumed in a different dress.

the premiere of *Come and Get It* shows her lack of tact and unwillingness to accept falsity. This scene brings back Mrs. Hillier to remind Frances of how she had previously told Frances, as a schoolgirl, that she would "go straight to hell." Frances tells Harry afterwards, "I'm not proud of it [being in *Come and Get It*]. I did what they told me. That's all they let me do." This ignores that we know how the film had started—with her collaboration with director Howard Hawks, of which evidence remains in the completed product— before her clash with the replacement William Wyler.

*Frances* shows the Mt. Kisco Playhouse 1937 summer production of *The Petrified Forest* that lead Harold Clurman and Clifford Odets to offer Frances the part in the Broadway production of *Golden Boy*. Interestingly, the sequence shows neither Clurman nor Odets applauding the performance (in which we see Frances has a supporting part), with Odets, in particular, disturbed by the standing ovation.

Jeffrey deMunn resembles the real Odets, and is pretentious but lacks the bile made apparent in the later Odets portrayals in *Will There Really Be a Morning?* and *Committed*. The idea that he has earned money from writing movies is only supported by the fact that his only produced screenplay appears to be for the Paramount crime thriller *The General Died at Dawn* (1936). Odets dropping red rose petals on the bed where he and Frances will make love suggests both his sensuality and perversity, and it is his influence that starts Frances on the road to drinking. As with its lack of coverage of her film performances, *Frances* also denies us a sample of Frances' stage acting, which is perhaps wise given Jessica Lange's lack of theater experience at the time.

The recreation of the mud scene from *Flowing Gold* has been discussed in that film's chapter; however, what is interesting is that the director (which we know to have been Alfred E. Green, though he's not named as such in the screenplay) is shown to be a lackey of Mr. Bebe's, who is deliberately making Frances do take after take just to humiliate her. This naturally causes Frances to dislike him, which becomes apparent in the party scene when she pulls a face upon seeing him. Frances' arrival at the party—with Bob Barnes, her studio-appointed guardian—is the only mention in the film of her use of Benzedrine, and here it is not named as such. ("Barn" gives Frances a pill, saying, "They make 'em in the studio basement; helps keep the fat off; make you feel nice and peppy.") The inclusion of the party is interesting on more than one level, partly as a forced studio obligation and also as the famous party Frances had attended before her dim-out zone arrest. The party is not said to be held by Deanna Durbin at Durbin's house, as one version of the real-life events has it. Nor does the film utilize the more acceptable notion that Frances had been at the house of her sister, Rita.

Frances taking a bath during the party and then appropriating a dress from the hostess are signs of Frances' defiance, since we have heard her complain to "Barn" how she hasn't had a chance to change out of the clothes in which she started the day. The party guests all stop to watch in silence as Frances walks down the staircase because she looks so beautiful—probably better than the hostess owner of the white gown.

The arrest sequence highlights the arrogance of the motorcycle cop, who provokes Frances by turning off her lights and shining his torch in her face. The bruises on her wrists suggest that there is more to the struggle that led to her arrest than we initially saw, with the bruises also suggesting that perhaps she was more than just man-handled. Clifford slows down his pacing for the accumulation of the scenes that show Frances' inescapable downward spiral, so that his deliberateness increases the dreaded impact. The scene with the hairdresser on the set of *No Escape*, like with the cop, shows Frances on the defensive, since the hairdresser is patronizing—"You're not the star of this show"—and treats Frances roughly. That comment is particularly amusing because Frances was the biggest matinee star in that film, even if Dean Jagger has the larger part. The comment and the hairdresser's employment on a Monogram picture also imply that the hairdresser has lost status—just like Frances had at this time by having to accept a part in a Poverty Row production. Frances looking in a mirror as her hair is brushed continues the mirror motif.

When Frances is shown arriving four-and-a-half hours late to the set of *No Escape*, the sequence doesn't read as believable for two reasons. First, assistant director Arthur Gardner had recalled in Tom Weaver's book on John Carradine that Gardner had gone to get Frances after she had failed to show up. Second, one would think that the production would have moved on to other setups in light of Frances' absence, particularly since she played only a supporting role. Although there is no verification in the biographical sources for the specific way Frances walked out on the production, her behavior here is believable given the context of her mental disturbance while making the film.

The reporters and photographers at the police station with Frances when she is arrested provide an ironic counterpoint to the attention a star actress would normally receive at work and in public. The screenplay makes Frances' reply to the Desk Sergeant's request for her name funny: "You jerks drag me down here in the middle of the night and you don't know who the hell I am?!" Frances' "cocksucker" response to his asking her occupation earns a laugh—not from the "Woo" reaction of the reporters, but from the facial tick of the Desk Sergeant. Lange in her prison cell recalls those photos taken of the real Frances, particularly when she lies on the cot, with the photographers' access an initial surprise. Regrettably, the film does not recreate the famous shot of her brawling with the police.

In court, Lange twists what looks like a paper clip in her hand, a piece of business that she will repeat later during her asylum hearing, effectively expressing neurosis. Unlike Susan Blakely in *Will There Really be a Morning?* Lange makes the famous Farmer remarks sound natural, believable and funny, even if her voice rising in pitch when she yells dilutes some of the impact. She also provides the suggestion of sleepless disorientation and potential madness in Frances' demeanor, with her messy, uncombed hair both an expression of her disturbance and her stance against Hollywood star grooming.

Frances has a line which mixes moviemaking and the reality of the situation when she responds to the sentencing judge's comment "You caused trouble on a movie set in Mexico," with, "I was fighting there, too; the same reason but a different scene." Lange delivers the line, which follows her prior "I was fighting for my country as well as myself," without any indication of sarcasm or irony.

In another, smaller courtroom, the shadow of Venetian blinds falls over Frances like prison stripes. This recalls the shadows cast by her porch fence railing in the beach house sequence, and also prefigures the use of Venetian blind shadows in the sanitarium. (Changing the sanitarium name to Meadow Wood, rather than using the real La Crescenta, was presumably done—like the Leif Erickson situation—to avoid potential legal difficulties.)

The first of two scenes between the sanitarium's Dr. Symington and Frances is a classic, with Lane Smith's unctuous performance matching the suppressed rage of Lange's Farmer. Clifford gives Lange a close-up reaction to Lillian telling Dr. Symington, "I have a lot of background material that you're going to find very important in treating my daughter." The climax of the struggle for power between Frances and the doctor comes with her mocking, "Those tiny little beads of sweat on your upper lip give you away," and her look of amused defiance and provocation at the casual way she stubs out her cigarette so that it falls out of the ashtray.

A leaf floating down a pathway, then falling into a pond, is a visual metaphor for Frances' plight. It is significant that, while Frances sadly observes the leaf's predicament, Lillian completely fails to notice.

Harry's rescue of Frances from the sanitarium includes a moment where we aren't sure whether Frances has understood his plan. Lange plays up this uncertainty, so we cannot read whether Frances really is mad or whether she is underplaying her complicity. Harry using an ice pick to threaten a sanitarium attendant prefigures the ice-pick lobotomy to come at the state hospital. Frances' explanation when she refuses Harry's marriage proposal offers a sad truth: "Nobody can screw things up the way I can," meaning that she would screw up their union. Clifford, in his DVD commentary, makes the point that the Harry York character may have been repeatedly rejected by Frances because Jacobson lacked the movie star looks of Sam Shepard.

When Harry drives Frances back to her mother's house, he questions why she would go back. Frances tells him, "I can't give up on her so easily." They then have a sweet exchange which also touches on the issue of whether or not she is suffering from mental illness, but in a light and clever way:

> HARRY: You're crazy [for wanting to go back home].
> FRANCES: Don't tell anybody.

A still of the real Frances can be seen in the scrapbook that Lillian works on, accompanied by other (recreated) photographs. After seeing herself in a mirror above the piano, Frances goes into a strange daze, which Clifford covers with an extreme close-up of her eyes. Although we will see that this is the moment in which she decides to visit her father at his office, the scene remains ambiguous, since we can also conclude that Frances is going into a crazy state. Lillian's assumption that this state is caused by Frances' need for a drink is handled with some humor, although, unlike in *Will There Really Be a Morning?* and *Committed*, we do not see Frances drinking at home at this time.

Frances' talk with her father has him raise the idea of Lillian's unrealized ambition being projected onto her daughter as an explanation (and prefiguring) of why Lillian will object to Frances' idea of abandoning Hollywood. Clifford shows Frances walking away via Ernest's point of view, imbuing it with a sad fatalism by having him see her as a blurred image through a rain-soaked glass window. This scene is perhaps Ernest's strongest with Frances, and presents him as an absent father figure who is unable to stop Lillian from committing their child. It is revealing that in spite of him being a lawyer, Lillian does not seek his legal advice, and his lack of objection to Lillian's actions reek of implicit approval and weakness. Clifford comments in his DVD audio commentary that the rain-soaked window is meant to match Ernest's tears, which are not as apparent.

Clifford's staging of the confrontation between Frances and Lillian, wherein Frances tells her how she wants to "live in the country, have dogs and plant a garden," has Lillian on the staircase with Frances looking up at her. The camera is positioned behind Lillian to show that she has higher status and that Frances is the weaker party—as if she needs her mother's approval to reject Hollywood. Lillian objecting to Frances' plans by saying "I think you've gone crazy" is, of course, ironic. (It carries additional resonance because actress Kim Stanley, playing Lillian, had done the some thing in her career.) That Frances should make this decision just when her agent has contacted her with a new offer is more irony.

Frances' protestations, "I'm not cured—I was never sick," expresses the screenplay's conceit that Frances is not mentally ill. Lillian's rationale for having her daughter committed, as told to Dr. Doyle, is revealing: "All my life I've been trying to live up to my parents' sense of excellence, the sense of independent thought and spirit that built our country. And I taught these things to Frances." Lillian rejects Dr. Doyle's supposition that she can no longer control Frances, and her unfinished sentence "The only way she'll…"— cut off by Alma Styles—suggests that her lawyer has advised Lillian to have Frances committed for reasons unknown.

Clifford makes an effective cut from Doyle's "Now perhaps you can tell us where to find Frances" to Frances in a strait-jacket being carried down a corridor and placed into a presumed hospital cell, screaming "Mamma" in a shameful way. A shock treatment sequence is followed by a shot of a woman on a gurney being brought into a ward—but it is not Frances, as the woman's long hair attests. Clifford then pans past the woman being placed on a bed to where Frances sits on the floor, out of her bed, with falling snow seen through the window behind her. The camera slowly zooms in on Lange in close-up and dissolves to scenes of what we presume are her memory of earlier days with Lillian, Lillian and Ernest, and Frances with Harry.

These scenes are not merely repeats of earlier shots. In his DVD audio commentary, Clifford advises that these moments came from deleted scenes that explained character, in particular the bond between Frances and Lillian to rationalize why Frances would repeatedly return to her mother. These sequences were cut because they were thought to slow the film's opening pace. In his book on Kim Stanley, *Female Brando*, Jon Krampner quotes Stanley saying that the scenes were among the forty-five to fifty minutes of footage cut by Clifford. Clifford would answer that he only excised ten minutes from the film, and that the deleted scenes were lost when the production company who stored them threw them away a few years after the film's release, without his permission.

A shot of soldiers being let out of the hospital ward alludes to the idea of them using it as a brothel. This moment of observation will echo later during the gang rape scene.

The contrivance of Harry rescuing Frances again by colluding with a hospital doctor to give her a drug (identified as reserpine by Clifford in the DVD audio commentary) to clear her head for the next day's hearing is countered by the shot of Frances' eyes and nose seen through the ward's door hole, with Lange's eyes expressing Frances' new lucidity and her pain at Harry having to leave her. The gothic excess of the female patients' performance is justified by the way Clifford presents Frances rehearsing her hearing speech. As she practices, the other patients' hyperbole amusingly matches the farce of Frances' act, although the fine line between their understanding of the joke and their madness is also implied. Clifford intercuts between Frances' rehearsal, flashbacks of the hydrotherapy baths she received, and what appears to be a flash-forward to the hearing. As in her court hearing, Frances twists something in her hands as she speaks—a sign of her artifice and neurosis, which the doctors do not pick up on.

An exhaled breath on the soundtrack underscores the news of her release, intercut with Frances emerging from the sea where she had been swimming. A close-up of Frances when she is returned to the Seattle house has Lange showing her suppressed rage at Lillian and a failed attempt at smiling. Her inability to have sex with Harry at the hotel is a spin on the usual scenario of the man being impotent, with Frances overcoming her fear of being touched in the eventual embrace with him.

Lange shows a cautious friendliness in Frances answering the questions of a hitchhiker she picks up. When Frances hides from a passing police car, and the hitchhiker asks her what she has done, she replies, "You know, I've never been able to figure that out." Of course, the obvious answer is that she has violated the terms of her parole by running away, and she will be arrested for vagrancy; however, the bigger answer is that she has not done what Lillian has asked.

Clifford stages Frances' confrontation with her parents as a reverse of the previous one. This time she stands in the position of dominance on the staircase, a position she will lose when she moves downstairs to meet the hospital attendants who come for her. Her speech to Lillian lacks anger but is still emotional:

> You can send me away and you can pretend I'm crazy and you can pretend I'm still your little girl who can't take care of herself. But Lillian, there is one thing that you cannot pretend anymore, and that is that I love you—because I don't. I can't. Not after what you've done to me. You see, because I am still me. I've been trying real hard all this time to be me. And you, little sister, you haven't been any help at all.

The indignity of Frances having her hair lopped off leads to the greater violation of her gang rape in the cave-like violent ward. This is represented by naked women and Frances' recitation of what sounds like a prayer to help her survive the assault she endures, as she is held down by a group of soldiers who comment on the bargain of "twenty dollars to fuck a movie star," and that "she really is crazy." Clifford advises in his DVD audio commentary that the rape scene as filmed was much longer, and was shortened in editing.

A subjective camera shows Frances being taken on a gurney into the room where she will be operated on by Dr. Walter Freeman. Although he is an observer, Dr. Doyle seen drinking at the sight of the procedure is both an indication of his professional detachment and his non-surgical attitude towards the treatment. One may question why Frances doesn't vocally resist the lobotomy, even when strapped to the gurney, since she is conscious when brought into the room. Lange's close-up shows an awareness of the horror that is to be inflicted upon her, but also an acceptance of her fate.

Freeman's comment that his cure comes with "loss of affect, an emotional flattening, with diminished creativity and imagination" prefigures Frances' zombified expression in the last scene with Harry. Clifford dissolves from Freeman's statement that "lobotomy gets 'em home" to a blackout and then to the *This Is Your Life* show recreation. Clifford comments that originally he had two additional sequences follow the lobotomy, both of which were lost in editing. The first used fiber optic technology to show the ice-pick entering lobes of the brain and its subsequent impact, and the second was a dream sequence with Frances bursting through the surface of water. He would use the latter image for the hospital release scene.

The *This Is Your Life* sequence is perhaps Lange's only disappointing part of her performance, since we have the real show's footage with which to compare. Lange overdoes the use of her eyes in her attempt to further the treatment's claim that Frances was lobotomized. Make-up also has trouble in making Lange look like a woman in her 40s (the real Frances was age 44 at the time).

Frances being alone as she leaves the Roosevelt Hotel is another false note, since her manager Lee Mikesell (who is missing from *Frances*) would have been with her. However, her being alone allows for the reunion with Harry, with her line about being "a faceless sinner" taken from William Arnold's book *Shadowland*. This last scene between Frances and Harry is moving because Lange's performance shows what Frances has lost, particularly in her blank face and slow reactions. Such a loss also applies to that which might have been between the two of them. Frances saying, "Don't be mad, Harry, some things happen for the best," is more of her acceptance of the situation, and recalls the platitudes she speaks on *This Is Your Life*. The film ends with a written scrawl that says Frances died alone, which ignores her relationship with Jean Ratcliffe; and a post-credit disclaimer reads as follows:

> In exchange for the use of certain facilities and per agreement with the California Department of Mental Health the producers have agreed to the following. "Since the 1940s there have been major advances in the care and treatment of the mentally ill. The reprehensible conditions experienced by Frances Farmer are not typical of mental health treatment today."

Clifford's DVD audio commentary mentions that at the time he became interested in directing the film, there were two other proposed productions on the life of Frances: one to be made by Francis Coppola, who abandoned his when the Clifford version went ahead; and the made-for-TV movie *Will There Really Be a Morning?* Clifford says that the main source for the *Frances* screenplay was Stewart Jacobson, since, due to the concurrent made-for-TV movie, Clifford could not use any of the material from the autobiography.

Apart from being a marketing tool for the film, the making-of featurette on the *Frances* DVD, *A Hollywood Life: Remembering Frances*, includes footage of the real Frances and provides some interesting comments by the filmmakers. There are portraits and stills of the real Frances not seen in the film (though some are recreated), Frances on the cover of *Picturergoer* magazine, and excerpts from the trailer for *Come and Get It*. Production Designer Richard Sylbert comments, "[Frances] couldn't dissimilate, which is a real problem in Hollywood, for anybody, at anytime, to not be able to back off." Jessica Lange also comments on the contentious issue of the lobotomy: "You talk to half a dozen people. Half would say yes she was lobotomized. The other half would say she was not. There's circumstantial evidence that it did happen."

On the *A&E Biography* episode on Frances, "Paradise Lost," Lange says of making the film *Frances*: "I really loved Frances. There was something about her that touched me so deeply. Sometimes I actually—and I know this sounds like kind of mumbo jumbo—I could actually feel her presence. I mean, it was a powerful entity." In the same documentary, David Farmer would comment on Lange playing Frances by saying, "I think what she captured was a large part of the inner sense of Frances—her intelligence, her strength. It was just uncanny. It was as though Frances' spirit had come into her."

An article on the website *The Misty One* about the making of *Frances* was assembled by Dario Recla from material featured in the book *Jessica Lange: A Biography* by J.T. Jeffries, the *Frances* pressbook, and the *Frances Original Motion Picture Score* CD booklet. The article gives a potted history of the production. Apparently it all started with William Arnold and Marie Yates. When Yates, a struggling Hollywood producer and agent, saw a 1973 article about Arnold's planned book on Frances—that which would become *Shadowland*—she became his agent and worked out a movie deal with Noel Marshall, the executive producer of *The Exorcist*. Arnold was to write the screenplay for the film. However, Yates supposedly also set up a deal with Jonathan Sanger and Mel Brooks' company Brooksfilms, who offered her a better position in the making of the film. Arnold was removed as screenwriter, and Brooks brought in the two Oscar-nominated screenwriters from his previous production, *The Elephant Man*, Christopher DeVore and Eric Bergren. Arnold sued on copyright infringement charges but lost when it was determined that the producers had used original material from a Seattle elevator operator and former worker for Marion

Zioncheck, Stewart Jacobson. Jacobson had approached Arnold and reportedly offered important secrets of Farmer's life for a fee, claiming a long romantic relationship with her. Arnold sent Jacobson to Yates. (Yates would later deny that she had met Jacobson via Arnold.) In *Shadowland*, Arnold makes mention of Jacobson but certainly does not present him as having the relationship with Frances that the screenplay would.

Fellow script consultant Lois Kibbee was dubious about Jacobson, who was sometimes known as Harry York. Kibbee said that Frances had never mentioned him to her in the interviews she held while working on the autobiography that she would subsequently abandon. Jacobson's extensive criminal history also created doubts. Charged with murder in 1939 and acquitted, he had also been arrested for vagrancy, witness tampering, and assault, as well as being charged with pimping and convicted as an unlicensed private investigator. Jacobson explained the lack of any photos of Frances with himself by claiming they had been destroyed; and he had also given orders that he not be mentioned in what would become the published autobiography *Will There Really Be a Morning?* Opposing Arnold's claim that the issue of the lobotomy had been taken from his book, Yates would say that it was confirmed by Jacobson and her own research with Seattle judges, who could not be named.

Jessica Lange came to the production after her own history with Frances. She had been told about the actress by an acting teacher, Warren Robertson, in 1974. In her class, Lange had seen Susan Blakely read dialogue from *Will There Really Be a Morning?* (an indication of Blakely's own interest that would lead her to produce the made-for-TV movie and play Farmer). Lange, too, became interested in developing Frances' story as a film, and worked with Robertson, while at the same time beginning her own film career. She came across some 8-millimeter home movies of Frances in summer stock and met with Kibbee. She had tried in vain to persuade both Bob Fosse, who had directed her in *All That Jazz* (1979), and Bob Rafelson, who had directed her in *The Postman Always Rings Twice* (1981), to make the film.

Production on the Brooksfilm *Frances* began after eight drafts of the screenplay had been written by DeVore and Bergren, and Nicholas Kazan had been brought in for a polish (Graeme Clifford in the DVD audio commentary says Kazan had been brought in by him). The budget was set at $10 million; former editor Clifford was hired to direct (marking his debut); and Lange was cast, on Clifford's recommendation after other actresses, like Diane Keaton, Jane Fonda, Tuesday Weld, Goldie Hawn, Sissy Spacek, Katharine Ross, Mia Farrow, Susan Sarandon, Lauren Hutton, Valerie Perrine, Cathy Lee Crosby, and Natalie Wood, had expressed interest. Lange had previously played leading roles in *King Kong* (1977), *How to Beat the High Cost of Living* (1980), and *The Postman Always Rings Twice*, on which Clifford was the editor and associate producer.

For *Frances*, Kim Stanley was cast in the role of Lillian Farmer, over other choices Kim Hunter and Celeste Holm. Legendary stage actress Stanley had not made a feature film since the 1966 Actors Studio production of *The Three Sisters*. She had previously been nominated for the Best Actress Academy Award for the crime drama *Séance on a Wet Afternoon* (1964). Stanley's best known role, as the self-destructive star of the drama *The Goddess* (1958), though based on Marilyn Monroe, recalls some of the torment of Frances Farmer.

Producer Jonathan Sanger and uncredited producer Mel Brooks had previously made another biographical drama, *The Elephant Man*. Sanger had also been associate producer on *Fatso* (1980), which was directed by Brook's wife, Anne Bancroft. *Frances* appears to be the only film that Marie Yates would produce.

Director Graeme Clifford with his star Jessica Lange on the set of *Frances* (1982).

## *Release*

December 3, 1982, with the tagline, "Her story is shocking, disturbing, compelling ... and true." A benefit screening of the film was held in Seattle, Washington, in January 1983, at the Liberty Theater, the same theater at which *Come and Get It* originally premiered and where this recreated scene in *Frances* had been shot. Jessica Lange was nominated for the Best Actress Academy Award for her work in *Frances*, as well as Best Supporting Actress for *Tootsie* (1982); it is thought that her winning the Best Supporting Actress Award was a consolation for losing the Best Actress Award to Meryl Streep for *Sophie's Choice* (1982). *Frances*' Kim Stanley was also nominated for the Best Supporting Actress Academy Award.

## *Reviews*

"Full credit must go to Lange, who truly rises far above the material. Usually, it's annoying to be constantly aware that the performer up on the screen is 'acting.' On the other hand, sometimes it's pure pleasure to watch."—*Variety*, November 22, 1982

"It contains a magnificent performance by Jessica Lange in the title role.... The excitement of watching her goes a long way toward transforming the film, which is a colossal downer, into an experience that is, if not exactly uplifting, genuinely memorable."—Vincent Canby, the *New York Times*, December 3, 1982

"A relentlessly depressing film bio.... Lange is believable.... Credit to Clifford for holding the lurid aspects as far down as he did."—Jay Robert Nash and Stanley Ralph Ross, *The Motion Picture Guide, 1927–1983*

"Well-made by Clifford, it is bleak without being unwatchable.... Jessica Lange plays Frances Farmer in a performance that is so driven, that contains so many different facets of a complex personality, that we feel she has an intuitive understanding of this tragic woman."—Roger Ebert, *Chicago Sun-Times*, January 28, 1983

"Farmer has become a small industry of late—this movie, a TV biography, three off–Broadway plays and three books—but no one has been able to turn those fascinating snippets of degradation into a coherent story line.... Jessica Lange emerges more than honorably ... she can be, like Frances Farmer, both vulnerable and powerful."—Richard Corliss, *Time* magazine, December 13, 1982

"[Gives Lange] the opportunities for brilliant nuances in a dud movie."—Pauline Kael, *Hooked*

# *Will There Really Be a Morning?* (1983)

## Orion TV Productions

**Credits:** A Production of Jaffe-Blakeley Films and Sama Productions, Inc., in association with Orion Television. Director: Fielder Cook; Producer: Everett Chambers; Executive Producers: Sandy Arcara, Stephen Jaffe; Executive in Charge of Production: Stanley Neufeld; Associate Producer: Steve Nicolaides; Supervising Producer: Richard M. Rosenbloom; Teleplay: Dalene Young, based on the autobiography by Frances Farmer; Photography: Michel Hugo; Editor: George Nicholson; Production Design: Karen Bromley; Music: Billy Goldenberg; Production Manager: Gwen Iveson; Toronto Set Decorator: Steve Shewchuk, Toronto Makeup: Anne Brodie; Toronto Hair: Paul LeBlanc; Los Angeles Art Director: Bill McAllister; Los Angeles Set Decorator: Peggy Cummings; Costumes: Linda Bishop, Jim Kessler; Los Angeles Makeup: Ed Butterworth; Los Angeles Hair: Carol Michaels, Lola Kemp; Sound: Richard Birnbaum; Color, 136 minutes. Filmed in Toronto, Canada, and Hollywood.

**Cast:** Susan Blakely (Frances Farmer); Lee Grant (Lillian Farmer); Royal Dano (Ernest Farmer); Joe Lambie (Bill Anderson); John Heard (Clifford Odets); Melanie Mayron (Sophie Rosenstein); Leonard Cimino (Adolph Zukor); Jack Creeley (Professor Williams); James Eckhouse (Harold Clurman); Jeanne Elms (Lottie); Joseph Maher (1st Hospital Doctor); Bruce Ornstein (John Garfield); Paul Perri (Luther Adler); Madeline Thornton-Sherwood (2nd Hospital Doctor); Ivor Frances (Drama Teacher); Roger Barton (Actor #1); Neil Affleck (Actor #2); Donnann Cavin (Actress #3); Joe Pagano (Actor #4); Sydney Armus (Judge); Frederick Rolf (Agent); Richard B. Shull (Publicist); Keith James (Reporter #1); Paddy Carol Brown (Reporter #2); Jim Chad (Reporter #3); Robert Hawkins (Franchot Tone); George Touliatos (Makeup Man); Dalene Young (Hairdresser); Joe Grifasi (Wyler); James Cahill (Howard Hawks); Michelle Leigh Stevens (Frances, Age 9); Thomas Barbour (Director); Martha Gibson (Script Girl); Neil Dainard (Justice of the Peace); Ray Powers

(Photographer #1); Eric Stine (Photographer #2); Bob Larkin (Reporter); Sean Moloney (Young Man); Alan Scarfe (Doctor #3); Joanne Strauss (Nurse); Meg Hogarth (Police Matron); Angus McInnes (Policeman #1); John Kirby (Sailor); Charles Prior (Reporter #4); Clark Stevens (Reporter #5); William B. Ward (Reporter #6). Uncredited: Hayley Taylor (Young Frances Farmer).

**VHS/DVD:** Not available in either format. A UK video was released by Rank Video in 1984 but appears to be out of print.

## Synopsis

*Will There Really Be a Morning?* details the life of Frances Farmer, tracing her childhood in Seattle; her college years, when she decided to become an actress; her success in films and the theater; her doomed love affair with playwright Clifford Odets; her physical and mental breakdown; and her ultimate emergence from an institution, where she spent five years.

## Notes

Susan Blakely in a publicity portrait for the made-for-TV movie *Will There Really Be a Morning?* (1983). Unfortunately, this attempt at recreation does not resemble the real Frances in any known studio portrait.

As equally disappointing as the feature film *Frances*—but for different reasons—this made-for-TV movie is hampered by the miscasting of Susan Blakely as Frances, a generic music score, and a treatment that trivializes her story and is historically inaccurate. Adapted from the contentious autobiography, the teleplay presents Frances as a woman suffering from ennui because of her distaste for acting and Hollywood, and whose fragile mental state is affected by her doomed affair with Clifford Odets and the struggle for independence from her mother (who appears to be even more mentally ill than her daughter). While there is some amusing dialogue, and the occasional interesting visual touch, director Fielder Cook succeeds best with the sadomasochistic relationship Frances is shown to have had with Odets, played with impressive egotism and nastiness by John Heard. Generally, this movie suffers from the repetition of material from *Frances*, although the teleplay fails to mention the attempted comeback, which is in the book and which *Frances* included, albeit briefly. Those familiar with the book can see an enactment of scenes that are done more literally than with inspiration, although some of the shorthand references in the teleplay assumes a prior knowledge of the events of Frances' life.

Blakely looks, acts and sounds nothing like the real Frances, who was petite and fleshy, with a deep, evocative voice and a stunningly beautiful face, and only in her twenties when her life fell apart. In her early thirties when the movie was made, Blakely is far too old (particularly when attempting to play a teenager), her beauty too conventional, and her intelligence too circumspect. Blakely's tall gangliness also gives her a different, and at times almost comic, body language, which is inappropriate for the tone of the piece. All this could have been overlooked if Blakely had brought something else to the part, the way Jessica Lange did in *Frances*; however, the role exposes Blakely's severe dramatic limitations. Her acting as Farmer on stage is particularly bad, which works against the praise the character receives. Blakely is good at listening, glares well, and has the technique to pull off some quiet and silent moments (e.g., her disbelief at Odets' boorishness, and when she contemptuously signs an autograph for a nurse in the asylum). However, her anger has no force, and she makes her Frances a shallow, self-indulgent and unlikable person. While it is conceivable that the real Frances possessed these qualities, presented in a dramatic vehicle, they don't engender empathy for someone in distress and pain.

As Frances, Blakely begins badly with an arch reading of the Emily Dickinson poem that inspired the book and movie's title, and makes it worse with her idea of playing a teenager like a cartoon—all attitude and pulling faces. Director Fielder Cook makes the Farmer home claustrophobic in its intimacy, and Lillian a controlling hysteric. However, Lillian scores a laugh with her first line, in spite of its negativity, when Frances runs into Ernest's arms: "Frances, your wrinkling your father's jacket." The treatment uses narration, some taken from the book, and sepia-colored faux photographs to delineate new chapters and locations, as if this device adds an element of mythology to Frances' tale.

Lillian's pleasure at her daughter winning the essay contest gives her character some dimension, so that she reads as more than a mere monster; but Lillian's appropriated fame adds a dark element to Frances' success. Lillian rejecting her daughter's wish for anonymity in regards to the press coverage is done under the guise of self-defense over the misconceptions of the essay. However, it is apparent that Lillian calls her own press conference simply to draw the spotlight onto *her* and to avoid the fear of being "a nobody" (a concept also touched on in *Frances*). This issue of personal integrity and independence will be the dividing wedge between mother and daughter, and will make Lillian a figure as dangerous as Clifford Odets will later prove to be to Frances. Lee Grant's performance as Lillian emphasizes the character's impulsivity, although Grant's slipping southern accent tends to dilute its effectiveness.

Frances in college allows us to meet Sophie Rosenstein, played by Melanie Mayron with sensuality, intensity and the suggestion of lesbianism. Sophie describes Frances as "you with the buttercup complexion and the shattered eyes." It's laughable that Sophie should be mesmerized by Frances' performance in *Alien Corn*, after Blakely garbles her words and uses amateurish gestures.

Frances' first encounter with Clifford Odets begins with a funny line when he goes to her and she initially says nothing. He comments, "Well, all this conversation is stifling me." The following exchange also raises a laugh:

> FRANCES: All I want—
> CLIFFORD: Is to act in an Odets play.
> FRANCES: Not necessarily. I can think of lots of authors I'd rather work with.
> CLIFFORD: Name one.
> FRANCES: Saroyan. Anderson. Howard.
> CLIFFORD: I said one.

Odets' acerbic approach is exemplified by the following: "What exactly are you offering? Talent? We've plenty of that. Beauty? Go to Hollywood. They adore peach and cream beauties out there. Now, would you like to go out to dinner, or not?" These mixed messages indicate his schizophrenic feelings towards Frances, which she will have trouble coping with (as Odets is the first man she has fallen in love with).

The *Golden Boy* read-through scene supplies more acerbic banter between Frances and Odets, following the Hollywood tradition of a squabbling couple destined to become lovers.

> CLIFFORD: What do you have on your legs?
> FRANCES: Cotton stockings.
> CLIFFORD: Lorna Moon wears silk.
> FRANCES: Frances Farmer doesn't.
> CLIFFORD: Stubborn. She won't take direction.
> FRANCES: When I'm in costume, I'll wear what the director tells me to.

The teleplay's reenactments of Frances making the movies *Too Many Parents* and *Come and Get It* are riddled with inaccuracies in staging, costume and dialogue. What is noteworthy about the *Come and Get It* sequence is the perplexing moment when Frances drifts away in Method madness when spoken to by Howard Hawks. This disorientation and lack of focus does not come from the autobiography, which paints this time in Frances' life as a happy one, and notes how pleased she was to be working with Hawks. The teleplay has Frances explain, "My life was becoming intolerable, so I stepped out of myself." In reply, Hawks delivers this sage advice: "You're a fine actress. But you've got to learn when to stop. This isn't real."

Cook uses the first of Frances' childhood flashbacks to express her mental turmoil, as a result of her rejection by Odets and her excessive drinking. These flashbacks feature a blue-tinted lighting scheme and echoed voices that would not be out of place in a horror movie. The first flashback shows the child Frances being berated by a presumably younger Lillian (Lee Grant with loose long hair) for walking into her mother's bedroom without knocking.

Publicity portrait of John Heard, who plays Clifford Odets in *Will There Really Be a Morning?* (1983).

Blakely wears a brunette wig for Frances' flight from New York to hide her famous blondeness (although she will later wear the wig at home as a sign of her mental deterioration). Her scene with a sailor in a hotel room is an indication of a period of promiscuity, presumably another sign of her lonely desperation and mental confusion. Frances' admission of promiscuity is met by stony silence from Lillian at the Seattle home—a form of denial—which is rather surprising and confirms Lillian as being as hard to read as Odets.

The first arrest scene has Blakely playing drunk badly, with the added detail that she punches the cop who stops her. Teleplay writer Dalene Young doubles as the hairdresser on *Ride a Crooked Mile* and *No Escape*, which we know were made for different studios. What makes Young's casting so delicious is the combination of her kewpie doll performance and her being hit by Frances.

The small size of the courtroom used for Frances' hearing is perhaps an indication of the production's budget constraints (and is much more cramped than the courtroom seen in *Frances*). The asylum surroundings seen later in the teleplay are equally minimal. Disappointingly, Blakely delivers Frances' famous courtroom dialogue in a staccato fashion, but the treatment's reveal of Frances being committed to the Montrose Sanitarium is perhaps better handled than in *Frances*, since here we just see the result and not the machinations.

The second flashback occurs at the sanitarium, which makes sense because it comes at a time when Frances would be introspective. In this flashback the child asks for her mother to hold her. Lillian's mental state here mirrors that of her adult daughter, with her wanting to be left alone an echo of what we saw Frances saying in her Hollywood home. This connects the daughter's mental illness to something inherited from her mother, triggered by her mother's rejection (shown by Lillian pushing the child away).

Frances' release to her mother's care comes with an infantile regression in her return to drinking. Lillian's failure to comment on the behavior or attempt to stop it are further signs of her denial. These tedious proceedings momentarily come to life in an argument between the women, with Blakely expressing Frances' anger in a believable fashion—until she goes over the top and her voice becomes a screech.

*Will There Really Be a Morning?* further deviates from reality in a pivotal scene in which Frances pushes Lillian and Ernest to the floor then *herself* suggests that they send her back. This is followed by Frances' peaceful acceptance of being taken away in a strait-jacket—the opposite of the autobiography's account. Frances' violent resistance to this committal would be better realized in *Committed* (this scenario in *Frances* lacks the ugliness of her mother's betrayal and the horror of Frances' entrapment).

Publicity portrait of Lee Grant, who plays Lillian Farmer in *Will There Really Be a Morning?* (1983).

The scene in which a nurse asks for Frances' autograph loses its impact because we cannot read the "Fuck you" that the autobiography tells us that Frances signed, although the nurse's reaction clues us in that something inappropriate had been written. Of course, the exclusion of the expletive was necessary for a made-for-TV movie; and, naturally, we don't hear Frances swear at any other time, something that she was known to do. (The closest she comes to swearing in the movie is telling Odets, "I don't give a damn," and saying to Lillian at the premiere of *Come and Get It*, "Last year I was the tramp of Seattle. Now the governor wants to shake my hand. Well, he can just kiss it, mamma. He can just kiss it.")

As seen in the asylum, Frances' seemingly curly brown hair chopped short is presumably a sign of her madness, which is highlighted in her interview scene with three doctors (taken almost verbatim from the autobiography). Cook adds expressionist camera angles to the blue-tinted lighting, although there is *real* horror and empathy in the following scene when Frances receives shock treatment. It's a pity that Cook felt the need to add horror movie music as well, since this scene—and the way the doors close at the end—effectively conveys the gothic horror of the asylum as described in the autobiography, and not the sanitized version that the real Frances tried to sell us on the *This Is Your Life* episode.

Another change in Frances' hairstyle—reverting to her previous blonde, straight locks—is the visual cue for her change of attitude. For the scene in which Lillian comes to visit Frances after this "transformation," the tone has been changed from the autobiography. In the book this event consists of practically all dialogue, whereas here Frances presents as less controlled in her new attitude. This is apparent in the way Blakely places her hands to the sides of her head to show confusion. The gallows humor of the book, which Cook mostly misses here, is Frances' repeated and failed attempts to appease Lillian, although Cook redeems himself with an extreme close-up of Blakely with a teary smile to show the effort of her act. It is noteworthy that the movie does not address the lobotomy issue (not surprising, perhaps, since it is not featured in the book).

Cook stages Frances' confrontation with her parents over the legal papers issue with suspense. Blakely enters the room, where a record is playing, and pauses before turning off the music and speaking. However, the information that her parole had been granted three years previously and her mental competency had been restored two years ago is more inaccuracy. It works for the purpose of drama, though, to empower the character and disempower those that had disempowered *her*. (The reality was much sadder, as Frances remained under the daily threat of being sent back to the asylum.) In the movie, Frances' promise to stay with her disempowered mother, despite what she had done to Frances, seems an incredible kindness. This is another inaccuracy, since the autobiography tells us that Frances left the Seattle home as soon as she was able.

The conclusion to the teleplay is a romanticized and inaccurate portrait of Frances living in Seattle, now a writer after having poems published. The inaccuracy continues with her statement that she turned down acting roles, and no mention is made of her going to California and marrying two more men (as noted in the autobiography). Rather, the teleplay ends with: "I would now live my life in simple pleasures. I had found my place. The beautiful sunlit morning for which I had waited so long." While this notion compliments the title of the book and the movie, it doesn't satisfy those who know the truth, and caps this poor treatment of Frances' life with further disappointment.

After starting in films in supporting roles, former model Susan Blakely scored leads

Frances (Susan Blakely) is disturbed when she sees that *Come and Get It* is screening at the asylum where she has been committed in *Will There Really Be a Morning?* (1983).

in *The Lords of Flatbush* (1974), *Report to the Commissioner* (1975), and *Capone* (1975). She then turned to television to make the miniseries *Rich Man, Poor Man* (1976), for which she was nominated for the Best Actress Emmy Award. Blakely would continue to make made-for-TV movies, along with the occasional theatrical film. Her role prior to Frances in *Will There Really Be a Morning?* had been Eva Braun in the biographical television drama *The Bunker* (1981). She would be nominated for the Best Actress Golden Globe Award for *Will There Really Be a Morning?* and it would be the only production to date on which she has been credited as producer. Glenda Jackson had been considered to play Frances when Ida Lupino was attached to direct a feature film adaptation. Apparently

Ann-Margret was also considered for the part when this made-for-TV movie production was confirmed, but chose to make the made-for-TV drama *Who Will Love My Children?* (1983) instead.

Fielder Cook was a veteran director of the *Hallmark Hall of Fame* television drama anthology series and had made the TV movies *A Love Affair: The Eleanor and Lou Gehrig Story* (1978), *Too Far to Go* (1979), *I Know Why the Caged Bird Sings* (1979), *Gauguin the Savage* (1980), and *Family Reunion* (1981), his project prior to *Will There Really Be a Morning?* Producer Everett Chambers was also an actor, writer and director, and veteran television producer. He had last produced the television crime drama *Turnover Smith* (1980), and supervised production on *Berlin Tunnel 21* (1981), which was produced by *Morning?*'s associate producer Steve Nicolaides and supervising producer Richard M. Rosenbloom. Nicolaides' prior title was the made-for-TV drama *Not in Front of the Children* (1982). *Will There Really Be a Morning?* is the only producing credit for executive producer Sandy Arcara. Co-executive producer Stephen Jaffe had previously worked on the made-for-TV movie comedy *Make Me an Offer* (1980) and drama *A Cry for Love* (1980), both of which starred Susan Blakely.

## Release

Broadcast February 22, 1983, with the tagline, "The life story of Frances Farmer, the glamorous star of the 1930s."

## Reviews

"One of the premises, never completely proved, of this production is that Miss Farmer was an exceptionally sensitive woman whose talent was too precious to be squandered on mere Hollywood movies.... Blakely provides a harrowing, in many ways memorable performance ... she fully captures the emotional turmoil of the woman."—John J. O'Connor, the *New York Times*, February 22, 1983

"Appears to be more accurate than the theatrical 1982 *Frances*, being adapted directly from Farmer's 1972 autobiography."—Alvin H. Marill, *Movies Made for Television, 1964–2004, Volume 2: 1980–1989*

"Whether Susan Blakely is superior to Jessica Lange in *Frances* is open to debate."—Hal Erickson, *All Movie Guide*

# *Committed* (1984)

Women Make Movies, Inc.

**Credits:** Story Films, in association with Channel Four (England), Presents. Directors/Producers/Screenplay/Editors: Sheila McLaughlin, Lynne Tillman; Photography: Heinz Emigholz; Additional Photography: Sheila McLaughlin, Elfi Mikeesch, Tom Chomont; Sound: Mary Bosakowski; Production Manager: Ruth Mullen; Makeup and Hair: Mark Clements; Costumes: Donna Henes, Dan Johnson.

B&W, 75 minutes. Partly filmed on location at the Collective for Living Cinema, Carnegie Hall Cinema, and the Chelsea Hotel.

**Songs:** "Lobster Leaps In (Phillip Johnston), "Honeysuckle Rose" (Phillip Johnston).

**Cast:** Sheila McLaughlin (Frances Farmer); Victoria Boothby (Lillian Farmer); Lee Breuer (Clifford Odets); John Erdman (Dr. Taylor); Heinz Emigholz (Dr. Kraus); Lucy Sanger (Nurse); John Nesci (Radio Announcer); Peter Walker (Judge); Jim Neu (Lawyer); Clove Breuer (Daughter Taylor); Diana White (Mrs. Taylor); Lute Breuer (Son Taylor); Devon Meade ("Movie Star" Patient); Rose Dreyer ("Shut Up" Patient); Bob Fleischner ("Strike" Man); John McGuire (Man in Rehearsal); Milton Lansky (Courtroom Judge); Peter Blegvad, Maryette Charlton, Paul Gibson, Jim Krell, Allen Robertson (Hospital Attendants); Helen Adam, Susan Berkson, Michelle Hurst, Lillian Kiesler, Lorraine Kennedy, Cynthia Kolbowski, Barbara Wise (Mental Patients); Kirsten Bates, Patricia Bates, Susan Berkson, Dorman Birmingham, Peter Bruno, Maryette Charlton, Rose Dreyer, Anne Friedberg, Seth M. Friedman, Rena Gill, Chantal Guilbaud, Jeanette Hans, Jean Holabird, Lillian Kiesler, Cynthia Kolbowski, Jane Smith, Ela Troyano, Barbara Wise (Strike Audience).

**VHS/DVD:** Video released November 6, 1999, by First Run Features.

## Synopsis

Imprisoned in an asylum, Hollywood actress Frances Farmer befriends a nurse and reflects on what has led her to this point, including her rocky relationship with her mother and an affair with the married playwright Clifford Odets.

## Notes

This generally abysmal independent biopic is marred by a screenplay that lacks dramatic action and attempts to compensate with slabs of exposition and pretentious direction that favors long static takes and expressionist camera angles. The non-linear treatment uses Frances' imprisonment in the asylum as a platform for flashbacks to her relationship with her mother, with the narrative points taken from the *Will There Really Be a Morning?* autobiography. Frances' affair with Clifford Odets is presented as one of sadomasochistic co-dependence, which, apart from some amusing dialogue, is the only redeeming aspect of this film.

The grainy black-and-white photography, with occasional flickering and over-exposed lighting in close-ups (meant to recall that of silent movies), reads more as pretension than an approximation of imagery seen in Frances' films. The film also employs un-synchronized sound in the opening scene of the strait-jacketed Frances being led down a hallway, and particularly in the arrest sentencing scene with the judge. This latter sequence comes off as especially odd, since Frances' dialogue is muted but his is not. The scene is also marred by jarring jump cuts—the only time they are employed in the film. Although the video cover blurb for the film describes it as "highly-stylized" and a "deconstruction," here these terms become synonyms for self-indulgence, pretension, and misguided technique and intention.

The opening scene's vaginal examination adds to the anguish of seeing someone in a strait-jacket, although this scene and the later horrific one in which she is strait-jacketed at home can't counterbalance the way Frances is otherwise presented as a self-indulgent, unlikable slob. This presentation may confirm the opinion stated by her doctors that she is insolent, foul-mouthed, and "an unpleasant person"; however, it makes the character hard to empathize with. Much of the blame for this unsympathetic presentation can be placed on the performance of Sheila McLaughlin, who fails to provide her Frances with any charm or humor (though humor may be a tough call, given the circumstances). McLaughlin's obvious plainness also undermines the repeated points made about how beautiful the character is supposed to be.

A scene between doctors suggests that Frances' commitment is politically motivated, an idea raised by William Arnold in *Shadowland*. However, the only subsequent follow-up to this idea comes when a nurse tells Frances about Clifford Odets being called to testify in front of the House Un-American Activities Committee (HUAC). The idea that her incarceration stops her from being called before the Committee is conveyed by her line, "I'm spared that, being insane." Frances follows this with a comment that's as much about her public behavior and general incarceration as the HUAC: "If I were sane, I wouldn't have told the truth. It's a good test of mental health—the ability to lie."

At the asylum, a camera moves around Frances as she sleeps on a cot before revealing a nurse watching her which comes as a surprise (although the narrative will present Frances' imprisonment as otherwise lacking in oppression). This casualness extends to her talks with the nurse, although eventually the nurse will comment that the two of them seen talking together has threatened her job.

Lillian playing "Silent Night" on the piano while talking to the camera is the first of many instances of Lillian's exposition, with the use of "Silent Night" troubling because its obvious association with Christmas connects the timeline with Frances' third and extended commitment. This narrative time-jumping obscures rather than clarifies the sequence of events for an audience unfamiliar with Frances' real story, something which the opening scene of Frances arriving in a strait jacket also does. However, the bigger concern is that the filmmakers must resort to a character talking directly to the camera, indicating they are not even clever enough to give Lillian a confidante (like Frances' nurse at the asylum). Lillian's awkward expositions continue, with her weeding her garden and later picking fruit.

The scene in which Lillian (referred to only as "Mrs. Farmer" in the screenplay) fastidiously makes a bed, then sits on it, and her obsessively picking lint from her dress, highlights Lillian's own mental instability, which, of course, makes Frances' plight all the more tragic. However, the film really only explores this tragedy in one scene—when Frances screams as she is strait-jacketed and taken away from Lillian's home. Further allusion to Lillian being a bigger whack job than her daughter comes in a scene between her and Frances. When Frances sits at a tiny table with Lillian, who eats breakfast (shown via an extreme close-up of her mouth from Frances' point of view), the following exchange occurs:

> FRANCES: You're driving me crazy.
> LILLIAN: You're the one who's crazy.

Lillian hearing Frances' line as "You're crazy" makes her both defensive and upset, so that Lillian over-pours a cup of coffee—a sign of both anxiety and nuttiness. Since Lillian over-pours Frances' coffee without being aware of what she's doing, the act cannot be considered an act of revenge—although Lillian having Frances recommitted *can*, after Frances comes home drunk. The breakfast scene, Frances' drunken return, and the morning after are perhaps the best sequences in the film, since the screenplay finally provides some dramatic conflict, with Lillian's "You make me sick" adding an element of camp due to the hilarious delivery of Victoria Boothby. As Frances is taken away, Lillian looks out the window, with Boothby's face in the bottom half of the frame. Her expression presents a horror movie mix of fear, madness, embarrassment, shame, pleasure and curiosity.

The scene in which Frances and Odets are in bed begins ambiguously, since we cannot tell whether he is reading from the manuscript he holds or is talking to her; however, her sullen attitude doesn't ring true. Despite her frustration over the relationship, it is known that Frances was happy to be away from Hollywood and working with the Group, even if the romance she had with Odets would prove to be unhealthy. This and the later scenes with Odets add dramatic tension to the treatment, although they also indulge in unrealistic exposition in their dialogue.

Odets' contempt for Frances is expressed in the inevitable comparison he makes between an actress and a whore, although his self-hatred is also apparent. She gets a good line with, "I can't change my face or my background any more than you can," which is also an unintentional and unfortunate comment on McLaughlin's casting. At the end of a performance of *Waiting for Lefty* (only recognized as such because of the famous "Strike" conclusion), there is a bizarre slow-motion slapping of Frances by Odets. One wonders why he would do that to her in public, and why at that moment? We don't see her say or do anything to motivate the slap, so it's hard to know what to think of it (apart from the literal presentation of a strike).

The slap does receive a form of payoff when Frances is seen sleeping in the asylum, surrounded by clapping hands. The clapping associates her with the applause due an actress, but this Ingmar Bergman–esque stylization also presents the madness of the other inmates. The filmmakers err in presenting the tediousness of prison life in boring fashion—via a two-and-a-half-minute shot of Frances lying on a cot while other inmates mingle, before panning around the room.

When Frances is back home with Lillian, Lillian responds to Frances trying to touch her by flinching, showing the kind of mother she is. The narrative undercuts Frances' real character by showing her to be as bored at home as she was at the asylum. The scene of Frances showing photographs and slides of herself to Lillian reads as unbelievable, given how Frances hated Hollywood and her time there. The slides also read as counterfeit since none of them attempt to emulate any known photos of the real Frances, and the shot supposedly from *Come and Get It* fails to replicate her hair or wardrobe from that film. Although some of the references in the screenplay demonstrate knowledge of Frances' film career, little is made of it.

The rehearsal for *Golden Boy* shows Odets berating Frances—in front of another actor—with, "You came all the way from Hollywood for your integrity as an actress. You can't act. You disgust me." Though such unprofessional behavior on the part of Odets rankles (and seems odd given that Odets is *not* the director), the glum performance McLaughlin gives during Frances' line reading makes her deserving of condemnation. The follow-up scene in which Odets tells Frances he will kill himself unless she lets him into her room—and their subsequent tortured makeup sex—disappoints, as once again McLaughlin's passivity as Frances makes you question why Odets would bother with her. However, at least this time there is no crippling exposition, as they enact a scene of present-tense drama.

There is a lyrical moment of Frances in the asylum grounds, where, standing in a sea of overgrown bushes as wind blows her hair, she talks about being "insane by reason of love." A long shot, with McLaughlin in half-shadow, makes her look almost attractive and soft; while her statement, "Maybe they're right to have me here," presents a quiet moment of honest reflection. However, the moment is ruined by the following medium shot during which Frances continues with a stagey monologue that outstays its welcome.

Dr. Walter Freeman is mentioned as having visited Frances at the asylum, with the lobotomy implied by Lillian's comment, "The doctors say she'll be quieter now, more peaceful." That line might also be interpreted as referring to the change in attitude the real Frances decided to make, but this Frances continues to be resistant at the parole hearing (proceedings presumably instigated at Lillian's request for Frances' release).

The film ends with Frances at the parole hearing, with McLaughlin in close-up, her face half in shadow and her eyes closed for a freeze frame. This image presumably presents Frances as a martyr to her suffering, with the closed eyes perhaps an indication of her limited future as a sleepwalker. Although history tells us that Frances was paroled because of her mother's request, the film does not make this apparent, so her closed eyes could also imply that her parole is not to be granted and she is to remain in the asylum forever. It's a shame the filmmakers don't mention the real Frances' comeback attempt and life outside the asylum after her release, wishing instead to keep her a metaphorical prisoner. Surely any feminist stance on Frances would include her freedom and triumph over adversity. By keeping her a tragic victim, this Women Make Movies production ironically portrays its heroine as even less empowered than in the previous two biopics made by men.

Like Susan Blakely in *Will There Really Be a Morning?* Sheila McLaughlin does not resemble the real Frances Farmer, and this affects the success of the biopic. McLaughlin looks more like Piper Laurie than Frances, although her dirty blonde hair color matches Frances' filmic hair color, and McLaughlin's fleshiness also matches Frances' inclination to be heavier than the Benzedrine-induced Hollywood slimness of the times. Also like Blakely, McLaughlin doesn't *sound* like the real Frances, with McLaughlin's arch intonation a poor contrast to Frances' deep contralto. The casting of Lillian and Odets is more visually accurate, with Lee Beuer bringing a resonant sliminess and pretentiousness to his Odets.

Women Make Movies is a non-profit feminist media arts organization established in 1972 whose multicultural programs provide resources for both users and producers of media by women. They were responsible for distributing the early work of Sally Potter and Jane Campion. *Committed* was the film debut of McLaughlin and Lynne Tillman; and in an interview with Pascale Lamache in the magazine *Framework*, McLaughlin said that the film's budget was $45,000. She would go on to write, produce and direct the low-budget lesbian drama *She Must Be Seeing Things* (1978), in which Tillman and Boothby would act. Tillman has not directed another title since *Committed*. McLaughlin had appeared in three earlier films in minor roles.

## *Release*

Unknown. The Video tagline is "The *True* Story of Frances Farmer."

## *Reviews*

"Superbly shot and acted ... more subtle than the sledgehammer Hollywood feature—and no less mythic"—J. Hoberman, *The Village Voice* (unverified—video cover)

"Packs a wallop that *Frances* lacks."—*The Independent* (unverified—video cover)

"Ambitious, low-budget but heartfelt film biography originally produced for British television."—Hal Erickson, *All Movie Guide*

"Although the extremely low budget sometimes gives the film an exceedingly rough look in its execution, [it] is a deeply felt work that captures the spiritual essence of Frances Farmer's isolation."—Pascale Lamache, *Framework*

"An original and stylish movie, austere and bitter."—John Pym, *TimeOut Film Guide, 2009*

## *Broadway's Dreamers: The Legacy of the Group Theatre* (1988)

American Masters

**Credits:** A production of WNET/New York. Director: David Heeley; Producers: Joan Kramer, David Heeley, Joanne Woodward; Associate Producer: Emily Grossman; Executive Producers: Jac Venza, Susan Lacy; Writer: Steve Lawson; Consultant: Helen Krich Chinoy; Editor: Alan Berliner; Music: Dick Hyman; Researcher: Blaine Smith; Photography: Rick Malkames; Makeup: Leslie Fuller, Karen Rudder, Toy Russell, Margaret Sunshine; Hair: Danny Cheng. Color, 87 minutes.

**Cast:** Joanne Woodward (Host); Stella Adler, Margaret Baker, Phoebe Brand, Morris Carnovsky, Harold Clurman, Cheryl Crawford, Mordecai Gorelik, Michael Gordon, Elia Kazan, Sidney Kingsley, Gerrit Tony Kraber, Robert Lewis, Sanford Meisner, Ruth Nelson, Martin Ritt, Sylvia Sidney, Eunice Stoddard, Lee Strasberg (The Players); Ellen Burstyn; Kate Burton; Katharine Hepburn; Margaret Klenck; Dylan McDermott; James Naughton; Paul Newman; Michael O'Flaherty; Maria Tucci; Shelley Winters; Ken Howard; Anne Jackson; Glynnis O'Connor; Austin Pendelton. Maureen Stapleton, Marlon Brando, Meryl Streep, Sydney Pollack, Gregory Peck, Roddy McDowall, Sally Field, Peter Bogdanovich, Jennifer Grey, Walter Matthau, Mary Steenburgen, Warren Beatty, Faye Dunaway, James Coburn, Henry Winkler, Julie Harris (End Credit Voices).

**VHS/DVD:** Not available in either format.

### Notes

This documentary about the rise and demise of the Group Theatre makes reference to Frances being cast as Lorna Moon in the stage production of *Golden Boy* in 1938 as a way to ensure box office success and a solid financial footing for the company by importing a Hollywood star. Although this strategy paid off—*Golden Boy* would be their biggest financial success (something which is attributed, rather strangely, to the production's sets by Mordecai Gorelik)—it would not allow the Group to continue for long. The strategy also placed Frances in the unenviable position of being resented by veteran members of the Group, particularly those actresses who believed they could have played her role just as well.

While the documentary doesn't present Frances' point of view, our knowledge of how important the casting was to her in light of her dislike of Hollywood leads us to draw parallels with the similar situation of Sylvia Sidney, the second Hollywood star imported to the Group. Sidney was cast in the 1939 production of *The Gentle People*, opposite Franchot Tone, who had left the Group earlier to pursue a Hollywood career. Unlike Frances, Sidney bemoaned the low salary she received working for the Group, although her marriage to actor Luther Adler at the time surely influenced her decision to stay. Ironically, after Sidney's return to Hollywood in the 1940s she would work less frequently.

The documentary shows Frances in advertising for the production of *Golden Boy*, most notably on the *Playbill* cover with Luther Adler, as well as in group photos of the company, although her subsequent appearances are never mentioned. Interestingly, footage is provided of Margaret Klenck playing Lorna Moon for a 1987 Williamstown Theatre Festival production of the play, with Klenck employing a New Jersey accent. It is presumed that such an accent was not affected by Frances, which perhaps feeds into the notion that she was miscast and that her casting was not the major reason for the play's Broadway success. A scene from a 1950 Dumont TV network production starring John Garfield and Kim Stanley shows Stanley also foregoing the New Jersey accent; while Barbara Stanwyck's Brooklyn accent heard in a scene included from the 1939 film version with William Holden acceptably conveys Lorna's status as a common tramp.

The documentary utilizes quotes from the Harold Clurman book *The Fervent Years* and interviews as many members of the Group as possible. The interviews were conducted by Joanne Woodward over a period of five years. (Woodward being one of the producers of the film explains why she gets reaction shots in all of the interviews.) It also presents photographs and period news footage for context, performance recreations, and, perhaps most valuably, archival film of performances and Hollywood screen tests of some of the Group's members. The latter are particularly amusing, given the mixed feelings the Group had about Hollywood, although we are told that part of the reason the Group folded was because the best actors left for Hollywood.

The history of the Group, shown through chapters in the documentary, lives up to the title of Clurman's book. Cheryl Crawford, Clurman and Lee Strasberg (all three employed by the New York Theatre Guild) formed a company to present new American plays with realistic acting that reflected the times they lived in. Inspired by the Moscow Art Theatre, who had come to New York in the 1920s, the Group is described as an "experiment," and said to be a reaction to the conservatism of the existing New York theater scene, which produced drawing room comedies and lightweight entertainment in the late 1920s. Strasberg would pioneer his own Method of acting based on the system devised by Constantin Stanislavsky.

The Group also copied the Moscow Art Theatre's focus on ensemble casts rather than stars. Interviewee Katharine Hepburn scores a laugh by telling how she went to one meeting of the Group before she had achieved any success. Upon hearing of this no-star policy, Hepburn decided to leave, telling the Group members, "I don't want to be a member of a group, I want to be a great big star." This policy, however, did not make the Group a democracy. Rather, the three creators were autocrats, and this would engender tension among their company (who all wanted to be stars, if truth be told). Their attempts to make it in Hollywood, although rationalized as a way to brings funds to the Group, reveal their true agenda.

After their first production, *The House of Connelly*, in 1931 received critical raves, the Group's next effort closed early. While the 1933 *Men in White* was applauded for being the first presentation of operation scenes on stage, and would win author Sidney Kingsley the Pulitzer Prize for Drama, it was a troubled production. The actors rebelled against Strasberg's use of "emotional memory" after Stella Adler had told the Group that Stanislavsky himself had stopped using it. This crisis of confidence came to a head when Ruth Nelson attacked Strasberg during rehearsal on the 1934 production *Gold Eagle Guy* after he had repeatedly berated her co-star. Strasberg's resistance to a production of the Clifford Odets play *Awake and Sing* would be ignored. Odets was a member of the acting company, and his play, written for his fellow members, was produced in 1935 and would prove to be the Group's signature play. Odets would go on to became the radical socialist voice of the Group, with the production of his other play, *Waiting for Lefty*, memorably calling for a strike at its end.

Odets' political activism is linked to the House Un-American Committee Hearings (HUAC) of the late 1940s and early 1950s, which occurred after the Group had folded. Although some members were aligned with the Communist Party, Harold Clurman admits that they were actors first and communists second, and that most were scared of being associated with Communism because it was such an unpopular cause. Martin Ritt, Tony Kraber, Ruth Nelson, Morris Carnovksy and Phoebe Brand would all have their careers in film affected by the blacklist, and Odets and Elia Kazan only survived because they were prepared to name names.

The Group suffered from having no money, no roster of new plays, and a disgruntled membership who refused to do the classics or revivals to help the company survive. The divisiveness would eventually see both Strasberg and Crawford resign, leaving Harold Clurman as the sole surviving creator, although he would close the company in 1941, leading to a memorable article printed in the *New York Times* on May 18, 1941. In this article Clurman would say that they had tried to "maintain a true theater policy artistically but proceeded economically on a show business basis," and it was this conflict between their means and the ends that ended the experiment. Twenty plays had been produced, but only three or four were financial successes, but the legacy of the Group can be seen in the influence the teachers, producers, directors, actors, designers, and playwrights had on American theater.

While actors Tony Kraber and Ruth Nelson become emotional in their interviews, it is the archival footage that is the most fascinating. We see Morris Carnovsky and Luther Adler in *Success Story*, Adler and Phoebe Brand in *Awake and Sing*, Ruth Nelson and an unidentified actor in *Waiting for Lefty*, and Nelson in *Weep for the Virgins*. Also included is a scene filmed in color from a 1972 TV production of *Awake and Sing*, with Walter Matthau and Felicia Fox, which highlights the so-called "organized street language" of Odets that actually reads as godawful.

The Hollywood screen tests made for Walter Wanger Productions include those of Morris Carnovsky, Luther Adler, Lee Cobb (later known as Lee J. Cobb), Ruth Nelson, and Elia Kazan. We see Stella Adler's film debut in Paramount's *Love on Toast* (1937) (although she is billed as "Stella Ardler"), and footage of John Garfield in *Four Daughters* (1938), he being the Group's most successful export once his name was changed from Jules Garfield.

*American Masters* is a PBS television series created by Susan Lacy and produced by Eagle Rock Entertainment, and has been broadcasting documentaries since 1983. It is dedicated to examining the lives, works and creative processes of America's most outstanding cultural artists. Other artists the series has profiled include Charlie Chaplin, Aaron

Copeland, Helen Hayes, Eugene O'Neill, Martha Graham, Billie Holliday, Leonard Bernstein, William Wyler, and Andy Warhol.

Director David Heeley had a history of directing, producing and writing biographical documentaries on show business personalities. He had won Emmys for *Fred Astaire: Change Partners and Dance* (1980) and *Spencer Tracy: A Tribute by Katharine Hepburn* (1986). Prior to *Broadway's Dreamers* he had helmed *Bacall on Bogart* (1988).

Writer Steve Lawson had penned numerous teleplays and the performing arts anthology series *Great Performances* episode "Edith Wharton: Looking Back" (1981). His prior title had been the made-for-TV drama *The Room Upstairs* (1987). He was nominated for the 1990 Outstanding Writing Emmy Award for *Broadway's Dreamers*.

## Release

Screened 1989, and won the 1990 Emmy for Outstanding Informational Special.

## Reviews

"A celebration.... The story of the Group Theater is noble, inspiring and, not infrequently, hilarious. Considering the sorry state of the Broadway theater today, this television tribute to past idealists is all the more valuable."—John J. O'Connor, the *New York Times*, June 26, 1989

# *Hollywood Scandals and Tragedies* (1988)

MPI Home Video

**Credits:** Producer: Ray Atherton; Executive Producers: Waleed Ali, Malik Ali; Associate Producer/Editor: Brian Graham; Writers: Ray Atherton, F.B. Vincinzo; Narration: Bill Thomas; Music: Debra Levine; Photography: Mark Gilman; Art Director: Joe Aguzzi; Graphics: Bruce Bolinger: Sound: Studio Media; Research: Linnea Aguzzi, Jim Blondin, Kathy Gildea, Kash McKewen, Mike O'Brian, Karin Sydney, Donald Wrzesinsk. Color and B&W, 77 minutes.

**Cast:** Sharon Tate; Roman Novarro; Sal Mineo; William Desmond Taylor; Ted Healy; Albert Dekker; Freddie Prinze; Lenny Bruce; George Reeves; Charles Laughton; Rock Hudson; Montgomery Clift; Roscoe "Fatty" Arbuckle; James Dean; Natalie Wood; Nick Adams; Thelma Todd; Peg Enthwistle; Jean Harlow; Lupe Velez; Bobby Clark and Paul McCullough; Carole Landis; Errol Flynn; Frances Farmer; Vivien Leigh; Clara Bow; Tyrone Power; Bela Lugosi; Jackie Coogan; Carl "Alfalfa" Switzer; Scotty Beckett; Jayne Mansfield.

**VHS/DVD Release:** Video released August 31, 1988. The video's back cover blurb reads:
> The highs of fame and fortune. The lows of drug addiction, odd sexual preferences and death. From casting couch to coffin, the stories unfold! The Hollywood Scandals and Tragedies detectives have gone beyond the glitter and

behind the headlines, exposing sordid secrets of the stars. These tantalizing truths will appeal to all movie lovers.

A thirty-minute version of this documentary was released on August 31, 1994, by MPI Home Video.

## Synopsis

In the late 1930s Frances Farmer was one of Hollywood's more promising new starlets. The moviegoing public became enchanted with her. She was on her way to becoming one of the most popular female stars in America. Then her fortunes drastically changed.

World War II had broken out. While driving to a party in Santa Monica a policeman stopped her for driving in a dim-out zone with her headlights on. Farmer harbored a dislike for police and she became abusive. She was arrested for drunk driving and given a suspended jail sentence of 180 days. The arrest for drunkenness created a serious scandal, and co-stars, agents and studios began to avoid Farmer and the bad publicity which accompanied her.

She began work on a new film, but early into the production she became embroiled in an argument with a studio hairdresser. Farmer struck the woman, dislocating her jaw. A few hours later, police, acting on an assault complaint, arrived to arrest her. Again she resisted arrest and had to be forcefully removed. At police headquarters she listed her occupation as "cocksucker." Now the tabloids accelerated the war against her, describing Farmer as a foul-mouthed troublemaker.In the court appearance following the arrest she was sarcastic and arrogant. An irritated judge sentenced her to 180 days in jail. A struggling, kicking Farmer was dragged out of the court as she shouted obscenities at the judge. Her behavior in jail led to a court-ordered transfer to the psychiatric ward of Los Angeles General Hospital.

Her next year saw her transferred from one mental institution to another. She was subjected to weekly electro-shock treatments, kept in strait-jackets and padded cells, and even tied naked to a toilet for long periods of time. She was raped dozens of times by inmates as well as male nurses. Farmer lived under these severe conditions for five years before her release from the sanitarium. There was a half-hearted comeback attempt made by her in 1957. She made one film appearance, with Bobby Driscoll in a B exploitation film, *The Party Crashers*. In April of 1970 she died a slow and painful death in the charity ward of an Indianapolis hospital.

## Notes

The synopsis provided is from this program's chapter on Frances, which is oddly positioned in a documentary that covers Hollywood murders, suicides, homosexuality, and untimely deaths. Frances (spelled Francis on the video cover) appears after Errol Flynn's first of two chapters (his first concentrating on his trial for rape, and his second addressing the claims about homosexual experiences). Using Paramount publicity stills, lobby cards for *Flowing Gold* and *World Premiere* (where Virginia Dale is presumed to be Frances), and stills for *The Toast of New York*, *Reunion*, and *The Party Crashers*, the two-and-a-half-minute segment prominently focuses on several of the famous arrest photographs. The ones of Frances being arrested in Antioch are used out of sequence, as is the still from *The Toast of New York*. The photograph of a Steilacoom ward reproduced in *Shadowland* is also shown here. The final image is a still from *Rhythm on the Range*; and Frances is mentioned in the closing chapter, accompanied by an arrest photograph describing her as a "sayer." The imagery and text repeat the stories from the *Shadowland* and *Will There Really Be a Morning?* books, but at least the episode does acknowledge Frances' acting career and doesn't just present her as a victim of her personal life.

One's appreciation of the documentary depends upon one's prior knowledge of the scandals covered, which might simply extend to a reading of *Hollywood Babylon*, from which it appears a lot of the images are taken. Some film footage is shown of the star in question, but mostly the imagery relies upon stills, newsreels for context, trailers and one outtake. Often the accompanying music has the tone of a bad horror movie score.

However, the writing and juxtaposition of images, taken out of context for deliberate effect, provides an occasional laugh. For instance, Sal Mineo's line, "I'm lookin' for a fella," comes right when the narration speaks of his homosexuality. Lupe Velez hides Jimmy Durante in a bathroom, just when we are told how she drowned in her toilet. The gun imagery from the opening credits of the *Superman* television series is shown when we are told how George Reeves was shot. The camera zooms in on the still image of a fireplace near which Rock Hudson sits as we learn how he was cremated. And Charles Laughton says, "All men are created equal," in the chapter on his hiring gay rent boys.

Rare nude photographs of Jean Harlow are shown, as well as the death scene pose of Lenny Bruce in his film *Dance Hall Racket*, which is said to prefigure Bruce's own death pose (the raised arm in the original and Bruce's beard in the real one, however, point out the differences). Errol Flynn is said to be buried under a naked statue of a woman with her legs crossed; the nude photo of James Dean with an erection from *Come Back to the Five and Dime, Jimmy Dean Jimmy Dean* (1982) is seen, and we get a Rock Hudson joke. After being described as the "cock of the walk" during his career at Universal, Hudson's post–AIDS reveal gives us the unfunny, "Did you hear about the new Rock Hudson jeans? The zipper is in the back."

A still of Vivien Leigh from *The Roman Spring of Mrs. Stone* (1963) is falsely identified as Leigh in *A Streetcar Named Desire* (1950), and there is rare television footage of the adult Carl "Alfalfa" Switzer on a Roy Rogers Western show. The chapters on William Desmond Taylor and Thelma Todd are probably the most interesting, since both deaths remain unsolved. The documentary ends with an unintentionally amusing apology for the way it documents the "sacrificial lambs slain on Hollywood's altar": "While some of the more exotic aspects detailed here may be considered in poor taste or insensitive to the memory of various celebrities, one must remember that in many cases these accounts remain the final signal that each has left for posterity."

Actor and writer Ray Atherton had previously produced the horror title *Meatcleaver Massacre* (1977), and would go on to make documentaries about Marilyn Monroe, John Wayne and Frank Sinatra. Waleed and Malik Ali had executive produced the horror title *Henry: Portrait of a Serial Killer* (1986), in which Waleed, Atherton, and associate producer/editor Brian Graham had small roles.

# Hollywood Undressed (1991)

Passport International Productions

**Credits:** Unknown. Color and B&W, 57 minutes.

**Cast:** James Dean; Frances Farmer; Marilyn Monroe; Jayne Mansfield; Lenny Bruce; Sharon Tate; Sal Mineo; John Belushi; Rock Hudson; Sean Penn; Kim Basinger; Madonna; Rob Lowe.

**VHS/DVD Release:** Video released October 18, 1991, from Amvest/Hotline Sales with the taglines, "Too Rough for Prime Time!" "Film clips you were never meant to see!" "The Ultimate Hollywood Expose!" and "Odd Sexual Preferences of the Stars!" The back cover blurb says, "This video is not to be compared to other Hollywood scandal tapes. This is the real authenticated stuff!"

## Synopsis

In 1935 a beautiful, sensitive and high-strung actress named Frances Farmer was signed for a seven-year contract at Paramount studios. Although the studio felt she was destined to become the new Garbo, Frances Farmer was given only less than Garbo-like roles. Soon she was loaned out to MGM where again she appeared in more films that fizzled at the box office. Farmer was a resolute individualist who refused to go Hollywood and was often quoted as saying she hated everything about the town except the money that could be made there. Her statements infuriated the moguls who hired her, and many felt Frances Farmer was poison to the Hollywood image.

She was arrested for a minor traffic violation in Santa Monica on October 19, 1942, and charged with drunk driving, operating an auto without a license, and having her lights on in a dim-out zone. She responded to the police with hostile aggression and wound up being tossed in jail. Farmer was sentenced to 180 days and put on probation. Later she was arrested at a hotel in Hollywood after failing to report to her parole officer. The incident took place after a manic fling in which she personally dislocated the jaw of a studio hairdresser and was later spotted running topless up Sunset Boulevard after losing her sweater in a drunken nightclub brawl. The Hollywood police caught up with her in a room at the Knickerbocker Hotel where they proceeded to drag her nude through the lobby and off to headquarters.

Frances demonstrated her hate for the police by signing "cocksucker" as her occupation on the police file. Once in court Frances was questioned by the judge about the extent of her drinking problem. She replied, "I put liquor in my milk. I put liquor in my coffee. And in my orange juice. What do you want me to do? Starve? I drink everything I can get, including Benzedrine." The judge rose from his chair and sentenced her to 180 days. Her request to make a phone call on leaving the courtroom was unconstitutionally denied, which enraged Frances so that she took a swing at a police matron and decked a nearby cop. Frances Farmer was then hauled off to her cell in a strait-jacket.

By this time Monogram Pictures released her from her latest loan-out contract, while the rest of the country learned of her bad girl antics in Tinseltown. It was clear that she desperately needed professional help, but none was forthcoming. Her mother soon declared her daughter a mental incompetent and had her institutionalized. She was placed in a private sanitarium to face a grueling schedule of daily insulin shock treatments, which lasted three long months.

In 1944 she was released, only to be declared insane once again. She was confined to a state mental hospital in Washington State. It was here that she spent ten more years in hell, with strait-jackets, leather straps, beatings and rapings by sadistic lesbian guards. But, remarkably, her downfall brought little compassion in a town which had helped exploit her from the beginning. She had been a so-called troublemaker, and Hollywood was glad to be rid of her. All this because a sensitive and high-strung girl, who was on the verge of a nervous breakdown, was arrested and denied her right to a fair trial. The terrible truth is that Frances Farmer stood alone in Hollywood and lost.

## Notes

As with *Hollywood Scandals and Tragedies*, the synopsis provided is that for the episode on Frances. While some of the information is incorrect (e.g., she never worked for MGM), and other myths are perpetuated, the coverage here is longer and more detailed than in the former documentary. The same Paramount publicity stills, arrest photographs, and *World Premiere* lobby cards are used, as are the Antioch photographs. "B" movie footage of two women fighting in a bar is shown to represent Frances' alleged attack on her hairdresser, with the blonde here seen to be the aggressor. The three-minute-and-forty-second segment repeats some images, and the manipulative generic music fights the narration all the way through the treatment.

Although some of the images seen throughout the program appear to be sourced from the prior documentary, this one offers some new trailers and footage. These include a Pepsi television commercial with James Dean, samples of Lenny Bruce performing on television, Rob Lowe's infamous home movie sex tape, and the trailer for *The Misfits* (1961), which offers quick edits of images of Marilyn Monroe. We also see the famous television Golden Globes award show footage of Jayne (spelled Jane on the video cover) Mansfield and Mickey Rooney, where the laughter derives from the sight of his diminutive Rooney's head barely reaching her bosom.

Each segment has its own music, but there are some odd choices. Marilyn gets a mournful vocal, Sharon Tate a sitar, and heavy breathing is heard for Sal Mineo. The treatment lacks the expressed homophobia of *Hollywood Scandals and Tragedies*, which is evident from the comparative sensitivity in the Rock Hudson episode. Oddly, there is no chapter on Freddie Prinze as advertised on the video box cover. The segment on James Dean tells how he spat at the portraits of Humphrey Bogart and James Cagney in the offices of Warner Bros., which some might say earned him his early death as poetic justice.

Although displaying its share of celebrity nudity, the chapters on the still living Sean Penn, Kim Basinger, Madonna, and Rob Lowe also attest to a different imperative than the earlier documentary, one less preoccupied with sordid period scandal and more with contemporary (for its time) relevance and notoriety. Amusingly, the reverb on the soundtrack gives the impression that the narrator lisps.

# *E! Mysteries and Scandals* (1998)

E! Entertainment Television

**Credits:** Producer/Director: Joel K. Rodgers; Producer: Liz Flynn; Associate Producer: Ann Nakamura; Writer: Laura Slobin; Music Coordinator: Steve Celi. Color, 21 minutes.

**Cast:** A. J. Benza (Host); Frank Farmer (Nephew of Frances Farmer); Bob Thomas (AP Hollywood Correspondent); Dalene Young (Screenwriter); Dr. Conrad Lane (Film Historian); Eric Bergren (Screenwriter); Susan Blakely (Actress); Stephen Jaffe (Producer); Dr. Jerry Dennis (CEO of Western State Hospital); Dr. Barry Kramer (Prof. of Clinical Psychiatry, USC School of Medicine); Frank Freeman (Son of Dr. Walter Freeman); Dr. Donald Becker (Chief Division of Neurosurgery, UCLA); Connie Stevens (Actress).

**VHS/DVD:** Not available in either format.

## *Synopsis*

In 1935 a young starlet named Frances Farmer dazzled Hollywood. The beautiful and gifted actress seemed to be living a charmed life. So how did this woman end up suffering years of bitter torture and profound humiliation? There is no star for Frances Farmer on Hollywood's Walk of Fame. Eight years after her film debut, Frances lost everything—her fame, her faith, and her freedom. Frances was locked up for more than five horrifying years in a public mental hospital. When she came out, doctors considered her cured, but her spirit was broken.... This is a story of a woman who refused to play the game and paid the ultimate price.

## *Notes*

The tone of this series is set by the pasted-on lettered titles that recall an anonymous ransom note; re-enactments shot with arty lighting; smoky streets where the host yells at the audience; and melodramatic music (although the music over the end credits offers both beauty and sadness). The coverage here includes genuine film and television footage from the *Come and Get It* trailer and the *This Is Your Life* show (where close-ups of Frances are freeze-framed), stills and publicity material, family photographs, and magazine covers and newspaper headlines. We see a printed copy of Frances' "God Dies" essay, a photographic collage of the arrest photographs (with a re-enactment of the famous flesh-exposing photo of Frances struggling with police), and rare stills from the *Will There Really Be a Morning?* made-for-TV movie and *Frances Farmer Presents*.

The program is plagued by inaccuracies. Frank Farmer incorrectly states that his aunt won her trip to Russia as a result of the essay contest. Frances' famous "cocksucker" occupation remark is incorrectly stated as "whore," and also mistakenly attached to her first arrest for driving in the dim-out zone. The assault on the *No Escape* hairdresser is said to have been a thrown hairbrush rather than the reported slap.

The episode offers plenty of drama, however. For instance, Stephen Jaffe's line, "By the time she was in Steilacoom her life had been shattered," is followed by a "shattered" image—a torn still of Frances, with cracked and broken glass placed over it as if it were framed.

The lobotomy issue once again proves divisive, with Frank Freeman, Conrad Lane, and (implicitly) Susan Blakely all agreeing that it happened, while Frank Farmer and Dr. Jerry Dennis denies it. The issue is further confused by the lobotomy being described as a frontal and not trans-orbital procedure (the type some believe Frances was given). Frank Freeman identifies Frances as the person being lobotomized by his father in the photograph that was first seen in William Arnold's book *Shadowland*, although Frank Freeman will later recant both claims in Jack El-Hai's book *The Lobotomist*. Frank Freeman will also report that after her release from Steilacoom, Frances was an alcoholic and when inebriated would speak in tongues. Blakely's belief in the lobotomy (although it is not covered in the made-for-TV movie that she produced, perhaps because it is not mentioned in the autobiography) is made implicit by her following comment: "If there was any passion, if there was any life left in her, it was gone. When you look at the film of her later, her eyes were just dead."

Publicity portrait of Frances that the television show *E! Mysteries and Scandals* optically "shatters" for dramatic effect.

This author does not agree with Blakely's assessment of Frances' eyes in her later work, specifically the *This Is Your Life* television episode and her last film, *The Party Crashers*.

Narrator A. J. Benza ends by stating that Frances died from throat cancer, since she had been a chain smoker since her 20s. He then provides an amusing coda by closing on the issue of Frances being considered crazy: "So was Frances Farmer really crazy? Look, if every celebrity with attitude and bad judgment or freaky behavior was locked in the nuthouse, there'd be no one left in this town."

Former gossip columnist for the *Daily News* A.J. Benza had previously played two minor roles in features. Director Joel K. Rodgers previously directed the television series *Fanatic* (1998). The *E! Mysteries and Scandals* series was the first producing work for writer Liz Flynn and associate producer Ann Nakamura.

## *Release*

Broadcast October 12, 1998, as episode 31 of season 1.

# *A&E Biography—*
# "Paradise Lost" (2000)

Van Ness Films/Foxstar Productions/
Prometheus Entertainment/Fox Television Studio/
A&E Network

**Credits:** Producer/Director: Lawrence Williams; Executive Producer: Kevin Burns; Supervising Producer: Kerry Jensen; Associate Producers: Hayley Briana, Colin Cotter; Coordinating Producer: Sonja Nelson; Writer: Gidion Phillips; Additional Research: G. Alexander Rossario; Editors: Laurie House, Martin Hilton; Music: Tom Jenkins, Chris Many. Photographs courtesy of David Farmer, William Arnold, Jack Randall Earles, Jeffrey Kauffman, et al. Color, 53 minutes.

**Cast:** Peter Graves (Narrator); David Farmer (Nephew); Patrick Agan (Biographer); Jeffrey Kauffman (Archivist); Jessica Lange (Actress); Joe Stockdale (Director); Dr. Jonathan Meyer (Psychiatrist, Oregon State Hospital); Gina Woods (Family Friend).

**VHS/DVD:** Not available in either format.

## Notes

"She was one of Hollywood's most beautiful and promising talents, but Frances Farmer's life was not a fairy tale. Her meteoric rise to the top was cut short by a debilitating addiction to alcohol, numerous arrests and years of confinement in a mental institution." These are the opening remarks in this documentary on Frances' life from the *A&E Biography* television series. Patrick Agan, author of *The Decline and Fall of the Love Goddesses*, which features a chapter on Frances, and Jessica Lange, who played Frances in the feature film *Frances*, both also make comments that are used in the introduction. Agan says, "I don't think that anyone has risen so fast or fallen as fast as Frances in the history of Hollywood." Lange comments, "It would be hard to survive everything that she went through with your spirit and intelligence in tact, but she had tremendous personal strength and reserve. She was a real warrior." The opening also features footage from Frances' films *Come and Get It*, *Rhythm on the Range*, *Son of Fury*, and *Too Many Parents*.

The program employs the irritating and unnecessary techniques of adding a photographic "click" sound effect whenever showing photos, and panning and zooming in on the subject of a photograph for a post-modern emphasis. Music plays over the talking head interviews, and our view of the speaker is interrupted by shots of film stills or star portraits. The intrusive music score is redeemed somewhat by the program closing with an orchestrated version of the *Come and Get It* song "Aura Lea," which actually provides some pathos, considering the resonance the song had for Frances' career. Thankfully, the eloquence of the interviewees survives the questionable choices of presentation style. Additionally, the opportunity to *see* Patrick Agan and Jeffrey Kauffman (as with seeing Edith Farmer on the *This Is Your Life* episode) adds another dimension to these authors of the source material used for this book.

For the specifics of this program, period newsreel film of Seattle, New York, Moscow, and Hollywood is shown, as well as family photos, theater stills, movie posters, lobby

A candid photograph of Frances at home circa 1940 seen in the *A&E Biography* television episode "Paradise Lost."

cards and stills, and newspaper headlines. We get screen captures of Frances' screen test, footage from *Too Many Parents*, the cover of *Motion Picture* magazine featuring Frances, and photos with Leif Erickson. About the start of her Hollywood career, the narrative offers:

> In only five months the dissident from Seattle had been transferred into a rising star with a handsome new husband. But Frances Farmer's dreams extended far beyond the boundaries of Hollywood, and her willful ambition would soon take her to the brink of disaster.

After footage from *Rhythm on the Range*, we get *Come and Get It*, with a still of Frances as a blonde Lotta Morgan with Howard Hawks. As Frances does not appear in the completed film like this, we presume that it is from a deleted scene. (Interestingly, the made-for-TV movie of *Will There Really Be a Morning?* has Susan Blakely as Frances also wearing a blonde wig as Lotta Morgan, appearing with the Howard Hawks character in what is presumably also a deleted scene from that title.) The narration says that Hawks was fired from *Come and Get It* "shortly after production began," which is incorrect, and it also claims that Frances did not get along with William Wyler because Wyler "belittled and rejected her suggestions," something which is not supported by the evidence. The footage of Frances singing "Aura Lea" in *Come and Get It* is shown so that it can be compared to her later singing the same song on *The Ed Sullivan Show*.

*The Toast of New York* is covered with a lobby card and stills, and Frances' resentment of the screenplay's romanticism of her character is touched upon (although the narration incorrectly reports that the film was a box office success). A still and poster for *Exclusive*, and a still and footage from *Ebb Tide* cover her next titles, although a still for *Border Flight* is also incorrectly placed among them. The same still of Lee Strasberg, Harold Clurman and Cheryl Crawford that appeared in the *Broadway Dreamers* documentary is shown here, along with stills and the *Playbill* cover for *Golden Boy*. An alternate version of the telegram Clifford Odets wrote to Frances when he rejected her is included (as mentioned in this book's Introduction). *Ride a Crooked Mile* is represented by stills and a lobby card, and lobby cards are shown for *Badlands of Dakota*, *World Premiere*, and *Among the Living*.

Frances' use of amphetamines and alcohol is mentioned, and her drinking commented on by David Farmer:

> I think there's a kind of personality shift that happens with alcoholics. At least some alcoholics, and Frances definitely fit that mold. When she was sober she was elegant and graceful and you would never hear an off-color remark, but when she was drinking you would think it was a truck driver.

Footage, stills and the poster for *Son of Fury* are included, and the claim is made that Frances had to wait a year after *Son of Fury* before being offered *Take a Letter, Darling*, in spite of the earlier title being a hit. This claim is not substantiated by the Turner Classic Movie database, which has *Take a Letter, Darling* going into production in November 1941, only twelve days after production on *Son of Fury* ended.

The version of Frances' dim-out zone arrest told here says she sped off after the "You bore me" comment made to the police officer, and a chase ensued; other versions of the incident don't mention any chase. Her arrest photos are also incorrectly presented timewise, since these were not taken until her second arrest. The incident in which Frances attacked her *No Escape* hairdresser is described here as Frances hitting the hairdresser with a hairbrush, in spite of the newspaper headline—presented here—that says the hairdresser was smacked. Frances' famous "cocksucker" remark is here described amusingly with, "She offended even the most seasoned of officers by describing her occupation with a shockingly lewd term." Although the exact term is tactfully omitted, David Farmer comments on her use of it by saying, "It was instinct for performance gone off. She knew a remark like that at a minimum would raise eyebrows. She did like to blow minds."

Frances leaving the "Kimbel" sanitarium (although it is otherwise called La Crescenta) is said to have occurred 8 months later, though what is not said is that she escaped by running away rather than being "released." A photo of Frances with the upswept hairdo she wore upon her return from her first commitment to Steilacoom is used incorrectly to represent her final release in 1950, in the same way that a publicity still for her *Playhouse 90* "Reunion" television drama is mistakenly employed to represent Frances in early the 1950s. Another photograph of a blonde Frances, said to be circa 1953, is valuable for its rarity, as is another candid of a brunette Frances holding groceries.

Accompanying clips from Frances' appearance on *This Is Your Life* is the comment, "Frances was unprepared for the difficulty of reliving her past in front of millions of viewers." *Frances Farmer Presents* is represented by footage of Frances interviewing Miss Indiana State Fair Queen Marilyn Louise Shaft. The *A&E Biography* show includes a picture of Frances with Jean, marking the first time Jean was seen in any of the documentaries featuring Frances.

As Frances was the actress in residence at Purdue University from 1962, we see play program covers for *Look Homeward, Angel*, *The Visit*, and *The Sea Gull*. Director Joe Stockdale comments on Frances as a stage actress:

> I felt she was very imaginative. I know she was sensitive and she could have a quality that they, many many years ago in the theater, called spirit and fire which was that wonderful kind of charismatic thing.

However, the narration tells us that her second stage career did not last, as Frances was unable to overcome her addiction to alcohol, a problem that also got her fired from her television show in 1965.

A second photograph of an older Jean is shown during Joe Stockdale's comments on the alleged autobiography, *Will There Really Be a Morning?* to illustrate his claim that Jean embellished the text to enhance the possibility of a movie sale. William Arnold's biography *Shadowland* (although the author is only identified as such by the book cover being shown) is said to have introduced the idea of Frances and Jean as a lesbian couple, *and* the lobotomy allegation. David Farmer comments on the lobotomy issue: "The doctor's son claims that he's got a photograph of Frances on a gurney either right before or after the operation. It's a woman on a gurney. I can't say it's not her. I can't say it is her." Gina Woods says:

> That's always been the rumor. [In *Will There Really Be a Morning?*] she talks about patients in the institution who beg to be lobotomized because they didn't want to feel anymore. So it's hard to believe that, if she herself had had a lobotomy, why didn't she just say that she did?

The treatment closes with an overview of Frances. The narration says "After 30 years her story is still clouded by controversy and conjecture, but what remains clear is that throughout Frances Farmer's life her indomitable spirit gave

Jessica Lange in *Frances* (1982). Lange talks about the real Frances in the *A&E Biography* episode "Paradise Lost."

her the strength to endure overwhelming hardship and personal despair." Jessica Lange comments, "It's a terribly sad story. It's a tragic waste of a brilliant human being." David Farmer states, "She had incredible wit. She had incredible intelligence. She had taste and grace. She was a magical creature." Jeffrey Kauffman ends the documentary with, "She was a survivor. I think the moral of her story is that she survived."

"Paradise Lost" is also the title of an epic poem by John Milton about the Christian story of the fall of man. Director Lawrence Williams was previously the associate producer and assistant editor on the made-for-TV documentary *Science Fiction: A Journey into the Unknown* (1994). He was also the director of the previous *Biography* episodes on Darryl F. Zanuck, Tyrone Power, Alice Faye, Carmen Miranda, Henry Fonda, Audrey Hepburn, Vincent Price, John Wayne, Barbara Eden, Fred Gwynne, Linda Darnell, and Yvonne DeCarlo. Executive producer Kevin Burns had previously written, produced and directed many made-for-TV documentaries on Hollywood and show business, and is the president of Prometheus Entertainment. Coordinating producer Kerry Jensen is also a story editor and director of other *Biography* episodes. *Biography* was the first credit for associate producer Hayley Briana and coordinating producer Sonja Nelson. Fellow associate producer Colin Cotter was previously a researcher on the made-for-TV documentary *Beyond Titanic* (1998).

## *Release*

Broadcast October 19, 2000.

# Bibliography

Aachen, George. *Popular Films of the Forties.* Sydney: Rastar Press, 1988.
Agan, Patrick. *The Decline and Fall of the Love Goddesses.* Los Angeles, CA: Pinnacle Books, 1979.
Andersen, Christopher P. *A Star, Is a Star, Is a Star! The Lives and Loves of Susan Hayward.* Garden City, NY: Doubleday, 1980.
Anger, Kenneth. *Hollywood Babylon.* San Francisco, CA: Straight Arrow Books, 1975.
Arnold, William. *Shadowland.* New York: McGraw-Hill, 1978.
Basinger, Jeanine. *The Star Machine.* New York: Alfred A. Knopf, 2007.
_____. *A Woman's View: How Hollywood Spoke to Women, 1930–1960.* New York: Alfred A. Knopf, 1993.
Baxter, John. *Hollywood in the Thirties.* London and New York: Tantivy Press and A. S. Barnes, 1968.
Belton, John. *The Hollywood Professionals, Volume 3: Howard Hawks, Frank Borzage, Edgar G. Ulmer.* London and New York: Tantivy Press and A.S. Barnes, 1974.
Berg, A. Scott. *Goldwyn: A Biography.* New York: Alfred A. Knopf, 1989.
Bloom, Ken. *Broadway: Its History, People, and Places, an Encyclopedia.* New York and London: Routledge, 2004.
Blottner, Gene. *Universal Sound Westerns, 1929–1946: The Complete Filmography.* Jefferson, NC: McFarland, 2003.
Bogdanovich, Peter. *Who the Devil Made It: Conversations with Robert Aldrich et al.* New York: Alfred A. Knopf, 1997.
Bookbinder, Robert. *The Films of Bing Crosby.* Secaucus, NJ: Citadel Press, 1977.
Bordman, Gerald. *The Oxford Companion to American Theatre.* New York: Oxford University Press, 1984.
Branson, Clark. *Howard Hawks: A Jungian Study.* Santa Barbara: Capra Press, 1987.
Breivold, Scott. *Howard Hawks Interviews.* Jackson: University of Mississippi Press, 2006.
Brennan-Gibson, Margaret. *Clifford Odets, American Playwright: The Years from 1906 to 1940.* New York: Atheneum, 1982.
Catalena, Mark A., and Peter Jones. *Goldwyn: The Man and His Movies.* Sony Pictures DVD, 2001.
Clifford, Graeme, and David Gregory. *Frances* DVD audio commentary. Starz/Anchor Bay, 2002.
Clurman, Harold. *The Fervent Years: The Group Theatre and the '30s.* New York: Da Capo Press, 1975.
_____. *The Naked Image.* New York: Macmillan, 1966.
Crawford, Cheryl. *One Naked Individual: My Fifty Years in the Theatre.* Indianapolis and New York: Bobbs-Merrill, 1977.
Crivello, Kirk. *Fallen Angels: The Lives and Untimely Deaths of 14 Hollywood Beauties.* Secaucus, NJ: Citadel Press, 1988.
_____. "Frances Farmer, Unlucky Lady." *Focus on Film*, no. 23, Winter 1975, 6:36–40.
Cross, Robin. *2000 Movies: The 1950s.* New York: Arlington House, 1988.
_____, and John Marriot. *The World's Greatest Hollywood Scandals.* London: Octopus Books, 1989.
Deschner, Donald. *Films of Cary Grant.* Secaucus, NJ: Citadel Press, 1973.
De Lafayette, Maximillien. *Hollywood Earth Shattering Scandals, the Infamous, Villains, Nymphomaniacs and Shady Characters in Motion Pictures: Showbiz, Entertainment and Cinema ... with Money, Fame, Sex, Gossip and Greed.* New York: Create Space, 2009.
Demastes, William W. *Clifford Odets: A Research and Production Source Book.* Westport, CT, and London: Greenwood Press, 1991.
DiBattista, Maria. *Fast-Talking Dames.* New Haven and London: Yale University Press, 2001.
Donati, William. *Ida Lupino: A Biography.* Kentucky: University Press of Kentucky, 1996.
Durham, Weldon B. *American Theatre Companies, 1931–1986.* Westport, CT, and London: Greenwood Press, 1989.

Eames, John Douglas. *The Paramount Story*. London: Octopus Books, 1985.
El-Hai, Jack. *The Lobotimist: A Maverick Medical Genius and His Tragic Quest to End the World of Mental Illness*. Hoboken, NJ: John Wiley, 2005.
Eliot, Marc. *Cary Grant: A Biography*. New York: Harmony Books, 2004.
Farmer, Frances. *Will There Really Be a Morning?* Great Britain: Fontana/Collins, 1972.
Farmer Elliot, Edith. *Look Back in Love*. Portland, OR: Gemaia Press, 1978.
Fitzgerald, Michael G., and Boyd Magers. *Ladies of the Western*. Jefferson, NC: McFarland, 2002.
Fortin, Noonie. *Memories of Maggie—Martha Raye: A Legend Spanning Three Wars*. San Antonio, TX: Langmarc Publishing, 1995.
Foster, Gwendolyn Audrey. *Women Film Directors: An International Bio-Critical Dictionary*. Westport, CT, and London: Greenwood Press, 1995.
Fowler, Gene. *Goodnight, Sweet Prince: The Life and Times of John Barrymore*. Philadelphia: Blakiston, 1945.
Frank, Gerold. *Judy*. London: W.H. Allen, 1975.
Garfield, Brian. *Western Films: A Complete Guide*. New York: Rawson, 1982.
Garton, Joseph W. *The Film Acting of John Barrymore*. New York: Arno Press, 1980.
Geller, Jeffrey L. *Women of the Asylum: Voices from Behind the Walls, 1840–1945*. New York: Anchor, 1994.
Giddins, Gary. *Bing Crosby, a Pocketful of Dreams: The Early Years, 1903–1940*. Boston, New York, and London: Little, Brown, 2001.
Giest, Kenneth L. *Pictures Will Talk: The Life and Films of Joseph L. Mankiewicz*. New York: Da Capo, 1978.
Godfrey, Lionel. *Cary Grant: The Light Touch*. London: Robert Hale, 1981.
Goodman, Barak, and John Maggio. *American Experience: The Lobotimist*. PBS DVD, 2008.
Govoni, Albert. *Cary Grant: An Unauthorized Biography*. London: Robert Hale, 1971.
Gow, Gordon. *Hollywood in the Fifties*. New York and London: A.S. Barnes & A. Zwemmer, 1971.
Gregory, David. *A Hollywood Life: Remembering Frances*. Blue Underground/Anchor Bay Entertainment DVD, 2002.
Gritten, David. *Halliwell's Film Guide, 2008*. London: HarperCollins, 2007.
Hadleigh, Boze. *Hollywood Lesbians*. Fort Lee, NJ: Barricade Books, 1996.
Halliwell, Leslie. *Mountain of Dreams: The Golden Years of Paramount Pictures*. London: Hart-Davis and MacGibbon, 1976.
\_\_\_\_. *Who's Who in the Movies: The Only Film Guide That Matters*. London: HarperCollins Entertainment, 2006.
Hannsberry, Karen Burrough. *Bad Boys: The Actors of Film Noir*. Jefferson, NC: McFarland, 2003.
\_\_\_\_. *Femme Noir: Bad Girls of Film*. Jefferson, NC: McFarland, 1998.
Harvey, James. *Romantic Comedy in Hollywood, from Lubitsch to Sturges*. New York: Alfred A. Knopf, 1987.
Herman, Jan. *A Talent for Trouble: The Life of Hollywood's Most Acclaimed Director, William Wyler*. New York: Putnam's, 1995.
Herr, Christopher J. *Clifford Odets and American Political Theatre*. Westport, CT, and London: Praeger, 2003.
Higham, Charles, and Joel Greenberg. *Hollywood in the Forties*. London and New York: A.S. Barnes & A. Zwemmer, 1968.
\_\_\_\_, and Roy Moseley. *Cary Grant: The Lonely Heart*. San Diego, New York, and London: Harcourt Brace Jovanovich, 1989.
Hillier, Jim, and Peter Wollen. *Howard Hawks, American Artist*. London: BFI Publishing, 1996.
Hirsch, Foster. *A Method to Their Madness: The History of the Actors Studio*. New York and London: W.W. Norton, 1984.
Hirschhorn, Clive. *The Universal Story*. Hong Kong: Octopus Books, 1983.
\_\_\_\_. *The Warner Brothers Story*. London: Octopus Books, 1979.
Inman, David M. *Performers' Television Credits, 1942–2000, Volume 1: A–F*. Jefferson, NC, and London: McFarland, 2001.
Jeffries, J.T. *Jessica Lange*. New York: St. Martins Press, 1987.
Jewell, Richard B., with Vernon Harbin. *The RKO Story*. London: Arlington House, 1982.
Kael, Pauline. *5001 Nights at the Movies: A Guide from A to Z*. New York: Holt, Rinehart and Winston, 1984.
\_\_\_\_. *Hooked*. New York: E.P. Dutton, 1989.
\_\_\_\_. *When the Lights Go Down*. New York: Holt, Rinehart and Winston, 1980.
Kazan, Elia. *A Life*. New York: Alfred A. Knopf, 1988.
Krampner, Jon. *Female Brando: The Legend of Kim Stanley*. New York: Back Stage Books, 2006.
LaGuardia, Robert, and Gene Arceri. *Red: The Tempestuous Life of Susan Hayward*. New York: Macmillan, 1985.
Lamache, Pascale. "Committed Women." *Framework*, 26–27 (1984): 36–43.
Lasky, Betty. *RKO: The Biggest Little Major of Them All*. New Jersey: Prentice Hall, 1984.
Loggia, Marjorie, and Glenn Young. *The Collected Works of Harold Clurman*. New York: Applause Books, 1994.
Maddern Pitrone, Jean. *Take It from the Big Mouth: The Life of Martha Raye*. Lexington, Kentucky: University Press of Kentucky, 1999.
Madsen, Axel. *William Wyler: The Authorized Biography*. London and New York: W.H. Allen, 1974.

Malden, Karl, with Carla Malden. *When do I start? A Memoir.* New York: Simon & Schuster, 1997.

Maltin, Leonard. *Movie and Video Guide.* New York: Plume, 1997.

Mank, Gregory William. *The Hollywood Hissables.* Metuchen, NJ, and London: Scarecrow Press, 1989.

Marill, Alvin H. *Movies Made for Television 1964–2004, Volume 2: 1980–1989.* Lanham, MD, Toronto, and Oxford: Scarecrow Press, 2005.

Martin, Mart. *Did She or Didn't She? Behind the Bedroom Doors of 201 Famous Women.* Secaucus, NJ: Citadel Press, 1996.

Marx, Arthur. *Goldwyn: The Man Behind the Myth.* London, Sydney, and Toronto: Bodley Head, 1976.

McBride, Joseph. *Hawks on Hawks.* Berkeley, Los Angeles, and London: University of California Press, 1982.

McCann, Graham. *Cary Grant: A Class Apart.* New York: Columbia University Press, 1996.

McCarthy, Todd. *Howard Hawks: The Grey Fox of Hollywood.* New York: Grove Press, 1997.

McCelland, Doug. "'Shadowland': The Fractured Fairy Tale of Frances Farmer." *After Dark*, November 1978: 70–75.

McIntosh, William Currie, and William Weaver. *The Private Cary Grant.* London: Sidgwick and Jackson, 1983.

McNally, Peter. *Bette Davis: The Performances That Made Her Great.* Jefferson, NC, and London: McFarland, 2008.

Milland, Ray. *Wide-Eyed in Babylon.* New York: Ballantine Books, 1974.

Miller, Gabriel. *Martin Ritt: Interviews (Conversations with Filmmakers Series).* Jackson, MS: University Press of Mississippi, 2002.

Miller, Lee O. *The Great Cowboy Stars of Movies and Television.* New York: Arlington House, 1979.

Morrison, Michael A. *John Barrymore, Shakespearean Actor.* Cambridge, England: Cambridge University Press, 1997.

Nash, Jay Robert, and Stanley Ralph Ross. *The Motion Picture Guide 1927–1983.* Chicago: Gnebooks, 1987.

Neibaur, James L. *The RKO Features: A Complete Filmography of the Feature Films Released or Produced by RKO Radio Pictures, 1929–1960.* Jefferson, NC, and London: McFarland, 1994.

Nott, Robert. *He Ran All the Way: The Life of John Garfield.* New York: Limelight Edition, 2003.

O'Brien, Pat. *The Wind at My Back: The Life and Times of Pat O'Brien.* Garden City, NY: Doubleday, 1964.

Odets, Clifford. *Golden Boy.* London: Victor Gollancz, 1938.

Okuda, Ted. *The Monogram Checklist: The Films of Monogram Pictures Corporation, 1931–1952.* Jefferson, NC, and London: McFarland, 1987.

Parish, James Robert. *The Slapstick Queens.* New York: Castle Books, 1973.

\_\_\_\_, and Michael R Pitts. *Hollywood Songsters.* New York: Routledge, 2003.

\_\_\_\_, and Ronald L. Bowers. *The MGM Stock Company: The Golden Era.* New York: Arlington House, 1973.

\_\_\_\_, and Vincent Terrace. *The Complete Actor's Television Credits, 1948–1988, Volume 2: Actresses.* Metuchen, NJ, and London: Scarecrow Press, 1990.

\_\_\_\_, and William T. Leonard. *Hollywood Players: The Thirties.* New Rochelle, NY: Arlington House, 1976.

\_\_\_\_, \_\_\_\_, and Charles Hoyt. *The Funsters.* New York: Arlington House, 1979.

\_\_\_\_, with Gregory W. Mank. *The Hollywood Reliables.* Westport, CT: Arlington House, 1980.

Peters, Margot. *The House of Barrymore.* New York: Alfred A. Knopf, 1990.

Pym, John. *TimeOut Film Guide, 2009.* London: Time Out Guides, 2009.

Reid, John Howard. *Academy Award-Winning Films of the Thirties.* Sydney: Rastar Press, 1989.

Sarf, Wayne Michael. *God Bless You, Buffalo Bill: A Layman's Guide to History and the Western Film.* New York and London: Associated University Press, 1983.

Schickel, Richard. *The Men Who Made the Movies: Howard Hawks.* Turner Home Entertainment DVD, 2005.

Sennett, Ted. *Warner Brothers Presents.* Castle Books, 1971.

Shipman, David. *The Great Movie Stars: The Golden Years.* London: Hamlyn, 1970.

Silver, Alain, and Elizabeth Ward. *Film Noir.* London: Secker and Warburg, 1979.

Slesin, Aviva. *Directed by William Wyler.* Kino Video DVD, 2002.

Slide, Anthony. *Selected Theatre Criticism, Volume 3: 1931–1950.* London: Scarecrow Press, 1986.

Solomon, Aubrey. *Twentieth Century–Fox: A Corporate and Financial History (Filmmakers, no. 20).* Metuchen, NJ, and London: Scarecrow Press, 1988.

Somerset-Ward, Richard. *An American Theatre: The Story of Westport Country Playhouse, 1931–2005.* New Haven, CT: Yale University Press, 2005.

Stack, Robert, with Mark Evans. *Straight Shooting.* New York: Berkley Books, 1980.

Tierney, Gene, with Mickey Herskowitz. *Self-Portrait.* Wyden Books, 1978.

Thomas, Bob. *The One and Only Bing.* London: Michael Joseph, 1977.

Thomas, Tony. *Cads and Cavaliers: The Film Adventurers.* South Brunswick and New York: A.S. Barnes, 1978.

\_\_\_\_, and Aubrey Solomon. *The Films of 20th*

*Century–Fox: A Pictorial History.* Secaucus, NJ: Citadel Press, 1979.

Thompson, Charles. *Bing: The Authorized Biography.* London: W. H. Allen, 1975.

Torregrossa, Richard. *Cary Grant: A Celebration of Style.* New York and Boston: Bullfinch Press, 2006.

Tranberg, Charles. *Fred MacMurray: A Biography.* Albany, GA: Bear Manor Media, 2007.

Trescott, Pamela. *Cary Grant: His Movies and His Life.* Washington, DC: Acropolis Books, 1987.

\_\_\_\_, and Chuck Ashman. *Cary Grant.* Oxford, England, and Santa Barbara, CA: Isis Large Print, 1988.

Vinson, James. *The International Dictionary of Films and Filmmakers, Vol. III: Actors and Actresses.* London: Papermac, 1986.

Vogel, Michelle. *Gene Tierney: A Biography.* Jefferson, NC, and London: McFarland, 2005.

Wansell, Geoffrey. *Cary Grant, Dark Angel.* London: Bloomsbury, 1996.

\_\_\_\_. *Cary Grant, Haunted Idol.* London: Collins, 1983.

Weales, Gerald. *Clifford Odets, Playwright.* New York: Pegasus, 1971.

Weaver, Tom. *John Carradine: The Films.* Jefferson, NC: McFarland, 1999.

Wiseman, Frederick. *Titicut Follies.* Zipporah Films, Inc. DVD, 1967.

# Index

A&E Biography 20, 22, 23, 32, 60, 63, 64, 179, 187, 192, 199, 202, 217, 242–246
Among the Living 24, 150, 158–165, 244
Arnold, Edward 13, 16, 90, 93, 95, 97, 98, 99, 108, 110, 111, 112, 113, 122, 129, 137

Badlands of Dakota 24, 142, 151–158, 159, 244
Barrymore, John 24, 144, 147, 148, 149, 150, 151
Bergren, Eric 22, 210, 217, 218
Blakely, Susan 210, 221, 222, 224, 225, 226, 227, 231, 241, 243
Border Flight 13, 73, 74–80, 131, 244
Brennan, Walter 13, 90, 96, 98, 99
Brian, Mary 30, 31, 175, 176, 177, 178, 179
Broadway Dreamers: The Legacy of the Group Theater 64, 232–235, 244

Carradine, John 171, 174, 175, 178, 179, 180, 213
Clifford, Graeme 202, 209, 210, 211, 212, 213, 214, 215, 216, 217, 218, 219, 220
Clurman, Harold 8, 17, 18, 19, 20, 22, 23, 24, 32, 212, 233, 234, 244
Come and Get It 3, 13, 15, 17, 23, 40, 44, 64, 87, 88–99, 102, 103, 108, 111, 112, 125, 129, 131, 167, 168, 191, 197, 203, 212, 217, 219, 223, 225, 226, 230, 240, 242, 243
Committed 64, 212, 214, 224, 227–232
Crawford, Broderick 24, 152, 156, 157
Crosby, Bing 10, 13, 19, 82, 83, 85, 86, 87, 88, 137

Damon, Mark 182, 184, 188, 189
Davis, Bette 23, 68, 126, 173
Dekker, Albert 159, 161, 164, 165
Driscoll, Bobby 47, 48, 150, 189, 236
Durbin, Deanna 27, 156, 212

E! Mysteries and Scandals 22, 64, 187, 199, 202, 240–241
Ebb Tide 16, 17, 113–121, 126, 129, 131, 169, 197, 203, 205, 244
Ed Sullivan Show 44, 45, 64, 191–193, 196, 202, 243
Erickson, Leif 11, 12, 17, 18, 19, 20, 22, 27, 32, 41, 58, 63, 79, 122, 123, 124, 127, 142, 197, 202, 209, 213, 243
Exclusive 16, 99–106, 120, 205, 244

Fitzgerald, Barry 115, 116, 120, 121
Flowing Gold 24, 86, 135–143, 152, 153, 154, 156, 167, 177, 203, 212, 236
Frances (film) 5, 20, 22, 28, 30, 33, 34, 37, 53, 57, 64, 65, 66, 86, 139, 142, 179, 196, 202, 207–220, 221, 222, 224, 242
Frances Farmer Presents 3, 48, 64, 201–205, 240, 244
Freeman, Walter 38, 63, 66, 67, 204, 208, 216, 231

Garbo, Greta 15, 19, 68, 118, 127, 238
Garfield, John 8, 18, 24, 137, 139, 140, 141, 142, 143, 156, 177, 233, 234
Golden Boy 17, 18, 19, 20, 140, 197, 203, 208, 212, 223, 230, 232, 233, 244
Goldwyn, Sam 13, 15, 87, 94, 95, 96, 98, 126, 134

Grant, Cary 16, 76, 107, 111, 112, 113
Green, Alfred E. 122, 124, 125, 126, 128, 129, 131, 132, 133, 134, 135, 137, 138, 139, 140, 141, 142, 152, 153, 154, 155, 156, 158, 159, 167, 212
Group Theatre 8, 17, 19, 20, 22, 23, 24, 29, 140, 142, 208, 230, 232, 233, 234, 235

Hall, Alexander 102, 103, 105, 111
Hall, Jon 24, 129, 130, 134
Hawks, Howard 3, 13, 15, 23, 88, 90, 92, 94, 95, 96, 97, 98, 111, 167, 203, 212, 223, 243
Hayward, Susan 3, 17, 24, 160, 163, 164, 165
Hepburn, Katharine 1, 10, 68, 98, 233, 235
Hollywood Babylon 1, 61–62, 164, 237
Hollywood Undressed 64, 238–239
Hollywood Scandals and Tragedies 64, 235–237, 239
Homolka, Oscar 115, 116, 120, 121, 129, 137
Howard, John 13, 74, 75, 76, 79

I Escaped from the Gestapo see No Escape
Indiana Epilogue (Frances Farmer Presents) 3, 48, 52, 53, 54, 58, 74, 87, 172, 203–205

Jagger, Dean 30, 31, 177, 179, 213

Kazan, Elia 8, 18, 19, 22, 234
Kibbee, Lois 5, 45, 58, 210, 218

Lange, Jessica 199, 208, 210, 211, 213, 214, 215, 216, 217,

251

218, 219, 220, 222, 242, 245, 246
Leisen, Mitchell 10, 26
Lombard, Carole 3, 72, 94, 105, 120, 146, 150
Lupino, Ida 46, 61, 171, 226

MacMurray, Fred 16, 101, 102, 104, 105, 106
McCrea, Joel 13, 98
McLagen, Victor 24, 129, 132, 134, 137
McLaughlin, Sheila 210, 229, 231
Milland, Ray 16, 115, 116, 117, 120, 121

*No Escape* 30, 31, 174–180, 212, 213, 224, 240, 244
Nolan, Lloyd 46, 102, 103, 104, 118, 120

O'Brien, Pat 137, 141, 142
Odets, Clifford 8, 18, 19, 20, 21, 22, 23, 32, 52, 57, 65, 208, 212, 221, 222, 223, 224, 225, 228, 229, 230, 231, 234, 244

Paramount Studios 9, 10, 11, 13, 15, 16, 17, 19, 20, 22, 23, 24, 27, 28, 69, 73, 74, 79, 80, 87, 88, 94, 97, 98, 99, 105, 106, 111, 112, 113, 118, 120, 121, 127, 133, 134, 139, 143, 145, 150, 158, 164, 165, 171, 179, 180, 187, 208, 210, 211, 212, 236, 238, 239
*The Party Crashers* 46, 48, 50, 150, 180–189, 202, 236, 237, 241
Power, Tyrone 26, 167, 168, 171, 173

Rainer, Luise 18, 20, 22
Raye, Martha 19, 82, 85, 87, 88
*Rhythm on the Range* 13, 14, 19, 62, 80–88, 92, 94, 105, 137, 197, 203, 205, 210, 237, 242, 243
*Ride a Crooked Mile* 17, 20, 21, 121–127, 131, 137, 142, 148, 167, 203, 205, 224, 244
Rose, Jane 9, 45, 197
Ruggles, Charlie 101, 102, 104, 105, 106
Rutherford, Anne 152, 154, 155, 156
Sanders, George 26, 167, 172, 173

*Son of Fury* 26, 62, 165–174, 180, 242, 244
*South of Pago Pago* 24, 25, 112, 127–135, 137, 153, 167, 169
Stack, Robert 24, 152, 155, 156, 157
Stanley, Kim 214, 215, 218, 219, 233

Stanwyck, Barbara 3, 16, 126, 140, 233
Stevens, Connie 187, 188, 189
Strasberg, Lee 19, 23, 233, 234, 244

*Take a Letter, Darling* 26, 27, 244
Tamiroff, Akim 122, 123, 124, 126, 127, 129, 137
Tierney, Gene 26, 167, 169, 170, 172, 173
*This Is Your Life* 46, 66, 195–200, 202, 204, 208, 216, 217, 225, 240, 241, 242, 244
*Titicut Follies* 56–57
*The Toast of New York* 16, 17, 98, 106–113, 117, 118, 197, 237, 244
*Too Many Parents* 12, 69–74, 76, 79, 105, 124, 131, 203, 223, 242, 243
Traube, Shepard 9, 10, 22

West, Mae 10, 105, 135
*Will There Really Be a Morning?* (made-for-TV movie) 61, 64, 68, 73, 168, 209, 212, 213, 214, 217, 218, 220–227, 240, 241, 243
*World Premiere* 24, 143–151, 164, 236, 239, 244
Wyler, William 13, 16, 23, 88, 95, 96, 97, 98, 111, 212, 235, 243

www.ingramcontent.com/pod-product-compliance
Ingram Content Group UK Ltd.
Pitfield, Milton Keynes, MK11 3LW, UK
UKHW050536150426
5217IPUK00026B/1956